INVENTING LORETA VELASQUEZ

INVENTING LORETA VELASQUEZ

CONFEDERATE SOLDIER IMPERSONATOR, MEDIA CELEBRITY,

CON ARTIST

WILLIAM C. DAVIS

Southern Illinois University Press • *Carbondale*

Southern Illinois University Press
www.siupress.com

Printed in the United States of America

19 18 17 16   4 3 2 1

Jacket illustrations: "Lieutenant Harry T. Buford" and Loreta Velasquez, engravings by Jeremiah Rea, 1875–76. *The Woman in Battle.*

Library of Congress Cataloging-in-Publication Data
Names: Davis, William C., 1946– author.
Title: Inventing Loreta Velasquez : Confederate soldier impersonator, media celebrity, and con artist / William C. Davis.
Description: Carbondale : Southern Illinois University Press, [2016] | Includes bibliographical references and index.
Identifiers: LCCN 2016004000 | ISBN 9780809335220 (hardback : alkaline paper) | ISBN 9780809335237 (e-book)
Subjects: LCSH: Velazquez, Loreta Janeta, 1842–1923. | Women soldiers—Confederate States of America—Biography. | Male impersonators—Confederate States of America—Biography. | United States—History—Civil War, 1861–1865—Biography. | Celebrities—United States—Biography. | Swindlers and swindling—United States—Biography. | Women social reformers—United States—Biography. | Women journalists—United States—Biography. | BISAC: HISTORY / United States / 19th Century. | HISTORY / United States / Civil War Period (1850–1877). | BIOGRAPHY & AUTOBIOGRAPHY / Women. | BIOGRAPHY & AUTOBIOGRAPHY / Historical.
Classification: LCC CT275.V4785 D38 2016 | DDC 973.7/82092 [B] —dc23 LC record available at https://lccn.loc.gov/2016004000

Printed on recycled paper. ♻

This paper meets the requirements of ANSI/NISO Z39.48-1992 (Permanence of Paper) 

For Bird, who I can happily attest has nothing in common with Lauretta

The biographer's cursed to limn his lives
by two besetting sins;
To fill the voids and fuse his facts,
with "probablys," and "might have beens."
—Anonymous

It is the penalty of a liar, that should he even tell the truth, he is not listened to.
—*Babylonian Talmud*, Sanhedrin, fourth century A.D.

CONTENTS

ILLUSTRATIONS

INVENTING LORETA VELASQUEZ

INTRODUCTION

MYSTERIES ON MYSTERIES

SHE HAS FASCINATED for more than 150 years. There is something eerily modern about her. To a current generation accustomed to media celebrities, people famous for little but their aptitude to attract public attention, she sounds familiar. She created her own myth by pioneering manipulation of the press in a way no American woman had done before, an aptitude she seems to have been born with. Wherever she went, she was her own living press release, and during the Civil War she made herself the Confederacy's first and arguably only true "media celebrity."

Her notoriety endures to the present thanks to her memoir, *The Woman in Battle*. Only one other of its ilk appeared.[1] Hence the rarity of her account invested it with importance far above that of most autobiographies in other genres and despite knowledge of serious problems lurking within her book. The conventional view has been that her adventures posing as "Lieutenant Harry T. Buford, C.S.A.," may be confused and exaggerated, but in broad compass they are authentic. Some have chosen to ignore the question of authenticity because her memoir is so rare, so dramatic, and so suitable to illustrate a variety of themes from women warriors to gender inequity in America. The virtually unknown woman offered a canvas for them to make of her what they wished.

Thus her claims to have fought as a man in the major battles of 1861 and 1862, her many wounds, her faithful slave Bob fighting at her side, her imprisonment in Union-occupied New Orleans, her crossing the lines as a courier, her running the blockade to Cuba and elsewhere, her later adventures in Richmond and Tennessee, her marriage to a Confederate cavalry officer who left her a widow, and her even more daring escapades as a spy in the North all have been in the main accepted, with apologies—and rationalizations—for obvious errors and impossibilities. Her experiences are cited as emblematic—if embellished—of those of scores of women who attempted to pose as men during the war.

It is for all this that she is known, her story still powerful enough to motivate books and articles, and now films, not to mention the devoted labors of a few energetic supporters who cannot countenance the notion that *The Woman in Battle* might be not merely exaggeration, but largely fiction. She is still influential on the Civil War scene because so many *want* to believe her. Therein lies her lasting achievement, what a longtime student of her life describes as "an incredible case study of myth-making."[2]

There is a fascination to myth, how it is born and nurtured, and the germs of truth that lie buried beneath the ignorance, imagination, rumor, prejudice, and sheer nonsense that nurture those seeds to bloom. It is what we choose to believe rather than what we should believe, and this says more about us than we realize. This book began as an effort to see if her story might have elements of verity. It became a quest to find the real woman behind the myth. In the process, it unearthed an unknown life that she led for nearly six decades after the war, a genuine story as dramatic as any of her fables. The result has been unexpected and will displease some and amaze others. She loses luster in the process, but her significance to her era and our understanding of it remains. Rather, her importance shifts to new and little explored ground, as she emerges as a different sort of archetype representing her age and presaging another to come.[3]

So much remains that we do not know and likely never will. Even though this book brings to light for the first time a score of her letters, the fact remains that we have nothing *reliable* from which to glean a personal portrait. She left nothing to illuminate her feelings as a woman. We have no sure idea of what made her laugh or weep. The family members she claimed in her lifetime—the multiple fathers, mothers, brothers—were fictions. Of the five men we know she married—occasionally inflated to seven in her stories—other than hints about the first, we do not how she felt about any of them, or whether she married from love or just self-interest. Her assembled statements total her children to five, yet three may have been inventions, and just one of the others is mentioned by name. Only a few self-serving declarations allow us to gauge any maternal interest.

We still do not know her true feelings toward any of her successive allegiances. She claimed to be Confederate to the core, yet 1863 saw her making bullets for Union soldiers to fire at Confederates. She claimed to be a Rebel spy in Washington, yet she and her husband offered to furnish valuable information to Union authorities. She claimed to be a partisan of Cuban independence, yet she promoted American annexation of Cuba. She publicly espoused rebuilding the South by white foreign immigration, yet she put as much or more real effort into Southerners expatriating themselves.

The most well-illuminated part of her life now is her near half century as a confidence woman, yet nothing allows us to judge her motivation as a pioneering female swindler on a scale that causes many of the male schemers of her day to pale by comparison. She virtually invented and refined techniques that confidence women would employ for a generation. Did she have any consciousness of law, or right and wrong, or did self-interest and survival justify to her anything she did? Neither has she left clues that might balance her larcenous acts with her interludes as a social reformer, crusading journalist, and champion of Southern reconstruction. She challenged leaders in the worlds of business and finance as an equal, testing their acumen as she conceived schemes on a continental scale.

What we can say with certainty is that in her the elements were truly mixed, giving her a complexity both challenging and fascinating. Her actions tell us much. They speak of a very intelligent woman, ambitious, fearless, combative, persistent, impressively ingenious, and above all a seasoned survivor. She was a formidable personality. No man or woman intimidated her, neither presidents, governors, nor generals. She took it as given that she could persuade any to do her bidding. Also erratic, inconsistent, and certainly impetuous, she was never dull.

She inhabited a no-woman's-land between fantasy and fact, and she generated puzzles still unsolved. Just who and what was she? Cuban? American? Confederate patriot? Apolitical opportunist? Narcissist? Fantasist? Cross-dressing transsexual? Lesbian? Feminist? Was she beyond eccentric and insane? What was her real influence on her time and place, if any? Ultimately, is she worth the study devoted to her over the years, and especially now that we know so much more of her?

The answers are no easier to find than for most of the myriad smaller conundrums pebbling the story of her day-to-day life. We may never know her real birth name or the true number and names of all her husbands and children. For all that now emerges about her schemes, more remains unknown. Certainly she was always a scheming opportunist, whether creating and marketing her Civil War story or trying to raise hundreds of millions of dollars in her startlingly ambitious swindles. Certainly, too, she was not very good at it, for she was caught out repeatedly, yet in some instances that was her intent, while in the rest discovery did not stop her. She genuinely seems to have pulled herself out of teenage prostitution and that profession's near-certain early death, but then only went on to pursue other seedy endeavors, punctuated by repeated bigamies, abandoned children, and decades flirting with actions promising imprisonment. There are so many blank pages in her real book, with little to fill them but those "probablys" and "might have beens."

Mysteries and more mysteries, those are her legacy. Not the least of them is whether she had any importance in herself or was at best a curiosity. Only telling her story can answer that, and she did not make it easy to tell.

Yet here it is.

CHAPTER ONE

WHO WAS SHE?

CALL HER LAURETTA.

History has known her imperfectly as Loreta, though when she first appeared in New Orleans in 1861, she actually went by Ann. However, from her first recorded use of Lauretta in October 1862, she clung to it—with variants like Laura, Loreta, even Lauratita—for over six decades. Later in life, when she used only initials, an "L." for Lauretta came first. In her younger years alternate versions appeared, thanks to the problems that inevitably dogged anyone who existed primarily in the press. Reporters and editors turned Ann into Anne or Annie, or Mary Ann, occasionally just Mary, and even Alice.[1] Her surname by birth is far more elusive. Everything she ever said or wrote of her origins may have been fabrication, as most surely was. The earliest recorded instance of her giving her full name came in November 1862, when she said she was born Lauretta J. Clark and that Williams was her married name. Yet she may actually have been born a Williams, a name definitely associated with her in April 1862 and the one she used more than any other through the summer of 1863. Less than two years later she said that Roach or Roche was her maiden name, only to change it to Clapp a few years later. She lived more than thirty years before her first recorded use of Velasquez, the name by which posterity has known her since 1876. It holds no better claim to authenticity than any others of her coinage.[2]

It is possible that she did not know her birth name or where or precisely when she was born. Women living in the circumstances in which Lauretta first appeared were often born out of wedlock from a casual liaison or as a consequence of an occupational hazard among prostitutes. She emerged as a teenaged prostitute in New Orleans, claiming her birthplace was New York, but within three years she changed that to Louisiana, Arkansas, Mississippi, Texas, and even the Bahamas. Years later she claimed nativity in Havana, yet Cuba was a late entrant in her birthplace sweepstakes, unveiled when she was over thirty and shortly before she assumed the name Velasquez. Not a jot of contemporary evidence supports either claim. A best guess would be that she was born in or near New Orleans, where she first appeared as a young woman of about seventeen. Her date of birth is just as cloudy, though there she was more consistent. In 1876 she claimed to have been born on June 26, 1842, and she cited that year more often than any other, though in later years she sometimes advanced her birth year to 1844.[3] A little mystery in a woman may be alluring, but Lauretta clearly overdid it.[4]

Only one salient fact of her youth is certain. She gained at least an average education for a young woman of her time, and a better one than was common among her associates when she first appeared. She was definitely literate, though not yet accustomed to writing much. She later claimed that an English governess helped her acquire "a fair knowledge of the English language" in Cuba until 1849, when she was sent to New Orleans to live with an aunt who taught her "an accurate knowledge of English, so as to be able to read, write, and speak it with fluency." Then in 1851 she supposedly commenced five years at the school of the Sisters of Charity to master "the ornamental branches" of learning.[5] There is no support for these claims, and much argues against them, not least the unlikelihood of a prostitute in her late teens having had a governess and a paid elementary education.

It seems probable that she spent her school-age years from about six to sixteen in Louisiana, and especially in New Orleans, where she had access after 1847 to free public schooling available to all white children. Louisiana briefly stood at the forefront of free public education until legislation in 1852 reduced accessibility. Though her later claim of Cuban birth is improbable, if she did come from Hispanic parents, then an elementary education in Louisiana would tend to have diluted any accent, something notably absent from nearly all accounts of her speech. Almost half of white children in New Orleans went to schools that stressed English in particular. Teachers emphasized learning to both read and write for boys, expecting girls to learn only to read.[6]

Lauretta appears to have been a product of such an education. She read well, and she certainly read newspapers, for no one as adept as she became at manipulating the press could have done so without being comfortably familiar with the medium. What she read beyond that, however, is uncertain. She inserted no quotations from literature in her later writings and only rarely referenced a written source she might have read. In her thirties she demonstrated some familiarity with the ancient and modern history of women warriors, especially Joan of Arc, but that could have been a ghost writer speaking, and in any event this did not mean she read of it in her school years. She also knew at least the title of Samuel L. Clemens's 1872 book, *Roughing It*, and certainly knew of his literary popularity as Mark Twain, but that does not mean she had read the book.

Most significant is her claim in 1876 that as a child of about seven she read Maria de Zayas y Sotomayor's collection of stories, *Novelas amorosas y ejemplares—Novels Amorous and Exemplary*—published in Spain in 1637, claiming that she found herself especially drawn to the novella titled "El juez de su causa" (The judge of her own case).[7] At the time of her childhood the book was available only in Spanish and in an 1847 French translation, but not in English. If the young Lauretta had really read it, then she read it in Spanish or French, or else someone read or recounted the story to her, and in multilingual Franco-Spanish New Orleans, thousands read in either language. Hence there is no certainty that she read it herself as she claimed, though it remains a possibility. Otherwise, nothing that she left behind in her own hand suggests familiarity with anything other than English, nor that it was not, in fact, her first and perhaps only language.

When it came to English, she amply demonstrated her ability to write from the age of twenty-one, which argues strongly for some degree of public school education, while the quality of her writing equally argues against English governesses, private tutors, or the Sisters of Charity. Her earliest known letter dates from 1863, though the fact of it surely argues that she wrote others earlier. It was riddled with misspellings and word confusions typical of a public elementary education of the time and atypical of the kind of education she later claimed to have had. She wrote "eavening" for *evening*, "commisary" for *commissary*, "criples" for *cripples*, "presedent" for *president*, "mater" for *matter*, "isue" for *issue*, "feild" for *field*, "posible" for *possible*, "adressing" for *addressing*, "depracate" for *deprecate*, "whoes" for *whose*, and "pleas" for *please*. Here and for the rest of her life, she confused "their" for *there*, "and" for *an*, and "oppinion" for *opinion*. Another letter five months later added "esure" for *ensure* and more to the list. She seemed to have a good vocabulary, and her orthography was entirely consonant with that of millions of other elementary-schooled Americans, but not with the level of spelling usually found among children from the affluence and high social position she later claimed as her own.

Her spelling placed her squarely in the lower-middle or working class, and so did the conversational idioms that crept into her letters and speech. In December 1863 she referred to a man who was "borned" in the North and how he and others "was forced" to enlist in what she later termed the

"Rebbel" service. In July 1864 she complained of being arrested "without I was guilty."[8] Clearly unaware of her misuse of the word, she always addressed letters to men as "respective sir." Meanwhile, she routinely wrote "bin" when she meant *been*, "secatary" instead of *secretary*, and "excepted" for *accepted*; she consistently mixed present and past tenses, confusing the use of "was" with "were"; and erratically employed the plural, as when she wrote in 1864 that "things looks very dark," "all kind of low people," and "as soon as my trial come off," or years later in writing "this cruel acts."[9]

None of this diminishes her intelligence. She wrote colloquially in the pronunciations, idioms, and word choices common among the working class of New Orleans and the rural people of America. She spoke the same way, in early 1864 calling a young man's mother his "Mammy" and referring to him with the colloquial "that there boy," which she pronounced "that 'ere boy."[10] Over the years her handwriting and spelling improved in small degree, but she never left behind the sentence structure and grammar that place her learning years squarely in a lower-middle or working-class environment. That does not reveal who her family was, but it does effectively preclude who it was not. She did not write, speak, or spell like the highly educated daughter of a Spanish grandee. It also seems evident that English was her native language, the products of her pen belying her later claims of patrician foreign birth.

Court records and newspaper accounts from the spring and fall of 1862 reveal she had lived in New Orleans for some years, probably since at least the later 1850s.[11] They identified her as Ann, Anne, Annie, or Mary Ann Williams, but unfortunately Ann Williamses were rather plentiful in New Orleans just then, which makes distinguishing the Ann who became Lauretta a challenging task. Some cases from the early 1850s can be dismissed because she would have been too young to fit.[12] By 1855, however, Lauretta might have been the Ann Williams arrested in February for shoplifting gingham from a store on Poydras Street and then again in May for stealing meat from a market on the same street.[13] Such petty theft was much in character for a girl of the streets in her early teens. In the fall of 1856 a court fined Mary Ann Williams $10 for disturbing the peace, probably meaning she was drunk or disorderly in a saloon or brothel.[14] Lauretta would have been fourteen at the time. Louisiana statute set the age of consent at twelve, so she could have been working legally in a brothel, though judges more often used sixteen as a benchmark.[15] In the fall of 1862 a journalist commented that the Ann Williams who was unquestionably Lauretta had been working for several years "in a house of questionable character." That meant that by 1856 Lauretta was very close to practicing the oldest profession, if not already so employed.[16]

If she was the Mary Ann Williams sent to the city workhouse for two months in April 1857 for being "very vagrant," then Lauretta was almost certainly "on the game" by that time, for in addition to vagrancy the court charged her with attempting to "steal" the husband of a woman in town and "threatening to exterminate her afterwards." That kind of bravado is redolent of the Lauretta who emerged a few years hence.[17] Then the Ann Williamses suddenly disappear from the court record for over two years.[18] Sometime during this period Lauretta changed her life, at least temporarily, or so she soon told people in New Orleans. In the first of her later tales of military adventure, she claimed to have joined a U.S. Army expedition in 1857 to put down the Mormon Rebellion. In July of that year, coincidentally just a few weeks after the workhouse released Mary Ann Williams in early June, U.S. troops left Fort Leavenworth, Kansas, on an expedition to deal with reports of anarchy and incipient revolt against Federal authority in Utah. The campaign was chiefly sound and fury but almost no action, and within a year it was done after no battles and no serious casualties. Whether they believed it or not, by 1862 people in New Orleans had heard that Lauretta was with the expedition and that during the campaign she had married a Lieutenant Arnold.[19]

Only Lauretta was a likely source for the story, and it was pure invention, for in 1857–58 there was a lamentable lack of Lieutenant Arnolds. Just two officers of that surname held commissions in the entire U.S. Army. Captain Lewis G. Arnold of the 2nd Artillery was a quarter century older than Lauretta, already married since 1843, and pinned at his post in Florida during the entire Utah business. Lieutenant Richard Arnold of the 3rd Artillery, then colloquially known as "Sherman's Battery" after its Mexican War commander, Thomas W. Sherman, spent the entire Mormon episode period on the staff of Brigadier General John E. Wool at Troy, New York.[20] This story of Lauretta's evolved over time. In November 1862, in a statement coming directly from her, she claimed that Williams was her married name, not Arnold, and then a dozen years later she claimed that it was Burnet. Unfortunately, the shortage of Burnets and Williamses in the army in 1857 was even greater than that of Arnolds, there being not one of either on the officer rolls. If she did go to Fort Leavenworth around the time of the Utah campaign, she went either attached to an unnamed enlisted man or else as a camp follower.[21]

What is significant is that this is the earliest known instance of Lauretta inventing a story about herself. Her motive is a mystery. Most of her future deceptions furthered some immediate purpose, but she could and did invent elaborate fictions purely for the fun of deceiving others. Her fabricated Utah experience may have presaged a burgeoning desire to associate herself with military life and glory, creating a fantasy world to take her away—if only vicariously—from the sordid reality of life on the streets of New Orleans. Though there is no record of what she read, she could have been influenced by works like Madeline Moore's 1851 story of a woman posing as a soldier, *The Female Officer*.[22]

Lauretta's apparent absence from the court record could reflect good behavior, or she might have created the Lieutenant Arnold story to cover an absence from New Orleans whose real explanation she preferred to keep secret. Throughout her life Lauretta speedily formed intimate relations with men, perhaps an artifact of her time in the brothels or evidence of a casual approach to men and sex that led her to the cribs in the first place. Regardless, now age sixteen to seventeen, she almost certainly worked at least intermittently as a prostitute. If she left New Orleans during 1857–59, it could have been to go to Fort Leavenworth to profit from the soldiers there assembled. If she wanted to make a break from her profession, then a fictional marriage made a good story to cover her absence and entitle her to some degree of stature among her peers. A prostitute who escaped to marriage and security would be the envy of others, and two dominant features of Lauretta's life would be her quest for respectability and a near obsession with attention and celebrity.[23]

All she got was growing notoriety, for once back in New Orleans her associations repeatedly put her name on the parish court docket. In June 1859 Mary Ann Williams charged a man and wife with physically assaulting her on Calliope Street in the red light district.[24] Two months later an Ann Williams went to the parish prison for two months for breach of the peace.[25] Then in October a man named Grumsbacher accosted her on Rampart Street on the fringe of the brothel section. After shouting insults at her, he grabbed her dress and threatened to disrobe her in public.[26] On May 25 the court handed down a fine of $5 or thirty days to a "Mrs. Williams," who, apparently unable to pay the fine, was sentenced to the thirty days. She was subsequently released on June 6 and three weeks later paid a bond to keep the peace.[27]

Again, more than one Ann or Mary Ann Williams probably accounted for these episodes and others. There can be no doubt, however, that on June

25, 1860, a nineteen-year-old Ann Williams, who gave her place of birth as New York, was a working prostitute in Clara Fisher's bordello at numbers 86 and 88 Dryades Street, a popular neighborhood for brothels. Ann was the fourth youngest of fourteen young women aged seventeen to twenty-four working for Fisher, who euphemistically gave her profession as providing "lodgings."[28] The house's takings allowed Fisher to festoon her fingers with diamonds, while those same fingers got her in trouble for lifting the occasional watch from a neighbor's house.[29] Just two months later, on August 28, the parish court sentenced an Ann Williams to the parish prison for "lewd & abandoned" behavior.[30]

The coming of the secession crisis in 1860 and the outbreak of war in April 1861 did nothing to retard business in the stews. The mobilization of thousands of men in the city just brought more demand to the marketplace; at the same time, that increased volume of business empowered younger and less jaded women to seek establishments where their share of the takings would improve. By the summer of 1861 Lauretta, still known chiefly as Ann or Mary Ann Williams, had left Fisher's concern and moved to another house.[31] In November 1862 a journalist recalled that she was "known also to have been an inmate of Nelly Bremer's."[32] Better known locally as "the notorious Nelly Bremer," the madam ran a bordello at 82 Dauphin Street.[33] Calling herself a "Furnished rooms Keeper," she had seven women aged twenty-one to twenty-eight working for her in 1860 and perhaps more the following year.[34] Besides being generally older than Lauretta's compeers at Fisher's, they were a rougher crowd. One had been arrested for theft in 1857, another of "loose character" for vagrancy and drunkenness that same year, and another for exposing herself indecently in public. One poor woman of just twenty-six would be confined for insanity in a few years.

At the same time, at least one was charged and fined for violating the city's March 1857 Ordinance concerning Lewd and Abandoned Women, commonly known as the Lorette Law after a section of Paris noted for its brothels.[35] Rather than curtail prostitution, which was one of the Crescent City's most profitable businesses, it tried to shift the trade away from the better neighborhoods, while at the same time mandating fines and licensing fees for those who insisted on remaining in the excluded areas.[36] For a generation or more, first in France and then elsewhere, the term *lorette* had been a euphemism for a prostitute one step above the street walker but not quite a courtesan. If Lauretta was not Ann Williams's real given name, then she may have revealed a delightful sense of irony when this *lorette* became Lauretta.

She probably fell afoul of the Lorette Law herself in July 1861 when city police made a sweeping arrest of thirty-nine women working in the brothels, including Bremer's. Among them was a Mary Ann Williams, arraigned and fined $10, then released along with the rest.[37] Perhaps motivated by that police harassment, Bremer moved to a two-story building on Customhouse Street in the Treme suburb immediately northwest of the old Vieux Carré. The local people were predominantly free people of color, but in the community of prostitution a social and occupational integration between whites and blacks had been common, if frowned upon. Either that or some other action by Bremer or her staff incurred someone's wrath, for in the middle of the night of August 23 someone set fire to the house. People extinguished the flames with little damage, but then at four o'clock in the morning on October 31 an arsonist set it alight again. The press noted rather cynically that the chief of police and his men "did not happen to be very far away" at that time of the morning, and they tried to quell the blaze, but to no avail. "The house of ill-fame kept by the notorious Nelly Bremer," valued at $24,000, was a complete loss. Police attributed the fire to an "incendiary," but no one was ever charged.[38]

Lauretta may have been done with Bremer's by that time. A year later common knowledge in the newspaper and law enforcement community recalled that a "well-to-do" man named Bachman from Arkansas had met her in New Orleans some time since, though clearly not as one of her customers, and took her back to Arkansas bent on matrimony.[39] Bachman did not keep her long. "On becoming acquainted with her character," as one journalist put it, he sent her back to New Orleans.[40]

One other thing might have kept Lauretta from being at Nelly Brewer's for that fire. New Orleans had nothing for her on her return from Arkansas but a return to a life she clearly wanted to escape. If her 1862 claims about the Mormon expedition revealed a genuine suppressed desire to be at the scene of action, the advent of war in 1861 offered an opportunity. Already by that summer seemingly everyone in the new Confederacy wanted to take part, including even free African Americans and some slaves. Why not women, then? The Southern press often published appeals from patriotic ladies wanting to do their part. "What shall we do?" wrote a Louisiana woman in late May. "Some one may imagine that we desire to mingle in the ranks of soldiers and rush headlong into the carnage of battle," she continued. Dismissing actually serving in the army, however, she begged someone to "devise a sphere in which they may contribute more than money and sewing."[41] Others went even farther. "Shall not woman, too, lay their best offerings upon the shrine of her country's honor?" asked an anonymous Memphis woman. She called on the city's women to organize associations of nurses for their regiments and to go with them to the front, declaring, "I will proudly stand in the footsteps of some fallen soldier, and prove to this age that the female virtue which was flanked about with chivalry, has not become extinct with the women of Boetia."[42]

Civil conflicts tend to be levelers and to become everyone's war rather quickly. North and South alike, women of 1861 knew the stories of Deborah Samson, a woman who undeniably posed as a soldier to fight the British in the American Revolution. Even earlier heroines like Hannah Snell, who reportedly dressed in her brother-in-law's clothes in 1745 to enlist in the Royal Marines and served for five years before revealing her gender, captured attention.[43] In a generation raised on the overblown romances of Sir Walter Scott, imaginations stirred at the notion of the daring and plucky woman—always in fiction a "girl" in her teens—who risked death for love or patriotism. Seeing brothers and fathers and sweethearts enlist to go to war in the first days of the conflict, before any battles had been fought, imbued sisters, daughters, even wives with a sudden impulse to try to share in the romance of it all. In the first weeks of April and May 1861 the subject assumed such prominence that a two-act musical drama titled *The Female Soldier* appeared on stage in several cities.[44] When a number of volunteer units put women in uniform as *vivandiers*—ceremonial "mascots" who marched with the regiment in parade but stayed behind when it went to the front—it was only a short step for some to want to go to war with the regiments, disguised as genuine soldiers.

They did so almost from the outset, impelled by a host of motives, from a desire to look after their husbands to the simple need for a private's pay. Some were prostitutes eyeing the bonanza of thousands of lonely young men away from home. Others hoped to profit from the experience otherwise if successful in their masquerade. A few suffered from genuine gender confusion, and one or two were mentally unbalanced. The most common aspiration, however, was simply to share in the adventure. Often these and other motives mixed and overlapped, and that is where the phenomenon intersects the trajectory of Lauretta's life in 1861. Sometime that summer she decided to become—or claim to become—a Confederate officer. After all, many swallowed her story of Lieutenant Arnold and accompanying the Utah expedition and continued to do so for years afterward. Even if she never saw Madeline Moore's book, being literate, Lauretta could read the stories of other daring women already appearing in the New Orleans press, such as that of the "Arkansas Heroine," whose name just happened also to be Miss Williams, helping her father arm a small company of men to resist the Yankees in June 1861.[45] Then there was the Baltimore woman who managed to get a Maryland regiment of Confederates armed and in doing so caught a Federal spy.[46]

If those young women could be heroines and become the darlings of the newspaper press, why not this Miss Williams too? There was certainly something in her that craved notoriety, and she also knew that fame, even if fleeting, might be parlayed into money. Both could lift her out of the brothel. Certainly prostitution offered adventurous women freedom of a sort, especially when they could make at least as much from one customer in an hour as a seamstress might earn in a day. Yet the trade proffered a double-edged sword, for the danger from violence, disease, and exploitation by men, as well as by female madams, dogged most women to premature aging and death. There was triumph in just escaping from prostitution alive.[47]

Just why, how, or when she decided on her escape is uncertain. Her myriad later explanations conflict with one another, sometimes dramatically. If she was or had been a prostitute, then trying to go to the army could have been just taking the commodity to the most promising marketplace, and her disguise a device meant to get her into the camps, while making herself an officer would give her more mobility and freedom of action. Yet there was likely more to it than that. She later claimed she had a desire for adventure, though subsequent events failed to demonstrate much of that. Rather, virtually everything in her recorded life revealed a dominant motivation to make money, and as quickly as possible. One path to respectability and renown that always appealed to her was being a writer, for both newspapers and the book press. The former was exclusively the realm of male journalists, precisely the sort of barrier she soon demonstrated a desire to break down. Going to the front with the soldiers could offer a vantage from which to write for the newspaper and periodical press—no doubt using a masculine pseudonym—and also provide the basis for much more money to be made from a book or books once the conflict closed. Somewhere in the mix of all that lay her real reason for taking the step—escape from her old life, excitement to be sure, a new career that might bring fame and fortune, and a chance to push back the boundaries placed on her as a woman.

She decided to leave the brothels behind her as early as September 1861. Though nothing conclusively links her with a mysterious woman who passed through Memphis on September 11, 1861, elements of the woman's story are suggestive. The mystery woman appeared dressed in a Confederate officer's uniform and was arrested on suspicion of being a spy, but as she explained to the editor of the local *Daily Appeal*, her husband had been captain of a company of volunteers and was killed at the First Battle of Manassas or Bull Run on July 21, whereupon his company "elected" her to succeed him. She was on her way now to join her command.[48]

The report raises possibilities. The presumed female officer's story could not have gotten into the Memphis press unless she told it herself, and commencing in June 1863 that would be Lauretta's modus of self-promotion for the rest of her life. Obviously the mystery woman did not attempt to pass for a man or she would not have attracted the attention of the editor, and if she went to him, then her act gainsaid any intention to deceive in the first place. In short, her uniform was a prop to gain attention, not a disguise to avert it, and that too would be mirrored in Lauretta's actions in days ahead. This woman wanted to be noticed, and she was, and well beyond Memphis. Within days, papers in Nashville, New Orleans, Richmond, Alabama, and North Carolina, among others, picked up the story. Soon it crossed the lines into the North, appearing in the press in Wisconsin, Indiana, Ohio, and elsewhere, so great was the interest in such a novel story this early in the war.[49] No one then or later connected this unnamed woman with Lauretta after her own impersonation became known, but it has features characteristic of claims she would soon be making, particularly of being the widow of an officer killed in action and drafted to command by his company.

That also presaged another hallmark of Lauretta's. The unidentified woman gave no hint as to the state her husband's company came from nor of the unit's identification. The fact that she was described as "passing through" the city established that she was not from Memphis. Thanks to the rail connections then available, the only travelers who had to go through Memphis to take trains to Virginia were those from western Tennessee, Arkansas, northern Mississippi, and Louisiana. A total of twelve units from those combined states were at or near that first battle in Virginia, and while a few of their officers suffered wounds, only one captain lost his life, Adam McWillie of the 18th Mississippi Infantry.[50] Yet the shortest rail route from his home to Virginia for his wife to travel, if she were the mystery woman, bypassed Memphis. In short, if the press quoted her accurately, the story told by the mystery woman in Memphis was pure invention.

That falsehood is redolent of the Lauretta soon to emerge. All her life she told lies, often apparently for the fun of it, and because by either natural gift or a skill developed, she was a born confidence artist. She could create convincing scenarios and "sell" them to others. That was the very marrow of prostitution, of course, selling an illusion of passion and romance for a few dollars. The "con woman" was a new and evolving phenomenon in mid-nineteenth-century America, and the war accelerated her numbers and development. She had much in common with her male counterparts. She would use her intellect and skill at pretense, including disguise, to deceive others and often just for the thrill of success in her portrayal. Mores of the time presented to her a challenge rather than a restraint, and the more intelligent or shrewd her victims, the greater the excitement in deception. Her tools would be her confidence in herself, her ability to handle a world run by men, and a perception of human nature and foible that enabled her to play on the fears, avarices, and gullibility of others. Most of all, whereas the confidence man usually sold a product, the emerging con woman sold herself and her story, hoping to profit thereby.[51] That was Lauretta to the life.

On her release, the mystery woman may or may not have continued her alleged journey to the army in Virginia, but it is beyond doubt that a woman did make just such a journey within days of the Memphis woman's release, and her story bore remarkable points of coincidence. If she boarded a train in Memphis, then she traveled east on the Memphis & Charleston to Chattanooga, changed there to the East Tennessee & Georgia to Knoxville, changed again for the East Tennessee & Virginia to Bristol, and there boarded a Virginia & Tennessee train to Lynchburg to change again for Richmond.

From Memphis she would have passed through Grand Junction and Corinth, Mississippi; Decatur and Stevenson, Alabama; Chattanooga, Knoxville, Bristol, and other smaller towns. She would have been on foot in public changing trains in Chattanooga, Knoxville, and Bristol. A woman in Confederate uniform on the platforms while changing trains ought certainly to have drawn notice, yet the press in those cities made no mention of such an apparition. That suggests strongly that wherever the woman began her rail journey, she did not actually change into her uniform until aboard the Virginia & Tennessee en route to Lynchburg, for that is where she was noticed, as indeed she clearly intended to be, for at least one observer soon noted that her uniform was so gaudy as to demand attention.[52]

On the evening of September 24, 1861, an officer stepped off the train and walked into Lynchburg's Piedmont House. He signed the hotel register as "Lt. Buford," the first recorded usage of Lauretta's later famed alias. That done, the lieutenant went back out to walk the streets and sidewalks of the

"Lieutenant Harry T. Buford," Jeremiah Rea's 1875–76 engraving, probably based either on a photo taken in early 1862 or, more likely, on Lauretta's Nashville sitting for Thomas Saltzman in June 1866. *The Woman in Battle.*

city with a haughty, if not pompous, air that to some proclaimed, "I am the master of the great Wellington and Bonaparte." The local *Lynchburg Republican* shortly noted that Buford's "gay and dashing appearance attracted universal attention, and led to the firm belief on the part of all that he was one of the chief dignitaries of the military world."[53] Soon people saw through what may have been an intentionally thin veneer of disguise, one witness declaring that "her dashing manners, fine appearance, gay uniform, and perfect *physique*, had caused her to be 'the observed of all observers.'"[54] Authorities realized that he was a she. Thus two weeks after a woman dressed as an officer passed through Memphis headed for Virginia, a woman dressed as an officer stopped in Lynchburg saying she had come from Memphis. The coincidence is almost conclusive, though what she might have been doing during the intervening fortnight is a mystery.[55] The mayor ordered her arrest on suspicion of being a spy, and police quickly brought her before a magistrate, who questioned her at some length. She admitted her charade and gave her name as Mary Ann Keith of Memphis. As her story unfolded, it revealed beyond doubt that she was Ann or Mary Ann Williams—Lauretta.[56]

Keith gave a brief history of herself, starting with two marriages. The first was to an unnamed man now in Company E, 3rd U.S. Artillery, or "Sherman's Battery." In short, her first husband—from whom she was presumably divorced, though she said nothing to that effect—was now an enemy soldier.[57] Then she claimed she had married a man now in the Confederate army, but from whom she had separated for reasons she did not divulge. However, she said nothing of being the widow of a fictional Louisiana officer slain at Manassas. Lauretta routinely changed details of her stories from one telling to the next, often for no apparent reason.

As for herself, she told a Lynchburg reporter that "she was all right on the southern question," and she certainly was no spy. Her real reason for impersonating an officer was that she felt "determined to fight the battles of her country, and thought such disguise more likely to enable her to accomplish her object." The *Republican*'s editor concluded that "she may be all sound as far as we know to the contrary," but still advised caution with "all such characters" found in the Confederacy.[58]

Richmond agreed, when notified of the suspicious woman, and ordered her sent to the Confederate capital by train the next morning for further investigation. Probably on the same train with her went copies of that day's *Republican*, whose coverage of her discovery soon spread across the Confederacy from Richmond to Memphis, and even to the North from Washington to Milwaukee, and faraway San Francisco in time.[59] From that first appearance in the press, Lieutenant Buford was on the way to becoming a media celebrity, the Confederacy's first and perhaps only one, and from now on Lauretta consciously reinforced her new persona's renown.

She should have arrived in the capital on the afternoon of September 25 but apparently was not under close arrest, for still as Lieutenant Buford in her uniform, she called at the War Department on John B. Jones, the chief clerk.[60] He soon described seeing before him "a gaudily dressed and rather diminutive lieutenant," who said he was returning home from leave and asked for a passport and rail transportation via Chattanooga back to his post under Brigadier General Leonidas Polk at Columbus, Kentucky,

Lynchburg, Virginia, circa 1875. The Virginia & Tennessee Railroad station stands immediately left of the end of the covered bridge crossing the James River. There on September 24, 1861, Lauretta, as Mary Ann Keith, stepped off her train and walked to the Piedmont House just right of the bridge to unveil Harry Buford for the first time. Courtesy of the Lynchburg Museum System.

on the Mississippi River. During their lengthy conversation, Jones found that Buford had no orders from the adjutant general's office for such travel, which was official procedure. Growing suspicious, he asked to see Buford's furlough but was refused. Still, Jones signed a passport, and Buford hastily grabbed it from his hand and hurried out of the office. When Buford left, Jones noted that instead of saluting—which was not necessary, since the clerk was a civilian—"he *courtesied*." It was only later that Jones began to think about the mysterious lieutenant, "the fineness of his speech, the fullness of his breast, his attitudes and his short steps," and concluded at last that this must have been a woman. Jones reported this to Provost Marshal General John H. Winder, and Winder promised to investigate and learn what he could of her.[61]

Meanwhile, the Richmond press heard of Keith's story and anxiously looked out for her arrival in the city. Armed with her new passport and orders for transportation, she left before some people knew she had been there.[62] She was headed back toward Lynchburg on September 27 when Winder wired an order to authorities there to be on the watch for her. When the Southside Railroad passenger train from Petersburg came into its Lynchburg station that evening, she was on it, and the mayor had her immediately taken into custody and brought to his office while he sent a telegram to Richmond asking for further instructions. "My mysterious lieutenant was arrested," Jones noted in his diary, "and proved, as I suspected, to be a woman."[63]

Keith told the mayor that she had visited the War Department, but not to see a mere clerk. Rather, she said, she met with Secretary of War Leroy Pope Walker himself and demanded a passport to the West. As if that were not enough, after Walker gave it to her, she left, changed clothes, and returned to his office dressed as a woman and secured another pass for herself, Mrs. Martha Keith. It was exactly the sort of prank Lauretta described herself doing repeatedly in her memoirs fifteen years later, playing the role of the "trickster," an ancient mythological entity or man/woman who used quick wits to make fools of people who obeyed conventional rules of society. The mayor spotted the holes in her story and sent her to the city jail pending notification of Winder's wishes. "We know nothing about Mrs. K," said the *Republican* the next day, "but we are inclined to the opinion that there is something suspicious about her movements, or she is [a] very erratic person."[64]

She spent several days in jail, until Winder sent orders for her release, Secretary Walker having determined that she was harmless.[65] She emerged from the cell dressed as Mrs. Keith once more and left on the next train for Chattanooga and the West, saying she would go home to Memphis. The *Republican* quipped that this female "will not again soon undertake to play the 'bowld solger boy.'"[66] At least Lauretta apparently did not again undertake to be Mary or Martha Ann Keith, for the name disappeared once she left Lynchburg. There is no reason to suppose that any part of the name was authentic, nor that Memphis was her home, and if she was in fact one and the same as that unidentified woman in uniform in Memphis in mid-September, it should be borne in mind that she was only "passing through" the city and not a resident.[67]

She learned two things from her Virginia adventure. First—and something she surely already knew—she could pull off a big bluff and get away with it, as she did with the clerk Jones. Hereafter, she demonstrated a quick and confident tongue that made her convincing even when marketing colossal lies. She already knew she could fool men, a necessary tool of her recent trade, and at least for a time she had deceived Bachman of Arkansas about her background. She had also, apparently, fooled enough people about the nonexistent Lieutenant Arnold and her supposed Utah trip that it was accepted knowledge by some in New Orleans. Her masquerade as Lieutenant Buford might have collapsed within a few hours of her arrival at Lynchburg, but still it lasted long enough, and was then so successful with Jones and perhaps with others in Richmond for a time, that she may have considered trying it for real in the army itself. At the same time, however, the gaudiness of her uniform and her exaggerated promenade around Lynchburg's streets are convincing evidence that evading discovery was the last thing she wanted. Without discovery there could be no celebrity.

That was the second thing she learned, for the notoriety came instantly and was practically universal. In addition to the *Republican*, all of the Richmond papers carried items on Keith/Buford, and within a week of her leaving the city, editorial exchanges saw her story in print for readers in Staunton, Virginia, Raleigh, North Carolina, Memphis, Nashville, and Baltimore. Then it jumped the battle lines to an even larger readership in Washington, Philadelphia, Boston, Cincinnati, Louisville, and Milwaukee, reaching San Francisco before the end of October. Virtually in an instant, hers had become the most widely circulated story of a Confederate woman thus far in the war, and she was its first celebrity created wholly by the press. And still no one knew her name.[68]

CHAPTER TWO

"HEROINE IN A FIX"

MARY ANN KEITH made no more appearances, which makes locating her for the next six months virtually impossible. One or more Mary Ann Williamses continued to occupy the court in New Orleans, beginning only days after Lauretta would have returned home. One was arraigned on October 17 with three other "*traviate* of Conti Street" charged with using obscene language to berate a respectable man. Two of them went to prison for streetwalking in "indecent attire," but Williams escaped by paying a bond.[1] In December a "Mrs. Williams" was convicted of larceny, and in February 1862 the court fined Mary Ann Williams $15 for abusing and insulting another woman on the same day that Lauretta's onetime madam Clara Fisher was arraigned for breach of the peace.[2]

With women like these in mind, and unaware that the Battle of Shiloh was then raging, the *Daily Picayune* on April 6, 1862, ran a sarcastic piece about women fighting each other in the street. "What a pity every body is too much prejudiced against the so-called weaker sex to raise in this city a battalion, nay a regiment or even a brigade of women," it lamented. There were enough of these combative Amazons to fill three or four companies in a month, "by offering a chance to those who are brought before the Recorder for assault and battery, let alone several other viragoes."[3]

If Lauretta was any or all of those Mary Ann Williamses, that would put her back in New Orleans for some period from mid-October 1861 to mid-February 1862. The only other grounds for locating her then are her own later claims, always risky at best. On April 23, 1862, she said that after fighting at First Manassas disguised as a soldier, she had been arrested and confined at Richmond on suspicion of being a traitor. Once released, she went to Polk's command at Columbus, Kentucky, and again saw action on November 7, when a small Union force led by Brigadier General Ulysses S. Grant drove Confederates out of their camps at Belmont, Missouri, only to be counterattacked and driven off by reinforcements from Columbus. During the ensuing winter she returned to New Orleans and made no claim to involvement in the pivotal Battle of Fort Donelson on February 13–16. Rather, she said she was in the city when General P. G. T. Beauregard issued an appeal for ninety-day volunteers on February 21, 1862, whereupon she volunteered as a man and joined fifteen hundred others who left to reinforce Beauregard and General Albert Sidney Johnston as they assembled an army at Murfreesboro, Tennessee. She claimed to have fought on April 6 and 7 in the ferocious Battle of Shiloh, where she took wounds in her foot and hand, then returned to New Orleans with other Louisiana wounded to recuperate.[4]

It was her first claim to have been at First Manassas, though she said nothing of being an officer, nor did she now call herself Buford. Her story of her arrest and visit to Richmond, and her subsequent travel to Polk's command in Kentucky, identifies her securely as Mary Ann Keith, which places her in Virginia in September–October 1861 and argues that wherever she was from November to mid-February 1862, she was not in New Orleans.

Her 1876 memoir actually provides some argument that she really was with or near the Confederate garrison at Columbus, Kentucky, briefly in the winter of 1861–62. Her changing accounts of her war activities from 1862 onward would often include a "backfire" set by her, a false story to cover up genuine episodes that she could expect to come back to haunt her. In 1876 she implied that in November 1861 she arrived at Columbus, where General Leonidas Polk set Lieutenant Buford to examining passes, leaves of absence, and furloughs of soldiers and civilians traveling the Mobile & Ohio trains running south into Tennessee. Giving no circumstantial details at all of this service, Lauretta abruptly turned to trouble caused when "one malicious scoundrel, because I would not permit him to travel without a pass, trumped up a most scandalous false charge against me." She provided no detail other than to say that the "scamp" accused her of being not "entirely trustworthy."[5]

If such a charge were made, it probably had nothing to do with the railroad, for it is hardly likely that Polk gave Buford any such assignment, if they even met. Far more likely is that Lauretta visited the Columbus garrison or its environs that winter, perhaps as Buford and perhaps not, and got into the sort of trouble that in the next several months saw her become first notorious and then imprisoned in New Orleans: prostitution or larceny. Inventing a disgruntled officer making a slanderous assault on her was an effective ex post facto counter to any in 1876 who might have remembered stories about her that circulated in the camps at Columbus in 1861–62. She later employed precisely this same deflective technique again and again.

If she did go to Columbus—which she later claimed was for three weeks—her knowledge of Beauregard's February 21, 1862, call for volunteers in New Orleans suggests that she was back in the city by then and that she left in the second week of March when those volunteers departed, either with them or on her own.[6] Had she remained in New Orleans from mid-February through late April, many people would have known it, endangering her story of being with the army.[7] She could have been anywhere in Louisiana or Mississippi after that, even in or near Shiloh, though only her own claims substantiate that. About two hundred of the less seriously wounded Louisiana volunteers returned to New Orleans on April 14, with a trickle of others coming thereafter.[8] Hence, if Lauretta really did go to New Orleans with the wounded, as she later claimed, it was most likely on that first train, but we have only her word for that. Still, a journalist with the *Daily Picayune* in January 1867 remembered seeing her on the street sometime that April, "dressed in a rough gray jacket and pants, the suit rather the worse for wear, with her hair cut short, and supporting a bandaged foot with a crutch of the most primitive pattern." Overall, she impressed him as "rather shabby."[9]

The journalist did not call her outfit a uniform, nor did he mention any rank. Also, the crutch was clearly homemade and hardly hospital issue. Her cropped hair spoke to an effort to pass for a male, yet it is implicit that the writer recognized her at the time as a woman, and he said nothing about any attempt to deceive. The rough clothes might bespeak heavy wear in camp and field, or they may have been throwaway men's clothes or even a worn and discarded uniform. A bandage on her foot hardly guaranteed a wound beneath, while the primitive crutch raises some suspicion, especially given the subsequent migrations of the supposed hand and foot wounds in her later accounts. In short, while she may have been wearing an old uniform, or something resembling a military suit, there were plenty of such to be had, as the number of secondhand uniforms being worn by body servants and slaves in the army with their owners gave proof. The crutch and the bandaged foot could have been genuine or affected to gain attention, and though it is possible that Lauretta had been somewhere in or around the army at Shiloh, she could simply have returned to New Orleans as part of the general exodus of Confederates from the now-lost western quadrant of Tennessee and northern Mississippi.

Why she chose to resume her impersonation of a soldier at this time is unclear, but having done so, she did not wait to be discovered.[10] In a typically bold move, she exposed herself. On April 23 she went to the office of Mayor

John T. Monroe and surrendered herself, dressed in her soldier clothing. New Orleans was in trouble. A Union fleet even then bombarded the two forts downriver that sought to deny passage to enemy gunboats. Confederate defenders had been reduced instead of reinforced, and the citizens felt justifiably nervous. In a matter of days, even hours, the city could be under the guns of the enemy fleet and occupied, and frightened people imagined Yankee spies lurking on every banquette. That could have made a woman posing as a soldier suspect. No record indicates that the authorities sought her, but the fact that Monroe immediately sent her to prison to await interrogation suggests that he might have been looking for her and that on hearing of it, she decided to turn herself in.

When Provost Marshal H. D. Ogden interviewed her, she first told him she was Mrs. M. M. Arnold and until recently had lived in Arkansas, where she owned a plantation. Saying nothing of any desire to be a soldier, she explained that she wanted to write a history of the war and figured that posing as a soldier would best enable her to collect the information necessary to the task. Her Keith story had given her the first taste of positive publicity and renown, and now she refined it, telling Ogden of her trip to Richmond and her brief arrest on suspicion of being a spy, and giving him some account of her time with the army at Manassas and Belmont, though without implying that she actually participated in the fighting. She added that she was back in New Orleans by that February to answer Beauregard's call for volunteers and subsequently was "in" the Battle of Shiloh, where she had received her wounds. She meant now to continue her peculiar mode of research if allowed, she said, and hinted that unnamed others worked on the project with her, though whether men or women, or in or out of disguise, she did not say. She had turned herself in, she explained, because she feared that her masquerade might get her into trouble, as it had in Virginia the year before.

Ogden found her story interesting, and to some degree convincing, but he remained skeptical and after their meeting concluded to talk with her again the next day. Before then, either he or someone present with him gave an account of her story later that day to a journalist with the *Daily True Delta*, which published it on the morrow. "She appears to be a woman of intelligence and gentle breeding," wrote the columnist, impressed that she had given the names of some respectable citizens of the city as references, a technique Lauretta employed then and later. "That she is an extraordinary woman there is no question," he went on, "and our curiosity is excited to know more of her history and her adventures in male attire."[11]

What Ogden's hasty investigation developed was not quite what the journalist had in mind. A little inquiry revealed that Mrs. Arnold had lived in the city under a number of aliases, including Gibbons and Lieutenant Buford. Ogden may have challenged her with this when they spoke again on April 24, but he apparently found none of it unlawful and ordered her release. "She is certainly a very extraordinary woman, and her history must have been an eventful one," concluded the *Daily True Delta* two days later, but by that time a shift in the fortunes of war seemed likely to defeat attempts to learn any more.[12] The day of Lauretta's second meeting with Ogden, Union gunboats bypassed the forts guarding the lower Mississippi. The next day the fleet arrived at the city waterfront, and the mayor was helpless to resist an occupation. On April 26 the Yankees took over.

Lauretta's explanation for going to the mayor is superficially convincing. New Orleans had been in a terror of enemy spies for weeks. In giving her name, she did not use Ann or Mary Ann Williams. Apparently she did not want her old identity in the brothel district known, and she presumably believed her disguise would prevent old associates from recognizing her. Nothing suggests that Ogden's investigation—necessarily cursory at the time—connected her to her former life, though he clearly suspected that Arnold might not be her real name. Instead, he found reason to believe that she was the Mary Ann Keith who used the alias Lieutenant Buford, though no details of the origin of the Gibbons identity were ever forthcoming.[13] Lauretta had to share in the common expectation that at any moment they might all be under Federal occupation. Revealing her impersonation was a means to avoid having to join the few remaining Confederate soldiers in the city when the order came to evacuate. Presumably she had no conventional female costume with her, or else she would need only change her clothes to embrace the protection her sex would have given her against being forced to leave as a soldier or being treated as a combatant by occupying Yankees.

The only hint as to what Lauretta did immediately after release is another recollection by that *Daily Picayune* journalist in January 1867. He stated that on April 25 people saw her in uniform, "dashing about the streets upon horseback."[14] That may be accurate or just postwar romanticism, but on November 8, 1862, she stated that as of that date she had been in the city for seven months, which covered all of the intervening time since her brief April appearance.[15] Confirmation of her stay came early that same November, when a court reporter noted that she had lived in the city "until recently" as Mrs. Arnold.[16] Meanwhile, the story of her revelation to Mayor Monroe spread at least as far as Georgia, though the confusion attendant on the fall of New Orleans probably prevented local press coverage circulating much in the Confederacy.[17] Mrs. Arnold then disappeared from the official record for six months just as Williams reappeared on the parish court docket.[18] A Mary Williams was arrested for fighting on Perdido Street in August and again a few weeks later, and she was sentenced to a month in the parish prison for assault.[19] Or Lauretta may have been the Adele Williams arrested on October 2 and charged with larceny.[20]

In a coincidental yet remarkable incident, on September 6 a woman registered at the Planter's Hotel in Augusta, Georgia, and later that day boarded a city omnibus. Riders quickly became suspicious and reported her to the authorities, who arrested her. She quickly broke down and admitted that she was a man, Charles Waters, about thirty years old. He had begun wearing feminine clothing as a teenager and maintained the impersonation for at least fifteen years, aided by his soft skin and smooth face. He continued cross-dressing after emigrating to Philadelphia but was discovered, so moved on to Charleston and then Savannah, then back to New York City, after repeatedly being found out. He crossed the lines into the new Confederacy, only to be arrested under suspicion of being a female spy, and thereafter traveled constantly. "This is one of the most singular cases that has ever occurred in this section of the country," claimed an Augusta editor, who believed the man should be watched, "as this is not the time to be indulging in such idiosyncracies or monomaniac freaks." More singular still, Waters's assumed female name was Anne Williams.[21]

Lauretta returned to feminine dress, though perhaps not to her old trade. Instead, she attached herself to a soldier in the occupying army, Private John Williams.[22] Perhaps she knew him, for he was a butcher in New Orleans, slightly younger than she at nineteen, and apparently a Union sympathizer. No record of any marriage survives, but she later said he was her husband, and it remains a possibility that he was the origin of the surname that she soon claimed to be her married name. On May 20, 1862, he enlisted in the 13th Connecticut Infantry, one of the occupying units stationed in the city.[23] It was a tough outfit, for its soldiers shot and stabbed civilians, stole personal goods from local women, and attacked and wounded city peace officers.[24]

A casual relationship developed between Williams and Lauretta, but as became her custom, her attachment was mostly one of convenience. She wanted to get out of the city and beyond Union lines, and Williams may have been a means to that end, as well as a source of some support. When his regiment moved to Camp Lewis outside the city at Carrollton on September 30, she went with him, and they lived as husband and wife for two weeks or more.[25] Soon a story emerged that she had persuaded him to desert one night and help her get through the lines, but finding their route blocked, they returned to Camp Lewis without being discovered. After that, she tried again, this time by boat on a bayou flowing into Lake Pontchartrain north of the city, the northern bank of which was Confederate-held territory. That too failed, and probably around October 20, when Williams was detached from his regiment and sent off on a march west to Donaldsonville, Lauretta returned to the city.[26]

She remained determined to get out of New Orleans. The city held little promise for her now but a return to her old profession, and however casual her personal relations with men might be, she wanted to escape a squalid life that promised only disease, violence, and an early death. She had experienced adventure and excitement as Buford. Her brief time in the limelight as Mary Ann Keith had passed, and few if any knew that she was Keith. Thanks to the interruption of the local editorial exchanges with papers elsewhere in the Confederacy, her April encounter with Provost Ogden barely got out of New Orleans, denying her the public notice she craved.[27] She likely wanted to try again for a bit of celebrity, though this time under her own name or a name by which she was known in New Orleans.

First she needed cash, and she used the female con artist's chief weapon of soliciting sympathy by posing as a weak woman in need of aid or protection, perhaps with a dollop of tears thrown in.[28] She conceived a convincing story of being a Unionist woman named Arnold traveling in the South, captured and subjected to rough treatment at the hands of Confederate irregulars when Louisiana seceded. Thereafter cut off from home or friends until the city's capture, she wanted to go home now to New York. She presented her new tale to several Unionists in the city who clearly did not know her as Ann Williams of old, and it is apparent that her skills of persuasion remained sharp. They gave her money for transportation, but instead of leaving right away, she persuaded a couple named Chester to give her temporary lodging in their home. Ever after she demonstrated this knack for talking her way into room and board at others' expense. By mid-October she decided it was time to make another attempt at leaving the city.

On the morning of October 16, after the Chesters left the house, Lauretta stole into their rooms and took a gold watch and chain, a gold thimble, and some other jewelry.[29] She immediately took it all to Solomon Jacobs's pawn shop at the corner of St. Charles and Poydras and sold it, giving her name as "Mrs. Williams" for the receipt.[30] Then she fled the city and went back to the old camp of the 13th Connecticut, where, even though Williams was gone, she settled in briefly and drew rations posing as his wife. The Chesters immediately lodged a complaint with police, and Officer J. D. O'Connell went looking for her. It took him a fortnight, but he started the search with a good idea of who she was, for someone who knew her rather well loaned him a photograph of Lauretta taken sometime during the past year, showing her in uniform as a Confederate soldier. Armed with that, and learning of her liaison with Private Williams, O'Connell went to Camp Lewis on October 30, where he identified her from the photo and arrested her.

He took her before the occupying forces' provost court immediately, and it remanded her to the parish prison.[31] Reporters immediately seized on her story, and the next day it hit the press, giving editors a chance for a heavy-handed pun on the theft of the watch when they quipped that "Ann Williams ought to be watchful, or she is likely to have enough of it before long." The papers joked about her over the following days as a familiar character, a "Heroine in a fix" caught in "a very unheroic attitude," as one put it, suggesting that she was well known to both press and public, regardless of what name she used.[32] This notoriety was hardly the sort of fame Lauretta craved.

She appeared before the provost court on November 1 and identified herself as Ann Williams, though she had been using the name Arnold for some time. Again the reporters treated her flippantly. "Annie is quite a character," one wrote the next day, "and has passed through adventures enough to fill a portly volume with exciting yellow-covered literature interest." Articles recounted her colorful past largely from local common knowledge rather than from anything she said now. Naturally, as is the way with rumors, variations emerged, though all agreed that hers had been a "checkered existence" and that she had spent some time "in a house of questionable character," the reputation of which was "not exceedingly high." One reporter mentioned Nelly Bremer's specifically. They detailed as well her brief interlude in Arkansas with Bachman and his sending her back on discovering her past. One journal had her marrying and leaving him before going to Utah rather than afterward, while one another declared that after she married the "Arkansas planter," it was she who left him when she tired of wedded life. One claimed that she used the alias Arnold on the Utah expedition but made no mention of marrying any such lieutenant. Another reporter said that by her own accounts, she had been "all over much of the far west," but since the occupation she had remained in the city as a woman and took up with Williams. Openly displaying his skepticism, one journalist wryly concluded that "in short, she has been everywhere."

Besides the new larceny charge, police cited multiple earlier charges that may tie her to the arrest of both Mrs. Williams the previous December and Adele Williams earlier that October. According to police, she was known to be "very free fingered," though she had escaped prosecution to date. There were also rumors that she carried letters from Confederate sympathizers in the city through the lines, and some people suspected her to be a Rebel spy, not to mention her claims to have been a soldier in disguise. The police report concluded, "She is a very dangerous character."

Lauretta pleaded her own case, and one reporter thought "she spoke right sharply in her own defence." She evolved her Keith story, admitting that she had been to Richmond and claimed service as a soldier at Manassas, Shiloh, and other fights. Then she displayed her Shiloh wound, only now the foot injury that had her on crutches in April had somehow migrated to her wrist. She also added new details that could only have come from her. At Manassas she fought with the 7th Louisiana Infantry, she said, while at Shiloh she was in the 11th Louisiana. She gave no account of her actions since the occupation and implied that authorities had arrested her the past April for appearing in male attire, but then released her in recognition of her "patriotic conduct." Patriotism for the Confederacy was treason to the Union court now trying her, so she denied ever being a spy. Despite her past actions, she declared that she supported the Union wholeheartedly and was "raising her children up to revere the old flag." Fortunately for her, no one asked her to produce those children in evidence. To demonstrate her loyalty even further, she claimed to be married to Private Williams of the 13th Connecticut.[33]

"Ann can talk glibly," one reporter had to admit. She certainly felt no qualms about committing perjury. She had no children. There was no ordinance prohibiting women from wearing men's clothing, and no one in New Orleans was arrested for so dressing. It had long been fashionable in France among the working-class *grisettes* and Bohemian types, including prostitutes, and New Orleans tastes always followed French fashion. There is no evidence of her marrying Private Williams, whose surname was conveniently and coincidentally consonant with the one she generally used.

Most important, only her own claim puts her at Manassas with the 7th Louisiana or at Shiloh with the 11th, but no Yankee court could check that.

If she was the Mary Ann Williams arrested on July 12, 1861, for violation of the Lorette Law, then she can hardly have been on the battlefield at Manassas nine days later, and no surviving record from the 7th Louisiana mentions a soldier named Buford or a woman posing as a soldier. Her Shiloh claim is equally impossible to verify, but evidence to dismiss it conclusively is also lacking. She seems to have been absent from New Orleans around that time, but nothing confirms her being in or near the 11th Louisiana in the battle.

"She is a little *passee*, but still quite a handsome woman," observed a reporter in the court, adding that hers was "a very masculine nature." It seems an odd assessment for a woman barely over twenty, but the life she had lived may well have been hard on her. The judge was unswayed by either her youth or her words. He sentenced her to six months in the parish prison, what one reporter called "a rather unromantic termination to a most romantic career." He added, "In our opinion, women should continue to be women, and whenever they unsex themselves should be treated, as they desire to be considered, like men under similar circumstances."[34]

All of the city's major papers gave the story more coverage than the usual case of larceny.[35] Yet again it was hardly the sort of attention Lauretta craved. She had made no recorded prior declarations of Confederate sympathy, though it was implicit in her claims of active service. Her open avowal of Union sympathy now made her a traitor to her fellow Southerners. Nothing in her known life thus far suggests that she thought beyond the moment. Her career had been one of seizing opportunities with little or no thought of future consequences, an approach common to both her youth and her recent profession. If she looked ahead at all, she had to recognize that the publicity from her trial would not be to her credit anywhere, South or North. Fortunately for her, it did not spread from New Orleans's Union-controlled press to the rest of the Confederacy, but within less than three weeks her story appeared in print in the New York *Evening Post* and thereafter spread to Connecticut, Boston, and Vermont, and west to Wisconsin and parts in between. Under headlines like "The Adventures of a Female Rebel" and "The Fate of a Heroine," Northerners read distinctly sarcastic accounts of her pretended escapades and the squalid facts of her larcenous ingratitude to the Chesters.[36]

It was some time before Lauretta learned what the outside public read about her. She had been in the parish prison before, but only for a few days or weeks at most. Half a year there held no appeal, and she determined to feign illness in hopes of being sent to the city's Charity Hospital. Security there would be more relaxed, and she might effect an escape. In her first week in prison she complained of having had abdominal pain since before her trial, and the ruse worked. Just after noon on November 8 authorities transferred her to the hospital, where she told the registrar her name was "Lauretta Williams born Clark," born at Nassau, New Providence, in the Bahamas. It was her earliest known instance of using Lauretta and the only time she mentioned the name Clark. She further added that she had been in Arkansas until April 1862, when she came to New Orleans, and said she was married. As always, any or all of the information she gave could have been false.[37]

The hospital doctor concluded that she suffered from "prolapsus of the womb," which could have been the result of childbirth at some past time and was impossible to feign. Either his examination was superficial or his diagnosis was wrong, for six days later she pretended to be recovered enough to take exercise and talked the surgeon into giving her a pass on November 14 to take a stroll in the city.[38] She was boldly parading in her old haunts on Poydras Street when she came face-to-face with Officer O'Connell, who demanded to know how she had gotten out. She lied, saying that Major General Benjamin F. Butler, commanding occupying forces in the city, had pardoned her. O'Connell wisely called her bluff and said he would take her to Butler's office to confirm her story. Lauretta balked at that and admitted she was only on a pass from the surgeon. O'Connell left her with a policeman, Lieutenant Boyd Robinson, while he went to the hospital, where the surgeon told him she really had not been very ill and he now suspected it was all a sham. Reporting on her attempt, the *Daily Delta* concluded, "She is a wily heroine."[39]

The police returned her to the Charity Hospital for confirmation, and two days later the doctor discharged her, whereupon she went back to the parish prison, a victim of her own compulsion to show herself off.[40] Had she stayed off the streets and undercover, she might have found a way out of the city. Instead, ingenious though she could be, she also demonstrated now and throughout her recorded life a recklessness and want of forethought that made her too smart for her own good. The local press loved it, running headlines like "Anne Williams Again" and "The Female Warrior." One paper ran her story atop its city news column, calling her "this celebrated fast one." Another facetiously referred to her as "the heroine of Shiloh and many other moving scenes, incidents and adventures by flood and field," evidence that her local notoriety in the past year went well beyond her latest scrape. Calling her "*alias* Arnold," one writer spoke humorously of

Orleans Parish Prison, circa 1866, where Ann Williams was an occasional "guest" and where, four years earlier, Lauretta spent six months for larceny. The Historic New Orleans Collection, accession no. 2010.0095.31.

O'Connell finding her "going on her way rejoicing" before he "took her in tow for the calaboose."[41] There was no concealing the fact that editors, if not their readers, regarded her as an object of ridicule.

Lauretta made no more escape attempts. She served her full six-month sentence without leaving a trace, the longest gap in her verifiable wartime record. With her behind bars, the number of Ann Williams incidents in the courts dwindled to just two, suggesting that Lauretta did account for a number of those before her most recent arrest.[42] She should have been released on or about May 1, 1863, though it might have been a few days later if her abortive escape effort earned her any extra days, and her six months could have concluded as late as May 16.[43] How she passed the time in the prison is unknown, but it seems clear that she had access to some local newspapers and possibly others from the North, since the city was occupied. On her release in May she also met the news that on April 27, the Federal commanding officer had issued a general order directing all "registered enemies" to leave the city by May 15.[44]

Lauretta could have been registered as an enemy with the provost's office by virtue of being a convicted criminal or because of her claims to have been a Confederate soldier. More likely the rumors of her being a mail runner and possible spy got her on the list. Besides the disloyal, people deemed "undesirable" were given passes to leave the city, and her criminal record certainly put her in that category.[45] Or she may not have been on the list at all, but may have simply attached herself to the people who gathered at the Pontchartrain Railroad terminus on Lake Pontchartrain's south shore at noon on May 17, 1863, just days after her release. It seems unlikely that she had much in the way of personal baggage after six months in prison, but such as she had she was allowed to take with her, probably just clothing and personal items left with friends when she went to jail. One thing she likely did not have was the tattered suit or "uniform" she claimed to have worn at Shiloh. She may have had material and buttons to make a new one, though where she got the money for any purchases is a mystery, as is her financing through much her life. Still she had only two definite skills to fall back on. One was sex. The other was her greatest "gift," her ability to talk people into giving her money.[46]

The undesirables gathered at Hickock's Hotel by the lake to be searched and have their baggage examined. A woman searched Lauretta, even forcing her to remove her stockings if she wore any, all to make certain no one smuggled information to the enemy. She boarded the steamer *A. G. Brown* and then passed down a little canal and into the lake for the three-hour crossing. On the other side they steamed up the Tchefuncte River for ten minutes to Madisonville, a sleepy settlement of a few streets, a hotel, and one or two closed shops. People on the riverbanks greeted them, and a nearby pole flew the Confederate "stars and bars."[47] Also there to greet them was a rumor that General Braxton Bragg's Army of Tennessee had been driven out of middle Tennessee into northern Alabama by the enemy, which was true, and another that General Robert E. Lee and his Army of Northern Virginia had been driven back to Richmond, which was false.[48]

A short trip took her to Meadville, Mississippi, a few miles east of Natchez, and from there by late May or the first week of June Lauretta reached the state capital at Jackson, only recently abandoned by U. S. Grant's forces as they advanced on Vicksburg to the west. The departing Federals had destroyed much of the town, but stores reopened and life returned to a semblance of normality. Most important to Lauretta, however, the local newspaper resumed operation.

Prison had given her time to reflect on what she wanted to do next, whom she wanted to be, and how to make it happen, and as with so much in her life, it probably began with the press. She certainly saw the coverage of her arrest and trial the previous October, and the newspapers' ridiculing tone, but she probably did not know that it saw little circulation elsewhere in the Confederacy. Still, it is quite probable that one or more of the Northern journals that picked up the story found their way to the occupying forces in New Orleans and hence into the prison, where she could read how she had been made a laughing stock.

Those same Northern papers treated another Southern woman more respectfully, and coincidentally her name was Anne or Anna Clark, two of the names Lauretta had used. As Clark told a correspondent of the New York *Daily World*, when her husband went into the Confederate army, she joined the 11th Tennessee posing as a man and fought at Shiloh, where she "performed prodigies of valor," even standing on the dead the better to take aim at Yankees.[49] It was all fantasy. In fact, Anne Clark's husband had abandoned her at the beginning of the war, and in her depression she unsuccessfully attempted to enlist in a Confederate cavalry unit. She was nowhere near Shiloh but probably did acquire somehow a semblance of a uniform, and she was arrested briefly as a result. That December, in her dementia, she told friends "what a good rebel soldier" she had been, warning them that she intended to help defend Vicksburg and saying, "I may get killed in battle."[50]

Every time she told her story, it changed, and Lauretta suspected that Clark based it in part on the republished accounts of her own adventures, for their stories shared multiple points of similarity. Both had used the name Ann, and Lauretta had claimed once to be a Clark. Both followed husbands into the Confederate army, Lauretta doing so in her Keith incarnation. Both claimed to have fought at Shiloh, Clark in the 11th Tennessee and Lauretta in the 11th Louisiana. Both claimed to have been arrested for wearing a man's uniform. It was bad enough for Lauretta to be the object of mockery at home and in the Yankee press, but it was even worse to see someone else borrowing elements of her story and being lionized in the papers as a heroine. Jackson's own *Mississippian* substantially republished the New York *Daily*

World article on Clark on December 30, 1862. Within weeks the story spread by editorial exchange to Atlanta, Montgomery, Charleston, and Virginia.[51]

If she had not seen it while in prison, Lauretta was not long in Jackson before she became aware of it, and the discovery confirmed her on a course she may already have determined during her time in prison. She would create new personas for herself, both as a woman and as a man, and use them to chase in the Confederacy the celebrity that something in her craved after her first taste of it in 1861 as Mary Ann Keith. She would take that original story and hone it to make it pay. Perhaps she saw it as a means to complete her break from prostitution, or maybe she was just drawn by the lure of celebrity. Either way, she realized at once that there was much in her past that she must recast favorably, and she could not wait for the press to come to her. Rather, she would have to launch her offensive by taking her story to the papers, and she needed to start by reclaiming her history from Anna Clark. Her natural gift for self-promotion was about to come to the fore.

CHAPTER THREE

THE SUMMER OF HARRY BUFORD

JACKSON AFFORDED LAURETTA a good platform from which to reinvent and launch herself. Twenty-five-year-old bachelor Robert H. Purdom, a member of the state legislature until he resigned in 1861, edited the Jackson *Mississippian*.[1] He had met Anne Clark and accepted her story when she passed through Jackson, and now Lauretta made him her first target.[2] She was well practiced at charming men and decidedly more feminine than the tobacco-chewing Clark.

She called on Purdom on June 4 or 5, explaining that she had left New Orleans with the registered enemies, and found him an eager listener as she set about expanding her small local mythology onto a broader stage.[3] She had seen the account of Anne Clark republished in the New York *Daily World* and emphasized to Purdom that what she told him now was "a true account of her remarkable career."[4] First there was her name, which he wrote down as Mrs. Laura J. Williams, though she probably told him Lauretta. Gone were the other aliases, for her goal now was to avoid connection with her sordid New Orleans past and to quell confusion with that other Clark woman. For the first time she unveiled the middle initial "J," which she used thereafter.

She continued crafting her new persona when she told Purdom that when the war broke out she was living in Arkansas, married to a man of Northern birth devoted to the Union, who left for his family's home in Connecticut and, as she afterward learned, joined the Yankee army. That established her surname Williams as one by marriage and also put the lie to claims in the New Orleans press that she had been sinfully cohabiting with John Williams of the 13th Connecticut. Outraged at her husband's betrayal of her and the South, she vowed to "offer her life upon the altar of her country" and become a soldier herself. She donned a Confederate uniform and assumed the name Buford, which she had used before when she was Mary Ann Keith and at one time in New Orleans as well. Now for the first time she gave her creation a given name, Harry, and implied without specifically saying so that "he" was an officer.

As Buford—Purdom's handwriting made the name look like "Benford," and so it would appear in print—she went to Texas to raise an independent company of infantry that she subsequently took to Virginia.[5] She led it in the engagement at Leesburg or Ball's Bluff on October 21, as well as in other skirmishes, but when authorities attached her company to the 5th Texas Infantry, its surgeon discovered her sex and forced her to return to Arkansas. Either she omitted all mention of the First Battle of Manassas, service in western Kentucky, the fight at Belmont, and her experience as Mary Ann Keith, or else Purdom failed to make note of them. Lauretta habitually spoke quickly, and as her story unfolded, he may have been too rushed to capture everything. At the same time, now and hereafter Lauretta was remarkably cavalier about omissions and contradictions as she retold her adventures. Connecting herself with the 5th Texas, for instance, was probably just a random choice, but it heralded innumerable future instances of her casually citing details that she—and likely her audience—did not know were impossible. There were no Texas units or independent companies at Ball's Bluff, and the 5th Texas only organized in Richmond on October 22, the day after that engagement.

Continuing to spin her story, Lauretta said she stayed home in Arkansas until shortly before Shiloh, thus covering the period from November 1861 to February 1862, which she had left blank in her earlier accounts. In the great battle of April 6 and 7, she told Purdom, she actually saw on the field her unnamed father, who was a Confederate soldier as well, but he did not recognize his daughter as Harry Buford, and she did not reveal herself to him. On April 7 she took a head wound and went to the rear, thus continuing the upward migration of the leg wound of the past April that turned into a wrist wound by October. After sending a note to her father, she went south to Grenada, Mississippi, to wait for him to come to her. Hearing nothing from him, she went on to New Orleans, where she fell ill and was still unwell when the Yankees occupied the city. She told Purdom nothing that linked her with the Arnold/Williams who turned herself in to the mayor on April 23.

Once recovered, she said, she escaped the occupied city and went to the Louisiana coast, where she spent the ensuing months carrying letters in and out of the city for Confederate sympathizers and running drugs and uniform cloth through the Union naval blockade of the coast, thus incorporating into her story the rumors that had surfaced the previous fall. After a treacherous black person informed on her, the Federals arrested her and took her to General Butler. She appeared as herself in woman's attire but defiantly told him that she "gloried in being a rebel," refused to take an oath of allegiance, and proudly declared that she "had fought side by side with Southern men for Southern rights" and would do so again. She told Purdom that Butler had denounced her as "the most incorrigible she-rebel he had ever met with" and sent her to prison for three months. Following release, she kept corresponding with Confederates outside Federal lines, and again the Yankees arrested her. Butler sent her to a "dungeon" to languish a fortnight "on bread and water," after which the Federals put her in the state prison as "a dangerous enemy."

Coincidentally, the 13th Connecticut was one of the occupying regiments in the city, and her Yankee husband, Williams, whom she now promoted to lieutenant, sent to ask if she would see him. She refused so long as he wore the hated blue, but he came to her cell nevertheless and insisted that she rejoin him, promising to secure her release if she would just take the oath. Then he would resign his commission and take her home to Connecticut. When she refused, he left her to her fate, and when Butler's successor, Major General Nathaniel Banks, assumed command in New Orleans, he kept her in confinement until May 17, when he sent her away with other registered enemies.

Lauretta thereby created more clouds to conceal unfortunate facts. Despite her November 1862 statement—and the published observations of others—that she had spent April through October 1862 in New Orleans professing her loyalty to the Union, now she put herself somewhere on the Louisiana coast working for the Confederacy. Thus she separated herself from that traitorous Ann Williams imprisoned for larceny. However, since she had put her name as Lauretta Williams on record that past November, and the press had made note of it at the time, now she turned her arrest to her credit by attributing it to her Confederate activities rather than stealing from the Chesters. At the same time, her proclamation before the provost court of wholehearted support for the Union she now transformed into defiant loyalty to the South. Her liaison with Private Williams, which was purported to be a respectable marriage the past November and evidence of her Union patriotism, now became proof of her Confederate solidarity as she turned him into a Yankee brute whom she spurned.

As for those embarrassing six months in the parish prison, she cleverly changed the cause and made herself a martyr to Butler's wrath, the bit about a bread and water diet being an inspired embellishment. Confederates universally demonized Butler after his famous general order in May 1862 that any New Orleans woman who behaved rudely to a soldier would be treated as a "woman of the town plying her avocation." Southerners immediately dubbed him "Beast Butler," and Lauretta shrewdly calculated her story of victimization by the "Beast" to gain even more credence and sympathy. Adding the claim that Williams tried to force himself on her, she relied on the confidence woman's ever-persuasive appeal for sympathy and protection, but there was something different, quite possibly unique, in her approach. Lauretta might present herself as a victim, but never as weak or helpless. Her defiance dared her enemies.

In closing her account, Lauretta told Purdom that on arriving in Jackson, she joined the surgeons' staff of an infantry brigade there and intended to "render all the assistance in her power" to Confederates wounded in the forthcoming struggle for Vicksburg. That meant acting as a nurse or caregiver, which implied that she would not resurrect Harry Buford in the immediate future. Purdom swallowed her story completely. In offering it to his readers on June 6, he called her "a lady whose adventures place her in the ranks of the Mollie Pitchers of the present revolution." He saw in her "little of the characteristic weakness of the sex, either in body or mind," but rather "her whole soul was enlisted in the struggle for independence."[6] Lauretta may have made her story more convincing by socializing with Purdom, for three years later he said he "knew her well during Confederate times," hinting at more time together than just an interview. Now he admitted that he found her "good looking and in speech and manner a perfect lady."[7]

Purdom's article was her first interview given directly to the press, far and away the fullest and most detailed from any source to date. It provided foundational elements of her future story, albeit one that continually evolved. If Lauretta hoped to get her own version on record around the Confederacy, while countering damage done by the New Orleans papers the past November, she estimated the press brilliantly. Through editorial exchange, it soon ran in newspapers all across the Confederacy. In fact, it appeared in two variants. Using the *Mississippian*'s headline "Adventures of a Young Lady in the Army," it appeared first in Natchez on June 13, then in Atlanta, then the capital in Richmond, followed by Houston, Dallas, Augusta, Raleigh, and Staunton, Virginia. The other variant changed the headline to "Career of a Female Volunteer" and traveled its own trajectory from Mobile to Richmond, Savannah, and on to Wilmington.

Allowing for the fact that the article surely ran in other papers now unidentifiable, Lauretta's creation was available to a quarter million or more Confederates either by reading or by word of mouth. It gained even more circulation in 1864, when Felix G. DeFontaine published his *Marginalia;*

or, Gleanings from an Army Note-book, a compilation of newspaper articles in which he included an edited version of the Mobile *Register & Advertiser*'s variant.[8] Purdom's piece prompted a surge of other stories of female soldiers in the Confederate press, forcing editors to confront the anomalous status of such women. "We admit as a general thing, such conduct is not countenanced by those who profess to possess a refined feeling," wrote a Knoxville editor. Still, he admitted that women like Lauretta surely acted "from the purest motives," and then added a backhanded compliment by saying that "it may be, in a secret way, *he, she* or *it*, as the case may be, is of valuable service to our cause."[9]

Lauretta and Harry Buford were soon back in public notice on a scale vastly larger than before, even though Purdom misprinted her alter ego's name as Benford. Though she spent the next two weeks in Jackson, there is no evidence of any effort to become a nurse with the army. Caring for the wounded, like her persecution by Butler, was just another calculated tug at the sympathy of potential benefactors, since by this time female nurses were widely hailed in both North and South for their sacrifices. Rather, she had now framed a plan to capitalize on past publicity and the more fully realized story she now had at hand for the press. She intended to become the first woman in American history to be not just a soldier, but a commissioned officer. She hoped to get from President Jefferson Davis a genuine commission as Lieutenant Buford. Such a distinction would be a catalyst for even more of the renown she craved and a vehicle that she could manipulate to provide more secure support than would a woman's pleas for charity. Only she knew if she really expected to get a commission to perform active service, but there is no doubt she intended to capitalize on the publicity Purdom gave her. Somehow she acquired gray fabric and shiny brass buttons, with which she made something approximating military pantaloons and perhaps a short uniform-style jacket.

Lauretta left Jackson as soon as she finished her "uniform," probably with copies of the *Mississippian* article in hand to show, and traveled first east to Meridian, and then south by rail to Mobile, arriving on or before June 16. The *Mississippian* interview appeared in the local press three days earlier, so the city was primed when she donned her gray suit and paraded its streets just as she had in Lynchburg in 1861, identifying herself as Lieutenant Buford. Thus she virtually announced that she was not a man, but the famed Lauretta Williams. Mobile and the rest of the Confederacy must have had no doubt that she was the heroine of Purdom's article. Now and for the rest of the summer she deliberately called attention to herself, proof enough that discovery was always her goal. She gained nothing if her masquerade succeeded but much if it did not.

From Mobile she wrote to the War Department in Richmond soliciting a commission and evolved her identity further by giving a full name to her newly assumed middle initial, signing as "Mrs. Lauretta Jennett Williams." She also mentioned that she already used the alias "H. T. Buford" and gave a return address in Mobile, at the moment a more secure location than Jackson.[10] She soon returned to Jackson, however, perhaps to inspire more press coverage in the *Mississippian*, but behind her she left troubling questions. A woman dressed as a man aroused suspicion, and impersonating an officer was a serious matter. Obvious though she made it that she was neither man nor officer, the local provost marshal felt uneasy about her, and shortly after she left Mobile he issued an order for her arrest and notified Richmond as well.[11]

Unaware of the brewing trouble, Lauretta displayed herself and her new uniform back on Jackson's streets on June 24. One local man described her that day on the sidewalks walking with "a very perceptible strut, and a trifle of a swagger," and later that day called her "a *rara avis*," adding that she was "a well made, but not pretty, Confederate lieutenant, of the *genus femina*." He and everyone else in Jackson knew her story by now, and though it was certainly romantic, he for one did not like the imposture. "We admire angels in calico, but we never could see the charm of dressing up 'the last and best gift of heaven' in pantaloons, though the trowsers were of nice Confederate gray, with brass buttons thrown in," he wrote. "It may be a splendid opportunity for showing a well turned ankle, but 'while it makes the unthinking laugh, it cannot but make the judicious grieve.'" The spectacle merited tears more than laughter.[12]

Coincidentally, the next day the War Department received her application, which immediately aroused suspicion, and a clerk docketed her letter with the notation "alias H. T. Buford Lt. C.S.A." Within hours a telegram speeded west ordering her detained and sent to Richmond for investigation.[13] Thus when she returned to Mobile, anticipating a response to her letter, the provost marshal arrested her and put her on a train for Virginia, still in her uniform, which did not fail to attract attention when she and her guard changed trains en route.[14] They reached Richmond on the morning of July 1, when her guard took her immediately to the office of Brigadier General John H. Winder, who apparently did not connect her with Mary Ann Keith of 1861, despite their common Buford alias.

Jackson, Mississippi, in late May 1863, only a week or two before Lauretta arrived to spin her new story for the press. The real notoriety of Harry T. Buford began here. *Illustrated London News*, August 8, 1863.

Brigadier General John H. Winder. Lauretta's bluff did not work on him when she was brought to Richmond under guard on July 1, 1863, and he ordered her to prison. Richmond *Southern Illustrated News*, September 12, 1863.

The *Mississippian* story had appeared in the city papers a dozen days earlier, so editors—and surely Winder's office—ought to have known her as Laura J. Williams, but when notice of her arrival hit the press, the Richmond *Enquirer* misidentified her as Alice Williams. The rest of the capital newspapers copied the *Enquirer*'s mistake, and Lauretta apparently did nothing to correct them. Given her appetite for publicity, Lauretta may have allowed the erroneous Alice to stand when she saw how much press coverage she got. Her focus always was on immediate publicity.[15]

Now confronting Winder, she again eschewed trying for sympathy and instead adopted what someone in the War Office regarded as "an independent air," warning that if he tried to press charges against her, she would "claim foreign protection" as a British subject over whom Confederate authorities had no authority. Thus, for the moment at least, she persisted in her claim that she had been born in the Bahamas. The bluff failed, however, for Winder concluded that "there was something wrong about her" and ordered her sent to Castle Thunder, the city's prison for suspected disloyal citizens, spies, and political prisoners. Meanwhile, the press learned of her arrival, not doubting that she was the *Mississippian*'s Laura J. Williams, as she claimed, for she seemed, in the *Enquirer*'s words, "not of the build to be frightened easily by either gun or goblin."

The next day newspaper coverage of her stay in Richmond commenced unsympathetically with that same paper's observation that she was "not quite as pretty as the romance of her case might admit."[16] Referring to her Purdom interview, the *Examiner* recalled that "recently a glowing account of a female, in Confederate uniform, went the rounds of the Southern press" and sarcastically commented that "she was a second Joan of Arc, and had done, and was to do more remarkable things," evidence that she was in danger of being ridiculed again. Still, so far as anyone knew, no specific charges faced her other than posing as a man and officer.[17] Within days Confederates read of "a female Lieutenant" imprisoned in the capital.[18] The appellation began to stick.

Captain George W. Alexander, commandant at Castle Thunder, took charge of Lauretta on her arrival. One of his officers found that Lieutenant Buford was "well formed, and had the bearing of a soldier," but Winder's statement that this was in fact a woman took the staff by surprise. They placed Lauretta in quarters with other female political prisoners, and there she made the best of her time in the "Castle." She obligingly told her latest amended version of the *Mississippian* story, now having her husband,

Williams, killed in action after joining the Yankees, and saying that after her Shiloh wound she remained on the field, where Federal surgeons discovered her sex and sent her to New Orleans.[19]

During her fortnight at Castle Thunder, Lauretta alternately charmed and bullied the inmates and superintendents. One officer recalled in 1879 that she wore her uniform constantly, probably having no other clothes with her when arrested, and though generally good-natured, she often became indignant at her treatment. Jailers allowed her to roam in the Castle and employed her in its office when they needed letters written. They also let her walk outside the prison occasionally under guard, and characteristically, she soon demanded that she be allowed to go out on her own, since no charges had been filed against her. One of her favorite officers asked Mayor Joseph Mayo if an exception could not be made to the statute prohibiting women from appearing in public in men's clothes, but he refused.[20] Mayo was apparently alone in not giving Lauretta her way, for "she quite took the Castle," one visitor discovered. "She got acquainted with everybody, ordered everybody about, and by her bustling manner and busy ways threw the commandant quite in the shade."[21]

She may have gotten acquainted with an inmate calling himself Harvey Birch, a sometime correspondent of the New York *Herald* who had been captured by Confederate cavalry. His real name was Charles Dunham, a lifelong impostor whose schemes in time rivaled Lauretta's. She seemed always drawn to men with a streak of charlatanry like her own, and though nothing Birch soon said of their brief acquaintance was accurate or reliable, still some of it resonates with her later activities.[22] Yet if they were acquainted, it must have been fleetingly, for now and later he knew her only as Alice Williams, suggesting that he knew only what appeared about her in the city press, mistakes and all.

Winder found nothing warranting further incarceration and ordered Lauretta's release on July 10.[23] She remained in the city for a few days, and according to Dunham, "the celebrated she Lieutenant Buford" actually lodged in Castle Thunder, perhaps because the room cost her nothing. According to him, Lauretta was "boarding, drinking, gambling and carousing with Capt. Alexander and other officers." Dunham wrote for a Northern audience, to whom he could expect Lauretta to be virtually unknown. He also hoped to be paid by Washington for information on Confederate spies. He saw in Lauretta a vehicle to that end and soon claimed that a guard told him she intended to go north via truce boat, pretending to be one of a number

Makeshift prison known as Castle Thunder, which would be Lauretta's "home" for two weeks until General Winder was finally persuaded she was not a spy. Library of Congress.

of Unionist women recently captured at Winchester. Dunham even later claimed that the day before she left prison, "the fair lieutenant" jokingly told him she would go to Baltimore and perhaps see him there after his release, implying that she intended to spy for the South.[24] As her actual movements demonstrated, that was pure invention, either his or hers, or both.[25]

One or two reporters got some brief details from her to flesh out the *Mississippian* profile, and Lauretta continued to hone her story. She added another turn to the maze of her claimed pedigrees. Discarding Nassau specifically, now she said she was born in the West Indies, a vastly broader territory. More significantly, forgetting or discarding her earlier claim to have been born Clark, she now for the first time named her father as Major J. B. Roche, then a wealthy Mississippi planter. Given her earlier claim to be a foreign national and her assertion of birth in the British islands, she may have meant to imply that he was English, but no one named Roche lived in Mississippi immediately before the war. There were many Roches and Roaches in Louisiana, but none with the initials J. B. and none from England or the West Indies.

She boasted that she had an annual income of $20,000 before the war, but that for the past two years she had spent most of that buying medicine for the Confederate government or following the marching army in her own ambulance loaded with medicines, bandages, and a slave, tending the wounded after every action. Thus she made herself a Florence Nightingale to wounded Confederates, a guise she would return to again. Meanwhile, based on rumor, the press, or Lauretta's own claims, one reporter declared that "she has been known to lend a helping hand with the musket at several battles in which she participated." Still, she said nothing about First Manassas now and only implied presence at Shiloh. Even now, added that reporter, "she persists in sporting her military costume and it was this that got her into trouble."[26] It was all invention, of course, and the claim to have spent the past two years following the army cavalierly contradicted her entire *Mississippian* account.

Her claim to have had a slave with her when she ministered to the wounded would be unique, the only time during the war that she mentioned a slave, and she would not do so again until 1876. The mention now demands a look at what may genuinely be said about her involvement with and attitude toward slavery. Her later assertion rests entirely with Bob, a "smart and mannerly negro boy" she claimed to have purchased in Montgomery, Alabama, around June 18, 1861. In that instant a problem arose. She also later said she met with Secretary of War Leroy Pope Walker the day before, on June 17, whereas he actually had left Montgomery weeks earlier and had been in Richmond since June 2. Thereafter, Lauretta put Bob with her when she arrived in Virginia prior to First Bull Run, adding that she threatened to kill him if he tried to run away from her, and soon he was with her in the skirmish at Blackburn's Ford on July 18. Yet there was no mention of a slave being with her when, as Mary Ann Keith, she had her first documented encounter with the authorities in Lynchburg and Richmond in September and October 1861, which initially brought her to the attention of the press and the Confederacy.[27] Her 1876 account made no mention of Bob being with her either.

Just over two weeks later, however, she recalled him at her side at the Battle of Ball's Bluff on October 22, where he took part in the fighting, and she found herself "proud of the darkey's pluck and enthusiasm." Thereafter, she placed him with her at Fort Donelson and Shiloh, and when he disappeared following the latter, she maintained that "this vexed me extremely, for Bob had become an invaluable servant, being very handy and entirely trustworthy." Meanwhile, the press reports of her appearance in New Orleans following Shiloh failed to mention any slave male with the ragged Buford on his crutch. Then in June 1863 she found Bob once more in Grenada, Mississippi.[28]

After that, he disappeared entirely without trace or explanation, as if Lauretta just forgot him. It is worth noting that in all of the wartime press accounts of her activities, there is no mention of her having a slave or traveling with a black male, nor did Bob appear anywhere else in her postwar interviews and accounts. He existed only in her 1876 narrative and only in her imagination. That she would ever have had the wherewithal to buy a slave before or during the war strains credulity. In 1860 she was a prostitute, a trade that could pay well but hardly provided sufficient discretionary income to save enough to cover the cost of a young male, and nothing in Lauretta's known history suggests that she ever saved money. Her financial condition when the war began is unknown, but in the summer and fall of 1862 she was destitute and reduced to conning room and board from the Chesters while stealing their jewelry to pawn. A slave male like Bob could cost $1,000 to $1,500 on the thriving and inflated New Orleans market.

Bob was just another fictional device reflecting nothing of Lauretta's reality. It did serve her pretensions of having been an antebellum lady of means, lending her the status of the slave-owning class, but if she regarded Bob as a truly significant trope, it seems hardly likely that her narrative would just leave him in limbo at Grenada and thereafter forget him. Never having been a slave owner in real life, Lauretta could not appreciate the depth of import that a slave held to his master. No real slaveholder would just forget about property that for many represented their largest capital investment.

Nevertheless, in 1876 Lauretta did place herself in the mainstream of American, and particularly Southern, attitudes toward slavery and blacks. She repeatedly referred to Bob as "my boy" or "the darkey." When she described other slaves or free black people, it was in terms like "grinning until he showed all his ivories" and had "eyes as big as saucers." She reinforced the belief that slaves could not be trusted when she blamed her betrayal to General Butler on a treacherous black person. During her spying visits to the North, she claimed to have met people there disgusted that the war had become one to achieve emancipation, and when she returned to New Orleans for the first time postwar, she found the South "in the hands of ignorant negroes."[29] Lauretta rarely revealed her attitudes toward race and slavery, but it is reasonable to assume that she shared the prevailing values of lower- and working-class New Orleanians in the 1860s.

Back at Castle Thunder a rumor soon circulated that Lauretta had become so popular that someone, Captain Alexander perhaps, offered her an appointment as a clerk and even that she may have accepted. "She longs for the wars, however," noted one journalist, "and will not be content to hold it long."[30] Indeed not, for sometime during the five days following her release, Lauretta called at the War Department to see Adjutant General Samuel Cooper, perhaps to inquire about her application for a commission—on which no action would be taken—or to offer her services as Mrs. Williams or Harry Buford alike. She certainly prevailed on him to give her a pass and some money for rail travel. The government had brought her to Richmond for no good reason, and she could rightfully demand that it return her at its expense at least as far as Atlanta. She also probably got his permission to write to him occasionally with any pertinent observations made as she traveled. He could expect little from that, but for her part, such letters ought to generate letters of acknowledgment in return, documents she could display as evidence of her connections and intimacy with high-ranking Confederates. As she soon demonstrated, she understood instinctively that the most mundane note from someone in authority could be parlayed into a document lending weight and legitimacy to almost any claim.

Armed with Cooper's pass, she boarded a train on July 16 to start for Atlanta. Behind her she left charmed newsmen entirely taken in by her story. "It is hardly probable that this brave but eccentric woman will be kept out of the fights in Mississippi," wrote one.[31] Vicksburg had fallen to Grant on July 4, and the most recent information was that the Federals were threatening Jackson once more. Noting on her departure that "she is brave, but eccentric, and certainly has an ambition to distinguish herself in the sphere allotted to man," another paper agreed that "if she is allowed the opportunity, she will doubtless take a hand in the fight at Jackson."[32] No one in Richmond yet knew that Confederate forces had abandoned Jackson that same day. Most fulsome of all was the *Enquirer*, which touted the valuable service of "the distinguished female lieutenant" as both nurse and soldier, concluding that "she appears to be all her published history represents her to be—a woman of heroic character, fearing no danger, dreading no trial, shunning no duty that her self-chosen fortune may send her." The writer wished her a long life "to enjoy her fame."[33]

In noticing her departure, the *Dispatch* and *Sentinel* adopted the *Enquirer*'s earlier—and continued—mistake of calling her Alice Williams, an error echoed elsewhere in the Confederate press, even though the authorities had in hand her application for a commission, which she had signed as Lauretta. More important from her point of view, the *Enquirer* gave her a new sobriquet that other papers copied, and which she immediately adopted herself. Hereafter, she would be "the female Lieutenant."[34]

After reporting on her throughout her incarceration, the press continued to cover her movements after she left Richmond.[35] When she changed trains on July 18 in Columbia, South Carolina, a local editor commented of "this far-famed female soldier" that "she has already been in the service a great while, and is represented to be a woman of heroic character, fearing no danger and shrinking from no undertaking." He added that "Mrs. Lt. Alice Williams" was now on her way to active service in the field, which is the story she would have given if asked.[36] Interestingly enough, a fellow passenger on her train out of Richmond was Confederate vice president Alexander H. Stephens. Neither left any statement to indicate that they met, but it would have been uncharacteristic of her to let pass an opportunity to corner an important man and press her case for a commission, or at least a note of recommendation to add to her rail pass and any other documents signed by important men. Her slight acquaintance with him years later thus may have begun before he got off at Columbia.[37] Brief speculation in that city suggested that she might have traveled with him as an aide, one editor extending to the mildest of innuendoes when he mentioned that Stephens "is a bachelor, we believe."[38]

Her whole Richmond experience attracted attention, from appearing in uniform under arrest, through incarceration at Castle Thunder, then release and departure once more, and that is just what she would have wanted. Moreover, many of her new embellishments to her story got into the papers, no doubt through her own agency. Soon the fame of Lieutenant Harry Buford, "the female Lieutenant," spread through the Confederacy. Articles from the Richmond papers found their way into journals elsewhere in Virginia, in South Carolina and Georgia, and probably as far as Alabama and Tennessee.[39] It was not all as she might have wished. As before, a few thought her story more deserving of sarcasm than celebration. One South Carolina editor dubbed this woman in uniform "Puss in Boots," calling her "the far famed female soldier, who we never heard of," and referred to the many "hair breadth 'scapes" in her adventures.[40]

In fact, she was doing a small service for the Confederacy now, though clearly unsolicited and entirely unofficial. On her trip back to Atlanta, Lauretta made note of the number of civilian men she saw on the trains and the further numbers of men in uniform she saw at quartermaster and commissary depots along the way. She thought they ought to have been with the armies in the field. When she reached Atlanta on the evening of July 19, she stopped first at the office of the city provost marshal, Captain George Washington Lee, to whom she told a sufficiently convincing story of her "mission" that he agreed to let her use his office address for her correspondence, a clever move that subtly reinforced her claims to be on official government business. The next day she returned to Lee's office to write a brief letter to Cooper to give him what she called "my oppinion of the war" and in particular noted the chagrin she felt at so many able-bodied young men being wasted in noncombatant roles. "There are plenty of Old Men & criples that can fill those positions," she told him, begging that he inform President Davis and get him to order all such men into the field, "or Else we will be lost." She believed as many as 110,000 soldiers could thus be added to their armies.

Her letter made it evident that she had no official sanction or mission as an agent of the War Department. In fact, she closed with an apology for sending unsolicited information. "I take this liberty of adressing you and hope you will not think me bold by so doing," she told Cooper. "Boldness in woman I depracate," she continued, while "the want of it in Man att the present crisis of times I deplore." As evidence that she closely followed the headlines about her, she closed her letter "the female Lieutenant whoes whole soul is Enlisted in her countrys cause." She signed it "Mrs. Laurretta J. Williams Alias Lieut H. T. Buford."[41] The press might call her Alice, but she expected Cooper to recognize her as Lauretta, more evidence that Alice was no alias of her invention.

She spent perhaps a week in Atlanta, maybe observing and sending more unsolicited letters to the War Department, and then took a train west to Montgomery, Alabama, arriving about the end of July. Whatever her purpose in going, she made no effort to conceal her identity. Montgomery had been kept abreast of her story thus far that summer by the Richmond papers, and the local press let its readers know that she was in town, where they saw her on the streets for several days into early August.[42] Then she returned to Atlanta, where her life was about to take a sudden, and bizarre, new turn.

CHAPTER FOUR

"IN SECRET SERVICE"

SOMEHOW LAURETTA MET a recuperating officer, Captain Thomas C. DeCaulp of Company D, 3rd Arkansas Cavalry. She later told conflicting stories of how and when they met, none more dramatic than her tale in 1876 of him serving in her late husband's company at Pensacola and of their later fighting together at Shiloh, their subsequent epistolary courtship, and their wooing here in Atlanta, all with DeCaulp unaware that his friend Lieutenant Buford was really Lauretta. The prosaic reality is that they probably met now while he convalesced in the city's Empire Hotel Hospital. Beyond that bare fact, little else about their meeting can be verified.

DeCaulp himself was a man of riddles, though his wartime service to date was straightforward enough. In July 1861 authorities organized the 1st Arkansas Mounted Volunteers, which included Solon Borland's 1st Arkansas Cavalry Battalion, raised chiefly from men in Little Rock and Pulaski County, though DeCaulp and some others actually enlisted at Pocahontas in northeastern Arkansas.[1] The War Department redesignated the outfit the 3rd Arkansas Cavalry on January 15, 1862, and during its career it saw more action than any other mounted unit from the state, though it never reached full strength in men or horses. In fact, only 395 men without mounts crossed the Mississippi River when the regiment transferred east in April 1862, and it remained dismounted for some months to come.

DeCaulp enlisted at the age of twenty-five in Borland's battalion on July 29, 1861, even though he claimed to be a native of Pennsylvania.[2] Soon he rose to corporal, then on May 26, 1862, the men in his company elected him second lieutenant, and on August 6 he won promotion to first lieutenant. At that time DeCaulp and other officers of the regiment petitioned for permission to return to Arkansas to get their horses, but they were still dismounted in the Battle of Iuka in September.[3] The Federals captured him in the Battle of Corinth on October 3–4 but paroled him the next day, coincidentally just as he was promoted captain to command of Company D of his regiment.[4] The terms of his parole provided that he could not engage in active service until properly exchanged, making him of no use to the army in the interim, so it sent him and other parolees back to Arkansas on November 23 to collect horses to mount their company. By December 11 he returned to his unit at Camp Rogers, near Waterford, Mississippi, there to learn—if he did not know it already—that he had been officially exchanged on December 2. He was still with his unit at Grenada, Mississippi, on the last day of the year.[5]

DeCaulp's whereabouts are uncertain for the next few months, though presumably he was with his regiment until May 14, 1863, when he was detached and sent to Atlanta to the Empire Hospital.[6] The cause appears to have been an illness, probably in his lungs, and it was serious enough that he was still there three months later when Lauretta came to town. Theirs was a whirlwind courtship, which became a habit with her in years ahead. Apparently a handsome man, DeCaulp stood almost six feet tall, with a fair complexion, gray eyes, and dark hair.[7] Sometime in early September Lauretta became his wife. Despite her claims to date, and many more to follow, it was probably her first marriage.

Unfortunately for the impostor "female lieutenant," she had been taken in by her male equivalent for a change. Her new husband was not Thomas C. DeCaulp. Within three months he would tell Union authorities that he was really William Irwin, a carpenter from the Philadelphia area. If he told the truth, then he was probably the carpenter W. L. Irwin, born in 1831–32, who lived in A. F. Dyer's boardinghouse in Little Rock in June 1860.[8] The outbreak of war had caught him in a seceded state, he said, and to avoid harassment as a disloyal alien, he had enlisted in a Confederate regiment under an assumed name.[9] Why he chose DeCaulp is especially puzzling, for it was entirely an invention. No one else in the divided nation carried that surname, unless it was his own misspelling of something else like DeKalb.[10]

His whole story seems improbable. Arkansas did not secede until May 6, and Irwin had ample time after the secession crisis arose the previous December to leave Little Rock and return to the North had he wished. His likely motive for remaining was something quite different, and perhaps another problem of which Lauretta as yet knew nothing. Not only was DeCaulp not DeCaulp, but she was not lawfully Mrs. DeCaulp. Thomas already had a wife.

During his time gathering horses in Arkansas, DeCaulp had wooed and won the prosperous thirty-eight-year-old widow Sarah Ann Hollingshead Haralson. Giving his name as Thomas R. DeCalp, age twenty-seven, he married her at her Little Rock home on December 8, 1862.[11] Given that a good horse on good road could travel up to forty or more miles a day, it was just barely possible for him to be married that day in Little Rock and still arrive back at Camp Rogers nearly 175 miles away by late December 11.[12] It is also possible that since the marriage was not registered until February 10, 1863, it was conveniently backdated to December after Sarah discovered that she was pregnant.[13] Certainly her pregnancy was not hypothetical. On September 5, 1863, exactly 271 days after the presumed marriage, she gave birth to a son she named Thomas Edwin DeCaulp.[14]

It is wonderfully coincidental that DeCaulp's son by Sarah Haralson, of whose anticipated existence he possibly knew nothing, was born at almost the same moment that the captain and Lauretta stood before the Rev. Samuel J. Pinkerton in the parlor of the Atlanta Hotel.[15] The wedding date was certainly during the first two weeks of September and possibly that same September 5.[16] Coincidentally, the Episcopalian Pinkerton was himself a Pennsylvanian, as Thomas claimed to be, from just the opposite side of Philadelphia, and he too claimed to have been driven from his home for his political beliefs.[17] DeCaulp seems to have been Episcopalian himself, and Lauretta now embraced that denomination.[18] News of the marriage spread, and before the end of the month a Savannah editor noted that "the female Lieutenant, 'Harry Bufford,' *nee* Mrs. Williams, whose history in connection with this war is full of romance, has, it is said, married a gentleman of Georgia by the name of DeCaulp, and has been commissioned with the rank of Captain." Confusing the place of their marriage for the state of DeCaulp's origin, the editor further indicated that Lauretta was a native of Mississippi.[19]

Some in the press were less friendly. "We know nothing of the character of these parties," an Augusta editor opined about ten days after the marriage.

> The matter is invested with an air of romance that may be captivating to the young and thoughtless, and mischievous in its influence, and we therefore allude to it to express regret that any Southern woman, however ardent her patriotism and pure her purposes, should so far discard the delicacy of her sex, and all regard for a public sense of decorum as to enter the army as a soldier.[20]

Almost as if reacting to that criticism, Lauretta now put aside Lieutenant Harry T. Buford for good. DeCaulp claimed a few months hence that he wanted her to give up the impersonation for her safety, and she later said the same, but there may have been more to it than that.[21] Despite her spreading publicity, no one in Confederate officialdom took her seriously. The War Department continued to ignore her application for a commission.[22] Many in the press doubted her claims, and male criticism even tarnished the notice of her wedding. Her pleas of Unionism in November 1862 stemmed from self-interest, but her loyalty to the Confederacy—like her later attachments to men, causes, and even children—was not much stronger and was driven as much by exigency as conviction. By early September she was perhaps already prepared to bolt if she did not get more respect and some recognition from the Confederacy, including an income. Years later she lauded Southerners who held out to the last, but her dedication now was nothing if not elastic.

As it happened, her new husband, DeCaulp, was fed up with the Confederacy as well, even as the hospital discharged him to return to his regiment with General Braxton Bragg's Army of Tennessee, then concentrating in north Georgia on the verge of a major battle. The newlyweds' discussions of their mutual frustrations are unrecorded, but when he left barely a week after their nuptials, they apparently had an understanding and some kind of plan to reunite soon, and in a radically different venue.

As soon as DeCaulp departed, Lauretta left for Richmond in search of money and perhaps a last attempt at the validation of an assignment to some useful duty.[23] She reached the capital around September 12 or 13, checked into the Ballard House, and immediately made her presence known to the press, which ran new headlines about "The Female Lieutenant." In womanly attire she held court in her hotel room, and she found that she was not the only person of note at the hotel. Pierre Soulé, author of the 1854 Ostend Manifesto, which proposed that the United States must acquire Cuba from Spain by purchase or force, was staying there after his return from a Northern prison. Her opportunity to meet Soulé is interesting in light of her postwar interest in Cuba and perhaps influenced her thinking. Also present was Major Juan Miangolara, commander of a small Louisiana partisan battalion, who somehow knew her, either from earlier acquaintance in New Orleans or meeting her now. On September 14 Miangolara met Henri Garidel, an exile from New Orleans stuck in Richmond, and took him to Lauretta's room to hear her recount yet again her adventures.

Garidel had read about her in the Richmond papers in July, so he knew of her as Alice Williams, and she made no correction during their interview, in which etiquette called for the use of surnames only. He saw before him "a fine-looking woman," in a black muslin skirt decorated with white flowers and a white blouse. She spoke well, with a slight lisp that others noted occasionally in later years, but he concluded that her speech aberration originated in some missing front teeth. She employed several ruses to win his confidence, starting with claiming to have a mutual friend in Dr. Felix Formento, an internationally distinguished physician of Europe and New Orleans who was well outside Lauretta's social orbit when she lived in that city. Then, presaging her later technique for establishing her bona fides, she displayed a collection of papers and documents, including what she called her "commission," which would have been something she created herself or one of her old passes from Winder or Cooper. Now and hereafter she became increasingly skilled at wringing apparent official endorsements from meaningless documents. Still, by now many people accepted her claim to be an officer, even if with slight reservation, as when the editor of the *Enquirer* noted that "Mrs. de Caulp, formerly Mrs. Williams, holds, it seems, a Captain's commission."[24]

Continuing the subtle yet constant amendment of her myth, Lauretta told Garidel that she had been the first lieutenant of a company commanded by her first husband, who was killed early in the war. She did not give his name, but it was implicit from other things she said that Williams had been his name and was not her maiden name. She often served as a spy as well as a soldier, and the number of her wounds now escalated to three. She was newly married to DeCaulp, who she said was still ill in Atlanta, and she had given up her uniform since he did not want her serving in the army anymore. Boasting of having collected considerable back pay on this trip to Richmond, she declared she would give it all to the ill and indigent in Atlanta. Garidel felt delighted after his interview. "I had heard a lot about her," he wrote that night in his diary, "and I had wanted to meet her." Already interested by her celebrity, thereafter he collected clippings about "the famous female lieutenant."[25]

With her customary indifference to self-contradiction, she told others that she had divorced her husband, John Williams, who she said was then in the Yankee army in Mississippi, and claimed that when she left Richmond two months earlier, she went not to Atlanta, but to Chattanooga, where she obtained a position on Major General A. P. Stewart's staff in Bragg's army to perform "secret service" work making important arrests of spies and "doing some very daring things." She also announced that she had been given a commission as a captain in the army, along with $1,600 in back pay, and soon would be leaving for her husband's home in Georgia.[26]

It was virtually all invention, probably including her claim now to be a native of Mississippi, though that was perhaps more probable than Nassau or the West Indies. In the eight weeks since she left Richmond on July 16, she was in Atlanta from July 20 until late in the month, then in Montgomery at least through the first week of August, then back in Atlanta long enough to meet, fall in love with, and marry DeCaulp in early September. That left no time for any trip to Chattanooga to serve on Stewart's staff or engage in secret service duty arresting spies.[27] Far from her gaining a captaincy in the Confederate army, her June 25 application for a commission had bounced around officialdom from the War Department to the president and back until August 4, when it was returned to Cooper's office to be filed without action.[28] Her husband was from Arkansas, not Georgia, and it seems hardly likely that the government gave her any money at all in return for a letter or two of unsolicited opinions.

Only the press seemed interested, even using her now as a point of reference.[29] A writer for the Richmond *Enquirer*, reflecting on the history of women taking arms in Europe against oppressors, commented that "here in the Confederacy we have seen some examples of the same female heroism" and offered her as his sole example.[30] Then dramatic news of victory at the Battle of Chickamauga on September 19–20 nudged her second Richmond sojourn from most front pages. By that time she was gone, only the *Examiner* noting her leaving, and few papers beyond Virginia and Georgia taking note.[31]

Lauretta left Richmond on September 17 or 18, probably on a train conveying men from Lieutenant General James Longstreet's corps west to reinforce Bragg's army at Chickamauga. When the train passed through Augusta, Georgia, she may even have seen the less-than-complimentary notice of her marriage that appeared in the city press a few days before. There was compensation, however, in being regarded as something of a celebrity on the train. Even though she wore a dress now and rode in the ladies' car, still word of who she was got around. Colonel Martin W. Gary of South Carolina discovered her there and soon brought some visiting British observers in to see her. She impressed them as "young, good-looking, and ladylike." For their benefit she promoted DeCaulp to major and regaled them with her own adventures in what one officer called "a pleasant quiet way." Gary came away convinced that she had "fairly earned her epaulettes," though she said she was now retired from military service. At every station on the route crowds cheered the passing soldiers, and most likely Lauretta regretted that she no longer wore her uniform so that some of the cheers might be for her.[32]

When the train reached Atlanta later that day, she passed out of sight for the next two months.[33] More than that, she passed out of the Confederacy. Lieutenant Harry T. Buford would be seen no more. Only the sketchiest of evidence hints at her movements or whereabouts. As long as DeCaulp stayed in Atlanta, she likely remained with him. When he left, so did she. Ten months later she gave a brief account in which it is implicit that when she left, she went by rail to Mobile, and thence north on the Mobile & Ohio to Okolona, Mississippi, the headquarters of Brigadier General Samuel W. Ferguson's cavalry brigade. There or in that vicinity she came into possession of two pistols and what she called "a Rebbel belt" that she somehow connected with Ferguson, though whether he gave them to her or she "captured" them from one of his couriers—she claimed both versions in time—is unknown. Then she traveled north overland and infiltrated Yankee lines outside Memphis or bluffed her way through a guard post, giving her name as Mrs. Lauretta J. DeCaulp.

By October she was in occupied Memphis, where she told a story convincing enough that the Union provost gave her passes and a permit to travel to Nashville.[34] That hardly means that she told the truth, of course, for in July 1864 she assured Union brigadier general Joseph D. Webster, "I have not bin in the Rebbel lines since last September," adding, "I was then sent through after my husband who was sick at Atlanta."[35] In short, she claimed that she had not spent the past two years and more in the Confederacy. Rather, she implied that she had been behind *Union* lines prior to September 1863 and only crossed into the Confederacy to tend to DeCaulp, to whom she was not actually married prior to September. Some of her contemporary accounts may be plausible, or they may all be pure invention, but it is certain that she did turn up in Memphis in October and had with her at least one pistol that she told Federal authorities she had captured from one of Ferguson's couriers. As for the "Rebbel belt," years later she claimed that she brought a captured dispatch to Memphis, and if the belt was designed for carrying documents, then she may have been in the vicinity of fact.

Her husband, Captain DeCaulp, was in Yankee territory too. He returned to his regiment with Bragg's army, though just when is unclear. He may not have been with it for the Battle of Chickamauga on September 19–20, but he certainly rejoined his regiment sometime in the three weeks following, though not for long. Illness and his recent marriage took away whatever stomach he had for continued Confederate service and probably for fighting itself. By this time he and Lauretta had a plan they had framed weeks earlier. On or about October 15 Thomas left his company and successfully passed through the lines to the Federal pickets outside the besieged Union army in Chattanooga. Surrendering himself as a deserter, he avowed his loyalty to the United States as a citizen of the North and swore an oath of allegiance. Then he told a good enough story to be taken to Major General William S. Rosecrans, commanding the Army of the Cumberland, who gave him a document attesting to his being a citizen in good standing. Sent first to Nashville, he was released on October 23.[36]

Just why he and his wife chose this moment for him to desert is puzzling. It could hardly have had anything to do with the birth of his son, Thomas Edwin DeCaulp, on September 5 in Little Rock, since the father made no effort now or later to return to Arkansas and probably did not yet know that he now had a son. He had closed the book on that chapter of his life. With DeCaulp, as with Lauretta, little was as it seemed. He claimed that he was a Union man trapped in a Confederate state in the summer of 1861, and his name change and enlistment were matters of self-preservation. Now he deserted to get back to the Union, and Lauretta soon echoed that same story. Yet his own recent experience makes that highly improbable. If he wanted to desert, he did not have to wait until September 1863 after more than two years of Confederate service and at least one wound. He and his regiment were frequently within easy reach of Union lines in Mississippi through much of 1862, or he could have crossed over in northern Arkansas when he was away from the army on parole in the fall of that year. Most telling of all, however, was his capture at Corinth that October. As a prisoner he was already safely inside Yankee lines, and all he had to do was what he did now, explain his case and take an oath of allegiance. Instead, he allowed himself to be paroled back to Confederate lines, and now in deserting, he took the risk of being executed as a deserter.

Ultimately, his real motive for deserting remains murky. It does not seem likely to have been a hasty or spur-of-the-moment decision. He had weeks in the Atlanta hospital to think about it, and making plans had to have involved careful forethought. Of course, Lauretta had a considerable power of persuasion with men. The year before, she had persuaded Private John Williams to desert his regiment in an attempt to escape New Orleans with her. If she had decided to cross the lines into the North now for her own purposes, she might have been able to lead DeCaulp in the same direction. Nevertheless, it seems clear that the primary decision to leave the Confederacy was his, and she adjusted her own course accordingly. She was just about twenty-one, young enough to make apparently strong—or advantageous—attachments quickly, as she would do again more than once in the future, and it appears that she genuinely loved DeCaulp. If he decided to desert, her choice to go north could have been motivated by nothing more than a compulsion to be with him. Just eight months later DeCaulp would gratefully remind her of how, in leaving the Confederacy, she had "forsaked suhor [sure] riches and dear friends to follow the object of her heart in the sight of *Almighty God*."[37]

In addition, the Confederate government's failure to provide some recognition led to disillusionment, if her later complaints are credited.[38] Throughout her life her loyalties were superficial. She adopted and dropped plans and causes with equal ease, so leaving the Confederacy may not have been wrenching. That she gave it up so readily reveals at best a lack of depth in her commitment and the forces of impulse and impetuosity that now and hereafter influenced her. If Thomas decided to desert at this moment, her devotion to him might have been enough to carry her across the lines to Yankeedom in her own act of desertion. Whatever her motives, it meant the end of the summer of Harry Buford. It had lasted barely four months from mid-June to October.

Somehow the couple reestablished contact in Nashville, which was close to midway between her entry point at Memphis and his at Chattanooga. She probably got there first and could have met him almost immediately after his release on October 23. Once together, their most direct route into the North was the railroad to Louisville, and thence north into Indiana. Surprisingly, DeCaulp did not take them to Philadelphia and his Irwin family, which raises more doubt about that part of his story. Instead, they stopped at Indianapolis, where for the next several weeks they established a semblance of housekeeping.[39] How they obtained the money even to travel that far is a mystery, yet Lauretta seemed always able to get by somehow. Now they had a compelling story to tell of love and loyalty and salvation from Rebeldom, which she could parlay into well-intentioned donations. Despite the reports that she probably created herself, it is highly unlikely that the Confederacy paid handsomely for past services she never performed. Still, she might have collected contributions from people given audiences in her room at the Ballard House, a recourse she would use again in the future.

Somehow they had enough to rent a room a long walk outside the city. DeCaulp found a job, but the illness in his lungs recurred, and his earnings could not support them. He put a brave face on it, telling her, "I am smiling at my affliction keeping from you nothing that was in my power to aid your comfort concealing my feelings and pain fearing that it would worry you." Over his objections, she got a job at the Indiana State Arsenal and began work on or about November 1.[40] It was not difficult, though monotonous, rolling paper into "cartridges" and filling them with gunpowder and a bullet. She earned $10 that month, more than many of the women employed but barely over half what a few made at more specialized tasks. In December her earnings dropped to just $6, evidence that illness or other causes reduced her essentially to part-time work.[41] The employees were mostly soldiers' wives or daughters, and few if any could live on their earnings.[42] The work could be dangerous too. The year before, an explosion at a Pennsylvania arsenal killed seventy-eight workers, most of them women.

No wonder Thomas did not like her being there. She had a long walk every morning and evening in the winter cold and faced constant hazard at work. "My minde was never easy during the day knowing the dangerous situation under which you were placed," he told her, and when he finished his own workday, "it was always a pleasure on returning at night to finde you safe at home."[43] The time they had together seems to have been placid and affectionate. She called him Thomas and he called her Nettie, a derivative of Jeanette, the middle name she now used.

Nettie was never reluctant to be assertive. After about five weeks, during a break from work at the arsenal on December 7, she wrote to Governor Oliver P. Morton with an idea that she and her husband probably conceived together. Thomas wanted to join the Union army and become a recruiter, but of Confederates. The government maintained a substantial prisoner-of-war facility at Camp Morton in Indianapolis. At the same time, it commenced a program of enlisting some prisoners into the Union army to send them to the Northwest, where the Sioux posed a constant threat. That promised to get men out of the squalor of the prison camps, requiring only their affidavit that they were Union men compelled into the Rebel service against their will and that they had escaped at the first opportunity.[44] It also freed northwestern regiments of loyal Northern men for the fronts in Tennessee and Virginia. Eventually about six thousand former Confederates thus became what were known as Galvanized Yankees.

Lauretta asked the governor to commission DeCaulp to go into Camp Morton to recruit, asserting that he could find and enlist at least a hundred men who, like himself, had been caught in the South when the war began. There was small risk of anyone noticing that he had been a prisoner in 1862 and could have "gone north" then. "He is a northern man borned in Philadelphia," she told Morton. Moreover, she said she could produce a letter from General Rosecrans attesting to her husband's loyalty, enjoining the governor to "pleas give this matter A thought."[45]

Apparently Morton did not act directly in the matter, or at least not as Lauretta requested. However, Thomas remained determined to find better employment for himself that might allow his wife to leave the arsenal, and the military seemed the surest means. As he reminded her a few months later, "It was on that account that I enlisted in the army, and to get you away from Indianapolis knowing that your health would not last if you continued at the arsenal."[46] He decided to go into the Union army as a substitute, a means whereby a drafted man could escape service by paying another to enlist in his place. A substitute could earn several hundred dollars if he made a good bargain, and that would free them from Indianapolis. DeCaulp traveled to Baltimore in mid-December, and there on the seventeenth he volunteered as a substitute. The next day he was enrolled for three years' service.[47] However, he had to wait until a draftee came forward to engage him and was ordered in the meantime to remain at Mason's Island in the Potomac opposite Washington.[48]

While there, DeCaulp resurrected his effort to secure a commission. He met with Assistant Adjutant General Major Louis H. Pelouze at the War Department to repeat his application and provided what he called "statements containing important informations of the so-called Confederate States." It is doubtful that Thomas had any useful intelligence from his perspective as a company commander of cavalry who had spent much of the year in the hospital. Pelouze interviewed him and apparently came to the same conclusion, for there would be no commission.[49] DeCaulp also approached a senator then in Washington for the session of Congress, explained that he had been "a good Union man" forced into the Confederate army, and asked for a letter of introduction to the commander of Union forces in Minnesota.[50] Why he chose Minnesota is unclear, but logically it would place him as far away from the Confederacy as possible to avert risk of capture and identification as a deserter. Then too, it is just possible that Lauretta knew people there, since back in November 1862 she told the provost court in New Orleans that she had known the Chesters in Minnesota before the war.[51] Instead, sometime in January 1864 DeCaulp received orders to go to Milwaukee to report to Brigadier General T. C. H. Smith, commanding the District of Wisconsin.

Back in Indianapolis Lauretta collected her pay at the arsenal on January 1 and left for Washington, expecting to rejoin Thomas there.[52] On her arrival she could not find him, though he might still have been there. If he had written to let her know he was ordered to Wisconsin, or if he left word of where she could find him, she failed to get the message. Genuinely distressed, she went to see Major Pelouze himself to learn where her man had been sent so she could go to him. Any civilians, including wives, wishing to go to the army first had to secure a pass from Pelouze, whose decision was final in such matters.[53] Whatever she came away with depended on her powers of persuasion, which were well practiced. Her goal was to find Thomas, and for her no exaggeration or untruth was too great in its pursuit. She had already written to Governor Morton about Thomas's potential for recruiting former Confederates. She could embellish that considerably. Then there was Thomas's statement to Pelouze, something else she could embellish to magnify the importance of his "informations."

Finally, for more than two years, she had been inventing and customizing her own story to suit her purposes. She told Pelouze she knew prominent Union generals in Tennessee, as well as many officers in Washington. She had traveled in and out of enemy lines and moved extensively inside Confederate armies. In fact, she had even been caught by the Confederates and imprisoned twice in Richmond. In a brilliant twist, she used the unfounded suspicions of her being a Yankee spy in New Orleans in 1862 and in Richmond in 1861 and 1863 as means to establish her loyalty and value to the Union.[54]

Pelouze or his superiors concluded that she might be useful. The Northwest, especially Indiana, Illinois, Ohio, and Michigan, as well as Wisconsin, caused great concern just then. There were rumors of traitorous plots to release and arm Confederate prisoners there to create havoc on the Union home front. If Lauretta heard these rumblings in Indianapolis, then her claim to be a widely traveled detective might recommend her as someone who could glean useful information. Authorities in Washington read captured Richmond papers, and hence the past summer's articles about Lieutenant Buford and her lionization as Mrs. DeCaulp seemingly confirmed her claims. In fact, her well-publicized persona as the Confederacy's "Female Lieutenant" would be an asset to win the confidence of plotters if she were sent to report on disloyal activities. She could be on "secret service" without needing her identity to be secret.

Somehow she learned that Thomas had left for the Northwest, and she might catch up to him in Columbus, Ohio. Pelouze gave her an order for rail transportation at government expense to Columbus, which was hardly customary procedure in such cases. She received something more too, a document that she could mould to support a claim to be a "detective" on government business. Whatever it was, it was enough. Then, despite her lack of experience at nursing, she called at the U.S. Army Medical Department and bluffed an acting director into giving her a letter recommending her as a hospital matron, presumably to get employment when she joined Thomas in Wisconsin.[55]

Thus when she left Washington on or about January 24, she was carrying a document acknowledging—or that she could manipulate to acknowledge—something rather dramatic. Nothing suggests that she was to be paid, though that might depend on what she discovered and reported. She might have been authorized to call at the Camp Chase prison in Columbus for some purpose related to Thomas's proposal of enlisting prisoners of war to be "galvanized." More likely, she convinced Pelouze that hers would be good eyes to report suspicious movements of people suspected of disloyalty in the Northwest. It was a common civilian assignment given to both men and women, especially in Maryland, Ohio, and southern Indiana and Illinois, one of a number of minor tasks sometimes described as "special agent."

Lauretta reached Wheeling in the new state of West Virginia on January 26 and called on the local commander, Captain Ewald Over. What she told him and what documents she may have brought with her remain a mystery. Certainly she had an order from Pelouze to provide her with transportation, and that may have been all she had, but with her skills at persuasion, that could easily be embellished into much more. Whatever she showed or told him, Captain Over gave orders that same day to issue "Mrs. Laurietta Decaulp" a pass on the Baltimore & Ohio Railroad to Columbus, Ohio, "in secret service."[56] Whatever the nature of her assignment, as described in papers she now carried, Lauretta was in some degree a U.S. agent.[57]

CHAPTER FIVE

"WIN MY GLORY BACK"

SHE REACHED COLUMBUS the next day and immediately registered a room at the Neil House, the residence of Major General Samuel P. Heintzelman, who six days earlier had taken command of the Northern Department, encompassing Ohio, Indiana, Michigan, and Illinois.[1] As was typical of Lauretta, after finding that Thomas was no longer in the city, she took her problem to the top. A hotel clerk soon informed the general that a "Mrs. Major De Caulp" wanted to see him on "some very private business." Heintzelman went to her room, where he met a woman dressed in black, of medium height and what he called "tolerably full," between twenty-five and thirty years old, "and apparently quite intelligent."

She began by telling him of her search for Thomas, and he thought her "ready to burst into tears" as she confessed that she did not know "when where or how to find him." He advised her to write or telegraph Pelouze for more information, and then she startled him by shifting abruptly to her own story in a manner such that "you would suppose that she had nothing to trouble her." She told him she had been a detective and knew important officers in Washington and several generals in the western theater. She likely told him she was a detective now and could show Over's "in secret service" pass as evidence. Heintzelman let her talk, patiently listening as "she passed from one thing to another for an hour and a half at the least." She regaled him with her adventures passing back and forth across the lines into the Confederacy, telling him how she had been all through the Rebel armies and had been arrested and sent to Richmond on suspicion of being a spy in the fall of 1861 and again the past summer. She even invented a meeting with two captured Union generals in her Richmond prison in 1861, though she had not been imprisoned on that occasion, and neither of the generals was there while she was in the city. Still, Heintzelman, like most Northern officers, would have known that those generals had been prisoners in Richmond after capture at First Manassas, lending authenticity to her claims.

"The accounts she gave of her adventures were really quite interesting," he reflected that evening, though he still thought she "told a queer tale." Nonetheless, in one of the earliest known examples of Lauretta's skill at convincing people with fast talking and ample common-knowledge details, she took him in. "From the names of places & people & events," Heintzelman concluded, "there is no doubt of the facts." He was still convinced a few days later when she asked him to call again. He found her "in distress" and seeking his help to get to Chicago. Lending her $20, he told himself that she would repay him, "as I think there is little doubt of the truth of her story." Only some days later did second thoughts arise. A week afterward, confessing that he felt "a little doubtful about her," he wrote to Pelouze, and Pelouze's reply apparently confirmed the general's mounting fear that "she is a scamp."[2]

As soon as she had the general's money, Lauretta boarded a train, but not for Chicago. Instead, she went to Detroit. Since she had remained in Columbus just three days, she may not have visited Camp Chase, or if she did it was brief and inconsequential. Whatever the nature of her "secret service," if there was any, the fact that her pass carried her no farther than Columbus argues that Washington regarded it as ending there, especially since she appeared to have no funds to travel farther. She reached Detroit late on January 29 and went the Michigan Exchange Hotel. Then she did the seemingly bizarre. She registered under yet another alias, "Mrs. Gates, Major, U.S.A.," and gave her home as Washington. Several stories of Lincoln giving commissions to women emerged during the war, the earliest in late spring of 1862, when he supposedly created a female major, only to have her husband insist on being made a colonel or else he would have to take orders from his wife.[3] Not long before Lauretta arrived in Detroit, a rumor spread through the press that Lincoln gave the widow of an officer named Gates a commission as major in reward for his bravery and her work tending wounded in an army hospital. No record of any such act has been found. A very genuine Mrs. Gage, not Gates, did gain some attention for tending wounded black soldiers the previous November, and press accounts said Lincoln rewarded her for services rendered to wounded soldiers "on several western battlefields."[4]

For some reason, Lauretta attached herself to that story and made rumor fact for the moment. It had been almost six months since she laid Harry Buford to rest, and her undeniable appetite for attention and celebrity had gone unsatisfied. She also needed money, and being taken for a heroine, even if briefly, might be parlayed into cash. If she did have a real secret service commission and it did not expire at Columbus, then she might now have assumed a false identity for security, but this was scarcely likely, for using a name well known to press and public defeated any such design, and within a week she would drop all pretense and publicly identify herself. In aid of her masquerade, she soon displayed the usual packet of documents, including alleged commissions signed by Secretary of War Edwin M. Stanton; a document from Pelouze or his superior, Adjutant General Lorenzo Thomas, that she managed to transform into an appointment to Thomas's staff; and a transportation pass. As if it made her seem more plausible, she also had portraits of several Union officers.

All this and her self-assurance convinced Detroit authorities that she was what she pretended to be, and the next day she was taken as an honored guest to nearby Camp Ward to inspect the 1st Michigan Colored Infantry, then being organized. She acted the part of a major, ordering junior officers to straighten up their companies, lunched with Captain Jonathan B. Tuttle of Company C, and took tea in the afternoon with the regimental quartermaster, meanwhile sharing a bite or two of hardtack with the enlisted men. "Her appearance there will long be looked back to as an era in the history of that regiment," wrote a reporter on the occasion.

Despite Mrs. Major Gates's documents and confidant air, some felt reservations. An informant who clearly had not met her in person told that same reporter that while Lauretta was "not represented as extremely captivating in appearance or features still there was much that was interesting in her red hair, ditto complexion and nose." Given that descriptions of Lauretta throughout her life represent her hair as black, this mention of her red hair might mean she wore a wig as disguise. The red complexion and nose were hardly compliments in that era and probably were meant to suggest that she was a drinker. Suspicion accelerated when she refused to say why she was in town. Rumors soon spread that she had come to look into raising a corps of women volunteers for the army. Some thought her brash and self-important manner meant she was a man in disguise, some thinking she might be the noted humorist Mortimer Thomson, who wrote under the pseudonym Q. K. Philander Doesticks. Others believed she might be Brigadier General John Hunt Morgan, the Confederate raider who nine weeks earlier had escaped from a Union prison at Columbus. "What command she has at present is only known to herself," said the Detroit press. "Where her headquarters are is also a mystery." So were her whereabouts Sunday morning, January 31, when it was found that she had left her hotel and the city.[5]

The next day she turned up in Cleveland, Ohio, now accompanied by another bizarre new twist. With her was a private soldier supposedly from the 49th New York Infantry, described as "a mere boy," whom she introduced as her husband, while witnesses described her as "upwards of thirty years of age."[6] It hardly sounds like Thomas DeCaulp, who, at twenty-seven years old and standing five feet, eleven inches tall, could hardly be described by any witness as a boy, but Lauretta could have met him here. Their first stop in the city was at the photographic studio of James F. Ryder, where Lauretta tried to bargain with the artist over the price of a cased image of the couple.

"If you knew who I am, perhaps you would give me a picture," she told him, then took out her packet of documents and pictures, declaring that she was the noted Mrs. Major Gates. It was her old game of trying to parlay her celebrity into free services.

"I can see no reason why you should not pay for a picture," said an unswayed Ryder, "and a good round price at that, for you are getting a pretty plump salary."

"That may be," Lauretta shot back, "but do you see that 'ere boy?" she said, pointing to her husband. "In all probability, besides having him to take care of, I shall have his dad and mammy on my hands soon!"[7]

If this new husband was not DeCaulp, then who he was and what he was to her are complete mysteries. The Cleveland press said she had married him there "recently," though she only arrived in the city that day. Within two weeks the story of the female major and her soldier boy husband ran in the press from Milwaukee to Massachusetts.[8] They left Cleveland almost immediately, however, passing through Chicago to reach Milwaukee on February 3, where Lauretta's story became even more peculiar. She ostentatiously promenaded along the sidewalks and streets just as she had in Lynchburg, Jackson, and Mobile, clad in a closely fitted basque, or hip-length military jacket, with major's insignia on its shoulder straps. Her intent was attention, not deception, for she wore a skirt beneath the basque, and the effect was as she intended. The local press commented that "the charming Major has evidently learned to stand fire, as every one that she passed on the street stopped and *shot* a glance at her," and a Janesville editor soon commented wryly that "the people of Milwaukee now have a nine days wonder in the shape of a lady wearing shoulder straps." The same speculations erupted about her as in Detroit, though now the press definitely identified her as Mrs. Gage.[9] There was no more mention of the boy husband.

Editors adopted the same patronizing tone she had seen in the Confederate press. A Milwaukee sheet called her "The Majoress" for two weeks afterward, and one article titled "A Female Major Gets Her Picture Taken" circulated widely.[10] "For the last two or three days our citizens may have noticed a lady, the wife of a military officer walking the streets wearing the regular shoulder-straps and star," said the *Daily Milwaukee News.*

> We are not posted in the mysteries of military insignia, but should judge she ranks as a *Brig-a-dear* at least. She carries a good deal of sail, and it is possible ranks as Major-General. We have no objection to arming any number of the fair sex, but would never fight with, against them, nor in any other way than *for* them. We don't like to see them countenance, much less study, the art of murder. When they fly to arms, men ought to surrender.
>
> We don't like that new style.[11]

Again there was speculation, now more tongue-in-cheek, that she was the escaped Morgan or that she had come to raise a regiment of women "to bring this rebellion to a speedy termination." One daily confessed abiding curiosity, admitting, "We are consuming to know what may be her whence, wherefore, whereby, whereupon, and how-come-you-so."[12] Perhaps that is what prompted her to end the masquerade. The next day, February 6, she sent a note to the editor of the *Daily Sentinel.* She was not General Morgan "or any other man," she said. She was Lauretta de Caulp, or "Major de Caulp," as she preferred.[13] Once again a story about her went abroad, appearing in Columbus, where Heintzelman could read it, as well as in Cleveland and even as far off as—ironically—New Orleans, which had been accustomed to her impersonating a *Confederate* soldier.[14]

Her reasons for the brief masquerade are obscure, for seemingly she had little to gain. As it happened, on the day she arrived in Milwaukee the papers there and elsewhere in the North carried stories lionizing the actress Pauline Cushman, who had been in the news for some time. A shameless self-promoter much like Lauretta, she called herself "Miss *Major* Pauline Cushman" and appeared in uniform, with claims to have been a Union scout and spy, virtually an echo of Harry Buford.[15] Lauretta may just have been jealous at seeing the attention she once knew going to someone else. Or it could have been a prank done solely for its own sake, for she liked fooling people, and with her customary lack of forethought about consequences.

Yet hers was no spur-of-the-moment act, for she had to have bought or made that blue basque and acquired the military insignia. Her action hardly furthered any observations she might make for Pelouze, if she was actually engaged in any business for him, but it certainly let Ohio and Michigan know that she had arrived.

Moreover, she traveled a peculiar route. Detroit and Cleveland had significant ties to the disloyal unrest then fermenting, but her stays in each were too brief to gather any useful information. Most likely she stopped in major cities hoping that publicity would alert Thomas to her proximity. The mysterious "boy" husband remains a mystery, perhaps a brief lover she met on her trip, or it could have been Thomas, though the description of him as a boy is baffling unless he had very youthful looks despite his stature.

Thomas was in the vicinity then. On February 1 Brigadier General T. C. H. Smith assigned him to Company C of the 30th Wisconsin Infantry, and one week later, on February 8, Private William Irwin reported to his company at Camp Washburn outside Milwaukee, where Lauretta joined him.[16] After a month the regiment shifted to Camp Reno, and Irwin made the move with the rest.[17] He seemed pleased with his company, and his officers with him, but having once been a captain, he wanted the rank of an officer again now. He asked his company commander, Captain Alexander A. Arnold, for a recommendation, and on March 31 Arnold obliged, saying, "He appears to be a gentleman & a good soldier being always ready & willing to do his duty."[18] The next day, April 1, Irwin appended Arnold's testimonial to a renewed application for a commission addressed to Major Pelouze. In it he affirmed his Confederate service, desertion, and subsequent volunteering as a substitute and reminded Pelouze of the "important informations of the so-called Confederate States" that he proffered in Washington. Once again, however, no commission was forthcoming.[19]

Married life in Milwaukee was not entirely tranquil. Lauretta was sensitive to any hint of criticism, even good-natured teasing, and Thomas teased for amusement. When she claimed wounded feelings, he took what he called "every pains to amend it even on my bended knee." Worse yet was what he referred to as "the little trouble at camp reano." In April some men of the regiment offended her. Just how is unknown, but it involved camp gossip about her that she thought insulting, and the most likely topic was her cross-dressing as Harry Buford, for it would have been unlike her not to boast of that. Irwin confessed to her, "I have suffered much in minde" over the episode, though he did nothing about it at the time, perhaps because of several companies being reassigned to frontier duty. Nevertheless, he promised her retribution. "Woe be unto them if i have the pleasure of meeting them on the plains this summer," he assured her. "I have all ready born to much from men and woe woe be unto all that has or will cross my path for I would rather suffer death than know you suffered insult from any."[20]

The couple spent considerable time together, and Thomas found Lauretta a lodging better than what they left in Indianapolis. "When I saw you best situated it was then my heart knew most joy," he told her. They made friends, including grocer Thomas Greenwood and his wife, as well as machinist Samuel Smeet and his dressmaker wife, Mary.[21] It was good that they were together, for Irwin apparently never fully recovered from whatever had hospitalized him in Atlanta. Men of his company told Lauretta that he seemed depressed, though he wore a brave face for her, and now he also suffered from rheumatism. "Nettie" nursed him when he felt so ill he could hardly care for himself. He called her "that devoted relenting heart that watched over me with cuch [such] care and anxiety during the long days and restless nights of my sickness."[22] It was no idyll, but they appeared happy.

Soon he would be transferred to Company B, which left in mid-April for Fort Snelling on the Mississippi near Minneapolis, to be part of an expedition to march into the Dakota territory.[23] It was a sad parting for Lauretta, who remained in Milwaukee until Thomas found her lodging near the fort. "What comfort is this world to me," she wrote him after a few weeks. "You no I love you dearly." Thomas promised to write every other day, but almost immediately that resolve faded, and after three weeks he had written only three letters, one of them just a hasty note, despite his having no duty to perform after reaching Fort Snelling.[24] When he wrote more fully on May 12, however, he demonstrated a command of ornate rhetoric—if not orthography—calculated to appeal to a romantic young woman:

> We ar designed to be separated by unavoidable circumstances which greives me much when I reflect over the past scenes of falisity that we have enjoyed to gather mitigating that blited love that like the early flowers of spring which ar niped by the late frosts of winter and left withered in cilence untill aroused by the genial sunshine of affection into its original state by womans love the only consoling friend of man when trials and advisities of this cheerless world gather around him.

Still not entirely well, he felt optimistic of full recovery. Yet he worried about her on her own in Milwaukee, especially since he had been months without pay. "I have suffered much solicitude of minde about your situation," he told her, "fearing that you would grieve yourself by being separated from me." He had hopes of better times, no doubt because his hoped-for commission would pay much more than a private's salary. "If I live to get out of the infernal servis," he said, "I will work to subort and be with you if I should be compelled to perform my daily labors bent double."[25] DeCaulp's grammar and spelling rather definitively put the lie to her later claims that he was highly educated.[26]

Lauretta was not at all happy by then. Every time mail came from the West, she went to the post office but usually returned to her lodging empty-handed. "I feel doomed to disappointment," she wrote him on May 12 after another day with no letter. "I wept bitterly to think you would treat me so unkind, after my being so kind to you when you were here not able to help yourself." Only two replies came to her last four letters, and one of those puzzled and disturbed her. Though she recognized his handwriting, he signed it "Benjamin F. Carter." No explanation illuminates that mystery, but given Thomas's past history—of which she may not have known all—he could certainly have had some other secret matter in hand and carelessly signed the wrong name to the wrong letter. "You thought I would not no your hand," she scolded. She felt hurt and angry but resolved to let the matter go until they could discuss it in person, "if we should ever meet again." She confessed, "Sometimes things looks very dark and gloomy to me." She was not pleased with his behavior, writing, "I love you dearly and have suffered a great deal for you and am suffering Everything almost woman could suffer for man."[27]

Finding herself a soldier's wife living in obscurity in a rented room in Milwaukee was a great step down from being Lieutenant Harry T. Buford and a celebrity all across the Confederacy. Surely she remembered when the Richmond *Enquirer* saluted her departure the past July with the wish that she might "live long to enjoy her fame."[28] Where was that fame now? "Separated from all I love," she told Thomas, "I am sometimes tempted to go to the front and try and win my glory back." Her "glory," of course, had been her notoriety, her place in the headlines in the Confederate press, which donning a uniform once more might resurrect. But then she added, "My present condition will not permit me for the present but by August or Sept. I will be able."

Just what she meant by "her condition" she did not say, but it is implicit that she expected Thomas to know. She might have been unwell, though any ordinary illness ought to be gone before the fall. She closed her letter by saying, "This leaves me well as could be expected." Shortage of funds might have been the "condition" on her mind, for in the absence of his pay she was dependent on charity, taking secondhand clothing from a local minister's wife. Or she could have been referring to a pregnancy. She and Thomas had been reunited in Nashville or possibly Indianapolis, at least since November 1863, if not earlier. Nine months from then would have been August or September 1864, the months that she referred to now. If she did mean a child was on the way, then even before its birth she was apparently willing to leave it with others while she pursued fame, something she would do again in years to come. The maternal instinct did not find fertile ground in her.

She still signed herself "your affectionate wife a kiss X." In a final note to a puzzling letter, she added that she addressed it "to your assumed name," whereas all of her earlier letters she had addressed to Thomas C. DeCaulp. Yet after she folded the letter, presumably to go into an envelope or be hand carried, she wrote "Thos C. Decaulp" and "Your Loveing Nettie" on the outside.[29] And so Lauretta too may have been unclear which of his names was the alias. And how would letters addressed to Thomas DeCaulp be delivered to the man known as William Irwin at Fort Snelling? He was very open about DeCaulp having been his alias in the Confederacy, but just who was he deceiving—the Union, Lauretta, or everyone? The letter signed Benjamin F. Carter, if really written by him, suggests yet another alias, and one unknown to her.[30] He was already a bigamist, assuming he and Sarah Haralson actually were married in December 1862, so the possibility that he had yet another secret life, though unlikely, is not altogether improbable. It would seem that Lauretta had met her match.

Private Irwin professed to be stunned by her "very abstruce complicated letter I recieved this morning which I am totaly at a loss to understand or fathom." He protested that he had filled the three letters he had written her to date with nothing but expressions of affection and husbandly advice. "I am also shure of signing my one name," he said. "If I signed any other I must have been delerious at the time." He professed to know nothing of the Carter letter, or of anyone by that name, then responded hotly, "When you receive this letter write amediatly and let me know the particulars of this letter you have recived and if there is a man here who dare to write you a letter good bad or indifferent he shall fight me for life or death the minit

I finde him." Thus, in his defense, he tried to deflect her anger toward the possibility that someone else had written to her, perhaps someone in some way connected with that earlier unpleasantness at Camp Reno.

Hoping to mollify his wife, Irwin let loose a torrent of high-flown romantic rhetoric, showing that whatever skill he lacked at spelling, he was skilled—and practiced—in the art of wooing:

> Your Thomas is a man of few words always concealing his feelings espechaly when they are such as to give sorrow and if you knew the long days spent in silent thought in regards to your whelfare, the fervent prayers and apeals to the *almighty* for your whelfare during the restless and silent midnight hours you would not have writen a letter acusing me of such gross crimes as being tired of you and not wishing to support you a thing that has never entered my mind . . . when I seace to love you it will be when the toung seaces to kiss the heart to beat and the mind unconscious of all wourldly things . . . it has rather been utmost in my mind how I could best promote your comfort and when I saw you best situated it was then my heart knew most joy.[31]

One problem he could not get around was the fact that since he had been in the army, he had not given Lauretta any money. He told her that he simply had not been paid since his enlistment, which by May meant five months without funds. In the Union army in 1864 that was an unusually long time for a regiment to go without pay, especially one doing duty in a fixed garrison. Still, it is possible, since they were almost on the frontier and payrolls had farther to travel. Yet it is also possible that if DeCaulp did have a secret life as Benjamin F. Carter or under some other alias, he could have been sending his pay in that direction and leaving Lauretta to fend for herself in Milwaukee. When dealing with two such practiced dissemblers, it is dangerous to take almost anything they said at face value. Now he told her that his inability to provide money to her was part of the reason his health had relapsed for a time at Camp Reno, but he expected to be paid any day.

Then he addressed something Lauretta did not mention in her May 12 letter, suggesting there were other, earlier complaints. "The most severe blow of all that went deepe into my heart which caused me to shed tears," he told her, "was the accusation of being unwilling to support my Infant the next dearest to me on earth and when I refuse to provide for you or it may the *almighty God* punnish me with the punishment he has promest those who shall offend them, which is, *Hell fire*." There seems only one explanation for his referring to "my Infant" as "next dearest to me" and for his reference to "you or it." He must have been talking about a baby probably due soon, just as she had hinted in her reference to her "condition."[32] Two months from now she would be buying clothing for small boys.[33]

If she had conceived in early August 1863, when they first met, she could have had a child as early as late April or early May 1864. Of course, DeCaulp was the father of an infant, Thomas Edwin DeCaulp in Arkansas, now eight months old, but there is no evidence that either he or Lauretta knew of the boy's existence. The "Infant" in his letter and the pregnancy suggested in hers could have meant that she had borne a child recently and was still recovering from the ordeal, but that too seems improbable. In early February 1864 she would have been six or seven months pregnant, a condition difficult to hide in that tight-fitting basque.[34]

Irwin signed his long letter "your loving devoted and sanguine husband until death non but thee and non without thee" and mirrored her X by way of sending a kiss when he signed as Thomas DeCaulp.[35] Nevertheless, from all appearances—and they are admittedly few—their romance had suffered a change in dynamic. The months ahead seemed to bear that out.

Several days earlier, on May 8, a company of "galvanized" Confederates now designated Company G, 1st Connecticut Cavalry, arrived at Fort Snelling, and DeCaulp and thirteen others from the 30th Wisconsin were detached to join them.[36] There had been no action on his application for a commission, but it is faintly possible that the men of Company G elected him briefly—and unofficially—their captain. When a new expedition against the Sioux was in the offing in June, however, a doctor found DeCaulp unfit for the campaign.[37] He remained behind at Fort Snelling through the summer and fall. Then in late October his lung disease relapsed to the extent that he was unfit for any duty.[38] Lauretta was not there to nurse him during much of that summer and perhaps not at all. Sometime following their exchange of letters in May she went to join him and moved near the fort, no doubt to care for him.[39] She called on Brigadier General Henry H. Sibley at his St. Paul headquarters, where she probably pressed the case for a captaincy and told him her husband's story of enlistment in 1861 under a false name and his desertion to become William Irwin once more. At the same time she told Sibley she was the daughter of J. B. Roach, only now said that he was a British admiral.[40] If she and Thomas addressed the issues between them, the resolution may not have been a happy one, for on June 14 she left Minnesota and her ailing husband.[41]

CHAPTER SIX

"YOU WILL LEARN A LITTLE MORE OF ME"

"HAVEING FRIENDS IN New York, I left and went to New York on a visit," Lauretta told Brigadier General Joseph D. Webster six weeks later.[1] Thus she began the most obscure period of her wartime life, and the only one whose empty pages *might* be partially filled by *some* of the activities she later claimed, though the likelihood is slim.

For a start, why did she leave Milwaukee? Things with Thomas may have been tense, but later events suggest she was not at the point of abandoning him, at least not yet. Nor does it appear that as of June 14 Thomas had orders that took him away from Fort Snelling, leaving her on her own to support herself elsewhere in his absence. Rather, it seems clear that she left him there, possibly with his knowledge and permission, perhaps even his blessing if she had a way to earn the cash the government failed to provide. Certainly she implied that to Webster when she told him that by the end of July her husband had not been paid for over eight months. Of course, Thomas had not been enlisted for a full eight months as yet, and she stretched the truth farther by claiming that the men in his regiment did not expect any pay before August or September, whereas in May he had told her they expected pay any day. "I wished to be doing something to for a livelihood and to assist my husband," she told Webster, "as I think it is Every ladies duty to help her husband in this hour of trouble." Hence she went to New York City.[2]

Taking her at her word, it follows to ponder why she did not just seek work in Milwaukee or St. Paul, close to Fort Snelling and her husband. Failing that, then why not in Chicago, Detroit, Cleveland, or even back in Indianapolis, all places much closer to Thomas than New York? Again there is no answer, but the fact that she went so far suggests that she was in correspondence with those "friends" before she departed and thus knew there was a promising reason to journey east. How she came to have friends in New York, if she did, is a mystery. In 1860 and again in 1862 she claimed to have come from New York.[3] Yet it seems unlikely that a young woman of her known background would know prominent businessmen.

The riddle grows deeper considering the men she claimed to have met: "my friends from Suspension bridge Col Young & Lady and Mr. Chamberlyn, the vice council to Mexico."[4] Colonel William H. Young was a veteran of the war with Mexico who raised one of the very first Union cavalry units in 1861, only to resign in a huff in October of that year when his regiment was handed to a more efficient commander. He had married well, and he and his wife, Dewellen, used much of her fortune to fund charitable works. In 1863 they organized the Volunteer Institute to educate and care for orphans of New York soldiers killed or disabled in action, with buildings at Suspension Bridge, on the east bank of the Niagara River across from Canada. By the summer of 1864 it had nearly a hundred boys enrolled, with demand for places growing.[5]

Despite their Southern birth, the Youngs both held unwaveringly to the Union. Chamberlyn, the supposed vice consul, is a complete mystery.[6] How twenty-two-year-old Lauretta would have known either of these dignitaries is puzzling, but if daring, bluff, and effrontery could do it, she had all three in abundance. Of course, her meeting with the Youngs and Chamberlyn could have been a cover if she planned to visit Suspension Bridge and cross to Canada, where Confederate agents plotted to unleash mayhem on the Northern home front.[7] Not a scrap of contemporary evidence supports that, but the theoretical possibility remains that she may have visited those agents to solicit a commission from them just as she apparently did Major Pelouze. Still, it seems certain that she met with Young, for he gave her a document that military authorities accepted as a commission. Given her false postwar claims to represent businesses and charities, it is possible that this commission was equally so and that any money she collected she intended to keep.[8]

Lauretta also claimed that one of them, probably Chamberlyn, introduced her to Orison Blunt, president of the newly created National Union Life and Limb Insurance Company, with offices at 243 Broadway in New York City.[9] If she read the local Milwaukee press, she would have seen a notice back in February that investors in New York were organizing the new insurance company, and perhaps that captured her interest.[10] Chartered in Albany in April to insure Union soldiers and sailors against loss of life and disability caused by loss of limbs, it was due to start selling policies in July.[11] Always adept at selling herself, Lauretta apparently convinced Blunt that she could sell insurance policies to soldiers, even though making a woman an agent was itself a notable break with custom, let alone sending her off to sell to men in the army. Nevertheless, the same statements she had made to Pelouze and Heintzelman about her acquaintance with Union generals in the East and West could have been enough to convince Blunt that she had entrée to camps and fortifications denied to other agents, even men.

She maintained that Blunt offered her what she called "an Agentcy," and she accepted. As evidence that he believed she could indeed use her influence to go where she wished, he gave her a commission for the territory commanded by Major General William T. Sherman, including virtually all of Tennessee, as well as northern Mississippi, Alabama, and Georgia. She was to go to Chattanooga immediately and there establish an office, then seek Sherman's permission to make day trips to the front lines to sell directly to soldiers.[12] She had company application forms, letters of introduction, and other evidence of intent to do business, but again these may have been a cover for her to make observations in army camps or another means for receiving cash she intended to keep.[13]

When she left New York on or around June 24, Lauretta went first to Baltimore, where on June 26 she called on Brigadier General Erastus B. Tyler and told him she was "on important business." Probably seeing the appointment from Blunt, he concluded that she gave "satisfactory evidence" of her purpose, and Tyler gave her a pass to travel to Fort Monroe and from thence to City Point, Virginia, where General Grant had recently established headquarters as his army besieged Petersburg.[14] Leaving Baltimore, Lauretta traveled through Washington on her way and called at Adjutant General Thomas's office. He agreed that she should make her office in Chattanooga rather than at the front, where there would be no proper accommodations for a lady.[15]

She probably went no farther. She carried an envelope of the National Life and Limb Insurance Company addressed in her hand to Grant and noted as "Official Business."[16] It likely held a letter from Blount seeking permission for her to sell policies within the lines of the Union armies, now that Grant was general in chief, or perhaps a request for a letter of introduction from him to General Sherman, then in command of all Union forces in Tennessee and north Georgia. Sherman could open all doors for her if he so chose. Grant was weary of vendors hanging around the army, however, and curtailed such traffic except in extreme cases. Lauretta's case was hardly extreme.[17]

Rebuffed, she returned to New York and went to Fort Columbus on Governor's Island on July 4, securing its commandant's permission to solicit donations for the Volunteer Institute from his men and officers. How much she collected and whether she sent it to Young or kept it herself remain unanswered questions, though this may be the germ of her story some years later of collecting contributions from Union sailors and then turning the proceeds over to the Confederacy.[18] She also met with Brigadier General Henry M. Judah, recently relieved of command of a division in Sherman's army, and cajoled from him a letter of introduction to use in her travels.[19]

The trip from New York to Chattanooga took her via Cincinnati and Louisville to Nashville, where she arrived by July 12. She first called on the general agent of the U.S. Military Railroads, showed her commissions, and asked for transportation to Chattanooga. He referred her to the special agent in charge, who in turn said he could not help her.[20] A few days later she tried to bypass them by applying to the assistant quartermaster, but again she failed.[21] Suspecting that Nashville was as far as she would get, she set up her enterprise there for the moment. She engaged an office at 52 North Summer Street, just two blocks from her room at the St. Cloud Hotel, and printed flyers announcing the "National Life and Limb Insurance Company of Nashville," with herself, "Mrs. Maj. L. J. DeCaulp," as agent. "Come one, Come all," it proclaimed, "for this may be the last opportunity you will have to insure your Limbs and Lives."[22]

She was in business barely a week. The company almost failed that year, signing only seventy-six policies nationwide, but she certainly gave evidence of effort.[23] Her letters of introduction to local commanders could gain access to their men and officers. She had blank application forms, brought from the New York office or sent by general agent Sylvester O. Post. She posted office hours from eight o'clock in the morning until six in the evening and put a notice on her office door announcing "No Admittance Except on Business." She even contacted a competitor, the Nashville agent for the New York Life Insurance Company, perhaps hoping to learn something of the insurance business.[24]

Meanwhile, she kept trying to reach Chattanooga. On July 23 she started writing a note to Colonel James L. Donaldson, chief quartermaster of the Department of the Cumberland, seeking an appointment one evening after she closed her office, and at his residence rather than his office. She would no doubt repeat her request for transportation, but this time in person where she could use her considerable skills of persuasion.[25] Lauretta never finished the letter.

Little business of interest came to the Union army's Nashville provost marshal's office that month.[26] Perhaps that made its officers more receptive to acting on vague rumors. Barely forty-eight hours after Lauretta started that letter, Federal soldiers appeared at her office or hotel on July 25 with an order for the arrest of "Mrs. L. J. DeCaulp," directing that she be kept under guard at her hotel. The order came from Captain Sidney A. Stockdale, assistant provost marshal to Sherman.[27] When the arresting officer delivered her to Stockdale's office, she demanded to know of what she was accused and by whom. Stockdale replied only that he had been ordered to detain her, promising to give her some details the next day. Meanwhile, she remained under house arrest in room number 49 at the St. Cloud.[28]

Several things could have put her under suspicion, not least her own craving for publicity. Authorities in Washington regularly saw the Richmond papers, and the coverage of her visit to the Confederate capital the past September was especially damaging. One article published her false claim to have gone to Chattanooga, where General Stewart employed her "in the secret service, effecting important arrests of spies, and doing some very daring things." That would hardly have endeared her to Union authorities, and the article identified her as Mrs. DeCaulp. It needed no leap of insight to connect her with Mrs. Lauretta J. DeCaulp, especially when other Southern papers at the same time spoke of her maiden name as Lauretta J. Williams.[29] Her transparent appearance as "Mrs. Major Gates" in Detroit and Cleveland, and her subsequent published admission that she was really Lauretta J. DeCaulp, only made the identification easier, while her thwarted effort to go to Grant's headquarters could have aroused suspicion, as might her repeated attempts now to get to Chattanooga, where she supposedly spied the year before.

Lauretta could only speculate on the cause of her detention. She believed the order must have come from Sherman, though Federal officers who visited her in her room said they thought he knew nothing of her or her case.[30] Initially she assumed she was accused of intent to "Injure the government," as she put it, and attributed this to statements by "malisious persons," and one in particular. She told Stockdale that a man in Chattanooga whose name she thought was Hubbards had told falsehoods about her.[31] There is no evidence that she was ever in Chattanooga, other than passing through it in September 1861 as Mary Ann Keith, and she certainly did not get there this summer, so this Hubbards must have seen and recognized her or her name somewhere else. There was little likelihood that anyone who had seen her in Richmond or Atlanta would now be at large behind Union lines, but when she gave her name, as surely she did, anyone could connect her with the Mrs. DeCaulp from both Confederate and Union press.

In particular, Lauretta felt uneasy about the circumstances of her appearance at Memphis the previous October.[32] The most logical suspicion

Nashville in the summer of 1864. Lauretta's brief sojourn there was not a happy one, as she was first under house arrest and then imprisoned by the Yankees. Worse, for a change, she did not know why. Library of Congress.

would be that she came as a civilian spy, making her movements since she crossed the lines a matter of importance, so she gave a general accounting of her travels. She had departed Confederate territory in September 1863, she said, and had not been back since. Then she was in Washington from December 1863 to January 1864 and in Milwaukee and Fort Snelling until June 14. She implied that she then went directly to New York to see Young, Chamberlyn, and Blount, then on to Washington. There is also a hint that she believed the Yankees thought her insurance agency might be a screen to mask activity of a less pacific nature, so she emphasized that she took the post only because her husband had not been paid in so long and she needed to support herself, her old appeal for sympathy to sway men.[33]

Starting on July 26, she bombarded Stockdale with daily written entreaties. "Investigate my case as soon as possible," she pleaded. Among other things, she had expenses to meet and she was not free to do business at her office, if in fact there was any business. "I am willing to meet any person or persons before and [any] court or jury in the U.S.," she continued, for she had not "by any act or word done anything that has any tendency to Injure the government" and would happily endure any punishment decreed if a court could find her guilty of anything.[34] A day later she sent Stockdale notice of a man about to leave Nashville who could corroborate her story of coming into Union lines at Memphis, and the day after that she begged him to come see her or else bring her to immediate trial.[35] "It is very unjust to keep [me] here under guard without I was guilty," she complained. Failing that, she asked for a parole pending trial so she could attend to her affairs, vowing that she had no desire to leave Nashville even if able. She added that she had neither her baggage nor any clothing, which is puzzling, since she was being confined to her hotel room.[36] By this time she had been in Nashville some seventeen days, begging the question of what she had worn during the two weeks prior to her arrest.

Lauretta also tried to meet Stockdale again face-to-face, perhaps counting on her power of persuasion to secure her release. She spoke with other Federal officers during her arrest, which means she could have callers, and she convinced them that she was under unjust duress. "You will learn a little more of me when you see me," she promised Stockdale on July 29, but if he came, she failed to move him.[37] In fact, the next day a guard came to her room and removed her instead to the city's U.S. Military Prison.

Suitably alarmed, Lauretta appealed on July 30 to General Webster, now Sherman's chief of staff, coordinating from Nashville all the logistics, transportation, and supply that kept Sherman's army in the field as he began a partial siege of Atlanta. "Have the kindness to have my case attended to as soon as posible as I feel sure that I am here under a false suposition," she implored. She still believed it was by Sherman's order and claimed, "I am able to answer any charges preferred against me," protesting that she was willing to go to Washington if necessary to seek a hearing. As was her custom, she added circumstantial details to her story to lend veracity, mentioning that General Sibley kept his headquarters at the International Hotel in St. Paul, and exaggerated as it suited her. She had already retroactively promoted her husband during his Confederate service, styling herself "Mrs. Major DeCaulp." Now she did the same for him in the Union army, telling Webster that the men of Company G of the 1st Connecticut Cavalry had elected Thomas their captain and implying that Sibley detached him for special duty at headquarters. As for leaving Nashville, despite her efforts to secure transportation to Chattanooga, she assured him she had no intention to leave until she heard from Thomas and received Sherman's permission to continue her work.[38]

Webster ordered Stockdale to report on her case in person.[39] There was much for them to consider. On the one hand, there were the unspecified allegations of Hubbards and whatever, if anything, the Federals knew of her former Confederate associations, including the claims to have helped unmask Union spies. On the other hand, the papers seized from her office or hotel room in the main supported her story. Her pass to visit Fort Columbus confirmed her as an agent of the Volunteer Institute. Other passes named her as an agent of the insurance company, as did some correspondence and her introductions from General Judah and others, not to mention the application form or forms she brought from New York. Then there was her pass from Wheeling to Columbus that said she was "in secret service." She no longer performed any such duty, or she would have offered it as a primary justification for her release, but the fact that she once held such a position seemingly spoke in her favor. Lauretta apparently thought it of no consequence, or else she would have emphasized it in her appeals, probably the surest evidence that her "secret service" was as minor as it was brief.

Three of her papers might have raised questions, however. Among the seized documents were her unhappy May 12 letter to Thomas DeCaulp, his own letter written immediately on receiving hers, and a seemingly innocent shopping order. In ordinary circumstances, Lauretta should have had only Thomas's letter to her. Why did she also have her own letter to him? And why an order for millinery supplies, which presumably ought to have been kept by the merchant addressee? The simplest explanation is that Thomas returned her offending letter when they met at Fort Snelling, and she did not have time to mail the shopping order before her arrest. Amid the evidence of a strained relationship, she had written these words: "I am sometimes tempted to go to the front and try and win my glory back." Did that mean an intent to return to the Confederacy and resume her guise as Harry Buford? If so, then maybe the stories of Buford the spy were true after all, in which case she might have done material injury to the Union.

As if to support that somewhat strained interpretation, there was the list of items ordered from the milliner. In among the stockings and handkerchiefs and papers of pins, there lurked potentially less innocuous items: ten yards of blue cloth, three "suites" of gray cloth in sizes for boys of three and four years, and one dozen "Staff buttons for coat." From that gray cloth and those buttons, could she have made herself another Confederate uniform jacket to seek out her "glory"? Might she have done the same with those ten yards of blue cloth to repeat her impersonation of "Mrs. Major Gates," only this time to spy or worse?[40] Given her craving for fame, it is just as likely that Lauretta had told any who would listen about her Confederate exploits. Learning that, military authorities in Nashville could have seen the germ of something suspicious in her ordering materials from which military disguises might be fashioned. All is conjecture, of course, as is one final, possibly coincidental, possibly meaningless fact: the Federals never returned the seized documents to her, not even the letters between her and Thomas. Instead, the papers remained on file and without regard to chronology. Someone, perhaps provost authorities or possibly a later government clerk, put this order for millinery goods on top of all the others.[41]

While Webster and Stockdale pondered, Lauretta addressed the captain one more time from prison to beg a hearing, still maintaining she knew not why they kept her "in this miserable place" without trial. "It is not fit for any Lady, thrown among all kind of low people," she protested. "It is not any place for a man['s] wife if they have any respect for a Lady." Abandoning any desire to get to Chattanooga, all Lauretta wanted was to "go home as soon as my trial come off." She had finally received a letter from Thomas, telling her he was at Fort Snelling and his health was failing, and she wanted to go to him.[42]

It seems clear that none of the suspicion directed at Lauretta was because of the much-feared Northwest Conspiracy to free Confederate prisoners in the North and loose them on the Union home front. The hysteria over that had begun to subside when the plot was exposed and supposed conspirators were arrested in Indiana and elsewhere on July 30. No evidence puts her in Canada, where the plot was funded, or in the company of any of the accused conspirators. Even if suspected because of her visit to Suspension Bridge, she would never have been more than a minor suspect.[43] In fact, her arrest and confinement were due to something altogether different, simple mistaken identity.

A young woman named Louise or Louisa Oyster, but known to have used the aliases Goodwin and Cline, had for the past year been suspected of carrying mail, medicines, and military goods out of Union-held Chattanooga to deliver behind Confederate lines. She was generally reputed in Chattanooga to be of bad character and "a woman of the town." Reports said she had come to Nashville in early July, presumably to continue her disloyal acts. Thus she and Lauretta had arrived in the city within days of each other. There may have been some physical similarity between them, but even if not, Lauretta's insistent efforts to get a pass to go to Chattanooga could have easily been mistaken for Oyster trying to go back to her old haunts. Whatever army authorities in Nashville knew or heard of Lauretta's Confederate activities only raised more suspicions, and if a man from Chattanooga named Hubbards really did make accusations about her, he most likely confused her for Oyster and so told the provost.

It was on such suspicions that Stockdale ordered Lauretta's detention on July 25 and then held her while he contacted Chattanooga to find someone who knew her. Four days later the Chattanooga provost put John Knoedler on a train to Nashville, promising that he knew and could identify the woman. On July 31 Knoedler reported to Stockdale, who immediately sent him to the prison "for the purpose of identifying Mrs. L. J. DeCaulp," by which he meant identifying her as Oyster.[44] After seeing Lauretta, Knoedler told Stockdale he had the wrong woman, and furthermore, Oyster had already left the city a few days earlier on her way to Louisville.[45] Stockdale had Lauretta brought to his office at three o'clock on August 1 and told her he had an order from Webster for the release of "Mrs. Major De Caulp, Citizen." At least she kept her promotion.[46] She was not free, however. She might not have been Oyster, but apparently the combination of whatever Hubbards said, what Lauretta and her documents revealed, and what if anything Stockdale might have read from her Confederate press reports convinced him that her presence was undesirable. General Sherman had recently adopted a practice of banishing from his department men and women suspected of disloyalty, and now Stockdale told her that she must leave Nashville on the next day's evening train and remove herself to somewhere north of the Ohio River, where she presented less of a risk. Until her train left, she would be free to collect her possessions and close any unfinished business.[47]

On the evening of August 2, on her trip to Louisville, Lauretta had much to consider. Banishment from Sherman's department nullified her commission as an agent to sell insurance to his soldiers. The Yankees scared her, and she had to know they did not regard her as entirely innocent, or they would not have expelled her. She could expect them to keep a watch on her activities hereafter. At last she had heard from Thomas, probably for the first time since she left Fort Snelling in mid-June.[48] At the moment, she had nowhere to go and no immediate option for support and subsistence. Even if she and Thomas were to some degree estranged, he was her best immediate prospect. As his wife, she could at least eat and get shelter until she devised something else.

On arriving in Louisville, on August 3 or 4 she called on Colonel M. D. Hascall, the quartermaster for the 2nd Division of the XXIII Corps, headquartered there. She found him a sympathetic and gullible ear when she told him she was looking for her husband, Private William Irwin, swearing that he "was a Union man forced to take up arms against his country or hang," and that he had "escaped as soon as an opportunity admited" by deserting in October 1863 near Chattanooga. She also told Hascall that her husband's real name was DeCaulp, but friends had advised him to change it for his own safety, hence Irwin was his alias. And then she let slip that she was the daughter of "Rear Admiral Rosche" of the British navy. She so convinced Hascall that he immediately wrote to General Sibley in Minnesota to ask if Private Irwin was still with his command, adding that he thought Lauretta deserved "great credit from the patriot in the field," presumably for her work for the Volunteer Institute or the Life and Limb Insurance Company, or some other story she spun him. "I do feel for her situation," Hascall told Sibley. He also gave her a letter of reference to present to an officer in Minneapolis to gain her aid when she arrived there en route to Fort Snelling.[49]

The references to her husband are slightly puzzling. If she really had gotten a letter from DeCaulp in late July, as she told Stockdale on August 1, then presumably she should have known he had never left Fort Snelling. There seems little reason for her appeal to Hascall and Sibley unless Thomas's letter was old and she feared he might have been sent elsewhere. Sibley received Hascall's letter on August 9, but before he could respond, Lauretta arrived in St. Paul, and when the general made inquiries, he found her reunited with her husband and set up in what he called "comfortable quarters" at Fort Snelling.[50] She arrived to find that Thomas's health had taken a dramatic downturn, just as she told General Webster, for he had recently been judged unfit for duty and was growing gradually worse, probably from tuberculosis.[51]

Alas, here they both disappear from the record. Thomas would not reemerge for five months, and Lauretta not for the next eighteen but for a few vague hints and one tantalizing glimpse. What does appear evident is that she made no more efforts on behalf of the National Union Life and Limb Insurance Company and seems to have had no further interest in the Volunteer Institute.[52] Once she rejoined Thomas, the isolation of the post easily accounts for her absence from the press. Moreover, if she were pregnant, as she implied in May, then she would have given birth around August or September, and that too could account for her silence for the next year and a half. Certainly something kept her out of sight, for her absence

Fort Snelling, near Minneapolis. Thomas DeCaulp, also known as William Irwin, was assigned to the garrison there. When Lauretta finally joined him in 1864, they had "comfortable quarters" for perhaps the only time in their brief marriage. Minnesota Historical Society.

from public view was wholly uncharacteristic. It had to be frustrating too, for she had been a genuine heroine of sorts in the Confederacy, its first and perhaps only celebrity created entirely in the media. Missing that attention is the only logical explanation for her brief career as Mrs. Major Gates.

Obscurity must have been more irritating as she read stories of other claimants to her kind of fame, most notably the Virginian Belle Boyd, a dime novel adventuress who actually did a little clandestine work and whose every movement the press, North and South alike, followed avidly. They certainly gave her more respect than they had Harry Buford. When Boyd was captured and imprisoned, it made headlines, whereas no one had even noticed Lauretta's week under arrest. Editors followed Boyd on her trip abroad after her release, and they reported every detail of her marriage in England to a Confederate officer whom they glorified, while no one paid attention to DeCaulp. Seeing all of that attention—hundreds of newspaper articles just from the time Lauretta left Nashville to the end of 1864—going to someone else might well have aroused enough of a craving for her former "glory" to impel her to action.

CHAPTER SEVEN

LOST MONTHS IN THE SHADOWS

ON THE AFTERNOON of September 29, 1864, a Charlotte & South Carolina Railroad train stopped in Charlotte, and passengers stepped onto the platform to change for the North Carolina Railroad to Richmond. Among them, people noticed "a beautiful dashing lady in the uniform of a Captain." She wore a straw hat at a rakish angle, topped with a black ostrich feather; a uniform blouse with two rows of miniature gilt buttons; and a black belt and chain. With her traveled a man of about forty years uniformed as a major. Rumor said she was from Mississippi, had been in "several hard fought battles, won promotion on the field for distinguished gallantry," had been home on furlough, and was now en route to rejoin her command. "There is some mystery yet unraveled about this heroine and her strange career," mused a local editor, "which will never see the light till the heart history of a love story is written."[1] The details are scant, but they all match Lauretta. This woman wanted attention. Though she might have been from Mississippi originally, she came now from eastern Georgia or possibly Charleston or Savannah, Charlotte's only major rail connections south. The two last points of origin meant she could have come from abroad on a blockade runner.

It hardly seems likely that this was Lauretta somehow returned to the Confederacy. For one thing, the mysterious captain gave no name, and Lauretta would not have waited to be asked. Certainly the major with her was not DeCaulp, for he was at Fort Snelling, growing steadily weaker. Yet still, it is just possible. Lauretta could not use either DeCaulp or Buford in the Confederacy now, for Thomas was a deserter and no glory would attach to his name. She always formed liaisons with men quickly and easily, and she might have found another companion if she had left Fort Snelling, or the mysterious major may have been only someone she had met on the train. If this was in fact Lauretta, though, nothing could have been more irritating to her than that the Charlotte *Times* headed its article "Another Belle Boyd."[2] One further tantalizing hint came late that October or early November, when a "Mrs. Williams" applied to Brigadier General James

Chesnut in Charleston, South Carolina, for a passport to go to the North. If Lauretta were in the Confederacy that fall, the most likely name for her to use would have been Williams. Apparently Chesnut granted the application.[3]

Only once in those eighteen months after early August 1864 did Lauretta definitely emerge from obscurity, and then in a cryptic manner suggesting she might have been back in Richmond, this mysterious female captain's destination. On December 22 the Richmond *Enquirer* carried a personal announcement written as a letter addressed to "Madame Laure De Caulp, formerly of St. James' Parish, LA":

> The following is an extract from a letter from Don Augustus V. Steinhosse of Havana.
>
>> Died, on the 20th November, at the residence of his sister, Mrs. Horatio Flagg, at Hayti, W. I., Commodore J. B. Roach, of the British Navy, aged 72 years and 4 months—In the distribution of his estate his daughter, residing in the Confederate States of America, is to receive at the expiration of five years the sum of $10,000, with interest. Her son is to be educated, at the expense of the estate, at the military school in London, and at the age of 21 years shall receive $30,000 with interest.
>>
>> The plate, valued at twenty thousand dollars ($20,000) was also left you, and your jewelry and manuscripts are on deposit in the Bank of England for you. The estate was valued at $1,810,000 and after deducting your own and your son's portion, it is to be equally divided between the remaining eight children. Your father expressed in his will a dissatisfaction with your late marriage, and acted accordingly. The only member of the family present at your father's death was your brother Harry, who is acting British Consul at Hayti. The remains were sent to Glasgow, Scotland, for interment.

In the next column, the first paragraph appeared again, but stating that she was to get $5,000 rather than $10,000, followed by notice that the paragraph came "from a letter received by a brother-in-law in Havana, Cuba," signed "Don Augustine V. Steinhosse."[4]

It did not appear again in the *Enquirer*, but a few days later the first long paragraph was published in Charleston. In it the inheritance was also $5,000 instead of $10,000; it said "his son" was to be educated, not hers; and this time the writer was identified as Don Augustine V. Stainhoss. There was no indication of where it came from, and on the last day of the year the Atlanta *Daily Constitution* presented it all under the wry headline, "In Luck," saying it came from the *Enquirer*. Where it should have mentioned $10,000, an error made it read "$10,00" instead, and further it said it was "her" son to be educated. Otherwise it matched the *Enquirer*.[5]

The sense of it appears to be that, writing from Havana, Steinhosse addressed an undated letter to Laure, or Lauretta, in which he copied the paragraph announcing the death—and in which she is spoken of in the third person—from a letter sent to a brother-in-law in that same city, though whose brother-in-law is unclear. In the second paragraph, now addressing her directly, Steinhosse added further details of her bequest and her family.

The letter raises myriad questions. Why would he tell Lauretta that her brother was British consul in Haiti when presumably she would know that already? Who was this son of hers? Had she really borne a child by DeCaulp? Who really was Commodore Roach? Why was the letter published in the Richmond press, and who placed it there? Was it, as the longer second paragraph clearly suggested, from a letter addressed directly to Lauretta, and if so, how did it get from her to the *Enquirer*?

Lauretta had already unveiled Roach as her father back in Richmond in July 1863, but then she said he was Major J. B. Roche, a wealthy Mississippi planter, with no mention of Haiti or the navy.[6] By August 1864 she had promoted him to "Rear Admiral Rosche" of the British navy.[7] Now in December he was Commodore J. B. Roach. This was his last appearance, but a little more than a year from now, she would again give her maiden name as Roach.[8] There has never been an admiral or lower-grade officer named J. B. Roach/Roche/Rosche in the British navy. Moreover, in this period, that navy did not use honorific titles like "commodore," unlike the U.S. Navy.[9] Roach was entirely Lauretta's invention. So was the brother Harry.[10] Britain had no diplomatic consul to Haiti at that time, only a *chargé d'affaires*, Sir Spenser B. St. John, from 1861 to 1872.[11] Horatio Flagg and wife equally defy identification, as does Augustus or Augustine V. Steinhosse, though the surname may be a mild joke, since in loose translation it comes from the German for "Stonepants."

The *Enquirer* did not publish it as news. Rather, it ran as a personal advertisement, meaning someone paid to insert it in the paper. Personals as a genre often ran for days and even weeks in hopes of being seen by the right people, yet this one appeared once and only once, hardly a serious

Died, on the 20th November, at the residence of his sister, Mrs. Horatio Flagg, at Hayti, W. I., Commodore J. B. Roach, of the British Navy, aged 72 years and 4 months. In the distribution of his estate his daughter, residing in the Confederate States of America, is to receive at the expiration of five years the sum of $5000, with interest. His son is to be educated at the expense of the estate, at the military school at London. and at the age of 21 years shall receive $30 000 with interest.

Copied from a letter received by a brother-in-law, in Havana, Cuba.

DON AUGUSTINE V. STAINHOSS,

Lauretta's first "inheritance scam" at work: the Charleston version of her fictitious father's death notice. Charleston *Daily Courier*, December 29, 1864.

effort at getting news to Lauretta. Furthermore, it said nothing about how to contact Steinhosse or anyone else. Instead, it appeared to be designed only to communicate information rather than elicit action or response, though again, the information mainly came from a letter originally addressed to Lauretta. The gist was that Lauretta was rich and soon to be richer, worth at least $20,000 now, not counting her jewelry, and sure to come into half again that amount in 1869, not to mention what she might manage to hold on to from her son's $30,000.

The only plausible explanation is that Lauretta fabricated the item herself and somehow got it to Richmond to establish a "back story," something she repeated more than once in years ahead. In this instance it established her as a well-born woman coming into a considerable sum and destined to have access to much more. Back in May Thomas had expressed his gratitude to her for abandoning "riches" to follow him, so she may have sold him her Roach and riches story and he believed it, meaning that each had lied to the other, she about her family and money, and he about that inconvenient pregnant wife back in Arkansas.

More questions arise immediately. How did she get the personal item to the *Enquirer*? She could have mailed it with payment enclosed, but doing so from Fort Snelling, or anywhere in the Union, would have been precarious at best. Such across-the-lines correspondence was mostly limited to letters home from prisoners of war and always subject to being opened and inspected. She might have given it to someone she knew who was making the hazardous trip through the lines, to be mailed once in the Confederacy, but by this period transportation and mail delivery in the South were breaking down seriously as Union advances steadily eroded Confederate infrastructure. The most secure way to see her information planted in the paper was to deliver it herself, a contingency reinforced by the fact that it appeared only once in the *Enquirer.* If she was going to use a clipping of the piece for some purpose, one appearance was all she needed, but then she must be there when it came off press to secure the clipping.

Her purpose had to have been cash. Now and later she demonstrated a shrewd understanding that the promise of wealth tomorrow could attract money today. Her pockets might have been bare at the moment, but showing someone this clipping was as good as proof that she had thousands if she could get access. That and her undeniable skill at persuasion might lure a wealthy suitor, act as collateral for a loan to take a blockade runner to England or elsewhere, even convince Thomas that it was worth her leaving him in his illness to pursue the fortune he already believed she was heir to. The mention of her "manuscripts" is also suggestive. She was on record as intending to write a memoir of the war. These papers might be just that, evidence enough to get a publisher here or abroad to advance cash for the exciting adventures of the "Female Lieutenant."

Unwittingly, Lauretta pioneered. For years she had been practicing a confidence game, presenting herself as something she was not, just as many other women attempted to pass as men to take part in the war.[12] With this personal advertisement, however, she anticipated ruses that criminal confidence women would be practicing in years to come. In 1871 an Elizabeth Bigley displayed a false statement that she was heir to $15,000, using it to persuade merchants to accept her promissory notes in return for goods. Later she showed a forged note from industrialist Andrew Carnegie, acknowledging her as his illegitimate heir to hundreds of millions, and with it defrauded banks of a fortune. A decade later Mary Hansen cited an inheritance as collateral to borrow cash for travel to collect it and pay attached fees, saying she would lose it otherwise and resorting to hysteria if necessary. Soon afterward Bertha Heyman of Milwaukee practiced the same sort of game, pretending to have wealth in order to cajole hotels and merchants, even banks and stock brokers, into advancing her credit and funds.[13] Lauretta was ahead of them all, however, and she needed no hysteria. Rather, she depended on her personality to sell the "con," and unlike those who came after her, she enhanced its seeming authenticity by making the press an unwitting accomplice.

What she sought to gain by this, her inaugural example is unknown. If the ploy worked, no hint survives, though it adds yet another layer to her increasingly sophisticated grasp of how to manipulate the press to create her own history. It is also her last certain wartime manifestation and just a shadow at that. At the risk of piling ifs upon ifs, if she were the female captain who passed through Charlotte in September, it could put her in Richmond in December to place her bait in the *Enquirer*, and if she were in the Confederate capital at the end of 1864, then she possibly could have been there until near the city's fall in April 1865.

Just three weeks following the personal letter's appearance in the *Enquirer*, surgeons discharged Private William Irwin at Fort Snelling on January 14, 1865. As of December 26 he had done no active duty for four months, since mid-August 1864. An examining physician diagnosed chronic sciatica and "hemorrhage of the lungs," which sounds like the onset of tuberculosis. He remained at Fort Snelling all that time, until the surgeon finally pronounced him two-thirds disabled and unfit for any further duty, not even healthy enough to transfer to the Veteran Reserve Corps, a unit made up of invalids. According to the forwarding address he gave the army at his discharge, he would be found thereafter at Holmesburg, a suburb of Philadelphia.[14] After that, he disappeared for good.[15] In late February 1866, just prior to her first postwar appearance in the press, she made no mention at all of her husband.[16] A week later, however, Lauretta would claim that he was captured in the fall of 1863 and sent to a prison in New York, where, "after a long and arduous siege," she got him paroled in January 1865, only to have him die eight days later.[17] Then in June 1866 she told another journalist that DeCaulp actually died in a Yankee prison.[18] Within less than a decade she moved his death up to September 1863 in a Union field hospital in Chattanooga.[19]

Hence the real question remains of just when and where he did die. If Lauretta substituted his fictional release from prison for the date of his discharge on January 14, then she would be saying that he died on January 22, 1865. If she was not actually with DeCaulp in Fort Snelling up to his discharge, she still had to be close enough to him to know that important release date, whose circumstances she just reshaped in 1866. That could argue that she was not in Richmond then, but with him up to the end or nearly so. Did she tell the truth when she said he died in New York? It is possible, though New York was well out of the way from the most direct rail connection to Philadelphia, where he said he was going at his discharge, and she gave no reason for them to go to New York instead. If he really died on January 22, they might not yet have closed housekeeping, and he could have been buried at Fort Snelling, though no such record survives.[20]

Until contemporary confirmation of his death can be found, it is at least a possibility that he did not die in 1865. If Lauretta abandoned him, as he had abandoned Sarah in Arkansas, he would likely have had no compunction about resuming his old life, even marrying again, and without benefit of divorce. Several William Irwins lived in the Philadelphia area from 1865 on, and a few were carpenters. One lived in Frankford, only about two miles from Holmesburg. He had been there in 1860 but not in 1861–64, when DeCaulp/Irwin was away at war and in Minnesota.[21] He was still there in 1870, now age twenty-eight, married, and with three children, the oldest born in 1864–65, and he continued in business at least as late as 1881.[22] His dates almost fit with William Irwin/Thomas DeCaulp, yet there are others, including a William D. Irwin in nearby Chester County, a carpenter born in 1834–35 in Pennsylvania, living with his wife, Sallie, and three children, the first born in 1866–67.[23] It would be fitting if Thomas DeCaulp, essentially a man who never was, should also be a man who never died.

Lauretta's earliest postwar accounts for the couple's blank war months are little help and contradictory. In late February 1866 she said that she spent the rest of the war "engaged in secret service," some in the Confederacy, then in England, and some in Canada. She claimed she spent several months in 1864 traveling in the Union, then in late January 1865 went to Columbus, where she looked after the welfare of Confederate prisoners at Camp Chase until war's end.[24]

Three months later, in May 1866, she changed her story to imply that she spent the last year of the war in Confederate service in the North and Europe, and that at or near the end she surrendered herself to authorities in Washington.[25] Then in June she elaborated, claiming that she also spent some time in prison, acted as a detective and spy for the Union, clerked in the War Department at Washington, and was in New York preparing to leave for Europe when the surrenders came. At the news, she turned herself in as a soldier and was so paroled.[26] Fourteen years later an officer she met at Castle Thunder claimed that he had seen her in Richmond in the fall of 1865 and that she told him she was on her way to New York for a job writing for a newspaper.[27]

Camp Chase, Columbus, Ohio. Lauretta claimed that acting as a Confederate spy, she visited Confederates imprisoned there, but on her only confirmed visit to Columbus, she spent her time looking for her first husband and borrowing money from a Yankee general. Library of Congress.

The most likely explanation, however, is that she spent some of those missing months at Fort Snelling caring for Thomas, probably up to his discharge in January 1865. Having left him once when she went to Nashville, she could have done so again, perhaps to get that advertisement in the Richmond press. The personal ad appeared just three weeks before Thomas's discharge, which he had to have known was coming, since a surgeon pronounced him disabled the previous December 26. However she got her notice in the *Enquirer*, Lauretta was setting up a future scheme that might support them both if he survived and support her if he did not. She was never without a plan.

CHAPTER EIGHT

THE RETURN OF MRS. DECAULP

PERHAPS LAURETTA DID go to Europe. In October 1865 the notorious journalist Charles Dunham, using the alias Sanford Conover, claimed to have heard stories about her and implied that he had met her recently at an undisclosed location while he was soliciting real and fabricated testimony to link former Confederates to the murder of Lincoln. He further claimed that he could secure her testimony about a plot to kill Lincoln in which she was to have poisoned the president. Dunham added that he would bring her to Washington to testify, but in all the voluminous archives surrounding the Lincoln murder and subsequent investigation, her name never appeared.[1] As with Lauretta, nothing Dunham said could be taken on his word alone. He was actively trying to make money by informing on as many people as possible, regardless of fact. In time he was found out and prosecuted for his actions. Moreover, the fact that he identified Lauretta as Alice Williams suggests he may not have seen her at all, since a number of officials in Washington such as Pelouze could recognize her as Lauretta DeCaulp. If Dunham had actually met her, and if she feared that authorities might act on his information, then she had good reason to leave the country. If she went overseas, she could well have been the twenty-four-year-old Laura Williams who returned to New York in steerage on the steamer *Moravian* out of Liverpool on January 11, 1866, seven weeks before Lauretta emerged once more.[2]

One fact is evident: wherever Lauretta DeCaulp was in those lost months, she gave considerable thought to ways to make some money quickly to support herself. Her mind went back to Mary Ann Keith's claim to be writing a history or memoir of the war. She could season it with the real and invented recollections she had already created for Harry Buford. The mention of "manuscripts" in her December 1864 notice in the *Enquirer* suggests that she already had a publication in mind. Embarrassing events in her real history had to be replaced, especially her six months in the Orleans Parish Prison. Thomas DeCaulp's desertion at Chattanooga needed recasting, as did her disappearance from the Confederacy at the same time. Invention never challenged her to date, so she could confidently create plausible stories to suit her purpose, but there always remained the problems inherent in piling one fiction atop another and keeping track of what lie she told when and to whom. She had not been at all good at that so far.

Just as Mary Ann Keith began her 1861 adventure in Memphis, so Lauretta launched her postwar career there. On or shortly before February 28, 1866, she appeared at the city's Commercial Hotel. Local journalists certainly knew of her as H. T. Buford, the one-time "Female Lieutenant," and if not she reminded them now and announced that she was on her way to St. Louis to buy dry goods and "plantation supplies" for a store she intended to open at Mulberry Grove in Jefferson County, Arkansas. She touted her service in several battles along with her wounds, which for the moment were two, and then added her first postwar layer of myth by averring that she "fought to the end" of the conflict. The *Daily Avalanche* identified her as "Mrs. L. D. Camp."[3] It may have been a typographical error, a compositor's misreading of the reporter's handwriting, or even Lauretta's invention if she feared using DeCaulp might awaken inconvenient recollection of Thomas's desertion or her own time in the North protesting her loyalty to the Union. The misappellation soon changed to DeCamp and remained so until mid-May in the press in Tennessee, Missouri, Georgia, and even Texas.

A few days after her appearance in Memphis, Lauretta reached St. Louis, took a room at the Southern Hotel, and called on a reporter from the St. Louis *Republican* to give him her story at some length. She recast her entire life to date into a cohesive narrative, the first of the uncountable cocoons of myth she would spin around the modest and often unseemly facts of her life.

Once again she appeared in print as "Mrs. Loretta De Camp," either yet another error between reporter and typesetter or a continuation of her uncharacteristic caution about possible problems with DeCaulp. She told the reporter she was born Roach in the West Indies, but in 1838, not 1842. Her family moved to St. James Parish in Louisiana when she was a child, and when the war started, a patriotic impulse inspired her to don a soldier's clothes. At her own expense, she raised and equipped a company of cavalry that she led to Virginia, but after eight months serving under the command of Colonel Charles Dreux, she was found out and sent back to Louisiana. Instead, as Buford she went to Kentucky and served under General Polk until he evacuated Columbus in February 1862 following the fall of Fort Donelson. She joined the Southern garrison at Island Number Ten in the

Mississippi River but almost immediately left for Fort Pillow, Tennessee, on the river some miles above Memphis. There the men of a Captain Phillips's company of "independent Tennessee cavalry" elected her their lieutenant, unaware of her gender. She fought with them at Shiloh, where Phillips was mortally wounded and she took command of the company. Leading it in a charge, she received two wounds and was taken from the field, then to New Orleans for surgical treatment. When the Yankees occupied the city in late April, she became their prisoner and spent several months in prison before being paroled and then exchanged.

She went to Richmond, where General Cooper gave her a lieutenancy and ordered her to report to Brigadier General Marcus J. Wright, commanding in Atlanta. He made her "chief of detectives" in the provost marshal's office and assigned her as a "military conductor" checking passports on trains. After several months she met her husband, "Major DeCamp." Now for the first time Lauretta claimed they were engaged before the war. When they married in Atlanta, "the dashing lieutenant Roach" became "the sober Mrs. Major DeCamp." Thomas was captured in the fall of 1863 and sent to prison in New York, where, "after a long and arduous siege," she got him paroled in January 1865, only to have him die eight days later. Meanwhile, marriage ended her services as an officer, but as herself she spent the rest of the war "in secret service" in the Confederacy, England, and Canada. In 1864 she traveled widely in the Union, including Minnesota, then after Thomas's death she went to Camp Chase for a period of time and remained in the North until January 1866. She then returned south to her home in Louisiana, staying only a few days before going on to Memphis.

Lauretta evolved her story considerably and revealed hallmarks of all her future variations—carelessness, confused chronology, and obfuscation to cover what she did not want known. She mentioned neither First Manassas nor Ball's Bluff, but claiming service in Virginia for eight months in 1861 implied her presence at both. Then she slipped badly when she said she had served under Lieutenant Colonel Charles Dreux. He had commanded no units but his own 1st Louisiana Infantry Battalion and was killed on July 4, well before Manassas or Ball's Bluff. Her claim of service with Polk at Columbus was unchanged, but being in Captain Phillips's company of "independent Tennessee cavalry" was something new—and false. There was no such company and no Captain Phillips, but virtually no one would know that. Making herself a prisoner of the Yankees in New Orleans from the fall of 1862 to the spring of 1863 neatly covered her actual time in the parish prison.

Absent was her arrest and incarceration at Castle Thunder in July 1863. Her claim then that she had joined General A. P. Stewart's staff as a spy she now changed to work for General Wright, checking passports on trains. She made no mention of her supposed husband Williams of the 13th Connecticut and continued Thomas's promotion to major that she had started in 1864 in the North.[4] She gave little detail on her career after the fall of 1863, for there was little hazard that anyone in the South might know what she had been doing after that time. Curiously, the reporter made no mention of Harry Buford, probably just an oversight, since she was already identified with Buford in the Memphis paper. Now she was "Lieutenant Roach."[5]

Lauretta's story demonstrated her Confederate patriotism and finished by appealing to the sympathy of readers, even here in St. Louis. The steamboat *Miami* had exploded in the Arkansas River on January 28. Only two of the few survivors were women.[6] Lauretta claimed now that she was one of them and that the cargo of goods she had bought in Memphis for her store in Arkansas was lost with the *Miami*, along with her personal baggage. Worse, the Memphis merchants neglected to insure her cargo, and "she lost her all." The *Republican* interview closed with a thinly veiled appeal to sympathetic readers to make contributions to cover the loss of such a self-sacrificing Confederate.[7]

Once more she employed the social and psychological stereotypes of the era, depicting women as weak and needing protection in order to convert sympathy to cash, a classic female confidence artist's pose. For a woman to be anything other than sincere, humble, and essentially powerless posed a threat to a hierarchy in which only men were seen as deceitful or manipulative. That was unthinkable, and Lauretta was only too ready to take advantage of that.[8] Only her confidence in that explains the careless mistakes she made. In Memphis in late February she said she was on her way to St. Louis to buy stock for her store. A week later in St. Louis she said she had already bought the goods in Memphis. Most glaring of all, how could she have lost everything on the *Miami* on January 28, a full month before she announced she intended to buy the stock? It was the same disregard she showed in her wartime accounts and something she never corrected.

Lauretta understood how the press worked. She expected the *Republican* article to spread quickly, as indeed it did.[9] Her friend from Jackson, editor Robert Purdom, even saw it in Dallas. "We knew her well during Confederate times," he asserted, recalling their brief acquaintance in June 1863. He happily contributed to her legend: "In the hour of battle she was ever among the foremost," he wrote, though he never saw a battlefield himself, "but when the carnage was over, she would drop the garb *militaire* and become an angel of mercy to the wounded and dying."[10] In time the interview appeared in faraway Mexico City to spread her fame and her need for money.[11]

In the process, descriptions of her evolved to make her "a young and beautiful woman," suiting expectations of the time, when men chose to believe all Southern women were modest, chaste, lovely, and of unquestioned character. That played into the hands of a trickster like Lauretta. When contributions dwindled in St. Louis, she returned to the Commercial Hotel in Memphis, knowing that potential contributors there had been primed by their press. To avoid mistake, she issued a correction that only added to the confusion when the local press bungled it too. Presumably telling it that she was Lauretta J. DeCaulp, not L. D. Camp, she appeared in print instead as Lauretta J. De Camp. Her wartime creation also appeared erroneously as "Lieutenant Harry S. Buford." Either that was still another typographical error, or else she briefly forgot that the lieutenant's middle initial had always been "T." The correction also multiplied her wounds to three, and she repeated that at the Commercial Hotel, "she will be happy to see any of her friends," meaning any who came with cash.[12]

By early March she moved her show to New Orleans and the St. James Hotel, the editorial errors coming with her as she was identified now as "Mrs. Major T. C. DeCamp better known as Lieut. H. T. Buford." Her war wounds doubled from two to four; "she has also been blown up on a steamboat," noted a reporter, and was in fact "the only lady passenger saved."[13] She soon realized the hazard of playing with facts about steamboats in a river city like New Orleans, however, for the story of the real survivors was well known by this time, as were their names, Mrs. S. Jacobs of Chicago and Mrs. Barret Brassius.[14] Lauretta never brought up the steamboat explosion again.

Soon she was off for the Atlantic coast. On May 9 she walked into the editorial office of the Atlanta *Daily Intelligencer* to meet a newsman she had known back in 1863. He saw before him "an elegantly dressed lady, still in the bloom of youth, and beautiful to behold, whom we soon recognized as the veritable *Lieutenant Buford*." She gave him her story but amended her most recent version by adding that at war's end she was either in Washington or went there to surrender herself. She also added that she had traveled twice to Europe and once to Canada on Confederate service, then revealed more about her plans for a book, promising that it would include public documents, unpublished military orders, and her own narrative. In fact, she was already writing it, promising to detail "the dangers through which she has passed in the tented, and in the battle field, on the high seas and amid the crowded cities of Europe, at Nassau, and in running the blockade."[15]

She needed subscribers and contributors now to support her while she finished her work, offering to display "very high testimonials" of her reliability and character to any potential donor.[16] Now the December 1864 personal item published in the *Enquirer* could be useful, putting her inheritance con into actual practice, for it promised surety that soon she could repay contributors. The postwar 1860s saw the dawn of a small wave of confidence women who flourished in their way, creating opportunities by sleight of hand and wits. Once more Lauretta rode in the vanguard.[17]

She made one more correction in Atlanta: her name was not De Camp but DeCaulp.[18] Just days earlier, her past had started to catch up with her. During a stop in Mobile, somehow she heard a rumor alleging that she had not been the Confederate she claimed, most likely a reference to her departure to the North in the fall of 1863. Instinctively in such situations, she took the offensive, resorting to the con man's exaggerated, even belligerent, denial.[19] She gave a public statement to the Mobile *Tribune*, which virtually endorsed her by saying she was "noted as a skilful officer and for indomitable perseverance and pluck." Pained by what she called the "circulation of slanders," she denounced them all as lies "and without shadow of foundation." She would happily refute them to any who asked, while any who spread the rumor "will do so at their personal peril." She signed it "Mrs. Loretta J. DeCaulp, Formerly Lieutenant T. Buford, C.S.A."

Within days her announcement spread through the press as far as Philadelphia and Massachusetts, as she expected it would.[20] In a few weeks her defiant challenge was being read across the Atlantic on the streets of Belfast, Edinburgh, and London.[21] To further demonstrate her loyalty, now she began wearing a Confederate military button on her dress.[22] Then even more disturbing stories came to her ears when she heard accusations that her late husband, Thomas, "had deserted the Confederate cause, and gone over to the other side." It was a base slander, she told the *Intelligencer*. She would defend his name "and will meet any one who dares or has dared to asperse his memory." Having been wounded twice—a sudden reduction from four—on the battlefield, she promised that bullets held no terrors for her, and she would "defy death itself" in vindication of her departed husband's honor. In other words, she would meet all slanderers on the dueling ground. "We do not envy the man who will accept this challenge," concluded the Atlanta reporter, "for though gentle in peace, 'in arms' this lady is sure to conquer."[23] No wonder the press elsewhere began calling her "the last 'lioness.'"[24] Yet again she broke new ground. Instead of resorting to artificial femininity, pleas of wounded innocence, or assumed weakness, to deflect problems with her fabrications, she boldly dared accusers, invoking the old code of honor to establish her claim to authenticity.[25]

After several days in Atlanta calling on old Confederates, she moved on to Savannah. The Northern press watched her progress now, usually reiterating excerpts from her *Republican* story, and soon after her arrival an Ohio paper announced that "'Lt. T. Buford' has reached Savannah."[26] During her trip she steadily evolved her undertaking and the potential base of support for subscriptions and donations. Now she declared she would write not one book, but three. One would be her aforementioned *The History of the Southern Confederacy*, including her own personal adventures. Another would be *The Cruise of the Shenandoah; or, the Last of the Confederacy*, the dramatic story of the Rebel commerce raider that continued taking Union merchant ships for months after Appomattox, unaware that the war had ended. The final volume would be a compilation of verse titled simply *Buford's Poems*, her first and only mention of poetry. She advised potential donors and subscribers that her visit was brief, so they should come to her hotel quickly before she left. Meanwhile, she tinkered with her story. The company of volunteers she raised in 1861 was actually composed of Texans, she said, and she bumped her two Shiloh wounds back up to three. For further details, she apparently handed out copies of the recent *Intelligencer* article.[27]

Then she left for Charleston, while coverage of her Savannah visit was being read in New York, Vermont, Pennsylvania, and elsewhere.[28] By the time she reached Charleston, news coverage of her journey should have prepared the city, but she took it by surprise, which was no doubt her object. Charlestonians one morning saw a woman riding the city streets dressed in a Confederate gray basque, or short tunic, "trimmed a la militaire, and with the insignia of a 1st Lieutenant on the collar." She even wore a derby hat cocked to one side of her head. "Her novel dress attracted considerable attention," said one citizen, and as Lauretta expected. People wondered who she was and if U.S. authorities knew about her. At last they discovered that she was "the celebrated Mrs. DeCamp alias Lieut. Buford." She immediately announced her object to obtain subscriptions for what she said would be a true and correct history of the war. According to her, several prominent men in the city made contributions, including former Confederate secretary of the treasury George A. Trenholm, and it appears that she gleaned a few letters of reference as well, which were always useful to her.[29] There could be no question about her reception. She was "the latest sensation here," wrote an observer, "the cynosure of all eyes." Another man saw that her appearance in Rebel gray pleased the unreconstructed among the citizens and wistfully added that "the fair lieutenant has flashed upon us like a dream that is past."[30]

Having crossed the Deep South, Lauretta headed west again, stopping first in Augusta, Georgia, and then in Atlanta, where she had left an agent authorized to collect donations for her. She claimed that the city had made "a liberal response" to her plea, but still there could be more. On May 21 she called at the *Daily Constitutionalist* to prime local donors with a reminder of her Confederate services. She showed the editor testimonials confirming that she was one and the same as Lieutenant Buford. Knowing the value of widowhood in eliciting sympathy and cash, she understood that there were different kinds of widows. Until now her husband had died after release from a prison camp, but today she told the *Daily Constitutionalist* reporter that DeCaulp had been "slain in the military service of the late Confederate States." Death in battle was a greater sacrifice than death from prison disease and deserved greater subscriptions. The word *psychology* may not have been in her vocabulary, yet she grasped its meaning instinctively and used that understanding cannily.

Expanding on her own service as well, she frosted her myth with cavalry service under the great Lieutenant General J. E. B. Stuart and Nathan Bedford Forrest, and she redistributed her Shiloh wounds. Now she said she had suffered the first in a cavalry skirmish several days after Shiloh and the second a few days later in a minor action at Stillwater, Mississippi. A wound in a forgotten skirmish was just as heroic as one in a major battle and offered fewer risks of inconvenient gainsaying witnesses. As for her books, she mentioned only the one general history, which she described now as a compilation of Federal documents on the causes and conduct of the war, and announced that Trenholm, a distinguished Carolinian, had made a large contribution.[31]

When the paper gave her several column inches under the heading "Joan of Arc," a reference becoming more and more common in articles about her, Lauretta called again at the *Daily Intelligencer* office. She showed new testimonials from Charleston and some evidence of the level of contributions received to date. Moreover, she now announced that she had arranged for the publication of her books, which now were back to two, the one on the *Shenandoah* and her memoir, now retitled *History of the Late War for Independence.* There was reassurance to those who had given her money, even if they had only her word for it, for a woman would not lie. In fact, she declared that she expected Atlanta to turn out even more subscribers, and the editor of the *Daily Intelligencer* concurred, calling on his readers to give generously and agreeing to accept cash on her behalf after her departure.[32]

Lauretta left for Montgomery on May 25, then moved on to Meridian, Mississippi, by June 1, where she reiterated her history and her current plans. She revised the title of her memoir yet again, to *History of the Southern Confederacy, with Personal Adventures of the Authoress*, suggesting that at these stops she intentionally experimented to find the title best suited to generate subscriptions. In Meridian she also broke with recent policy and cited the *Miami* disaster as the reason she "will ask the Southern public to assist her with the means to get her books out." Overconfidence and underestimation of her audience, classic pitfalls of the con artist, made her careless with conflicting claims, but she was usually lucky that no one noticed.[33]

By mid-June she reached Nashville. She met with the editor of the *Union and American* but may have offered little in her own words, for his account mostly reiterated what had appeared elsewhere, including features she had abandoned, such as a husband prior to DeCaulp and Thomas's death in prison. But she did say that at war's end she was not in Washington, but in New York preparing to leave for Europe, and that she turned herself in to the authorities and received a parole that she still carried, her first and only mention of such a document. As for male attire, she had given it up entirely but still wore that Confederate uniform button on her dress. She gave no details of her contemplated books, saying only that she intended to publish one or more. Entirely convinced, the editor added that "if nothing more than her own romantic experience is given in the simple language of truth, they will possess unusual interest."

He noted something else, the most perceptive evaluation to date of the woman before him: she demonstrated "the eccentricities of a strongly marked character, extreme shrewdness and readiness of address, combined with great energy and self-possession."[34] Before long Lauretta echoed those words when she declared, "I had unlimited faith in my own tact and skill, and did not doubt my ability."[35] That certainly described a heroine, but one distinctly outside conventional expectation. They just as easily described the confidence woman.

She soon revealed an even greater grasp of self-promotion and manipulation of opinion. Shortly after arriving, she went to the Union Street studio of Thomas F. Saltzman, perhaps Nashville's premier photographer. There she sat for a portrait from which Saltzman produced several hundred copies for her to market from both his studio and her room at the St. Cloud Hotel. For almost a fortnight she advertised them in the local press under the headline "Photographs of Lt. Buford," adding that she would be pleased to receive her "old comrades in arms" at her room every evening from five until eight o'clock.[36] The portrait photos, probably small *cartes-de-visite* in size, would be lasting reminders of her story. Not only would she make money from their sale, but they would also keep her story alive to promote future subscriptions.

Before long, she moved on. Pulaski, Tennessee, welcomed her as "the world-renowned heroine and Confederate officer." She solicited subscribers for her book of poetry and her history. Instinctively understanding that the con artist needed always to announce progress to keep people mollified, now she announced that she had just completed both, whereas it is clear that she had not put pen to paper.[37] Indeed, it is uncertain at this point that she intended ever to write a book or do more than string out her collection of donations and subscriptions as long as she could, then disappear or announce that some new catastrophe like the *Miami* disaster had consumed her manuscripts, a customary resort for con men who had run their game to its reasonable conclusion.

At last she returned to Memphis, where her fund-raising tour had begun. The press coverage of her travels made her better known than before and raised even more sympathy. Former Confederates in the city planned a benefit ball in her honor at the Charleston Hotel for the evening of June 28. "Her many friends in this city have tendered her this benefit, as an appreciation of her merits," read an announcement that appealed to people to turn out their pockets and come.[38] No estimate is possible of how much the ball raised or how much cash she took in from subscriptions and outright donations since the previous February. It may have been considerable, probably several hundred dollars at least, even a few thousand, though cash was dear in the still-stricken South, and she might not have realized as much as hoped.

After a month of inactivity she made one more journey, this time to the former Confederate capital at Richmond. There she called on the editor of the Richmond *Whig* on August 9, saying not a word about her books or her career as Buford, but simply announcing that she was at the Spotswood Hotel and would gladly receive any former Confederates, no doubt relying on her persuasive ability to press her case for money more personally. She claimed now that she lived in Dallas County, Arkansas, two counties southwest of Jefferson, her supposed home the previous February. Almost as an aside, she mentioned that she planned to visit Europe in the fall.[39]

A few days later she arrived at the Kirkwood House in Washington and announced that she had come to meet with President Andrew Johnson. There was no mention of books or subscriptions or her career, other than that she had been known during the war as Lieutenant Buford. Rather, she pursued an entirely new interest. She wanted to build an "asylum for the disabled and destitute of the South."[40] That simple notice saw wide republication, yet while the press expected that she would "doubtless be extensively *feted* before she leaves," nothing more was heard of her or her asylum.[41] In light of her activities over the next thirty years, the projected asylum was almost certainly an embryonic confidence swindle, her announcement a trial balloon to see if it generated enough interest for her to pursue the matter. Assuming that her recent tour had gleaned as much as she could expect, it would be time to look for another project, and charitable enterprises held the same emotional appeal as a heroic widow. Should she get an audience with Johnson, she could manipulate anything he said into an endorsement.

Instead, she went to ground, disappearing altogether for four months. Given her appetite for notoriety and her growing skill at drawing attention, only something compelling could have made her disappear again as she had after August 1864. Since she reemerged in New York City, perhaps she did go abroad, since New York was the major embarkation point for trans-Atlantic voyages, and her tour should have raised enough money for her passage. If there were any truth to her occasional claims to have spent much of the last year of the war abroad, then she might have been revisiting familiar scenes or friends. She could have met a man and accompanied him, or she might have gone on her own. Perhaps she dropped out of sight because of her health. Hereafter, she periodically disappeared from view for a few months, and her behavior and reports of her actions in coming years manifested that she occasionally dealt with an as-yet-undiagnosed condition. One thing her later actions make clear is that she was not closeted writing her memoir.

However occupied, Lauretta kept abreast with the news. During her tour across the South, she had to have seen the wide press coverage of a scheme to colonize former Confederates in lands granted by the ruling regime in Venezuela. A number of emigration projects erupted in those years to relocate people in Brazil, Mexico, and Central America, where they might rebuild their lives. The organizers garnered large land grants and then sold substantial plots for prices that included the expense of passage and a good fee for the leader. Most projects fell through quickly, and some were frauds, but a successful impresario could make thousands. Men ran all of them.

In 1865 Dr. Henry Price secured a grant of 240,000 square miles of land along the Orinoco River, promising to introduce colonists to develop and populate the territory. They would establish a state government "which shall be moral, social, and purely Southern in all its characteristics," he declared in March 1866.[42] That September he announced that the "Venezuelan Emigration Company" would provide homes for ex-Confederates who "cannot remain in their old homes under the domination of their heartless victors." For $1,000 a buyer got title to 1,280 acres of land, but Price set aside three hundred thousand shares to be given outright to former Confederate soldiers who agreed to emigrate and settle the country. There would be no taxes and complete freedom of religion despite Catholicism being Venezuela's state faith. Moreover, the mineral and agricultural wealth of the region was to be theirs, and there was talk of gold strikes in the interior.[43] By December 20 news circulated in the East that the first group of emigrants had formed in St. Louis and was on its way to New Orleans.[44]

It seems more than coincidental that Lauretta reemerged on December 22, 1866, just as the impending departure of those colonists made the press. That day she boarded the steamer *Montgomery* in New York, bound for the Crescent City.[45] On January 2, 1867, the *Montgomery* tied up at the New Orleans landing, and Lauretta moved into the City Hotel. Two days later she called on the mayor, and then called on a correspondent of the *Daily Picayune* who remembered her from 1862.[46] He saw in her now a "rather graceful and elegantly attired lady in black," who picked up where she left off the previous summer retelling the story of Lieutenant Buford, or "Bufort," as the journalist wrote it carelessly. She stayed with being lieutenant of a Texas cavalry company that she had led at First Manassas, then went to the western army and suffered just one wound at Shiloh, "in which memorable engagement she claims to have performed splendid service."[47] Back in New Orleans, she said, she lived with a regiment camped on the edge of town, implying that this was before the Union occupation, and hence she did not mention that it was a Yankee regiment with which she billeted. Saying she was then arrested for violating the nonexistent ordinance against women appearing in men's clothing, she added that no charges were pressed and she then purchased a fashionable female wardrobe from a city dressmaker.

Conventionally attired, she left the city and went to an unspecified place upriver, but she came back just before the city fell to the enemy and was arrested for being again in uniform, "dashing about the streets upon horseback." After that, General Butler arrested her "for some indiscretion." Being "subsequently released"—she made no mention of six months in prison for larceny—she went to Richmond only to be assigned as "passport agent" on the railroad between Atlanta and Chattanooga, which she did for six months or more. Then she married Captain DeCaulp—she demoted him from major for the moment—and continued her passport duty apparently until the last year of the war, which she spent as a special agent to Europe buying uniforms and equipment for the Confederate army.

The journalist wrote what she told him, yet when his article appeared the next day, he hinted that her story seemed a bit much. "Her descriptions of campaign life, both in Virginia and Tennessee, would impress one with the idea that she certainly saw a good deal of active service," he concluded, but then added that her life, "according to her account, and what is generally known, has been quite an adventurous one, and would furnish data for half a dozen such books as 'Belle Boyd in Prison,' and other sensational biographies of that class." That "what is generally known" presented a problem. She wisely customized the early part of her story to fit press reports that she knew appeared in the city in 1862 but still took a risk hoping that memory of details would be dim after half a dozen years. Yet she was lucky again, for no one came forward to gainsay her account, only reinforcing her confidence that she could sell any story if boldly told.

The journalist was more skeptical when he announced that she claimed "to be the agent for the southern States for a Venezuelan Emigration Company," adding that she had no other evidence of authorization. Instead of Price, she said John Walker of St. Louis was president of the organization, and she would open an office shortly to handle its business. Pressed for details, she equivocated, and the reporter concluded that "her ideas about the matter appear to be yet quite crude and vague." Lauretta promised she would soon have documents to explain all. She skillfully impressed him with her enthusiasm about the benefits awaiting enrolled emigrants, but he hesitated when she spoke "only in general terms, and is apparently not sufficiently versed to enter into those minor details which emigrants of a curious or inquiring turn of mind would like to converse about a little before setting sail with their families for the new Eldorado."

Personal facts stood out by omission. She made no mention of the books she claimed to be writing, nor of subscriptions and donations, and said nothing of a soldiers' asylum. Her full name appeared only in the article's headline, and as "Mrs. Mary De Caulp."[48] It could have been an editorial error or confusion with one of the aliases he knew her to have used in 1862 and earlier. Thereafter, of course, she was Lauretta, but there had been those rumors the year before in Mobile and perhaps elsewhere questioning Lauretta DeCaulp's loyalty to the Confederacy, which would hardly help her persuade former Confederates to invest with her. She may have used Mary for temporary cover, for she had to have known that her impersonation as an agent would be short-lived. Most likely she had exhausted her cash and done little or nothing toward producing the books, so she needed a new moneymaking scheme and perhaps some time out of the country if her past contributors were growing uneasy. She could make serious money selling $1,000 shares in the company if she peddled them before Price discovered and exposed her swindle.

If she seemed vague to the newsman, it was because she had nothing to do with the "Venezuelan Emigration Company," which had actually restyled itself as "The Venezuela Company," and unbeknownst to her, it already had a Southern agent in the city. There was a John Walker associated with it, but in London, not St. Louis, and as a company director and overseas agent, not president. Lauretta played this game so close to the calendar that the first group of emigrants from St. Louis reached New Orleans two weeks before she did, most of them Missourians and Kentuckians whom one cynical editor regarded as "dissatisfied rebels."[49]

Three weeks after her interview a clipping reached Price's company, and he sent an immediate refutation, which the *Daily Picayune* published under the headline "Mrs. De Caulp and the Venezuela Company." Price said he had never heard of her. "Mrs. De Caulp is a self-constituted agent," he declared, "and does not know even the title of our company." The *Picayune*'s editor sarcastically commented that "Mrs. De C. must be connected with some other company."[50] Nine years later, in glossing over this episode, she claimed that she had actually meant to start her own company and was only investigating Price's on behalf of her prospective clients. The fact is that she had no land grants to sell, and using Walker's name and the title of Price's company make clear her effort to gain fleeting legitimacy while swindling buyers before being forced to stop.[51] In its way it was the Volunteer Institute and the National Union Life and Limb Insurance Company all over again as Lauretta sought to capitalize on a genuine enterprise by connecting with it to pursue her own ends. She would do so again in the future, and in the process she pioneered once more. Confidence women, such as they were, tended to sell themselves to lure their victims, as she certainly did, while confidence men usually sold a product. Yet Lauretta intended to sell both, covering a broader base of activity.[52]

Price's letter would have rendered further effort pointless, but Lauretta had abandoned her plans weeks earlier when she realized she was too ill prepared to succeed. In a typical lightning turnabout, she got married instead. As she described it several years later, she stepped onto a streetcar one day and saw "a young Confederate officer, Major Wasson," whom she described as "a remarkably fine-looking man." She claimed to be smitten at once, though it may have been because he was one of Price's emigrants. "After that I saw a great deal of Major Wasson, and a strong attachment sprang up," she recalled. Within days he proposed, and she accepted. "I did so willingly," she said, "for not only did I admire him greatly, but I felt it would be better in every way that I should accompany the expedition as a married woman."[53] Wasson was a means to an end.

On January 17, 1867, just a fortnight after her arrival, "Lauretta J. De Caulp" went before Justice of the Peace Paul Collins and married John W. Wasson of Missouri.[54] As with Thomas DeCaulp, Lauretta promoted Wasson on her own, for there is no record of a Major John Wasson in the Confederate service.[55] She later claimed that they kept their marriage secret for several days, probably because her recent claim to be an agent of the company could have made her persona non grata among the emigrants.[56] The new Mrs. Wasson was always impulsive with men and attracted to those who, like her, were preoccupied with get-rich-quick schemes. Her marriage to Wasson after only a few days' acquaintance may have been a romantic whirlwind, but it would also get her out of the country and away from people who might want back the money advanced for her unpublished book. If she had little or none of that money left for the $1,000 fee to join the company and receive a warrant for 1,280 acres, then Wasson might have paid it for her.[57] Marriage would get her to Venezuela as Mrs. Wasson, and not as DeCaulp, a name known to Price as an impostor. Besides, no single women joined this first emigrant group. The only two adult females were wives, making a speedy marriage to a single man the only way she could join the party.

She and forty-nine other emigrants were aboard the chartered schooner *Elizabeth* awaiting departure when the police arrested all of them without warning and charged them with taking unlawful possession of the vessel. It took a day or two to settle the confusion before their release.[58] Finally the *Elizabeth* set sail on the morning of January 29, and two days later the ship anchored off the South Pass of the Mississippi, ready to embark on the Gulf. "All were in good spirits that at last all our troubles were over, and we were in a fair way to bid farewell to the once happy 'Sunny South,'" a man in the party recalled six weeks later. He also noted that one of the three women aboard was a "Mrs. Wasson."

They made slow passage, taking six weeks, beset alternately by storms and calms and seasickness, before they anchored at the mouth of the Orinoco River. At last, on March 14 they arrived upriver at Ciudad Bolivar, the capital.[59] If Lauretta's marriage to Wasson had been a speedy one, others in the group now showed equal haste in forming unions with local women. Seven other men took wives before the end of the month. Meanwhile, Lauretta Wasson became something of a favorite in the enclave, described by one of the group as "a widow lady, young, gay and fascinating." For the first time she referred to herself as "Madame," perhaps because she told them all that her father was an admiral in the British navy. The same writer sent word home to Missouri in March that their prospects in the new country were as yet uncertain, but none felt discouraged.[60]

Barely a week later they began to disintegrate. Dissent and dissatisfaction spread, and eventually seventeen decided to go home. "All these were Yankees . . . who smuggled themselves among us," claimed Price, but two who wanted to leave were Confederates, and one of those might have been Lauretta.[61] Many were outraged at finding free blacks in charge of much day-to-day administration, expressing the feeling that "it would have been just as well to have remained at home and fought the battle for supremacy with the free negroes and carpet-baggers on familiar ground."[62] Lauretta attributed that sentiment to the other emigrants, though she was silent as to whether she felt it herself.

She later claimed that she had come to scout the potential for her own emigration scheme, and as soon as the *Elizabeth* reached Ciudad Bolivar, she left the schooner while everyone else remained aboard, pending moving upriver. Wasson refused to go with her, and her leaving him after less than two months argues more than anything that for her this was a marriage of convenience to achieve her private end. She later claimed she called on the American consul and the governor of the province to explore the possibility of launching her own emigration scheme, and then spent the next several months in the agreeable city.[63] If she had any command of Spanish, it would have made her a valuable intermediary between the colonists and the authorities, but she never mentioned it.

She probably never saw Wasson again. A small gold rush swept Venezuela at the moment, and a number of the colonists were far more interested in gold than planting. On March 23 fourteen men on the schooner formed the Della Costa Mining Company and left Ciudad Bolivar for the strike area 125 miles into the interior. One of them was John W. Wasson.[64] All Lauretta said on the matter years later was that "he left, and started for the gold mines." All of them fell ill, and at least three died at the mines. To escape the epidemic, Wasson returned and went to Caracas, apparently without his wife, but the virus went with him. "Shortly after his arrival, he was taken ill with the black vomit," Lauretta recalled, "and died." In writing of it later, she showed no sadness at Wasson's death. Rather, she spoke only of lamenting the money wasted on the adventure.[65]

Now she was twice a widow and still only about twenty-five. Of course, there is only her later word for it that Wasson was in fact dead, just as her postwar statements are all that establish that DeCaulp was deceased. In both instances, the men probably were no longer living, but as always, when Lauretta is the only authority for her assertions, facts rest uneasily on the record.

Having determined, as she later said, that Venezuela "was no place for poor Americans to go," she decided that fall to return to the United States. She claimed that sometime in October she took ship for Demerara, then on to Barbados, St. Lucia, St. Thomas, and then Cuba.[66] Finally, on or about October 31 "Laura Wasson," occupation "lady," booked as the only passenger on the 424-ton American merchant bark *Elba*. After a brief stop at Matanzas and a passage of about a dozen days, she reached New York on November 12, 1867. Lost on her, apparently, was the irony of her deliverance from a sort of exile in Venezuela aboard a vessel named *Elba*.[67]

CHAPTER NINE

GOLD, SILVER, AND BIGAMY

YEARS LATER LAURETTA claimed that she hoped to settle in the South on leaving Venezuela. If so, it is curious that she took ship for New York instead.[1] Several motives probably changed her direction. After two years her subscribers still had nothing to show for their money, and inevitably she would encounter some demanding redress if she returned to the South. Her financial condition at this point is unknown, but she had funds to travel to the United States and cash left to choose a less risky option.

Just days after her arrival the city's press announced completion of the Union Pacific Railroad as far west as Cheyenne, Wyoming, with stagecoach connections on to Denver and Salt Lake City. Lauretta remained only a few days and then bought a seat on a train to Omaha, Nebraska, where for $275 she boarded a Wells Fargo stage to cross the Great Plains to Salt Lake.[2] The New York to Salt Lake trip took just eleven days, but she made layovers for sightseeing along the way. Then, just a day out of Salt Lake, her coach found that heavy rains had washed out the only bridge over the Box Elder River. The driver tried to cross at a nearby ford late on Christmas Day, but the coach mired in the mud and capsized. Lauretta and the others swam to the bank to spend the night in a Mormon home. A fresh team freed the coach the next day, and they resumed the journey.[3]

Lauretta spent a couple of days in Salt Lake, then boarded another coach headed across Nevada toward Virginia City, near the California border. If she had not already determined to try her fortune among the gold strikes in the West, she did so now. There was money to be had, and she would be well away from the South. Now named Laura or Lauretta Wasson, she need fear no one in Nevada connecting her with DeCaulp, Williams, or even Buford, names now well publicized.[4]

About two days out, the coach stopped at Ruby Valley in northeastern Nevada. Lauretta later claimed that a miner there told her the best prospects for finding gold at the moment were on the Reese River in and around Austin, Nevada, more than four hundred miles west of Salt Lake. She heard much the same from others and made that her goal.[5] Ideally, the coach trip from Salt Lake to Austin would be just over seventy hours, a grueling ride from dawn to dusk, with thirty stops at stations along the way to change horses and allow passengers to stretch and eat a bite, plus at least four nights spent at the stations. The fare from Omaha to Austin was another $100 or more, not counting at least $20 for meals, so Lauretta made a significant investment in the journey, more than $400 in all, unless someone else paid it for her.[6] She did not travel with anyone, so most likely she paid her own way, perhaps with money Wasson left when they parted.

Another two days from Ruby Valley brought her to Austin around the end of the year.[7] It was a fairly rowdy, typical mining boom town. It had only one hotel, the International, where she took a room, but a number of saloons, including the Bank Exchange Saloon next door.[8] A competitor, the Reese River Saloon, advertised "Lager Beer and Pretty Girls" and promised that "pretty girls are continually in attendance" for "the lovers of Pleasure and comfort."[9] The town was also known nationally, thanks to Ruel Colt Gridley, who less than four years earlier carried a fifty-pound sack of flour through the town when he lost a bet, then auctioned the sack for $250 to donate to the U.S. Sanitary Commission, a charitable organization that brought small comforts and medical care to ill and wounded Union soldiers. Gridley took his sack to nearby towns, then San Francisco, and eventually the East, auctioning it again and again, raising more than a quarter million dollars. Though he left Austin in 1866, his fame remained, and a newspaperman in nearby Virginia City, Nevada, Samuel L. Clemens, soon included Gridley's story in his 1872 book, *Roughing It*, written under the pen name Mark Twain.

When Lauretta stepped out of the coach in Austin, her interest was not the town's notoriety, but its mineral wealth and the men who had it. A few years later a resident named Adam Wilson recalled that on arriving, she spread the story that she had once owned "a vast amount of property," an echo of her wartime claims to plantation lands in Arkansas and elsewhere. It had all been confiscated, she said, presumably because of her Confederate service, and she was even then in litigation for its recovery.[10] In other words, she might have little or no money at the moment, but it was only a matter of time before she was wealthy again, a new variation on her inheritance con. A clipping from the Richmond *Enquirer* virtually proved that in December 1869, just two years hence, she would come into at least $10,000, not to mention $20,000 worth of silver plate, jewelry of unspecified worth, and perhaps even more of what was left to her supposed son by DeCaulp. Whether the boy ever

Austin, Nevada, photographed by Timothy O'Sullivan in June 1868, just six months after Lauretta arrived. The spire seen at center is the Methodist church where she and third husband Hardy Bonner were married on January 29. Library of Congress.

existed meant nothing in terms of the clipping's import in establishing that she had great wealth just beyond her reach. It was a fine gambit to convince a prosperous man that she was not after him for his money.

She soon found her prosperous man, "a gentleman who paid me attention, and to whom I became sincerely attached," as she wrote a few years later.[11] Edward Hardy Bonner, more often known as Hardy or just E. H., had been born in Mississippi in May 1826, then went to the California gold rush as a forty-niner, settling on the Yuba River in the placer mining country where he lived with seventeen other miners on their claim.[12] He prospected for silver in California's Death Valley when the war neared its close, then searched for diggings lost or abandoned by others and invested in one or more operating mines. He moved about too, spending some time at Prescott, Arizona Territory, but by the fall of 1867 he settled in Austin. Friends knew him as a quiet, modest man who kept to himself. He took no part in civic affairs and did not even vote. Instead, he worked hard at his trade.[13] As a result, he was also known to be prosperous. If he had not been mining profitable ore when he met Lauretta, he soon would be.

His worth caught her interest, and in turn she caught Bonner's. Their romance was not quite as much of a whirlwind as her fortnight courtship with Wasson, but it was still fast even by frontier standards. Scarcely four weeks after arriving in Austin, she and Hardy Bonner went before the new Methodist minister in Austin, the Reverend A. Taylor, only recently authorized to perform marriages.[14] On January 29, 1868, he joined them in wedlock.[15] The next day J. D. Fairchild, editor and publisher of the Austin *Daily Reese River Reveille*, announced to his readers, "Married in this city, Jan. 29th, by Rev. A. Taylor, E. H. Bonner and Lauretta J. Wasson." Fairchild went on to mention that the couple had given his paper "substantial compliments," in return for which he wished a long and happy life together "to the hardy prospector and his bride."[16] The pun on Hardy Bonner's name was of minor note. Within a month of her arrival Lauretta had not only found a well-to-do husband but also ingratiated herself with the local press.

"We were married in a very quiet manner," she recalled seven years later, "for neither of us desired, any more than we could help, to be made the subjects of the gossip of a mining town."[17] That fear was another of her backfires, an ex post facto defense to blunt any lingering damage from gossip that started soon after the wedding. The newlyweds set up housekeeping and remained contentedly enough for about eight weeks, though Hardy Bonner was probably away working one of his claims after their first month together, the first of many such absences.[18] Then on March 27 they both boarded an overland coach to go west on a visit.[19] Where they went is uncertain, and they may have been away until early June, quite probably on a honeymoon.

Whenever they returned, they did not stay long, and this was Lauretta's doing. Seven years later she claimed that soon after their marriage, she went to New Orleans, ostensibly to visit a brother and other relatives.[20] That may have been the March 1868 trip, and if Bonner left with her, it might only have been to escort her to a ship in San Francisco to take her to New Orleans. It remains doubtful that she really had a brother or any living relatives, and Bonner's friends in Austin remembered her departure quite differently. His prospecting had yielded him "a large amount of money in 1868–69," said Adam Wilson, "and as often as he got enough ore to make a crushing, she would receive a letter from her lawyer that she must come immediately to San Francisco with money to prosecute her suit, sign papers, etc."[21] Clearly Bonner believed her story of suing to reclaim her land and of the fictitious inheritance from the equally fictional Admiral Roach.

"Hardy Bonner and wife" left again on September 2, but he returned three weeks later.[22] Lauretta did not come back until October 4, meaning she spent some time in San Francisco or elsewhere on her own.[23] These trips were not inexpensive. Just the 325-mile leg from Austin to Sacramento cost from $45 to $51.[24] Soon she wanted to go yet again, and to set up the need for another visit—and no doubt more money from Bonner—she employed a variation of her December 1864 inheritance scam by placing a personal advertisement in the press for her to find and show to Bonner as evidence. On January 9, 1869, the San Francisco *Daily Alta California* ran the following:

> Obituary. Mazatlan, November 10, 1868. The remains of Colonel R. D. Clapp arrived here to-day, en route for their last resting place, San Luis Potosi. He leaves a wife and four children, and one married sister—Mrs. Lauretta J. Bonner, of Austin—to mourn his sad loss. Died from injuries received at the fall of Fort Arequipa, Peru, 13th of August, by the earthquake. Leopold Begocha.

A note at the bottom specifically requested that the New Orleans and Vicksburg papers and the *Daily Reese River Reveille* copy the notice.[25]

It was another confidence game. There was no mention of an inheritance, but she could add that orally when she showed the personal to Bonner. Suddenly Lauretta had also changed fathers. Gone was Admiral J. B. Roach. Now, four years later, her father had become a man named Clapp, assuming that her "brother" carried their father's surname. Whereas in 1864 she was one of nine siblings, now in 1868 she was apparently but one of two. Arequipa on the Peruvian coast did recently suffer a devastating earthquake, a convenient occasion for a family loss requiring her presence in New Orleans or perhaps even Mazatlán.[26] Surely this was the brother that Adam Wilson recalled a few years later as the reason for her trips. She was not done with this new Clapp paternity, and it would reappear in a few years. Meanwhile, the request that the notice be picked up by the *Daily Reese River Reveille* was a clever means to ensure that her husband and others saw it for themselves, though it does not seem to have been published there after all. Nevertheless, Lauretta would have had a copy from the *Daily Alta California* to show her husband. The visits to New Orleans or San Francisco continued periodically, and she even may have prevailed on Bonner to go to Paris in pursuit of her fictional inheritance, for "Mr. and Mrs. E. H. Bonner" registered with the Paris banking house of Drexel, Harjes & Co. in January 1869, and she could have sent Clapp's death notice to the San Francisco paper when they boarded ship there for the journey.[27]

The newly invented father Clapp soon gained a grandchild, for sometime that winter the Bonners had a son. If Lauretta did have a child by DeCaulp in 1864, by some means that infant was clearly out of her life before she went to Venezuela, if not before the end of the war. In a few years she would claim that she had lost three infant children by her first "husband," the fictional Lieutenant Arnold, though they were probably as imaginary as he was. This Bonner baby was incontestably genuine, however, and hereafter turned up ghostlike in her life for several years before he too disappeared.[28]

By this time she and Hardy Bonner were Californians. Lauretta later admitted that he "for a time prospered in his mining operations," while she claimed that she worked at "advancing [her] husband's interests." However, several years hence she would protest that she felt unhappy with the unscrupulous nature of the local mining community and finally persuaded Bonner to move to the Sacramento Valley.[29] Letters held at the San Francisco post office for her as "Miss L. J. Bonner," "Mrs. L. J. Bonner," and other variants testify that she was expected to be there from October through December 1869, and the fact that they were all claimed within a few days attests that she was in fact in the city at that time.[30] In mid-December, however, people addressed letters to her in Sacramento. How long the Bonners remained is unclear, but they lived in or near Sacramento at least through the later months of 1870.[31]

If Lauretta is to be believed, Bonner's gold fever led him to new claims in Utah, and he departed for Salt Lake City in February 1871, leaving her to follow. Soon he prospected and lived not far from town, making occasional trips to the city to look for letters advising him of when she expected to come. On March 19 she arrived from Sacramento to meet him.[32] At first they stayed at the Salt Lake House, but she soon found a room boarding with the Mormon bishop Milo Andrews and his family, where she remained for the next eighteen months while Bonner spent most of his time at the diggings some miles distant at East Cañon, making frequent trips in to the city to see her.[33] When he came to visit, he took a room at the Salt Lake House rather than stay where she boarded.

He worked in northwestern Utah's Box Elder County for a year with no success, and she later complained that he "expended all his money without achieving anything." However, Adam Wilson accounted for their financial straits by declaring that Lauretta "by one excuse and another beat Bonner out of a great many thousand dollars," until she had gotten it all and he had worked out his claim.[34] Bonner then took a job as foreman at one of the Wellington mines in the Lucine district of the county, after which he worked mines in Little Cottonwood and the Alta City region not far from Salt Lake City.[35] Still they did not prosper, and Lauretta later claimed that she disliked the atmosphere of sham and swindle hanging about the mines.

It looked as though the marriage was failing, not unlike the strains in her marriage to DeCaulp. Lauretta still traveled often, but by September 1871 she was living with Bonner again when he prospected at Tintic, hailed as "the New Eldorado."[36] Two months later they moved temporarily to Silver City, New Mexico Territory, returning frequently to Salt Lake but separately rather than together. Bonner may have remained in Utah while she spent her time in New Mexico.[37] Lauretta continued her extended visits to San Francisco, one in April 1872, as she supposedly sought to settle the legal impediments to regaining her alleged wealth.[38] She actually did some prospecting herself in the city by the bay, seeking a likely replacement for Bonner and showing her documents to establish that she was no fortune hunter. She even directed potential suitors to General James Longstreet in New Orleans as a reference, though they had never met and he knew nothing of her except what she told him in a letter or two. How she justified this to Longstreet remains a mystery, but she could always claim that she rode on the same train as part of his reinforcement to Bragg in September 1863, or even that DeCaulp, or herself as Buford, served under him at Chickamauga. Any polite response from him, of course, only added to her dossier of supposed endorsements.[39]

By the fall the Bonners changed base one more time. Utah had played out, and Hardy decided to try his luck back in Silver City, where a strike in 1870 launched a new boom.[40] In fact, it was a swindle. Speculators had opened the Burro Burro Mine near Tucson in June, and its ore averaged less than $100 a ton, not enough to make it profitable. Then the operators began "salting" the mine with high-grade ore from other sources and sending it out to attract investors, enabling them to capitalize a new company for $9 million.[41] By 1871 the scheme had collapsed and one of its principals, Philip Arnold, was about to move on to a far greater fraud.[42]

Lauretta had some personal acquaintance with Arnold. In 1871 he conceived a gigantic diamond swindle that put him in the world news for some time when it all unraveled.[43] It was probably on her April 1872 visit to San Francisco that she met Arnold and possibly discussed his defunct Burro

Burro scheme, though she later affected not to suspect him of involvement.[44] Men like Arnold attracted her. Out of a sort of confidence artists' professional courtesy, she later said that she thought him "a very energetic miner, prospector, and adventurer; one who has taken more chances to prospect and develop the great mineral sources of the West than [any] other miner in the West."[45]

Settling in Silver City around November 1872, the Bonners tried business for a change and opened a small hotel they called the Keystone House in January 1873.[46] It would be the first, but not last, time Lauretta tried being a landlord. Advertising that they were "prepared to accommodate travelers and regular boarders with the best the market affords, in the line of a first-class hotel," they promised modest rates and comfortable rooms.[47] Silver City prided itself on its good dances and fair ladies, and the Bonners catered balls at nearby Porter Hall, receiving compliments for the "fine supper" they served.[48] Business ran brisk, thanks to the silver rush. By the first week in April they had every room filled and were renting the parlors as well, but Silver City disappointed them, or at least Lauretta. She may have been honest a few years later when she wrote that she was "anxious to be among a different class of people from those who, for the most part, make up the population of the mining districts." All around her she saw "outrageous swindling," a clear case of one cooking utensil maligning the color of another.[49] In less than three months the Bonners sold the hotel, and by late April or May Lauretta had left Bonner for good and returned to Salt Lake.[50]

In her later memoir Lauretta never mentioned Bonner by name and implied that she left him because of his near abandonment during their Utah years. Bonner's friend Wilson, however, told another version, charging that after draining every dollar her husband earned, she went to Salt Lake City and applied for a divorce, then left for San Francisco with a wealthy Jew whom she intended to marry.[51] Certainly the Bonners were no longer together the last time she went to Salt Lake. It appears that he went prospecting near Fort Barnard, New Mexico Territory, and then on to Southern California, while his wife and their son probably went to Sonoma and from there to San Francisco, arriving late in May.[52] There is no record of any divorce.[53] As for the Jewish man in the story, he could have been one of those suitors referred to Longstreet. Having decided to return to the South, Lauretta needed money now if Bonner was cleaned out, and Wilson's suggestion of the Jew's affluence matched her purpose. If she left with such a fellow, however, he was no longer with her that fall when she met another man.

One man notably missing from her life during her entire sojourn in the West was Lieutenant Harry T. Buford. For a change, Lauretta consciously called no attention to herself. Even though editor Fairchild of the *Daily Reese River Reveille* told his readers that he knew the Bonners well, she apparently said nothing to him of her earlier notoriety, for his pages carried not a hint of Buford. During the war Austin had been a pro-Union community, and in Lauretta's time there it supported then-president Grant, so she may have thought it prudent not to parade her Confederate associations. During her trips to San Francisco she resisted any impulse to call on editors, and Buford was no more heard from there than in Austin. She may have been wise, especially if her reason for going west was to avoid disgruntled subscribers. Still, it had to have been frustrating to remain anonymous, just as in 1864 in Milwaukee when she dreamed of regained glory. If she is to be believed, she began making notes and perhaps portions of written narrative for the long-promised memoir, to which she could add her travels in Venezuela and the West. A book might yield enough income to buy her freedom from the dull life of a miner's wife.[54]

Until now she had written nothing more than letters, and though she felt at ease inventing a life for others to limn in the press, she was literate enough to recognize her own writing as rough and ungrammatical. Nevertheless, if she could produce an outline and extensive notes or, better yet, a rough draft, then a competent editor or ghost writer could turn it into a book for her. To accomplish that, she needed to get both herself and anything she wrote to the East to find an editor and publisher.

After she arrived in San Francisco in May 1873, her movements for the next several months are obscure. Then she traveled eastward to Denver, then south through Pueblo and Albuquerque, reaching Santa Fe in the New Mexico Territory by November. From there she went on to El Paso, Texas, to catch the eastbound overland stage.[55] Significantly, if all she intended to do was return to the East, she could have traveled there faster and with less difficulty via Denver and Cheyenne and then by train. Leaving from El Paso meant she intended to return to the South, which in turn suggests that she took with her enough of her memoir in outline and notes to approach a writer and publisher, and at the same time have something substantial to display to angry subscribers as evidence that their investment was about to blossom.

The twice-weekly four-horse coaches of the El Paso Mail Company's line went to Fort Concho in west Texas, where transfer to another coach took mail and passengers on to San Antonio.[56] Companies of U.S. soldiers stationed at or near most of the stops along the way offered some degree of protection for passengers and mail, but in the main both traveled at the mercy of roads, weather, and local natives, their most immediate protection being the coaches' drivers.[57] The El Paso coach that took Lauretta east that November was known as a "rebel concern," and it must have been there that she quickly struck an acquaintance with the former Confederate who drove her coach.[58]

This new man was Andrew Jackson Bobo, born at Cleburne, Alabama, on December 2, 1844, the son of a slave overseer.[59] During the late war he and his father, William, enlisted in Company E of the 22nd Alabama Infantry, but he served virtually his entire time as a wagon teamster until captured near Atlanta on August 3, 1864. The Federals sent him to Camp Chase prison at Columbus until March 1865, when he was paroled and sent home.[60] If Lauretta really did spend time at Columbus in 1865 looking to prisoners' welfare, she might have met Bobo there, but it is far more likely that they first met now in El Paso. Bobo went west after the war, first to Monroe County, Louisiana, where he was sheriff in 1869, but by July 1870 his skill with wagon teams found him driving coaches for the U.S. Mail Line out of Fort Concho in Texas's Bexar District.[61]

By the time Bobo and Lauretta met in late November 1873, he was one of the senior "gentlemanly" employees driving the El Paso line's "superb conveyances."[62] A territorial editor claimed that "a better set of men cannot be found."[63] They drove over what one traveler described as "the very worst, that is, most dangerous, roads in the country."[64] Stage driving was an uncertain business at best. The animals were prone to several diseases, lumped together as "the epizootic," occasionally forcing the mail line to close for indefinite periods.[65] Coaches overturned on the rough roads, as one did outside Fort McKinney in 1871, breaking the driver's leg and requiring its amputation.[66] Sometimes the stages upset in flooded creeks, drowning the animals, nearly drowning passengers, and soaking mail and baggage. Indians frequently raided stage stations for horses and mules, and there were occasional mail robberies by both Indians and white people.[67]

Bobo himself was a plucky veteran of such an attack back about June 1, 1870, when twenty-five Indians confronted his coach on a return trip to the Concho Station a few miles distant. Bobo and a passenger opened fire with their Winchester Model 1866 repeating rifles, and after hesitating briefly, the Indians rode in a circle around the stage, sniping with rifles and arrows. When one turned and rode straight for the coach, Bobo held the reins in

Lauretta's until now unknown fourth husband, the "jovial" Andrew Jackson Bobo, as a private in the 22nd Alabama Infantry, circa 1863. Their marriage was Lauretta's briefest. Ancestry.com.

one hand to steady the animals and aimed and fired with the other, bringing the man down. Later accounts said Bobo and the passenger killed or wounded nine Indians before the team panicked and broke into a run for the station with the attackers in chase. Bobo brought the team to a halt, then jumped to the ground with rifle in hand, ready to continue the fight, which persuaded the pursuers to give up the chase.[68]

Acquaintances described Bobo as "jovial," and perhaps that helped attract Lauretta's notice.[69] What she told him of herself is a mystery; evidently she left Bonner out of it, for she told Bobo her name was L. J. Wasson.[70] A stage driver in west Texas was hardly likely to have the kind of wealth or status that drew her to the supposed planter DeCaulp, the impostor "Major" Wasson, the genuinely prosperous Bonner, or the mysterious affluent Jew.

Nevertheless, by the time they crossed the Pecos River and reached Bobo's station on the Concho, probably early in December, they had grown more than companionable. When the stage reached San Antonio, Lauretta went on to Galveston, probably intending to complete her trip to the South by steamboat to New Orleans, but it is evident that they planned for him to meet her before long.[71]

By late January 1874 Lauretta "Wasson" and her son—she never gave his name—roomed temporarily in Galveston with no apparent plan other than to wait for Bobo. He wrote to her at least once, perhaps to say that he expected to arrive in mid-February.[72] When she felt the time was right, Lauretta placed a personal advertisement in the Galveston *Daily News* on February 19 requesting that "Mr. A. J. Bobo will please call at Tucker & Campbell's [attorneys] office, Number 122 Postoffice street, and inquire for Mrs. Wasson." The editor of the paper even called attention to her announcement by adding his own comment in another column that "Mr. A. J. Bobo is interested in a card elsewhere."[73] He must have arrived that same day, for February 20 saw them making the hundred-mile rail trip to Houston and from there to Hempstead in Waller County. The following day, February 21, 1874, they appeared before justice of the peace J. H. Adams, where she identified herself as "Mrs. Loretta J. Wasson" of Galveston and gave her age as thirty-one, while Bobo gave his as thirty and his home as Concho. Those details completed, Adams joined them in marriage.[74] Two days later "A. G. Bobo, lady and child," returned to Galveston and checked into the Cosmopolitan Hotel.[75]

For the fourth time Lauretta rushed into a marriage, this time bigamously, and not for the first time if William Irwin still lived. Perhaps that is why they went to Hempstead when it would have been easier and faster for them to wed in Galveston, where a press notice might have appeared that could reach Hardy Bonner. It is apparent that they did not intend to stay long in Galveston, for just two days after their return, her mail began to accumulate at the post office, and a week later it was still there.[76] Most likely she and her son went back to Concho with Bobo, which would explain her disappearance from notice of any kind for the next several months.

What happened then is one of her many mysteries. Perhaps she rued acting on impulse or tired of life at an isolated coach station in the wilderness. Maybe Bobo learned somehow that she had another husband or that any stories she told him of wealth around the corner were false. Possibly events just pulled them apart. Barely two months into their marriage, Bobo joined two other men tracking a black man they believed had stolen a horse. On April 24 they caught him about thirty miles north of Waco. As they brought the man back to face charges, Bobo and the prisoner rode together some distance ahead of the others and out of immediate sight. Near the village of Dresden in western Navarro County, the men in the rear heard a gunshot. They rode up to find the prisoner dead, and Bobo explained that the man had either tried to escape or "offered insult" and he shot him. Word soon spread that Bobo left immediately for "parts unknown."[77]

Perhaps it was Bobo's precipitate departure that impelled his wife to a decision. In a remarkably short time the marriage was over, though once again she eschewed the formality of a divorce.[78] Within three months Lauretta was east of the Mississippi on her way to New York. Just as she had expunged Bonner from her life when she gave her name as Wasson on her recent marriage license, now she erased Bobo as well, traveling once again as "Mrs. E. H. Bonner."[79] In the nearly half century ahead of her, she made no mention of A. J. Bobo by either name or inference. If she wrote Bonner out of her history, she never wrote Bobo into it.

CHAPTER TEN

"AN IMPOSTER OF NO ORDINARY RANK"

LAURETTA PASSED THOSE months in Texas before leaving Bobo by contemplating two frauds, one her own conception based on her Venezuela experience and the other a genuine project that still embraced an element of deception in its service. First she settled on announcing herself as an agent of the fictitious Gila Valley Colonization Society, its goal to get Southern immigrants to purchase shares in return for grants of land in the small valley at the southwest corner of Arizona Territory. Her inducements would be samples of the rich ores supposedly taken from its earth, and she may well have had some to display collected by Bonner in his prospecting. Whereas the Price expedition to Venezuela tried to downplay fortune hunting, she intended to encourage it to sell shares.[1]

Meanwhile, it was time for Harry Buford to reappear, and in a new and expanded version befitting his creator's intentions for her future. Clearly Lauretta had given a good deal of thought over the past months or even years to reshaping and filling out not only Buford's history but also her own. She had not written the narrative for her book, though she might have made some extended notes, perhaps even an outline. She understood that she did not have the narrative or stylistic skill to produce the actual book itself. "I am struggling along to get it ready but I am now compelled to have some assistance," she confessed that summer. She needed a ghost writer or, better yet, a well-known coauthor who could write the work while his reputation helped boost sales.

She would claim that she contacted the University Publishing Company of New York and Baltimore, a firm largely owned by former Confederates, including Major General John B. Gordon, and also the venerable New York firm of D. Appleton and Company. The University was a favored publisher of schoolbooks for Southern states, with a growing list of titles by former Confederates, while Appleton had a good force of sales agents in the South and also had an interest in books by onetime Rebels. Given that, Lauretta probably did solicit them, as she later claimed, since either gave good promise of wide sales. Encouraged, when she left Texas in the summer of 1874 she traveled to New York City to see the publishers in person and took up residence in a boardinghouse at 155 East 29th Street. Appleton's editor saw the potential in her story, agreed that she needed a professional writer to turn her notes into a salable book, and advised her to approach one of the nation's fastest-rising authors, Samuel L. Clemens, or so she claimed. Hence she wrote to the man known as Mark Twain. She gave him a rough outline of what she described as two years and eight months in the Confederate army, four years in the western mining camps, eighteen months among the Mormons, and seven months in Apache territory. To add extra spice, she proposed to include an exposé of banking and enlistment bounty frauds during the war and what she had seen of mining swindles.

"Could you in the spring take hold of my Book," she told him, "if written up by you it will have a large sale in the South and the West." She was in bad financial straits and needed the income from the book, she said, which was probably more manipulation than fact. "You can readily understand how we Californians stand when we say we are almost to the bed Rock," she added, then employed the same tactic she probably used with Longstreet and others. "I knew you at Virginia City, Karson, and Sanfrancisco," she wrote, implying an acquaintance that they never had. Lauretta relied on men to be gentlemen, not gainsaying a lady even if they thought her mistaken.[2]

Just as she had referred suitors to Longstreet, she now used Brigadier General M. Jefferson Thompson, a former Confederate from Missouri, as a reference, but when Clemens wrote to Thompson, he got no response. In any event, he declined Lauretta's request to, as he put it, "join her in dishing up an account of her adventures as a spy during the war." Persistent, she wrote again. Once more he refused, though he did suggest that she think of his old journalist friend James S. Bowman of San Francisco as a possible collaborator.[3] After that, Clemens probably forgot the matter, but Lauretta rarely took a first or even second no for an answer. Counting on her powers of face-to-face persuasion, she decided to meet Clemens in person if she could, but first she had something else in mind. Early in August she packed her son and what notes she had completed and left for New Orleans. She would go on tour again just as she had in 1866, raising money and an appetite for her book that might weigh heavily with Clemens when finally she saw him. Despite her plea of poverty, it seems evident that her purse had cash enough to fund several weeks on the road, perhaps the last of Bonner's mining profits or else money from Bobo. As usual, she could expect to stretch its buying power by relying on sympathy from former Confederates along the way to cover her room and board.

New Orleans was a logical place to commence her publicity campaign, and it was expecting her, but on arriving she found the local press uninterested. Hence she was soon eager to leave again.[4] She set aside her usual modus or she would have approached the editors herself, and the only logical explanation is that she still feared her story might spark local memories connecting her with her past as Ann Williams. Exposure as a onetime prostitute and prison inmate would hardly be an auspicious beginning for her campaign, especially when those memories could also challenge the latest version of her story. How long she remained in the Crescent City and what she did while there is unknown, though she did call on General Longstreet, the only time they ever met, and left him struck that "her adventures as she gave them and as given by her western suitors were remarkable."[5] Otherwise, her only known act was leaving her five-year-old son there with friends.[6] Whom she left him with, in fact, is an open question, but she seems to have had little to do with him thereafter and did not mention him again publicly for almost four years.

Lauretta reached Mobile on August 22, and there she began her campaign first with a few calls on influential men "whose connection with the war rendered her desirous of forming their acquaintance," surely the motive for her visit to Longstreet. She wanted letters of introduction to use later in her tour, as well as possible investment in her book. Then she called on the editor of the *Daily Register*, who saw in her "an intelligent-looking lady, of about 35 years of age." She seemed unusually refined for a woman who had lived the soldier life "and performed the duties of a man for more than four years."

She introduced herself as Mrs. E. H. Bonner, making no mention at all of her earlier names Williams or DeCaulp, both of which risked identification with her old self. Neither did she mention Wasson or Bobo. She was on her way to New York, she said, to discuss her book with a publisher, and then she shared some of its highlights. "This distinguished lady has, perhaps, gone through more hardships and done more for the Confederate States," the editor soon concluded, "than any woman." The war had barely begun when she determined to take an active part in it, she told him, and in June 1861 she dressed as a recruiting officer and left New Orleans for Arkansas, where she raised a company of volunteers with herself as first lieutenant, all to serve under a Captain Weatherford. In a new detail, she described how she took the company to Key West, Florida, but the local commander accused her of incompetence and forced her to give up her command. So she went to Virginia, joined Dreux's battalion on July 20, and fought in the great battle at Manassas the next day. It was all false or contradicted her earlier stories. Her myth was still evolving.

Soon afterward she joined the 8th Louisiana Infantry, she continued, only to have her impersonation suspected, whereupon authorities arrested her and sent her briefly to prison pending an investigation. Though she did not say where she was imprisoned, other details in her story make it clear that she spoke of her fall 1861 arrest and brief confinement in Richmond as Mary Ann Keith. While incarcerated, she said, she received a committee of ladies sent to make a final determination as to her gender, but after they saw the dashing young Buford, they decided not to make an "inspection." For the first time in her accounts, Lauretta introduced the recurring theme of Buford as a fatally attractive charmer. Finally the mayor interviewed Buford and released him, and then an unnamed authority commissioned him to "perform any services for the Confederacy, which she might be called upon to perform." General Winder subsequently ordered her west to scouting duty around Okolona, Mississippi, where she did such fine work that "General" William C. Quantrill sent her as a spy to Missouri.

After "inestimable service" in Missouri, Buford returned to New Orleans and joined the 21st Louisiana, then being organized, and reported to Brigadier General James Villepigue in northern Mississippi. Given a new commission as first lieutenant, Buford went to Memphis and then Shiloh, to be severely wounded in the right shoulder on the first day, which led to discovery of Lauretta's true gender. Ultimately her superiors gave in to her refusal to stay out of active operations and ordered her to Atlanta, then to pass through the lines to the North but not as a spy. Awaiting orders in Atlanta, she went north to Dalton, Georgia, and Chattanooga and engaged in battles at both places.

On returning to Atlanta, she received orders to board blockade runners departing from several ports for Caribbean islands, sometimes carrying communications to the commanders of the daring Confederate commerce raiders CSS *Florida* and CSS *Shenandoah*. On one occasion at Bridgetown in Barbados, she collected $780 in donations from the Yankee fleet there under command of a Commodore Brissel, saying it would go to benefit Union soldiers, whereas she actually sent it to Confederate hospitals. Next she was sent to San Diego and Havana to buy coffee and sugar, and then, as she described it, she traveled "to South America, in the interest of the

Confederate Government, with Price's expedition." From there she went to the West Indies, "charged with some important mission for the country she loved so well and served so faithfully," and without actually saying so, she implied that at this point the war ended. She also told the Mobile journalist that during the war she gave considerable aid to Confederate prisoners of war at Camp Chase, though she did not chronologically fit it into her narrative.

In support of her story, of course, Lauretta had documents to show. "From all of them it can be seen that she was trusted unhesitatingly, and bore an unblemished character from the beginning to the close of the war," wrote the *Daily Register* interviewer. Following Appomattox, she went to New Mexico to become a mining speculator, from which she "realized a handsome fortune." Meanwhile, she completed her memoir, "a truthful account of her adventures during her connection with the Confederacy," and now she was going to New York with introductions to prominent men from the North and South, along with "other evidences of an irreproachable reputation."[7]

It was a major recasting of the Buford story, and at the same time it bore more than ever before the hallmarks of Lauretta's oral statements, at least as reported—confused or nonexistent chronology, contradictions of previous accounts, and easily demonstrated impossibilities. Except for June 1861 and the mention of the Battle of Shiloh, no dates appeared in her narrative to place events in their proper order, and many were out of sequence. There was no Captain Weatherford in Dreux's 1st Special Battalion or in any other Louisiana regiment, and Dreux's unit went to Pensacola, Florida, in April 1861, not Key West in June, and was not engaged at all in the First Battle of Manassas. No soldier named Buford served in the 8th Louisiana Infantry. Quantrill was never more than a captain at best, and at the time she spoke of, which context placed roughly in the fall of 1861, he was in western Missouri, hundreds of miles from Okolona.

There was no Buford in the 21st Louisiana either, and far from being sent to Villepigue after enlistment, it never left New Orleans and was captured at the city's fall in April 1862. Lauretta then jumped abruptly from April 1862 to the fall of 1863, placing herself in either the Battle of Chickamauga in September or the several engagements around Chattanooga that November, when she was really already working in the Indianapolis arsenal. The only engagements in or around Dalton, Georgia, took place in May 1864, when she was demonstrably in Milwaukee. There was no Commodore Brissel, nor anyone by that name, in the Union navy during the war, and most confused of all was her reference to going to South America on behalf of the

Confederacy with "Price's expedition." That was the Venezuelan colonization enterprise that left New Orleans in January 1867 more than a year and a half after the end of the war.

Several things may account for the impossibilities in Lauretta's account. First, the newspaperman might have confused the chronology as he rushed to write down everything she said while trying to keep up with her oral narrative. This seems especially likely in the absurd placement of the 1867 Price expedition during the war period as a Confederate operation. As for the rest of the problems, Lauretta was the source. She habitually left out dates and always confused chronology. Moreover, she usually avoided making statements of solid fact about real people, places, or organizations to leave herself room for maneuver should she be challenged. Beyond that, there may be early hints, even here in 1874, when she was only about thirty-two, that her mental grasp of facts and dates and chronology was unsteady, that she could not remember accurately what she had seen and done only a few years before.

Lauretta could use the press to her advantage better than any woman in the country. The Mobile *Daily Register* headlined her story "An Adventurous Lady," and within a week her interview was being read in Indiana. Inside a fortnight readers in New York and Chicago saw her adventures, and by mid-October presses in Michigan, Kansas, South Carolina, Tennessee, Connecticut, and New Jersey repeated the story, sometimes retitled "A Confederate Amazon." Soon readers in Louisiana and North Carolina joined the list of Harry T. Buford's admirers.[8] She did not wait for that, however, and soon left Mobile for Atlanta, arriving about September 1. The next day she called on a correspondent for the *Daily Constitution*, who did a more than typically careless job of noting details in the oral account she gave him, calling her "Mrs. E. W. Bonner" and her alter ego "Harry F. Bufort." He found her to be a bit above average height, "thoroughly educated, and very fluent," adding that her face "lights up with interest" when speaking. Rather than just dictate her story, as she did in Mobile, she allowed the *Daily Constitution*'s man to ask her questions, and he found that "she has no hesitancy in talking about the strange events of her life."

In the process, she made more important additions to her story. Done with Roach, she claimed she was born "Loretta Jeanett Clapp" in Havana, Cuba, in 1842 or 1843. Her new origins echoed the bogus personal ad she had placed in the San Francisco paper in 1869, but this was the first time she publicly changed her birthplace from Nassau to Havana. Her father had been Samuel S. Clapp, who moved his family to Mississippi when she was young and later to Texas, where she grew to young womanhood. She had no living siblings, her mother died in 1860 in Texas, and her father died in 1863 as a prisoner of war at Fort Hamilton, New York. Of special note, however, was the fact that her father's brother had been Theodore Clapp, a famed Universalist minister in New Orleans.

Then she gave even more details. In Texas the Clapps lived next to the family of young William E. Burnett of Galveston, then a cadet at the U.S. Military Academy. In 1857 the two were secretly married, though she was barely fifteen years old and her husband scarcely older. When Burnett graduated, the army sent him to Pennsylvania and she went there to be with him, but when secession came, he resigned his commission and returned to Texas to raise a company, which he then led to Pensacola. That was when Lauretta first got the idea of posing as a man, and she and Burnett agreed that she would raise a company of her own and take it to Pensacola to join his, whereupon he would assume command of the combined battalion. She put on a second lieutenant's uniform and went to Arkansas, calling herself Harry T. Buford, and enlisted 136 men. Finding that Burnett's company had been posted back to New Orleans, she joined him there, and they called their battalion the Louisiana Greys.

Then somehow she wound up at First Manassas in Dreux's battalion and was close to him when he was killed, but she was apparently back with her husband's command when, late in 1861, Burnett was killed too, though she did not say how or where. She subsequently took her battalion to Fort Pillow on the Mississippi, some miles above Memphis, where Brigadier General Gideon J. Pillow promoted her to first lieutenant at an unnamed time, though given her earlier statements, this should have been in the fall of 1861. The next spring at Shiloh her severe shoulder wound came not on the first day, but on the evening of April 7, after the battle was almost done, and now the shell burst injured her hand as well. Then by July 1862 she was in Virginia in the Battle of Malvern Hill at the close of the famous Seven Days' Battles in Colonel Tailor's 12th Mississippi Infantry. Thereafter, she did not stay long in any one place, calling herself "an independent officer," and so she remained until 1864, carrying dispatches for the government.

On November 30, 1864, after the Battle of Franklin, Tennessee, she met "Capt. Byron DeCamp of Van Dorn's cavalry" on the battlefield. She had known him before the war, when he was an officer in the U.S. Army, and following Burnett's death, DeCamp courted her by letters, but they did not meet again until now. He did not see through her disguise as Lieutenant

Buford, and she did not reveal herself to him just yet. The next time she passed through Atlanta, however, she learned that DeCamp was there sick in a military hospital, and she went to him and gave up her secret. Soon a Methodist minister married them at the Atlanta Hotel, but she had orders to carry dispatches to some faraway destination, and he received orders to rejoin his regiment in Mississippi. Later, when she traveled to Corinth to rejoin him, she learned that he had died in camp and was already buried. After that, she asked to be assigned to blockade running duty and made several trips to and from Havana, importing desperately needed supplies. At the same time, she often crossed the lines into the North to smuggle back supplies and valuable military information, and she rendered aid and succor to suffering Confederate prisoners.

Since the war she had married John W. Wasson of Kentucky and went with him on the Venezuelan expedition, where he died. She then went to New York and from there to Austin, where she met and married the miner Bonner, who she said was "her present husband," at that moment in New Mexico on a prospecting expedition. She also mentioned her five-year-old son, who was staying in New Orleans, and added for the first time that she had lost two children previously, without mentioning who the fathers of any might have been. If not entirely fictional, one of the two could have been the child by DeCaulp.

She completely took in the journalist. Once again she displayed her parcel of authenticating documents, this time expanding her new theme of Harry Buford's irresistibility to women by showing a number of "love letters" the lieutenant had received from women and girls during the war. It helped that the reporter knew people who remembered her as Buford, including a few who said they attended her wedding. Though he did not say that he had seen her during the war himself, he did add that she had been a frequent sight at the city's railroad depot in her lieutenant's uniform and sporting a "lovely imperial" beard. "She certainly made a handsome officer," he added, noting that during her short time in Atlanta, she was the object of considerable attention on the part of people and city officials. He concluded, "It would take a book to hold all of her travels from point to point while on this duty." Of course, a book is just what she hoped readers would soon be buying. To stimulate sales, she now made a startling new announcement. Her recollections would be turned into a book by Mark Twain himself. She was on her way even now to see the great humorist and find a publisher.[9]

Lauretta left Atlanta on September 3, promising to return in a month to participate in a riding contest at the annual state fair, as well as to deliver a series of lectures at the invitation of its managers. Some would likely deal with Buford's adventures, but she also intended to deliver one titled "The Agricultural and Mineral Resources of New Mexico and Arizona as Compared with Those of the Southern States," on behalf of her Gila Valley Colonization Society, to be illustrated with samples of the minerals to be found.[10] These would be her first apparent efforts to break into the remunerative lecture circuit, where other women were already relating exaggerated wartime adventures.

She left behind her a host of new and reckless enhancements to her story. Prior to this interview she was almost always sufficiently vague to make refutation and exposure difficult, if not impossible, in an era when few had access to information. Now, however, she had given a series of concrete claims about genuine people that were subject to verification. For a start, her "uncle" Theodore Clapp was a very real person, a hero in New Orleans thanks to his tireless work caring for the sick during fever epidemics. He had died in 1866 in Kentucky, so he was no longer around to refute her claims of kinship, but he had no brother Samuel, nor was there a Samuel Clapp living in Mississippi or Texas or serving in the Confederate army and dying in a Northern prison camp. Though Lauretta had invented Samuel Clapp in 1869, she first claimed kinship to Theodore only after her recent visit to New Orleans, where she might just have learned of Clapp's death.

Her reference to William E. Burnett was even riskier. Lauretta's description closely fit a real person, and one from a prominent family. William E. Burnet was the son of David G. Burnet, the first provisional president of the Republic of Texas in 1836 and thereafter a prominent man in state affairs and longtime resident of Galveston, where he died in 1870. His son was a first lieutenant in the 1st U.S. Infantry. Instead of being a teenager in 1857, when Lauretta said they had wed, William was in fact born in 1833, and he never went to West Point, being directly commissioned into the army in 1856, though he did graduate from the Kentucky Military Academy. After the war broke out in 1861, he resigned his commission in July and went home to Texas against his father's wishes, but he did not get a commission in the Confederate army until September, long after Lauretta's alleged husband was supposedly killed at Pensacola. This William E. Burnet served almost the entire war at Mobile until, as a colonel of artillery, he was killed on March 31, 1865, in the very last days of the conflict, and he never married. Lauretta could have met him during the war, when she was arrested in Mobile in 1863 or later when she claimed to be involved in cotton smuggling in 1864–65, an enterprise that the real Burnet himself flirted with in January 1865.[11] In her brief time in Galveston in 1874, she also could have learned about the Burnets and later amalgamated their William into her story, now that neither he nor his father lived to gainsay her.

After having invented this first husband, her efforts to completely obfuscate her second marriage spoke eloquently of her fears of those 1866 rumors of DeCaulp's desertion. No amount of careless transcription was likely to turn Thomas C. DeCaulp of Forrest's cavalry into Byron DeCamp of Van Dorn's. That had to have been deliberate. Moreover, she now claimed twice that they were married in 1864 rather than 1863, and she said that he died at Corinth, Mississippi, presumably in 1864, rather than in New York in 1865. The whole business of their having known each other before the war and their courtship was also new, a feature she clearly liked, as she retained it for future use. Also interesting is that now she fully identified Bonner, even giving their wedding date, and spoke of him as if they were still married—as indeed they were.

She confused her chronology more than ever in Atlanta. She took her company to Pensacola now, not Key West as she had said in Mobile just a week earlier. Once again she was by Dreux's side when he was killed on July 21, 1861, at Manassas, even though he actually died sixteen days earlier and more than one hundred miles away. The real Louisiana Grays were part of the 5th Louisiana Infantry, with which she had no connection. The 12th Mississippi Infantry was in the Battle of Malvern Hill on July 1, 1862, and it did have a colonel named William H. Taylor, but no Lieutenant Buford. Her peripatetic wounds shifted from infliction on April 6 back to April 7, and were again two rather than one, with no mention at all of the leg wound that supposedly had her on crutches in New Orleans. Most reckless of all was her declaration that Clemens was to be her coauthor and would turn her story into a book that she predicted "will sell well." She even displayed documents appearing to confirm Clemens as a partner.[12] Mark Twain was very much alive, and if she were lying, he could call her to account and serious embarrassment.

Lauretta next stopped at Louisville on September 4, to find that her Mobile *Daily Register* interview had preceded her in the city's press, so there was no reason to call on the local editors. Instead, she attended the races at the city fairgrounds and soon found that not everyone was impressed by her recent celebrity. H. M. McCarty, publisher of the Louisville *Western Ruralist,* challenged her to don a soldier's uniform to see if it would fit, but she declined, "unreasonably," he thought.[13] In the same city, an article in the

Courier-Journal sounded less gallant than recent press reports, noting that at about thirty-five years of age, she "is not particularly handsome, yet there is something striking about her countenance that renders it rather attractive." All she said there was that she had spent eight months with her unnamed husband's Confederate company in 1861, adding the new tidbit that the premature firing of a defective gun had killed him. Whenever she heard the sounds of a battle, she rushed to take part, she testified, and suffered three wounds in all during the war. Afterward, she married "a second time," skipping over DeCaulp and Wasson entirely, and her "present husband" was a miner.

She introduced an entirely new personal claim, revealing that she was "a newspaper correspondent" who was "constantly writing for the papers."[14] Journalism was a profession still denied to women in the main. If any women regularly wrote newspaper articles, they used pseudonyms to conceal their gender, which ran counter to Lauretta's craving for attention and renown. She loved challenging conventions, but her writing ability was too crude for any serious editor to accept work from her pen. Yet it is clear from here on that she was interested in writing for publication and in publishing itself. This claim represented not a reality, but an aspiration.

Coincidentally, almost immediately an opportunity arose for her to prepare her first known example of writing for publication. Before she left for Lexington, she learned on the morning of September 6 that an acquaintance of hers, the swindler Philip Arnold, was in jail in Louisville, being held for extradition to California. Knowing him slightly, and believing him innocent, she prepared a public statement to that effect. Her longest written creation to date, and clearly intended for the press, her statement was also the earliest instance of another instinct developing in her, the impulse to adopt—or be seen as adopting—the cause of an underdog. Her motives in later instances were invariably intermixed with self-interest, but it is hard to see what she had to gain from defending Arnold. Still, coming as this did within days of announcing that she was a journalist, her letter suggests that she felt some instinct to blend journalism with the adoption of a cause. In her very small way now, she stood on the outer fringes of pioneering women in journalism.

Disclaiming any interest in Arnold's plight except for his being an acquaintance, she addressed her statement "To the Public Press." She began with a history of Arnold's connection with the Burro Burro Mine and how it was eventually parlayed into hundreds of thousands of dollars before discovery of the fraud, by which time Arnold had no interest in the mine. Still, when a former partner had to refund more than half a million dollars to English investors, he wanted redress and sued Arnold's former partners, meanwhile securing a warrant for Arnold's arrest and extradition on the old diamond fraud charge, thinking that his partners would pay the contested money to free Arnold.

Lauretta laid out what she saw as a fact of life in the speculation-happy West:

> I have lived, with my husband, in the mining regions of Nevada, California, Colorado, New Mexico (my husband is now on the headwaters of the Gila on a mining expedition) and I have never heard of a miner being arrested for selling a mine to a speculator. We sell a mine for what we have in sight and the purchaser takes his chances for its being a success. The miner sells for all he can get from speculators, and it is considered a legitimate transaction. This rule holds good throughout all mining regions where I have been.

It might as well have been a statement of her own attitude toward her past and future schemes and deceptions, a caveat emptor, in short, or as she said, "the purchaser takes his chances." She believed Arnold to be "the victim of a swindle and a shameful outrage." As for herself, "I have been a witness to so many swindling tricks that I am not surprised at anything they may do." Her mention of Bonner prospecting on the Gila was faint evidence of a trick of her own that she hoped to play soon enough.

Given other claims she was soon to make, her calling the salted mine "the Burra" is significant. "I do not know how to spell the name of the mine," she explained, going on to say that "burra" was "the Spanish pronunciation of the word, which is donkey in English." She did not know that the Spanish pronunciation was in fact "burr*o*," not "burra," nor that "burro" actually was the Spanish spelling of the word. It seemed a curious mistake, for her suggested pronunciation was closer to the way rural Americans might say the word. Any Hispanic people she met in her western travels would have said "burr*o*." She was claiming now to have been Cuban-born in Havana, even if her Clapp parentage was wholly American, yet she did not know basic Spanish pronunciation of a common word, and if she had any accent as a vestige of her Cuban birth, no one to date had commented on the anomaly of a British-American woman speaking so.

She signed her letter "Mrs. E. H. Bonner, New Mexico," and apparently gave it to the press in person, for a writer for the *Courier-Journal* declared that "she is a woman of remarkable intelligence" with "a business manner which will carry her through thick and thin, having already experienced a little of both." Moreover, the writer swallowed everything she said about her extensive travels there and abroad and her high reputation in the West, concluding that she seemed "entirely truthful in her statements."[15] Lauretta's power to impress men with her sincerity remained sharp as ever. Nevertheless, given that Arnold had swindled some important people in recent years, her endorsement drew mainly skepticism elsewhere and cast her own reliability somewhat in doubt. It also revealed once more Lauretta's unusual affinity for shady characters.[16]

She continued her progress east and northward, unaware that her lies were on her heels. Early in October she called on West Virginia newspaperman Owen S. McKinney and boldly gave him Clemens's name as a reference, claiming to have known him in California. She displayed letters she said Mark Twain wrote her on his publisher's letterhead to establish that he was her joint proprietor in a book Clemens was then completing, to be titled "Harry Bufords Adventures during the War." She showed more letters commending her to the "courtesy of the members of the press to whom she might apply during her travels." One was on the letterhead of Port of New Orleans collector of customs General James F. Casey, asking President Grant to assist her in securing mineral specimens from the Smithsonian. She explained that she was an agent of the Colonization Society of the Gila Valley, authorized to enlist Southern immigrants, and needed mineral samples to display when she addressed audiences of prospective settlers.

After she left him, McKinney began to suspect that her documents were forgeries and soon felt certain of it, concluding that she had somehow persuaded editors to publish her unproven claims, which is exactly what she had been doing for more than a decade. As she would do in the future, she most likely pilfered the publishers' stationery when calling on them in New York and collected Casey's letterhead during a visit to his office when she was in New Orleans, for Casey had written no such letter to Grant.[17]

"She is certainly a very great imposter," McKinney warned Clemens, "or a *remarkable* woman."[18] He found her story "well calculated from its plausibility" and told Clemens he had to admit that "she is one of the most intelligent as well as one of the 'cheekiest' women I ever saw." Among other things she carried were recent articles extolling her story as Buford. "She is an imposter of no ordinary rank," he continued. "Her story is admirably constructed, and remarkably well told—being connected and coherent in all its details." When he received McKinney's letters, Clemens scribbled on the envelope, "Mrs Bonner the fraud."[19]

Samuel L. Clemens, who did not hesitate to pronounce Lauretta a fraud when she declared he would coauthor her book. Wikimedia.

He also decided that it was time to take action. In typical humorous fashion, he told the editor of the Louisville *Courier-Journal*, "I do not want the public defrauded in my name except when I do it myself," and then on October 9 wrote a disclaimer for the press.[20] "There is a large mistake here somewhere," he stated emphatically, denying that he had sent any letters to her agreeing to coauthorship and emphasizing, "I am not joint proprietor in any book with any woman."[21] He replied to McKinney that "the woman is a fraud," fearing that she had forged his handwriting on those spurious letters, and McKinney agreed.[22] "The woman is a fraud," McKinney replied, "though her representations were of the most plausible character," adding that "the tale she tells is well calculated from its plausibility."[23] Lauretta felt the same, apparently, for she kept telling it, even writing to Atlanta to tell the *Daily Constitution* that Mark Twain not only had agreed to be her writer but also was actually at work on the book even then.

Already newspapers were beginning to react to her claims. While republishing her Mobile interview, editors called her "a veritable Belle Lamar," an uncomplimentary reference to a new melodrama of the same name that one reviewer found "feeble and flimsy," concluding that "it has next to no literary merit, and as a work of dramatic art it is insignificant."[24] A New York editor intended no kudos when he observed now that "as far as devotion to the Confederate cause was concerned, it seems that Mrs. Bonner was a double concentrated *Belle Lamar*, with the additional advantage of never having indulged in 'the wild utterances of despeah!'"[25] An Augusta, Georgia, editor found that the claims of "the female Confederate Lieutenant" bore the fragrance of invention. Even as he published notice of her dispatch to the *Daily Constitution* about Clemens writing her book, he added that "due allowance for exaggeration must however be made weighing this announcement of this Confederate Joan D'Arc."[26]

For all of her undeniable skill at manipulating the press, Lauretta's carelessness always bordered on the foolhardy. She had to have known that anything in print about Clemens being her writer must reach him eventually and produce an inevitable and embarrassing disclaimer. It had happened to her more than enough times in the past that she should have been conscious of the possibility of it happening again, yet she ignored her own experience. Either she just did not care or her intellect lacked the critical element of forethought. Even bad publicity could sell books, of course, but like most confidence artists, she trusted her ability to extemporize new lies to explain away old ones.

Soon she had to do just that. It was January 15, 1875, before Clemens's disclaimer saw print in the Atlanta *Daily Constitution*. The very same issue ran a letter to the editor from faraway Utah. If Lauretta thought it safe to use the name Bonner now that she was hundreds of miles from the mining camps, she miscalculated. A copy of the *Daily Constitution* issue with her September 1874 interview had found its way to Salt Lake City and into the hands of Hardy Bonner's friend Adam Wilson, who wrote a brief but incendiary letter telling another version of Lauretta's marriage to Bonner and how she had drained him of "a great many thousand dollars" during her sojourn in Utah and Nevada. "She is without doubt a low, vulgar, unprincipled adventurer," he concluded. "Her ideas of morals are of the loosest kind, and no one in this country would believe her under oath." In a word, he said, "she is what the people in this country call an old blister." As for her claims about Mark Twain, Wilson doubted that the writer would have anything to do with her and ended by declaring that "she will prove a dead beat, that I am sure." Already suspicious of her since the past fall, the *Daily Constitution*'s editors now disavowed her story entirely. "The woman was adroit," they said, "but she had not long left the city before it became known that she was an imposter."[27]

The Wilson letter and Clemens's disclaimer seriously compromised the story Lauretta had built to promote herself and her proposed book. From the time they appeared, she dropped out of sight for several months, her movements largely unknown. She spent some time in New York, corresponding with William Ramsay, editor of the Atlanta *Sunny South* and owner of the Southern Publishing Company. Perhaps she wrote some chapters as best she could. Sometime in the spring of 1875 she signed a contract for Ramsay's company to publish her book.[28]

CHAPTER ELEVEN

THE APPEARANCE OF "MADAME VELASQUEZ"

ONCE AGAIN LAURETTA re-created herself. Being DeCaulp had led to embarrassment in 1866 because of Thomas's desertion. Now being Bonner backfired on her as well. She concluded to put some distance between herself and earlier connections that might lead to questions about her Confederate loyalty or what she would say in her memoir. At the same time, she took the opportunity to assume a more exotic persona, an identity with allure to attract more attention. She invented a new name and with it a new version of her personal history. In April 1875 she announced through the Memphis *Daily Avalanche* that henceforth she was to be addressed as "Madame L. J. Velazquex." Editorial error accounted for the peculiar spelling, for she customarily—but not always—spelled it Velasquez. Fittingly, the same announcement misspelled her wartime alter ego, calling him "Lieutenant Harry Benford," surely another editorial error, for a change in spelling would hardly disassociate her from Lauretta J. Bonner and Harry Buford. In the public mind Madame Velasquez and Harry Buford must be one and the same.

In her interview with the *Daily Constitution* in September 1874, she had changed her parentage from Admiral Roach to Samuel S. Clapp and her birthplace from Nassau, Bahamas, to Havana, Cuba. She said nothing about her parentage now but kept the Cuban connection, claiming that after the war she posed as a man once again and tried unsuccessfully to join Cuban insurgents seeking to overthrow Spanish rule, the first time she associated herself with the island's revolt. The editor of the *Daily Avalanche* confessed that "she was of decided masculine appearance," but the revolutionaries were not to be fooled. Returning to feminine attire, she went to New York to become a sales agent in that city for the Paris firm of Charles Eabre and Company, importers of artificial flowers, a position she currently retained.[1] Gone were Wasson, Bonner, and Bobo; her Southern tours of 1866 and the year just past; steamboat explosions; Venezuela, Nevada, California, Utah, and New Mexico; and apparently even her son. The content of her *Daily Constitution* interview was almost all new—and false. Her reincarnation lacked shape as yet. Finding nothing of lasting utility in these new details, she soon abandoned virtually all of them. Still, she was laying a foundation for her future fictional life.

William "Gus" Ramsay was a necessary part of that transformation. He operated on the relatively new subscription basis, rather than relying on bookstore sales. His agents solicited subscribers well ahead of a book's publication, and their payments helped him defray in advance the costs of printing, paper, and ink. It was what Lauretta had done in 1866, only she had no book then and no publisher. As a result, books were published that might otherwise have required too great an expenditure. When books came off the press, he sent copies to the subscribers and to commission-earning agents who canvassed the country, often to places that had no bookstores. He paid the author a royalty on each copy sold, just as did conventional publishers.[2] The major center for such publishing was Hartford, Connecticut, where Samuel Clemens lived. Fully a dozen companies operated in Hartford, all but one on the same street and six of them under one roof.[3]

What Ramsay apparently did not tell Lauretta was that earlier that year he had dissolved a partnership in his Southern Publishing Company and now intended to continue operating it on his own, meaning he was seriously undercapitalized. In May creditors seized his presses and equipment to sell at auction to satisfy a judgment in debt against him, forcing Ramsay to revert temporarily to his prior occupation of auctioneer. In June he advertised for a new partner to invest up to $10,000 in rebuilding the firm, and apparently he found some or all of the money he needed. Meanwhile, he had to tell Lauretta that there would be a delay in issuing her book, and then another, and another.[4] He was also something of a Lothario, if local rumor is to be believed. "Gus is so popular a ladies man when business is on hand he is 'going-gone' in a moment," an Atlanta paper said in September. "Traveling around with belles suits him well."[5]

Lauretta Bonner knew how to handle a man who liked women. In early August she released to the New York press word that her memoir was done, to be titled *The Woman in Battle; a Narrative of the Exploits, Adventures, &c, of Madame L. J. Velasquez, Otherwise Known as Lieutenant Harry T. Buford, C.S.A.* It would come off the press in September 1875 and be, she said, "the most intensely interesting and exciting war book ever published in America." Readers North and South alike well knew the exploits of Harry Buford and would thrill to the author's "dauntless courage in the face of extraordinary perils."[6]

Portrait of Velasquez engraved by Jeremiah Rea from a photo in 1875–76. In April 1875 Lauretta announced that henceforth she was to be Madame Loreta Janeta Velasquez. *The Woman in Battle.*

September came and waned with no book. Late that month she went to Atlanta, and on October 2 she confronted Ramsay, who had taken to referring to her as "Madame Velasquez, or 'the woman in battle.'"[7] In days everyone knew she was the same Bonner who had been in the city the year before. As was typical, she defended herself by going on the offense. Within forty-eight hours she called on the editor of the *Daily Constitution* and told him the Adam Wilson letter was "false in every particular," claiming that no one in Utah knew anything of him and that "there is no such man."[8]

When she and Ramsay met, each blamed the other for delay, whereas in fact the manuscript may not yet have been completed. Jointly they announced that she was in Atlanta now to supervise the work, yet they backed away from a precise publication date, saying only that "the book will soon be out." They also announced that she had now "resumed her maiden name of Velasquez."[9] A week later, on October 21, Lauretta suddenly fell ill and for several days was confined to her hotel room. Then on October 30 a series of convulsions lasting almost nine hours seized her. The next day a doctor said she was "some better now" and predicted she would recover.[10]

Perhaps she was ill, but the fact that her indisposition was announced to the press could also have been a means to keep her out of sight to finish her part of writing the book. Certainly she generated no news or comment for another fortnight after her presumed recovery. If she did rush the writing to completion, she must have finished by mid-November, for on November 18 she went to Marietta, Georgia, on other business for Ramsay. Having fired his sales agent for a city directory for Atlanta, Marietta, and other towns, he sent Lauretta out to solicit business, a distraction they could not have afforded if her work was unfinished. While selling his books, she promoted her own, and as evidence that it was nearly ready for the press, she boasted that it would run to 600 pages.[11] The type had been set and the pages "electrotyped" in Boston, a printing process that created a single press plate for each page rather than printing from unwieldy original type, and their number in fact came to 606. By December 18 the plates were ready, as well as illustrations, and Ramsay pronounced aspects of the book "very unique."[12]

In Marietta she also unveiled her complete restyled name. She was "Madame Loreta Jauneta Velazquez," having already explained that "Velazquez is my fathers name, which I have chose for the Title of my Book, now in Prep."[13] The new Madame Loreta made another faint effort to link Clemens to her book when she wrote to the Louisville *Courier-Journal* on October 7, demanding to see his letter denying any connection with her and claiming, "I am in Posession of Several Letters from Mark Twain denying the writing [of] said Letters, to your Paper." It was a bold lie, but in the process she admitted that he had nothing to do with her book and demanded that the paper retract his disclaimer. If she could discredit Clemens's disclaimer, then she would be free still to hint at some connection with him. She wrote her letter on Ramsay's Southern Publishing Company letterhead to lend some authority. The editor of the *Courier-Journal* sent it to Clemens with the amused comment, "what have you been doing to this woman?" Clemens scribbled "female fraud" on the envelope and filed it away.[14] Lauretta wrote to him one more time on October 30, but evidently he made no response and discarded her letter.[15] Unfazed by the repeated rejections, she still hinted to Ramsay when he announced her book was ready for press that "Mark Twain is reported to have said that it will be *the* book of the season."[16] One way or another, she was intent on using Clemens to sell books for her.

Meanwhile, the advance promotion of subscription sales continued. In December flyers solicited agents to apply for commissions to sell the book, promising that *The Woman in Battle* would be "the best selling Agents' book ever published." Touting Madame Velasquez as "a True Southern Heroine" of "extraordinary valor," the leaflet proclaimed her to be "the heroine of a number of exploits even more interesting than those of the battle-field." Testimonials asserted that the book's facts were "substantiated by leading men both South and North." In short, "no book of such varied and intense interest as the Woman in Battle has ever been issued in America."[17] At the same time, Lauretta happily related sundry stories from it in conversation, as when she told the noted Methodist minister Simon Peter Richardson how she had the opportunity to assassinate General Grant at Shiloh. In her book she asserted that a change of heart stopped her, but she told Richardson only that "something prevented her from firing."[18]

The Woman in Battle still met with delays into February 1876. Now it carried the cumbersome subtitle *A Narrative of the Exploits, Adventures, and Travels of Madame Loreta Janeta Velazquez, Otherwise Known as Lieutenant Harry T. Buford, Confederate States Army. In Which Is Given Full Descriptions of the Numerous Battles in Which She Participated as a Confederate Officer; of Her Perilous Performances as a Spy, as a Bearer of Dispatches, as a Secret-Service Agent, and as a Blockade-Runner; of Her Adventures behind the Scenes at Washington, Including the Bond Swindle; of Her Career as a Bounty and Substitute Broker in New York; of Her Travels in Europe and South America; Her Mining Adventures on the Pacific Slope; Her Residence among the Mormons; Her Love Affairs, Courtships, Marriages, &c., &c.* Lauretta and Ramsay left nothing off the title page that might titillate a buyer. Though he would apparently print all copies as actual publisher, he subcontracted the book to appear under a number of different regional subscription publishers' imprints, all of them affiliated with Dustin, Gilman & Co., which had offices in Cincinnati, Chicago, Richmond, and Hartford.[19]

Peculiarities about the book should have been apparent before it went to press. Throughout the work Lauretta's name appears as "Velazquez," even though she signed all of her correspondence as Velasquez from the time she adopted the surname. The single exception in the book is on the frontispiece, where her name is spelled as she signed it and not as it appears everywhere else in the volume. Clearly not everyone was paying close attention. In fact, it showed abundant evidence of haste and carelessness in preparation for press and intent to publish it as cheaply as possible.

The publisher engaged an artist to create two sizes of initial capital letters set into woodcut engravings to begin the first words of the fifty-two chapters. The larger placed the letter within a scene of stacked rifles in camp, the inside of a fortification, or a battle. Yet only five such letters were commissioned: F, H, I, T, and W. All of the other initial capitals appeared on a smaller scale, set into bland floral arrangements connoting nothing relevant. The larger letters appear just eight times, seven in the first third of the book, and the eighth beginning chapter forty-one. The smaller letters open forty-four chapters, an odd imbalance made stranger still by the fact that in several instances the first word of a chapter begins with a letter represented among the five larger commissioned pieces, but instead the publisher used the smaller. It suggests that Ramsay paid an artist and engraver for custom letters but stopped when he saw the cost, and then for the rest of the book just borrowed generic graphics from some other source. Meanwhile, whoever designed the pages failed to make full use of the commissioned letters by apparently forgetting they were available and using the smaller ones instead.

The maps and illustrations show the same lack of concern for detail. Not one of the maps was created for the book. In fact, Ramsay lifted them all from some previous work on the *Union* side of the war, for they depict only Northern campaigns or units. He also borrowed most of the illustrations, especially for the chapters covering Lauretta postwar, where they all came from sources such as *Harper's Weekly Illustrated Newspaper* and Francis Fuller Victor's *The River of the West.*[20] Elsewhere in the book, he used woodcuts of Havana and Cienfuegos, Cuba, from an 1871 set of illustrations of Central and South America, and then threw in irrelevant fillers—an engraving of a Confederate treasury note, the great seal of the Confederacy, crude woodcuts of leading Confederate generals—taken from other works, with no credits, and likely no use fees paid, to the original sources. Any savings Ramsay probably applied to ten special woodcuts depicting Buford's war exploits. They were crude to the point of cartoonish, though two or three met better standards of the time, evidence that Ramsay commissioned more than one artist.[21] However, he did spend money on half a dozen steel engravings from which some illustrations would be printed, hiring Jeremiah Rea of Philadelphia, one of the finest engravers of the time, especially of human faces.[22]

It may not have been coincidence that previously Rea had done illustrations for Belle Boyd's sensational memoir, *Belle Boyd in Camp and Prison*.

Rea also made engravings of three portraits, and the finished work strongly suggests that he worked from photographs. All three raise interesting questions. The first is the frontispiece of Lauretta, identified as "Madam Velasquez in Female Attire." Besides its conflict with the spelling of her name on the facing title page, the caption also conflicts in its spelling of "Madam" versus "Madame" in the title. Here again was the carelessness. The face in the portrait raises even more questions. The photo is clearly postwar and probably was taken specifically for the book in 1875–76, but otherwise it cannot be dated. Even if taken late in 1875, the woman in the image appears middle-aged, worn, and tired, her jowls sagging, whereas Lauretta cannot have been more than about thirty-three years old at the time. She had seen some hard living, and more than one reporter had spoken of her as looking older than her years. She enhanced the impression by wearing her hair pulled back in a style often associated with Hispanic women. A striped ribbon attached to her bodice by either a button or a brooch had a star pinned to the bottom. Contrary to reports that she wore the symbol of her lieutenant's rank—which would have been a single horizontal bar for a second lieutenant or two bars for a first lieutenant—the single star signified a major, a rank she never claimed. The button, if it was a button, could have been Confederate military issue.

The second Rea engraving was captioned in Lauretta's handwriting, "Harry T. Buford 1st Lt Indpt Scouts C.S.A." The bust portrait showed her in an officer's uniform blouse with a kepi on her head, her hair clipped short to ear length, and a resplendent imperial beard and mustache on her face. She certainly looked younger than the woman on the frontispiece, and the quality of the engraving suggests that Rea worked from either the 1862 photograph known to have been taken of Lauretta or a print from her sitting for Saltzman in 1866 if, as seems likely, she posed in uniform.

Most puzzling of all is the third Rea portrait, also done from a photo. Readers might expect it to be her tragic love, Thomas C. DeCaulp, or someone else equally important in her life. Instead it was her onetime jailer, Captain George W. Alexander of Castle Thunder. He figured on just two pages of her narrative, though she made it clear that she entertained high regard for him for his kindnesses. That may have been genuine, but it could also be because there was something to Charles Dunham's insinuations back in 1863 that she became overly friendly with the captain from the Castle. The most likely reason was more recent, however. Alexander currently edited the Washington *Sunday Gazette* at the nation's capital. Lauretta had already announced that she was writing for the newspapers. Her acquaintance with Alexander might have gotten her commissions to write for the *Sunday Gazette*, or perhaps she hoped to parlay flattery in her book into commissions to launch the journalistic career that loomed large in her ambitions.

By far the biggest mystery about *The Woman in Battle* appears on the title page, which does not actually list Madame Velasquez as author. It states that the book was "edited by C. J. Worthington." He is a complete cipher, if he even existed. If Lauretta is to be believed, she realized by mid-1874 that she could not manage writing her memoir, and as she told Clemens, a publisher advised her to engage a collaborator to turn her recollections into a manuscript. In August 1875 she announced that her book was to be edited by "J. C. Worthington."[23]

The transposition of initials was probably just a printer's error, though if Worthington was an invention, then Lauretta or Ramsay may not have been settled yet on his name. In December Ramsay announced that "the book is written by a distinguished Northern writer," and that same month, when advertising for agents, he added that C. J. Worthington had served in the U.S. Navy during the late war.[24] In the "author's prefatory notice," admittedly written by Lauretta herself, she said only that "although during the war he was on the other side, he has interested himself most heartily in assisting to get my narrative into the best shape for presentation to the public, and has shown a remarkable skill in detecting and correcting errors into which I had inadvertently fallen" In his own "editor's prefatory notice," Worthington spoke glowingly of Lauretta's character and graces typical of a Southern woman, going on to plead for sectional reconciliation, pointing out that he had been in the U.S. naval service "from near the beginning to the end of the civil war."[25] In a few months Ramsay also let drop that Worthington lived in Philadelphia.[26] The title page of copies for Northern sale would show Worthington as "Late of the United States Navy," but copies for sale in the South omitted that. Surely the difference signified nothing more than an awareness of some sensitivity on the part of buyers in both sections.

If C. J. Worthington was indeed a "distinguished Northern writer," then something else written by him ought to have been current in that generation, but *The Woman in Battle* is the only book ever published under his name. He cannot be found living in or near Philadelphia in the 1870s. If he did serve in the recent war, there should be some evidence of his service, but no such man served in the Union navy at any level. Worthington is seemingly a man who never was, making him a literal "ghost writer" telling the story of a woman who in large part never was either.

He may have been a complete fiction, invented for some as yet unperceived purpose by Lauretta or Ramsay, though there is an arresting coincidence. Until 1874 Dustin's partner in the subscription business had been Alfred D. Worthington, who then went out on his own and enjoyed great success with a sensational book titled *Tell It All: The Story of a Life's Experience in Mormonism*, written by a woman who recounted her twenty years as the wife of a Mormon elder. Lauretta's book included her time among the Mormons, perhaps hoping to capitalize on the popularity of *Tell It All*. Worthington was also the sort of character Lauretta gravitated toward, for his next title was a pirated edition of a British book that bankrupted him in 1876. It is possible that he was involved with Lauretta and Ramsay and rewrote her narrative under a thin alias.

Another possibility is George W. Alexander. Lauretta was certainly in touch with him, since he provided one of the endorsements she used in advertising her book. Certainly he could write, and he had reason to resent some Confederate officials whom *The Woman in Battle* treated unkindly, for he went before a court more than once while executing his duties at Castle Thunder. That would also explain the anomalous inclusion of his portrait as one of only three in the book. Then there was Charles A. Dunham, that same congenital con artist who, as Harvey Birch in 1863, had treated Lauretta rather harshly in his letters to the editor sent from Castle Thunder and, as Sanford Conover two years later, tried to implicate her as Alice Williams in the Lincoln assassination. They were two of a kind, to be sure, and might naturally have gravitated toward one another. He lived in Philadelphia as recently as 1874, publishing the *Market Journal*, and was certainly an able writer.[27]

One final alternative is that Worthington was just another alias for Lauretta. She lacked the command of grammar and style to produce a finished narrative, but any competent schoolteacher ought to have been able to correct and expand her rude prose into publishable text, working right behind her as she turned out the chapters.[28] It was a long book, to be sure, about 235,000 words, but if Lauretta began when Clemens turned her down, that would have given her at least six months to finish the draft after contracting with Ramsay, writing about three book pages per day. For someone of Lauretta's skill at extended verbal improvisation, such an output posed small challenge, since she made up most of her story as she went along. It may be significant that this same February she claimed to know three different methods of shorthand to aid her as a journalist. Certainly she was intelligent enough to learn shorthand, so if her claim was true, then speedy writing would have been familiar to her.[29]

Whatever Lauretta's creative involvement, she likely wrote bits and pieces over several years, and then handed it all to an unnamed editor to create a coherent narrative. Still, the fact that the finished text agreed with most of her post-1874 accounts suggests that the bulk of the book was of very recent origin or else heavily revised.

It began with Lauretta's own five-paragraph preface, apologizing for her book's "many faults of style" and hoping that her story's interest compensated for its "lack of literary elegance." She had lived "a life too busily occupied in other matters," she went on, "for me to cultivate the graces of authorship." The loss of her early notes—no mention now of the *Miami* disaster—forced her to rely solely on memory, though later in the book she claimed that she had kept a diary during the war.[30] She explained any errors of fact or chronology by saying "memory is apt to be very treacherous." Moreover, "I have been compelled to write hurriedly," she claimed, amid long interruptions due to earning a living. None of that was conducive to literary quality.

She frankly confessed that she cared little about her book's want of art. Her real interest was, as she put it, "the money that I hope this book will bring in to me," for "the money I want badly." Her candor had its purpose, for she also employed the poor weak woman pleading for help motif, echoing her plea to Clemens in 1874 and presaging such appeals in years ahead. Lauretta was canny. She meant to tell a good story and knew that lurid detail and thinly veiled sexual innuendo attracted readers. Her cross-dressing as Harry Buford, the tales she would tell of encouraging women to fall in love with "him," the titillating aspects of a woman exposed to the rough behavior of soldiers in camp and field all served greater sales. She felt no embarrassment at anything in her war career posing as a man but said nothing about nearly half of the book that dealt with her movements after she permanently retired Buford. She thanked "my editor," Worthington, who helped "to get my narrative into the best shape for presentation," and especially for correcting errors in her accounts. "The book, such as it is," she concluded, "is now, for good or ill, out of my hands," and in another reassertion of her supposed foreign birth, she left it to "my adopted country people" to decide if it had been worth the effort.[31]

There followed an editor's preface in which Worthington said Lauretta had handed him a completed manuscript that was unbalanced, detailed in some places and perfunctory in others. He claimed that they had corresponded about these points and then met several times. In their discussions they decided that he should have the final say on content, calling on her for material to expand the meager passages. Where he found errors in chronology or facts, he called them to her attention and made corrections with her approval. While filling out some passages, he cut out much that was extraneous, promising that "nothing has been omitted that is of value or importance." Lauretta's preface mentioned only lost notes, but Worthington specifically said she had lost her diary—meaning that is what she told him—which forced her to write "entirely from memory." He then apologized for any false recollections, for "considering the multiplicity of events, it is very remarkable that she has been able to relate her story with any degree of accuracy." That both cited her memory emphasizes that she or they knew well of such mistakes, an implicit admission of the rush to press. "A few errors may have been permitted to remain uncorrected," he added, but they were "not material" and did not compromise the story's interest. He said nothing about compromising accuracy.

Worthington concluded with a few words about her. "Madame Velazquez is a very remarkable woman," he wrote. Slender and slightly over medium height, she was quite physically fit and above the average in good looks, an interesting assessment if she wrote it herself. She moved quickly and purposefully, direct and vivacious in speaking. Successful as she had been at disguise as a man, there was nothing masculine about her. "She is a shrewd, enterprising, and energetic business woman," he added. He had left as much of the text in her words as he could, for her style had "a certain flavor which is far from unpleasant." She had also a flair for entertaining conversation and even "a fund of racy anecdotes" that she told with a flair for mimicry, suggesting that she could imitate gestures, manners, and most important, with her claims of Cuban birth, accents.[32]

The actual mix of Lauretta's and Worthington's contributions in the finished product is incalculable, but one thing is certain: a reading of the few dozen of her surviving letters and other writings before and following publication of the book makes it clear that she did not write much of what finally appeared on her pages. At the very least, Worthington, or whoever acted under his name, edited everything she wrote with a heavy pencil and apparently complete freedom to substitute words and phrases, perhaps even incidents, in the interest of a better narrative. That and the mistakes and omissions the editor made in handling conflicts and chronology in effect made him virtually a coauthor, meaning that at least some of the problems of the book are just as likely to have originated with him as with her.

That is important because the remaining 573 pages of *The Woman in Battle* were to be an exercise in the bizarre.

CHAPTER TWELVE

THE WOMAN IN BATTLE

THOSE "FEW ERRORS" that Worthington dismissed as "not material" were legion, infecting virtually every chapter and episode admitting any corroboration, and are too numerous to address in toto. The chronology that both he and Lauretta called to readers' attention was a dog's breakfast of undated events misplaced out of order by weeks, months, and in a few cases even years. The editor's claim of assiduous effort to correct misstatements and anomalies was simply false, for the most rudimentary checking could not have missed so many glaring mistakes, artifacts of the rush to get the book finished and of Lauretta's instinct to avoid precision. The more fluid her chronology, the easier to rationalize conflicts of times, places, and dates. By her account, whatever she wrote herself was composed mostly in 1874–75, so she acted on memories from a distance of a dozen years down to just a few months, which begs the question of how her memory could have been so appallingly bad. Of course, she invented much and in places obfuscated to cover her real activity. As well, just as some of her recent newspaper statements might have been hints of incipient mental problems, so could the myriad and often remarkable confusions in her book.

For a second time, now, she claimed birth as Loreta Janeta Velazquez in Havana, in a house on the Calle Velaggas, on June 26, 1842. Gone from her paternity were both Roach and Clapp, but she stopped short of giving her new father's full name, saying only that he came of noble blood and descended from Diego Velazquez, the first Spanish governor of Cuba. Educated in Europe, he spoke several languages and became a diplomat. He married the daughter of a French naval officer and an American mother. The couple had six children, of which Lauretta was the last, as opposed to Roach's nine children and Clapp's two. In 1840 Spain sent Velazquez to Havana, where his daughter appeared two years later. Then in 1844 the family moved to San Luis Potosí in central Mexico, where he inherited a large plantation that he later lost to the United States in the 1846–48 war. He returned to Cuba, made a fortune in coffee and sugar at Puerto de Palmas, and hired an English governess to give Lauretta "a fair knowledge of the English language."[1]

In 1849 Velazquez sent her to New Orleans for further schooling with an aunt identified only as "Madame R."[2] There Lauretta acquired "an accurate knowledge of English, so as to be able to read, write, and speak it with fluency." What really consumed her, however, was a passion to achieve greatness in world opinion. She claimed that she identified with Joan of Arc, asserting, "My soul burned with an overwhelming desire to emulate her deeds of valor." She wrote, "I wished that I was a man, such a man as Columbus or Captain Cook." The idea haunted her, and at nights she sometimes donned a male cousin's clothing and stood before a mirror practicing a man's swagger.

So far, it was nonsensical. Then romance appeared, first an arranged engagement for which she felt no zest, then an infatuation with a young officer who was courting her schoolmate, a Miss "Nellie V." The story is unimportant save for being the book's first instance of Lauretta lighting a backfire to deflect recollections of her youth still lingering in New Orleans. She wrote that she and "Nellie V." were close friends until Lauretta took the handsome officer away from her, whereupon "she said a great many disagreeable things about me."[3] When Lauretta first unmistakably appeared on the documentary record in New Orleans, she was generally known to have been a prostitute working in the house of "the notorious Nellie Bremer." If the two Nellies were one and the same, Lauretta muted the effect of anything Bremer said about her old profession by creating a framework of spite and disappointed romance as the basis for such slanders.

Lauretta identified her new love simply as William, saying nothing of the William Burnet she first named in September 1874. After a rapid courtship, they married secretly in New Orleans on April 5, 1856, when she had not yet turned fourteen. The parallel with the rumors in 1862 of Anne Williams marrying an army officer named Lieutenant Arnold is unmistakable, and the claim that her father disinherited her when he heard of the marriage retroactively confirmed her December 1864 personal ad in Richmond regarding the death of Admiral Roach, even though she now wrote him out of her story.

William left on the 1857 Mormon expedition—as had Lieutenant Arnold—but she was pregnant and unable to go. The birth of her child led to a reconciliation with her parents, however, thanks to a brother, possibly named Josea, who flitted in and out of the succeeding pages under different names. After William returned, they moved to Fort Leavenworth in the Kansas Territory. There she remained until the spring of 1860 and bore another child. William then went to Fort Arbuckle in the Indian Territory, but she went to St. Louis, once more pregnant, and there gave birth to their third child, who soon died. When he returned in October, his father wanted him to resign his commission and come home to Galveston, expecting a war. Soon a fever took their two remaining children, and in her grief Lauretta returned to her youthful dreams of glory.[4]

Nothing thus far was confirmable, though already she had created multiple conflicts with established facts and her own prior claims. Thereafter, the pace of those conflicts accelerated. On April 5, 1861, the couple was in Memphis preparing for William to go to Richmond as a Confederate officer, where he expected to see old friends like Robert E. Lee, "who had linked their fortunes with those of the South," though as of that date Lee was still in the U.S. Army and Virginia in the Union. No sooner did William leave than she bought two Confederate uniforms and went to New Orleans to have them fitted along with the rest of her disguise, concluding to identify herself as "Lieutenant H. T. Buford, C.S.A." Then she returned to Memphis and crossed the Mississippi to Hopefield, Arkansas, where she boarded a train for the short, ten-mile trip to Hurlburt Station.[5] There she raised a company of volunteers she called the "Arkansas Grays" and for the first time amused herself beguiling the local women as Harry Buford.

This vanity in her attraction to women of all ages became a repetitive fixture throughout the narrative. "I was accounted an uncommonly good-looking fellow, when dressed in my best uniform," she boasted. Time after time Buford allured young women into offering him their wealth, affections, even chastity and reputation, until such episodes in the narrative became predictable and tedious. She recounted at least five such encounters, which she found "immensely amusing," hinting broadly that at least two of her conquests wanted more than a squeeze of the hand. She even described stealing the beloved of one of her male comrades in arms and twice detailed leaving groups of several young women swooning, attributing her power over women to her "fascinating figure and manner." She received love letters by the dozen, and she stopped breaking female hearts only when she put Harry Buford to rest in late summer of 1863. Then, as a woman, she proved equally irresistible to men, with two more of them beguiled by war's end, not to mention capturing DeCaulp's heart, followed after the war by another unnamed suitor, as well as husbands Wasson and Bonner.[6]

It is tempting but unwise to read this as evidence of a suppressed aberrant sexuality—cross-dressing, transgenderism, even penis envy—in Lauretta.

Her four or more marriages as of 1876 argue that she preferred traditional male-female relationships, even if hers were less romance than means to other ends. Moreover, while her male conquests appear in chapters before, during, and after the war, her dalliances with women ended abruptly when she retired Buford. Nothing in the balance of the book or in her recorded years following even hints at a renewal of such activity except that one now-abandoned claim to have posed as a man to enlist with Cuban rebels. She omitted her January–February 1864 Mrs. Major Gates episode from the book for obvious reasons, but in that very genuine instance, though wearing a military-style basque, she made no effort whatever to conceal her gender. At least one and perhaps two or more serious male relationships after 1876 reinforce her healthy, and very conventional, sexuality.

Lieutenant Buford the Lothario was a fictional device shrewdly designed to titillate mid-Victorian tastes and sell more books. Crafty chapter titles and subheads in her table of contents enticed purchasers with promises of "Love Matches and Marriages of Convenience," "Love's Young Dream," "Bashful Maidens," "A Nice Little Flirtation," "A Bit of Flirtation with a Columbia Belle," "Another Lady in Love with Me," "A Little Love Affair," "An Unfortunate Love Affair," and more. Best of all was "Lieutenant H. T. Buford as a Lady-killer."[7] Skilled as she was at "selling" herself to the press, she instinctively grasped how to appeal to public tastes in marketing her book.

The confirmed time that Lauretta spent in a uniform is limited to those occasions when she was caught at it: a few days in the fall of 1861, a few more in April 1862, and brief periods in June and July 1863. Yet during her time in Jackson and Mobile that June, she made no effort to conceal her identity or gender as she paraded in her pantaloons. Rather, being "caught" was always her design, something she inadvertently gave away in her book when she described her uniform as "well calculated to attract attention."[8] There was no fame in anonymity; only discovery served her purpose.

She led her company to Pensacola, financing their equipment and travel from her own pocket, and on arrival handed over to her husband command of her volunteers, one of whom was none other than Thomas C. DeCaulp, now first lieutenant. William sent her back to New Orleans for more supplies, and while she was away a carbine exploded accidentally in his hands, killing him. Lauretta rushed to Pensacola, turned command of her husband's battalion over to DeCaulp, and then left with other officers on June 16 for Richmond and anticipated action. Along the way she mentally made "some very uncomplimentary notes" about Confederate soldiers and their "utterly revolting" conversation, "fouled with blasphemy and obscenity." Blotting the image of soldiers whom she otherwise lauded made her book racier, which she lost no opportunity to do, just as she now portrayed Buford as breaking a pretty widow's heart, despite the lady's hints that "a little more love-making would be more than agreeable."[9]

On the way to Richmond, she stopped in Montgomery for an extended conversation with Secretary of War Walker—who at that time actually was in Richmond, not Montgomery—then stopped long enough in Columbia, South Carolina, to attract the attentions of yet another young lady. Stopping again in Lynchburg, she amused herself as Buford by regaling people with her intimate knowledge of the Rebel army forming back in the Mississippi valley. "A good deal of the information I gave them was fictitious, while the rest was made up from telegrams, the newspapers, and conversations I had overheard," she confessed, unaware that she thereby revealed her own technique for convincing newspapermen of her authenticity. Before she left Lynchburg, a local lady sent a note inviting the irresistible Buford to her bedchamber, but he did not respond, being put off by "such a forward specimen of my sex."[10]

On reaching Virginia, Buford rushed to Manassas. His explanation then and later was that he was "an independent," essentially fighting his own personal war. Placed in command of a company whose captain had fallen, though in reality there had been no action yet, he fought in the skirmish at Blackburn's Ford on July 18, 1861. Miraculously, he awoke the next morning more than forty miles from where he had bedded down to join the army of General Joseph E. Johnston for its march . . . back to Manassas. He fought in the great battle on July 21, but the battlefield is unrecognizable from Lauretta's description. Then he "attached" himself to Brigadier General Barnard E. Bee in time to hear Bee bestow an immortal sobriquet on Brigadier General Thomas J. Jackson. After the battle Buford spent some time with the 5th and 8th Louisiana Infantries, then left for Richmond.[11]

Two months passed, and then suddenly Buford had a pass to go west and stopped at Lynchburg on the way. Now Lauretta's story intersected with her Mary Ann Keith story, though she changed it in every respect. Keith had not claimed to have fought at Manassas or even in Virginia that summer, but Lauretta now had Buford taking a side trip to Leesburg for some time and then participating in the Battle of Ball's Bluff on October 21, whereas Lauretta as Keith was really going back and forth from Lynchburg to Richmond and spent several days in jail. Keith left Lynchburg on a train for Tennessee a week before Ball's Bluff, which action Lauretta now misdated.[12]

To fill the blank space in her known movements from late October until April 1862, she devoted several chapters to a spying mission to the North and then a trip west to Columbus, Kentucky, to offer her services to Brigadier General Lucius M. Polk. He assigned her to a—nonexistent—"detective corps" and put her to work as a military conductor examining passports on the railroad. Then she raised the matter of that "most scandalous false charge" made against her to General Polk, as she lit another backfire to counter rumors and accusations. What she did or heard said against her at Columbus is lost, if in fact she was ever there, but now her refutation was on record.[13]

Soon Lieutenant Buford took part in the defense of Fort Donelson, and after its surrender she tended Confederate wounded. At that point, of course, they were all in Union hands, yet miraculously she nursed them without becoming a prisoner. A page later she was free and on her way to join the Army of Tennessee under General Albert Sidney Johnston, who immediately put her in another nonexistent "detective corps," but in a subsequent unnamed skirmish she took a painful wound in her foot and left the army for New Orleans to recuperate.

It was there that her new narrative again intersected with a published record she could not change, forcing her to adapt her story around the facts. She had appeared at the mayor's office on April 23 to surrender. Now she muddled the chronology to suit her story. People suspected something amiss with soldier Buford on his crutch, she claimed, and the provost arrested her on suspicion of being a spy. She talked her way out of that only to be arrested again the next day, this time on suspicion of being a woman, though dressing as a man was not in fact a crime in the city. Only then did she appear before Mayor Monroe, who ordered her to admit her masquerade and dress as a woman. Sticking to the claim of being Harry Buford, Lauretta refused, and Monroe sent her to prison until she changed her mind. The next day a reporter did come to see her, though now she did not identify him as being from the *Daily True Delta*. Claiming that he wanted to write "a sensational article for the paper," she added that "this sort of thing did not increase my amiability." Hence she told the man very little, and indeed the article that actually did appear was barely a paragraph.

Deciding at last that admitting her sex would be the fastest way to get free, Lauretta sent a note to Monroe with her confession, though it cost a fine of $10 and an additional ten days in jail. Once again her chronology collapsed as she skated over events. Being arrested on April 23 and held for at least two days before admitting her gender would mean her additional ten-day sentence would have had her released on May 5 at the earliest, by which time New Orleans was completely under Union occupation. Yet her next claim was that on leaving the parish prison dressed as a woman, she went to a *Confederate* recruiting station on Jefferson Street and enlisted as a private in Captain B. Moses's company of the 21st Louisiana Infantry, with which she soon left for Fort Pillow.[14]

At this point Lauretta launched into the most critical episode of her entire memoir regarding establishing her service in the field as a man at any time during the war, for this was the only period for which any Confederate officer or soldier claimed eyewitness knowledge of Harry Buford in the ranks or of Lauretta being Buford.

Her evidence rested on the testimonials in that four-page leaflet promoting the book. It brimmed with hyperbole: "the most intensely interesting war book ever published," it said, written by "the most remarkable woman of the day."[15] The leaflet offered five statements about her service as Buford, all consonant with Lauretta's old technique of massaging letters from important men into evidence of more than they said.[16] First Brigadier General George Anderson of Atlanta attested that Velasquez "is the person known during the late war between the South and North as Lieut. Harry T. Buford." It was a meaningless acknowledgment that she was Buford, which was common knowledge, but said nothing of knowing Buford during the war or of witnessing any of her presumed activities. Dr. Lorme McLeod of Atlanta, a supposed Confederate colonel who himself defied efforts at identification, said he found her descriptions of the far West "true and life-like" and attested that she was "a lady of unsullied character, and of acknowledged ability." Once again, it was a meaningless endorsement so far as Buford was concerned. George W. Alexander did assert that she was "well known to me during the late war," as she certainly was when a prisoner at Castle Thunder in July 1863, but beyond that said only that he knew she was Buford. Yet again, there was no confirmation of her claims of service in the army.[17]

The remaining testimonials seemed to say more at first glance. Signing himself "J. F. Hammond, M.D., Asst. Surgeon Empire Hospital," the first testified that "no one knew Madame Laureta Juaneta Velasquez under her assumed *pseudonym* (Lieut. Harry T. Buford) better than I did" and added that he "knew much of her history, especially that part which relates to the field service." He even stated specifically that she was admitted to his hospital on July 26, 1863, "suffering at the time from a wound," and that he attended her wedding to DeCaulp, who was another of his patients. Thus Hammond confirmed two very specific details of her narrative, making him the only verifiable wartime witness to her being Buford, her wounding in battle, and her marriage.

Unfortunately, he was not all that he seemed. Joel F. Hammond enlisted as a private at age twenty-four in the 35th Georgia Infantry in 1861. He may have had some medical schooling, for by March 1862 he was detached as a nurse in Richmond, then that October was detailed as a nurse and steward to Atlanta's Empire Hotel Hospital. His duties included procuring milk, butter, chickens and eggs for the patients; overseeing preparation of meals; dispensing medicines; and applying bandages and dressings. When he was made master of a hospital ward on October 13, 1863, his responsibilities would also have expanded to general supervisory functions to oversee lighting, heat, and ventilation, though by that time Thomas and Lauretta were both gone from Atlanta. However, he definitely was not a doctor, let alone assistant surgeon, as he styled himself in 1875.[18]

As herself, Lauretta passed through the city briefly on one occasion prior to July 1863, so he could have known of her from the newspapers at the time and what she subsequently told him, though in 1863 neither he nor anyone else knew her as Velasquez, an alias she had not yet invented. Hammond further compromised his statement by saying she was admitted to his hospital on July 26, 1863. That he would have a precise recollection of the admission date of one out of hundreds, or even thousands, of patients who passed through his ward strains credulity. The only reasonable explanation is that she furnished him the date when she wrote him in 1875 to request a testimonial. His statement suffers further from the fact that, by all of Lauretta's accounts, fifteen months had passed since her supposed Shiloh wounding when she arrived in Atlanta on July 20, 1863. She was "sent" to Atlanta, she wrote, because she had "severely hurt the foot which had been wounded at Fort Donelson."[19] However, her actions there, and her letter to Adjutant General Cooper, suggested nothing of a wound or ill health, a claim further undermined by the fact that she remained in the city only about ten days before leaving for Montgomery. (In her book she said she had been behind enemy lines at Martinsburg, West Virginia, then made her way to Chattanooga, crossed the lines, and rode south on horseback to Dalton, Georgia, and from thence went to Atlanta presumably by train, all of which was a fiction.) In mentioning that "wound," Hammond merely parroted what Lauretta told him in 1875.

Even more suspect is his statement that "her work is founded on facts," given that "her work" may not have been in print yet when he provided his testimonial. If she did show him any of the book in advance, he might have read in it her statement that "Dr. Hammond is still living, and I am glad of such an opportunity as this of testifying to his noble qualities."[20] Perhaps one good testimonial deserved another. Hammond also said that Thomas DeCaulp had been a patient of his and that he had witnessed their marriage at the "Thompson Hotel." There was no such hotel in 1863, but the Atlanta Hotel had been operated by Dr. Joseph Thompson until May of that year.[21] Hammond closed by saying he knew Lauretta's character, giving his oath that she was "above suspicion" and that "her conduct was that of a brave soldier, whose life was at the disposal of home and country."[22] Yet Hammond could have seen or known nothing firsthand of what she did or did not do in the field. He knew only what he read in the press and what she told him.

That last was particularly important in light of Hammond's postwar career. When he wrote the testimonial, he was a physician in Atlanta practicing "eclectic Medicine," essentially herbalism mixed with physical therapy. Some years later he was embroiled in an embarrassing public scandal when he rented space in his practice to a charlatan practicing quack remedies, even though he believed the man was insane. Worse, at the fellow's request, Hammond wrote a testimonial for wide distribution endorsing the man and recommending people to use him. As Hammond later admitted, he provided the endorsement in return for $250, "for the use of my name and influence." In short, Hammond was willing to sell testimonials. That and the clear influence of information supplied by Lauretta seriously undercut his reliability.[23]

Only the final testimonial appeared to confirm eyewitness observation of Lauretta serving in the field as Buford. John Newman, formerly major of the 21st Louisiana Infantry, stated that "Madame L. J. Velasquez is a lady of the most unblemished character," that he had known her for thirteen years, and that "she has served under me with distinction as a soldier, for three months, and was afterwards promoted for her great efficiency and integrity to the position of 1st Lieutenant in the Confederate Service." That said, he concluded by adding, "I therefore take great pride in recommending her to parties to whom her services may be available."[24]

Immediately apparent is that this was not written to endorse her book, which was not yet published and of which he said nothing. This was a personal recommendation, and the fact that he spoke of her as Velasquez—assuming that is what he originally wrote and she did not change it for publication—dated his statement to sometime after April 1875, when she adopted her new alias. That put his acquaintance with her sometime in early 1862. It may or may not be remarkable that even after so many years he could recall one soldier specifically or that said soldier had been under him for three months. It has the sound of Newman confirming a statement made to him in a prior communication, typical of Lauretta's prompting people to "remember" things that she told them and soliciting their confirmation in reply. It was the same technique she had tried with Clemens, who declined to remember meetings he knew they never had. In a few months she would try it again with another old Confederate, Colonel William L. DeRosset, formerly of the 3rd North Carolina Infantry. Passing through his town, she sent him a note. "I would be pleased to see you if convenient upon receipt of this," she told him, adding that she had "not had the pleasure of seeing you since 1862 at Richmond."[25]

There is no evidence that she set foot in Virginia at any time between October 1861 and June 1863, and her own book implied that she left Virginia in November 1861 and did not return again until 1862 was long past.[26] Then she added a teaser, telling DeRosset that when they met, "you will be some what surprised." It is not difficult to surmise the promised revelation, for several times before this, she had "surprised" men who supposedly knew her—or knew of her—as Buford by revealing her real gender and identity. She could simply claim to have met him in Richmond in her guise as Buford and count on him not to let the absence of any such recollection keep him from doing the gentlemanly thing and pretending to remember, and then confirm it by saying so in writing. Thus she would have yet another testimonial. DeRosset was not to be duped, however. He pasted her note inside the cover of a copy of her book with this annotation: "I must say that I have not the slightest recollection of ever having seen the 'Lieutenant' before and it is at least probable, if I had, I would not have forgotten it."[27]

That is probably how Lauretta got the statement from Major Newman. The context of her own narrative places her alleged enlistment in April 1862, though it certainly was not after the fall of New Orleans to the Yankees. In fact, in February and March Newman had been advertising in the local press, offering a $50 bounty for ten to fifteen men to fill out his Company D of the 21st Louisiana. However, his recruiting office was on Customs House Street, not Jefferson, and Captain Moses was not involved, having a different company of his own.[28] In any case, of the 202 men known to have served in their two companies, almost all enlisted in July–September 1861.

Only four men signed the rolls in 1862, two in March and two in April, the latest being April 12. Three of them were German, whereas during the war Lauretta claimed no foreign identity other than that of a British national, and none signed on as Buford. Moreover, the company was disbanded with the rest of the regiment on July 15 due to crippling desertions.[29]

That established the latest limit for any time she might have served under Newman, and thus her alleged three months had to have fallen between April and mid-July 1862. She was certainly in New Orleans as late as April 25 when released from the parish prison, so even if she went immediately to Newman's regiment, she could not have been with him more than about eleven weeks. In her book Lauretta reduced Newman's three months to what she called a "short time," then further compromised Newman's statement by asserting that she did not relish serving in his regiment as an enlisted man and quickly obtained a transfer to East Tennessee. "The officers and men of the regiment, of course, knew nothing," she claimed, "of my previous history."[30] Then she left them, her entire account of serving with the 21st Louisiana occupying just two brief paragraphs, with not one anecdote or detail and not a single mention of Major Newman, who was, and remains, the sole authority for Lauretta as Harry Buford ever being with Confederates in the field anywhere. His comment about her subsequently being promoted to first lieutenant in reward for her services clearly repeated what he read of her in the press during or after the war, for nowhere in *The Woman in Battle* did Lauretta make such a claim, averring only that she had a commission to enlist volunteers in 1861, long before she ever encountered Newman. Meanwhile, placing her at any time with Newman's regiment in the summer of 1862 conflicts directly with her own statement to the Charity Hospital registrar that from late April through the end of October 1862 she did not leave New Orleans, a statement circumstantially supported by others at the time.

She invented her service under Newman and manipulated him into confirming it in order to fill otherwise unaccounted for time after the fall of New Orleans, ignoring her earlier accounts of being a mail runner and smuggler for the Confederacy in those months. According to her April 1862 statement, she was in New Orleans in February, and thus she could have been hanging around Newman's company as it formed before going to Fort Pillow, just as she resided with the 13th Connecticut that fall. Newman might have remembered her from that period or from her claims published in the press at the time.[31] Or else she invented the entire story, including Newman's affidavit, or maneuvered him into his testimonial. In *The Woman in Battle* she referred to his and the other statements, claiming that "some of the most distinguished officers of the Confederate army, and many equally distinguished civilians, can and will testify to the truthfulness of the story I am about to relate."[32] They had done no such thing.

There followed an account of her involvement at Shiloh, of her chance to kill General Grant, of being wounded during a skirmish on April 9 when an exploding shell dislocated her right shoulder and lacerated her arm and a finger, and of her wounds leading to the discovery of her sex by a surgeon who sent her to New Orleans to recuperate.[33] In fact there was no artillery skirmishing between the Shiloh armies on April 9. Continuing her chronological confusion, she stayed in New Orleans until its fall in late April, and then spent fifty pages spinning a fictional tale of smuggling drugs into the city and information out of it and running the blockade to Havana, all of this during the only period when she could have served with Newman if there had been any truth in his statement. Then she ran afoul of the Union occupation commander, Major General Benjamin F. Butler, who had her imprisoned. Her six months in the parish prison did not figure in *The Woman in Battle*, and neither did her expulsion from the city in May 1863. Instead, she claimed that a fisherman took her across Lake Pontchartrain and to reach Jackson.

Lauretta then provided an "eyewitness" account of the burning of the city's Bowman House Hotel and her escape from the blaze on June 17, though she had actually left Jackson two days earlier. Whereas authorities arrested her in Mobile on suspicion of being a spy and sent her to Richmond, now she wrote that she went there on her own. Then General Winder supposedly made her a special agent and ordered her back to the West; in fact she left for Atlanta with no official duty at all. There followed several pages of nonsense about being arrested and confined in Lynchburg before she could return to Richmond, and then it was suddenly September 1863 and she tried to join General Longstreet and his corps on their way to help Braxton Bragg face a Yankee army at Chickamauga. Then she set out on a trip through the Federal lines that, though fictional, contained elements mirroring her crossing the lines to Memphis in October.[34]

Only then, months out of sequence, did she detail her courtship with DeCaulp. She neatly disposed of his desertion and service in the Union army by having him die in a Federal hospital shortly after being captured just three weeks after their marriage. She added that he had a brother, also a captain in the Confederate army, who died in Nashville just after the end of the war. She created this fictional Captain DeCaulp as a foil in case word leaked out in 1876 that her husband had deserted or equally in case people learned of Thomas's other wife and child in Arkansas. Should such a problem arise, she could claim confusion of her Confederate hero with his brother. After that, Lauretta said she returned to Richmond, then went on another spy mission to the West, and she gave an account of her passage through the lines to Memphis that echoed her actual experience.[35]

Her narrative covering the rest of the war is muddled and confused, all but impossible to pin down chronologically and mostly fiction. She claimed that as of the summer of 1863 her identity as Buford was still undiscovered, ignoring the fact that it had been in the press across the Confederacy from late 1861 onward. Nevertheless she set Harry Buford aside and went North in female garb "with my womanly reputation unblemished by even a suspicion of impropriety." She briefly covered her time at the Indianapolis Arsenal but placed it a year too late, and she launched into her extended supposed relations with Colonel Lafayette C. Baker, a special provost marshal for the War Department whose deceptions matched Lauretta's.[36] She gave more personal background on Baker than on any other person in her narrative, but it was all readily available in Baker's own book, *History of the United States Secret Service*, which came out in 1867, most of which could also be found in *The Secret Service in the Late War*, a shorter posthumous version published in 1874.[37] Much of the balance of her account of spying for and against Baker she based loosely on his memoirs.

She completely omitted everything in her experience from January through August 1864, instead inventing Baker sending her on a trip to Richmond as a spy, after which she went to Canada as part of the plans behind the Northwest Conspiracy. She then gave a confused tangle of lurid inventions that included Baker actually assigning her to find herself. Nothing in her war account thereafter can be corroborated. She supposedly commenced a career of blockade running, getting supplies purchased in Philadelphia by boat to Cuba and then running them into the Confederacy. She claimed that she was in St. Thomas when the Confederate commerce raider CSS *Florida* came into port, but the *Florida* did not put into St Thomas at any time in 1864.[38] The notion that a Confederate government that had declined to employ her in any prior capacity would now entrust her with considerable sums of money as a purchasing agent overburdens credulity.

The bulk of her narrative covering the actual period from late 1863 through the end of the war is wholly invented. Whereas the narrative covering the

1861–63 period offered some dates and references subject to corroboration, this next portion is characterized by a complete absence of dates putting her in particular places at specific times, a hopeless jumbling of chronology even worse than in the earlier chapters.

The three chapters giving an account of her work for Baker typify her method of creating a story in the absence of one. She implied that she arrived in New York in late September 1864 and launched into a career of encouraging men to enlist in the Union army in return for cash bounties, and then deserting to repeat the process, while she also worked with "substitute brokers," who sold drafted men forged enlistment papers naming often nonexistent men willing to go into the army as substitutes in return for payments, all of which the brokers themselves kept. She paraphrased the whole account from four chapters in Baker's 1874 book.[39] There was word-for-word plagiarism, and her dependence on Baker is unmistakable.[40] His description of his means of gathering evidence is mirrored precisely in her narrative, even to the mention of Baker disguising himself as a bounty jumper to call on a corrupt recruiter.[41] Her only original additions were some anecdotal bits that do not admit of corroboration.

Among the most fantastic claims in *The Woman in Battle* is her account of obtaining electrotype copies of the printing plates for new $100 Treasury notes, already known as "greenbacks," then using them to print millions of dollars in counterfeit notes to buy materiel for the Confederacy and fund its agents in the North, herself included. She got them by blackmailing an unnamed victim easily identified as Spencer M. Clark, chief of the Bank Note Printing Bureau, boasting, "It is impossible for me to give any idea of the enormous amount of the kind of counterfeiting that was done."[42] The wartime press had carried more than enough stories on counterfeiting operations for Lauretta to compile a fiction involving millions.[43] Baker's 1867 book gave in just five pages all of the detail needed. Moreover, all of this took place when Lauretta was in Milwaukee, and the government's own investigation and settlement of the counterfeiting scandal concluded by July 31, 1864, when she was still under arrest in Nashville.[44] She could not have been in Washington or Philadelphia, and no hint of any such Confederate counterfeiting enterprise in the North ever emerged then or later.[45]

In another aspect of her alleged work for Baker, she did mention Clark. He made a convenient foil, since he had been in the national news for another sort of scandal when he and G. A. Henderson, chief clerk of the Treasury Department's Warrant Bureau, carried on illicit affairs in 1863 and into 1864 with female Treasury employees, sometimes at their office. According to Lauretta, Baker pointed out to her the women involved sometime prior to December 1863, but the clandestine trysts actually occurred from September 1863 onward, and she was in Atlanta, Memphis, and Indianapolis during that entire period.[46] Meanwhile, everything in the scandal that came out during the subsequent investigation occurred while she was demonstrably in Milwaukee, then Minneapolis, and finally Nashville. No wonder that in her account of the story, which according to her happened while she was in Washington working for Baker, she is entirely absent as either participant or witness, though she represents herself as knowing all about it firsthand. "I know that the men were guilty of the offenses with which they were charged by Baker," she wrote, "for I was one of their associates."[47]

In fact, her account of the Clark-Henderson scandal, like her story of the bounty and substitute frauds, contains nothing she could not have found in published form in 1875, when her book was being compiled. Everything she wrote about the Treasury scandal appeared in a published House of Representatives report that in her book she claimed to have read.[48] Whether she actually did or not, its influence on her account is clear.[49]

Her whole handling of the Baker episodes is a template for her approach to creating a story. When writing of actual events and places, she mixed up chronology, changed facts, and ignored the unflattering, but she still gave a framework that was in some degree genuine. In dealing with a period like 1864–65, when nothing of use really happened, she resorted to gossamer invention or claimed that she provided no details because it would make her book longer "without adding to its interest," saying merely, "I was coming and going constantly." In early 1865 she placed herself in New York, supposedly collecting money for a Union soldiers' aid society, which she claimed she actually sent to what she called the Southern Relief Fund, an obvious reworking of her 1874 story about collecting $780 from the sailors of the nonexistent Commodore Brissel's fleet. Then she went to London on Confederate business and was just entering New York Harbor on her return on April 10 when she got the news that Robert E. Lee had surrendered.

Unwilling to give up hope, she went to Missouri, shifting to the end of the war her August 1874 claim to have served with Quantrill in late 1861, taking secret papers to him and consulting other agents on continuing resistance. In fact, Quantrill—whom she promoted to general—was then in hiding in Kentucky. Then she went to Columbus, Ohio, by context placing her arrival on April 14. She slept well that night, she said, "on account of a

Confederate victory of which I had heard," though she must have been the only person to hear of it, for the South had no victories in the days after Appomattox.[50] In the morning she learned of the assassination of Lincoln.

Returning to Washington at once to confer with fellow Confederate agents, she agreed to make one more trip west but said nothing of its purpose or where she went. She stopped again in Columbus on her return while Lincoln's body lay in state there, dating her supposed arrival to April 29. Soon Baker gave her one last job, finding a female Confederate agent then operating in the North. According to Lauretta, for the second time Baker assigned her to find herself. In a book filled with repetitive and unimaginative melodramas about fooling every Yankee, it was by far her best plot twist.[51] Instead, she claimed, she went to New York to meet her brother and they sailed for Europe to put the war, the Confederacy, and her career as a spy behind them.

The final eight chapters of *The Woman in Battle*, covering her life after the war, contain more genuine recollection of actual events and experiences, and less invention, than all the rest combined. The chronic problem with chronology remained, and so did the motives for her to omit or misshape certain episodes, but in the main she presented a fair representation in broad compass. Her inventions included tours of Europe and the late Confederacy to gauge its condition, and thereafter she said she traveled to Charlotte and Columbia, then Charleston, Atlanta, and finally to New Orleans, the reverse order of the tour she really did make in 1866. She skipped over the last five months of 1865, on which her actual record remains silent, and then appeared in New Orleans for her version of the Venezuelan emigration scheme, maintaining that she went on the expedition to protect the interests of innocent colonists who might be taken in. She acknowledged marrying Wasson, then dismissed him with a passing mention of his death as impersonal as her brief accounts of the deaths of William and DeCaulp.

Leaving Venezuela, she said, she then visited Havana. Given her recent claim of attempting to enlist with Cuban revolutionaries, it is peculiar that she said nothing of the uprising against Spain, while instead saying she was quite friendly with Spanish military authorities, particularly General Joaquin Manzana.[52] On reaching New York she left immediately for the West, and though her subsequent account in *The Woman in Battle* is a chronological mess, she gave a somewhat accurate story of her travels, with notable exceptions. She covered her marriage but never mentioned Bonner by name, no doubt wary of readers connecting him with Adam Wilson's

1875 revelations, and portrayed her husband as gold hungry and neglectful, setting another backfire to explain her frequent absences and further discredit the Wilson letter.

The book ended with an account of her stagecoach trip across the Southwest and abruptly closed with her heading for the Concho and the station run by A. J. Bobo, of whom she wrote not a syllable. "This journey," she concluded, "was the last of my adventures that is likely to be of interest to the majority of readers." She left it to her readers to decide whether her story had been worth telling. "I did what I thought to be right," she went on, "and, while anxious for the good opinion of all honorable and right-thinking people, a consciousness of the purity of my motives will be an ample protection against the censure of those who may be disposed to censure."[53]

It was a remarkable work, not for its writing or believability, though it presented good and sometimes vivid descriptions of characters such as Benjamin F. Butler and Lafayette C. Baker and effectively told anecdotal material. Truly arresting was the fact that she cavalierly contradicted almost everything she had said about her life from her first appearance in print as Mary Ann Keith fifteen years earlier. Setting aside obvious cover-ups like DeCaulp's desertion or her imprisonment for larceny, it seems incredible that she overlooked at least the more glaring inconsistencies among her several accounts. Worthington cannot be blamed, for that inconsistency hallmarked all of her statements from the beginning, whereas her editor—if she actually had one—was involved only in *The Woman in Battle*. Even though she had learned that some of her older fictions could haunt her, she went on contradicting herself. It is hard to dismiss her as unconcerned, for her clear revision of some facts to obscure embarrassing episodes argues otherwise.

Lauretta demonstrated yet again classic traits of the female confidence artist. Her book came from the same mold as other fictional female memoirs, but hers was bolder. She completely concealed her real self behind her creation, for an accurate autobiography would have presented her as a woman no sane person would trust or believe. She delighted in flouting conventional ideas about womanly behavior. She also employed humor rather skillfully, adding to the appeal then common in sensational novels. It was all like playing a game, especially her episodes as the "trickster," as when she fooled Baker.[54] Indeed, she revealed more than once a certain contempt for men. "Women have the reputation of being bad secret-keepers," she wrote in passing. Lauretta always succeeded in keeping hers, she averred, adding, "I have always found it more difficult to beguile women than men into telling me what I wanted to know." When it came to clandestine work, she declared that "women are, out of all comparison, superior to men."[55]

On a broader canvas, she revealed the con artist's contempt for her "audience," an assumption that she could make anyone believe anything by using her femininity and gift of gab to explain her way out of any difficulty. In her life to date, as now in her book, her solution when caught in a lie was to tell an even bigger one, counting on the gullibility of others. In a blatant echo of her attempt to imply collaboration with Mark Twain, she even titled one of her chapters "Roughing It." If her life prior to 1876 demonstrated the instincts and predilections of a classic con artist, *The Woman in Battle* confirmed it on a six-hundred-page scale.

Remaining to be seen now was how far she could take those skills, and just how far they might take her.

CHAPTER THIRTEEN
EMBATTLED WOMAN

FINALLY IN LATE July 1876 *The Woman in Battle* began delivery to subscription agents for their customers and the newspaper press for review.[1] Meanwhile, Lauretta and Ramsay had fallen out, almost violently, and for a time she really was a woman in battle. She deposited two proof copies of the book with the Library of Congress on March 3 and one week later registered her claim for copyright in the title *The Woman in Battle*, listing herself as "author & proprietor" rather than just as author.[2] Three days earlier in Atlanta she swore out a warrant against Ramsay, charging him with fraud. Since signing their contract in the spring of 1875, he had given her one date after another for publication but always postponed. Soon enough she knew why he missed press dates, and now she charged him with misrepresenting his assets and abilities. His failure to publish when promised voided their contract, she contended, and all rights to the book belonged to her.

Ramsay pleaded that all the suits against him had caused delays, but in good faith he had done the best he could. Then he blamed delay on having to deal at long distance with the Philadelphia editor Lauretta engaged.[3] Concluding that Ramsay demonstrated no intent to deceive, the judge dismissed the warrant.[4] The litigants met to discuss Lauretta buying back the rights to sell the book but could not agree on a figure, and it seems unlikely that she had enough cash in any case. Notwithstanding, on March 26 she published a notice in the *Daily Constitution* that Ramsay and his nearly defunct Southern Publishing Company no longer had any right to grant agencies to sell *The Woman in Battle*.[5] Henceforth, all parties interested in buying copies or becoming agents for its sale must come directly to her at her Marietta Street address.[6] Two weeks later, on April 9, Ramsay published his own notice that he still owned the rights and that she had not yet come to terms. Should they finally agree on a purchase, he would notify the public.[7]

The next day, Monday, April 10, they encountered each other by chance on Marietta Street. Incensed by his exposure of her false claim of exclusive rights just the day before, she loudly abused him for it, waving her arms wildly with clenched fists. Then she hit him under the eye, knocked his hat from his head, and felled him to the gutter, after which she drew a small knife from her purse. Yelling, "Murder! Police!" Ramsay got to his feet and ran away, with Lauretta running after him and laughing at his flight until a policeman stopped her. When he let her go, she left in high spirits. "Poor fellow!" wrote one reporter of Ramsay. "He has apparently read Madam's adventures in 'The Woman in Battle' to such good effect that he has imbibed a holy terror of her prowess." A journalist quipped that Lauretta should write a new book titled "A Woman in a Street Fight."[8]

The first printing of *The Woman in Battle* appeared under the imprint of Dustin, Gilman & Co. of Richmond. Perhaps Ramsay entered a joint venture with them or Lauretta finally recovered the rights and placed it herself. Reviews soon appeared, and thanks to the publicity Lauretta had attracted during her 1866 and 1874 tours, the press and readers readily received the book. The Atlanta *Daily Constitution*, noting that but for a series of reverses the book "would have been published several years ago," said that "it is rather a readable book," going on to say that the author's services to the Confederacy—which it did not question—ought to entitle her to a good sale.[9] Certainly she needed a good sale, for she had not lied when she said she wrote the book for money. Early in May 1876 she unsuccessfully applied to the Tax Committee of Atlanta's General Council for permission to hold a "gift concert," with herself as beneficiary.[10]

More reviews followed, first in Georgia, then across the South, and they continued to appear sporadically for two years, while Lauretta placed advertisements in dozens of Southern newspapers. In the main the reviews were complimentary. Her story of unreconstructed heroism and making fools of the Yankees appealed to Confederates anxious to salvage pride from defeat. Moreover, her elastic approach to history and autobiography were not excessively wide of the norm among other current memoirs, notably Sarah Edmonds's *Nurse and Spy in the Union Army*, an account by a woman who unquestionably did pass for a soldier, and the only other such book-length work.

Like the *Daily Constitution*'s, other reviews were good but rather tepid. Everyone remembered the stories about Lieutenant Harry Buford, and some reviewers felt the new work did not live up to the subject. "Much of the book is tame," said one, the narrative simple and straightforward but too detailed, though he added the backhanded compliment that "female readers will be pleased with it."[11] Recalling that "absurdly exaggerated" stories had been told about Buford, another reviewer averred that some Southerners simply

THE WOMAN IN BATTLE:

A NARRATIVE OF THE

Exploits, Adventures, and Travels

OF

MADAME LORETA JANETA VELAZQUEZ,

OTHERWISE KNOWN AS

LIEUTENANT HARRY T. BUFORD,

CONFEDERATE STATES ARMY.

IN WHICH IS GIVEN

Full Descriptions of the numerous Battles in which she participated as a Confederate Officer; of her Perilous Performances as a Spy, as a Bearer of Despatches, as a Secret-Service Agent, and as a Blockade-Runner; of her Adventures Behind the Scenes at Washington, including the Bond Swindle; of her Career as a Bounty and Substitute Broker in New York; of her Travels in Europe and South America; her Mining Adventures on the Pacific Slope; her Residence among the Mormons; her Love Affairs, Courtships, Marriages, &c., &c.

EDITED BY

C. J. WORTHINGTON,

LATE OF THE UNITED STATES NAVY.

Command the trumpets of the war to sound!
This stillness doth perplex and harass me;
An inward impulse drives me from repose,
It still impels me to achieve my work.
SCHILLER — *The Maid of Orleans.*

PROFUSELY ILLUSTRATED.

HARTFORD:
T. BELKNAP.
1876.

Title page of Lauretta's book, which appeared in 1876: a milestone but not the end of her historical journey. *The Woman in Battle.*

refused to believe there ever was such a person. Still, *The Woman in Battle* "is a volume of romantic interest," he concluded, "written in that fascinating style that never fails to enlist the deepest interest." He believed, however, that a reader "can with difficulty persuade himself that the story is real, and not a wild creation of fantasy."[12] In Salt Lake City, local press mentioned that "the madame, who acquired considerable notoriety by her adventures and exploits while serving in the confederate army, spent some time in Utah a few years ago," though it did not connect her with the miner's wife Lauretta Bonner.[13]

Reviewers in North Carolina proved more effusive, perhaps because Lauretta moved to Raleigh to promote the book. "It has been promised to the public a long time and has come at last," declared one, calling it "an autobiography of a most adventurous woman" that "the reader of a few pages will not willingly lay it down."[14] Another Tar Heel reviewer called it "a pleasant and animated personal narrative that thrills the reader," adding that after Lauretta won a reputation as "Lieut. Harry Bufford," her "name alone is sufficient to arrest the attention."[15]

The first real rave came at the end of the year. "Madame Velasquez can wield the pen as well as the sword," said the Raleigh *Observer*. "Written in a peculiar, trenchant, facile and attractive style," the book was superior to other recent writings by women because it was unpretentious and easy to read. "Her finesse, singleness of purpose, heroism and patriotism can best be admired among all the intelligent people North and South," gushed the reviewer, who welcomed the "first reliable *exposé*" of the Confederate secret service in operation. "It is no wishy-washy, sensational tale, but real matters-of-fact alone, told in an able and eloquent manner, in simple, pure, chaste and elegant language." He went on to declare that "in her rare elements of character are concentrated, quickness of perception, love of glory and country, true courage and chivalry, love of danger and the finesse necessary to self-preservation." Madame Velasquez was a "truly remarkable woman."[16] Another Raleigh paper was equally enthusiastic, calling it "one of the most remarkable books of the age."[17]

Lauretta knew how much of her wartime account was invention, so a prime concern was how former Confederates received the work, since many might know enough to catch her in falsehoods. The new magazine *Southern Historical Society Papers* was the first hurdle. It began publication that same year and quickly became the journal of record for the Confederate side of the war. In the October 1876 issue editor John William Jones struck at the heart of her problem. *The Woman in Battle* was interesting, but "how far it can be received as *history*, is altogether another question." He asked how it was possible for Buford to be fighting at Blackburn's Ford on July 18, 1861, and yet the next morning to be forty miles east with the reinforcement coming to Manassas. Jones wondered how Buford could "be at so many battles fought by the different armies in different sections of the country—or how he managed to accomplish various other physical impossibilities."[18] Jones's restrained condemnation did not dismiss the book as a humbug, for that would be ungentlemanly, and Lauretta knew that she could hide her real self and her book behind the womanly ideal that Southern male culture preferred.[19] Hence Jones concluded with the anodyne comment that "we can only say that it is a very *readable* book, and would serve well to while away a winter's evening."[20]

He was the first, but certainly not the last, to spot the essential weaknesses of *The Woman in Battle*. The narrative strained credulity until it snapped under scrutiny. Even casually knowledgeable readers could see the problems. A poor notice in the *Southern Historical Society Papers*, even one as genteel as Jones's, risked compromising sales. Lauretta confronted Jones directly, and in her typical fashion she skirted the issues he raised, writing him that "the work was not intended as a history of the late war between the states," a response to a criticism he had not made. She dodged his query about putting herself in two places at once with a diversion to the question of who really held overall command at First Manassas, Johnston or Beauregard, yet another matter that Jones had not challenged. Recklessly, she built her response on a statement she claimed was on page 98 of her book, when no such statement appeared there. It was her old "big lie" bluff.

Two weeks later she wrote to Jones again, complaining, "Your notice is unfair and unjust to me and I would ask you to reconsider the matter." She asked him to cite instances of the "physical impossibilities" he mentioned, promising "it will afford me much pleasure to give you a satisfactory solution of what appears to you as a 'physical impossibility,'" still ignoring the instance he already had pointed out. As if it would make up for the book's problems, she repeatedly offered to send copies of her growing collection of "testimonials" from prominent former Confederates.[21] Jones did not pursue the matter, and that ended the business of the *Southern Historical Society Papers*.

With the book out, she attended to selling more. For several weeks she stayed in Atlanta personally soliciting sales, and then announced that she would tour the South seeking subscribers.[22] The new Madame Velasquez had kept busy selling advertising for Ramsay's forthcoming directory until their break, meanwhile assaying to make good her earlier claims to be a newspaper reporter. Early in 1876 she began attending the debates in the Georgia state house, probably for Ramsay's *Sunny South*, and was frequently seen in the capitol with notebook in hand. A colleague referred to her as one of "our fair reporters," marveling that "she can write *three* kinds of short hand."

She seemingly expanded her horizons of interest, as befit a newswoman, and began talking spiritedly about the so-called "Great War" for Cuban liberation that had started in 1868 and was just then petering out as Spain finally quashed the insurgents. Moreover, that February Atlantans heard a rumor that she was soon to marry a titled officer in the insurgent army, a rumor she likely started herself to give cachet to her claim to be Cuban.[23] This interest in Cuban affairs was sudden. She had only added the island to her list of claimed birthplaces sixteen months earlier, and even then she still represented her parents as being the Clapps of Mississippi. She traded them for Hispanic parents with the appearance of her book several months after she took up the Cuban struggle. Stranger still, after having gone on record in February as a supporter of the Cuban insurrection, she said not a syllable about it in *The Woman in Battle* five months later.[24]

Though she did not name her latest set of parents, she made it clear that her father had been a native of Spain and a military and administrative official in Cuba. In short, she claimed to come from the same ruling elite that her newly—and briefly—adopted revolutionaries now battled. She never gave an explanation for this sudden and contradictory empathy for the insurrection, though she rarely did anything without a motive founded on self-interest. Most likely it was to bolster her new identity as a Cuban, to sell more books by capitalizing on widespread empathy for the insurgents in the United States, and perhaps to advance her journalistic ambition by making herself a presumed authority on a topic of current public interest. This interest in Cuban freedom would wax and wane over the next two decades, with no discernible logic. In fact, she showed more interest in Cuban annexation by the United States than in its independence.

Her Cuban concerns reflected a hitherto unseen—and inconsistent—side to her personality. In February 1876 she also attempted to add social reformer to her growing portfolio. Postwar Georgia leased convicts to railroads and other labor-based enterprises to make the state money rather than spend it building a prison. The program commenced in 1868, and there were immediate complaints of inhumane treatment. A year later employers were found guilty of overworking, beating, whipping, and even murdering prisoners. Conditions improved briefly in 1870, and then regressed, and by 1873 fully one-tenth of the leased convicts either escaped or died. The next year 26 out of 39 at one mine died, and in 1876 at least 174 were lost. Early that year the legislature authorized new contracts to lease prisoners for up to twenty years, with the promise of as much as half a million dollars for state coffers, but as the program became more profitable, contractors worked laborers all the harder, while the abuses accelerated.[25]

Into that situation Madame Velasquez inserted herself, even though most of the prisoners were former slaves for whom she never demonstrated any concern. On February 24 she wrote a letter to President Ulysses S. Grant complaining that the leased prisoners were "used most brutally under the lash and starvation," badly clothed and housed, and if one asked for food he was liable to be stripped and whipped "till the blood trickles to his feet." She implored the president to investigate. "In the name of humanity and Christianity for god sake put the stop to this human cruelty and murder," she implored, telling of one convict whipped until he collapsed, only to be drenched with water while two prison guards rubbed salt and turpentine into his lacerated back, then repeated the whole brutal business the next day until he died. The cruel irony was that that man's family paid taxes to support the penitentiary.

If someone called the guards on their conduct, they accused the man—or woman—of being a Yankee, hurled vile epithets, and made murderous threats of retaliation. She did not actually say she had been so threatened, and she probably wrote from hearsay, but she told Grant that she wrote under threat of being forced to leave the state. Was there no law to protect the prisoners and those who tried to stop their mistreatment? she asked. In closing, she asserted that she was "one who does not fear to express the truth before her god and man" and felt certain that if protected from violence, others would add their voices. She genuinely may have feared some retaliation, for she signed not as Velazquez, nor even as Bonner, but reached three husbands back to close as "your friend Mrs. L. J. Wasson." Since her book carried an account of her opportunity to assassinate Grant at Shiloh, she perhaps doubly felt need of an alias.

Grant referred her letter to the attorney general and the U.S. attorney for the District of Georgia, as well as Senator Powell Clayton of Arkansas, chairman of the Senate Judiciary Committee, which promised an investigation but in the end took no action. Nothing would be done about the abuse for another forty years, and Lauretta was soon too busy with other concerns to pursue it further.[26] However, when the attorney general conveyed her letter to Clayton, copies leaked out. The correspondent of the Atlanta *Daily Constitution* saw one—though clearly not the original—and his paper printed it on March 23 as an example of the Republican administration's desire to insert itself into state prerogatives such as prison and convict management. "The Jacobins are already beginning to call for the usual budget of lies from their Georgia allies for campaign purposes," wrote the correspondent, referring to the next election.[27] For several weeks the Georgia papers fulminated over the business. "We fail to see what the Federal Government has to do with the matter," complained one. "The United States Government has no jurisdiction in the premises."

By then "Mrs. Wasson's" anonymity was crumbling. A New Jersey reporter saw the original letter, and his paper printed an extract even before it appeared in the Georgia press, making passing note of a seemingly unimportant fact: Mrs. Wasson had written the letter on stationery headed "Southern Publishing Company."[28] It became a newspaper fray momentarily, the *Daily Constitution* asserting that the Southern Publishing Company no longer existed, no doubt recollecting the previous year's notices of seizure of assets for debt, and perhaps knowing already that the sale was scheduled just a few weeks hence—and somewhat embarrassingly forgetting its own reporting of the company's renewal under Ramsay and his occasional advertising in its pages.[29] The same day that the *Daily Constitution* printed her letter, an Augusta paper picked up the news of the letterhead. Many Georgians believed that their popular senator, former Confederate general John B. Gordon, was or had been president of the Southern Publishing Company, and the Augusta *Chronicle & Sentinel* called on him to investigate the whole business, since they looked to him to safeguard the state from onerous federal intrusion.[30] In Atlanta the *Daily Constitution* indignantly asked, "Who and what is this Mrs. Wasson?" opining that she was probably "a lineal descendant of that worthy couple Ananias and Saphire, the biblical couple who lied to Peter in *Acts* and died for their sin."[31] Another editor dismissed Mrs. Wasson as "some wretched creature, of course, trying to curry favor with the paternal Government at Washington."[32]

After a week of back and forth, the confusion was finally settled when it was remembered that Senator Gordon had been an officer of the University Publishing Company, which issued schoolbooks.[33] Still, as late as the end of March Ramsay did not know the identity of Mrs. Wasson and already wished he had never known Madame Velasquez.[34] He entered the controversy by issuing a statement: "we positively deny having been a party to such a vile letter," saying the mysterious Mrs. Wasson had no connection with his company and "must have stolen the stationery upon which she wrote her letter."[35] It echoed her episode with Mark Twain and the eastern publishers' stationery. Evidently Ramsay, like many publishers, did not carefully read what he published, for Lauretta twice gave the surname of her late husband "Major Wasson" in her narrative.[36] Had he remembered that, Ramsay ought to have been able to make the connection. Perhaps he did finally, for he told a reporter of the Macon *Telegraph* that he suspected who it might be and had detectives looking into the matter. In a wonderful unintentional coincidence, the *Telegraph* published a note on Ramsay's detectives, and then in the very next sentence went on to say, "Ramsay is unlucky with the women—he has got into terrible trouble with Madame Velasquez about her 'Woman in Battle'—and now this female is using his paper, with printed address."[37] Just days after the street encounter, from which neither pressed charges apparently, a Savannah newspaper announced that it had somehow concluded that the elusive Mrs. L. J. Wasson was in fact the combative Madame Velasquez.[38] The revelation attracted little attention.

A few weeks after the book appeared in print Lauretta moved to North Carolina, on August 23 checking into the Yarborough House at Raleigh, where she remained for the next several months engaging commissioning agents to sell the book.[39] *The Woman in Battle* was available in three different versions, from a cheap binding at $3.50 to a leather-bound edition at $4.50.[40] Soon she established a separate office in the Grange Hotel at Wilmington and Davie Streets to sell "one of the most intensely interesting books ever published," with herself as overseeing agent for North Carolina.[41] By November she moved on to Charlotte, and in January 1877 she set up in Wilmington to take orders from her lodgings at a boardinghouse. Lauretta felt encouraged at her progress and began looking ahead to future projects, including a work on commerce, finance, and manufacturing in the South. She even began touring manufacturing establishments to collect information.[42] However erratic and shady her business affairs often were, she possessed the instincts of the genuine entrepreneur. By spring of 1877 she moved to Baltimore, and she may well have spent much of the rest of that year traveling the country to market the book.[43] That summer she also hinted that she had written a stage drama based on her adventures, due to be produced in the fall, though no stage production materialized.[44]

Meanwhile, the encomia continued, now from New Orleans, where the *Daily Picayune* called Lauretta's account the "romantic—we might say most romantic—career of a most remarkable woman," written modestly but "with vivacious candor." Again there was praise for the light supposedly shed on Confederate clandestine operations.[45] The word used more often than any other to describe her book was "romance," which carried with it the implication of fiction as much as history. Few reviewers were more restrained than the Galveston writer who said simply that it was well printed and bound, the illustrations were good, and it might "be attractive to lovers of that particular style of literature." A Chicago editor wrote only that it was "a remarkably interesting romance," and in Washington, DC, one paper dismissed it as a "curious volume."[46] A Texas reviewer referring to her notoriety during and since the war added that stories about her were "often absurdly exaggerated" and that "some have refused to believe there was such a person." Still, he averred, "there is the most abundant testimony of a kind that cannot be disputed, to the effect that she did succeed in disguising herself as a man." Readers might not approve of her actions, but all had to admire "her courage in undertaking the perilous adventures she passed through."[47] An editor in Kansas, more from carelessness than insight, referred to her book as "a novel."[48]

By January 1878 she lived full- or part-time in Washington, determined to realize her ambition to be a journalist. Another reporter in that city—a woman, as it happened—found that she was "of the dark, Spanish type, and seems to be one of the persons of note here this winter." Evidence of that came when she attended a women's suffrage convention at the Riggs House Hotel that month and found herself among a number of colorful attendees. Dr. Mary Walker, the noted Medal of Honor–winning female surgeon of the Union army, was there, as was Mary Tillotson, who shocked society with her short dresses and bloomers. So was Julia Evelina Smith of Glastonbury, Connecticut, who, with her sisters, refused to pay taxes in their town since they could not vote and thus had no representation. Lillie Devereaux Blake, president of the New York State Woman's Suffrage Association, attended, and Phoebe Cozzens represented suffragettes from Missouri. Isabella Beecher Hooker, who proclaimed that the Constitution already guaranteed women the vote, was also present. Perhaps the only women's rights luminary not there was Susan B. Anthony, and she sent a contribution of $200 to their efforts. However, the greatest press attention went to a member of the audience at the proceedings, Madame Velasquez, whom one female reporter described as "a Cuban woman of the adventurous type." Kate King, reporting for the Cleveland *Leader*, touched on highlights from Lauretta's book including the counterfeiting and concluded that "if everything set forth in her work be true, she has earned the plaudits of rascals the world over, and for herself a good, quiet nook in the Penitentiary."[49]

A few weeks later the Washington correspondent of the Charleston *News* met Lauretta, whom he described as "one of the most notable feminines now in Washington." He found her slim and youthful, and could only have gotten from her the fact that she currently weighed 128 pounds, whereas years earlier when she posed as Buford she had weighed 20 pounds more. Somehow her weight seemed important to her, for she brought it up soon with another newspaperman as well. She was as "loquacious as a mimic," this reporter found. She told him her story, and if he reported it accurately, she had not stopped evolving her narrative with the publication of *The Woman in Battle*. Born in Cuba, she had come to the United States at age five and at seventeen married an officer who resigned in 1861, only to be killed early in the war. Now for the first time she implied that President Davis had given her a commission in 1861 through "army influence," after which she served with Bragg's army, went to Atlanta sick, and there met and married an officer who was later killed, though she did not name Decaulp. On going to Richmond as Buford, she was discovered and imprisoned by Davis's order, but his wife, Varina, secured her release, things she had never before claimed.

More startling still, he reported her as saying that she later married a man named Velasquez, who died or got killed, "or someone and somehow else was put out of the way, and now she is here espousing the cause of Cuba."[50] It had been two years since the rumor of her engagement to a Cuban, and she had said and done nothing more with regard to Cuba. Meanwhile, in at least sixteen years of a life largely lived in public, no one to date had commented on there being anything Hispanic about her. None of her interviewers mentioned Spanish features until the reporter Kate King this January, nor did anyone seem to notice any trace of an accent in her spoken English. Lauretta made certain to explain that in her book, writing, "My Spanish accent was none of the best, my long non-use of the language having caused me to lose the facility of speaking it in such a manner as to do entire credit to my ancestry."[51]

Now she stepped once more into the public eye on behalf of the island insurgents. Early in the year she drafted what she titled an "Address to the American Congress on 'Cuba.'" Speaking to "Citizens and Patriots of my adopted country," she protested that the revolution on "my dear native island, Cuba," had been sputtering for more than nine years. The course of the war seemed to be going well now, with rebel forces in control of much of Colon and plans to advance next on Matanzas and Havana, while Spain had relieved several of its commanders for failure. Still, the insurgents desperately needed forty-five thousand new volunteers. With American support, they could succeed. As a new world power, the United States had an obligation to support other peoples striving to secure their rights, she argued. Moreover, the rebels seemed consonant with the nation's stand now against slavery. Quoting from recent importation figures of Cuban goods, she also appealed to commercial instincts for aid in preserving and enhancing such trade, the first time she demonstrated an awareness of Cuban exports. She reminded congressmen that a few years earlier the Spaniards had captured and executed a number of Americans caught on a vessel taking arms to the insurgents, and for a time war talk ensued. Now if only America would intervene to halt the butchery so near its shores, she said, "our blood-stained banner will float to the breeze over a free and independent country, and to the honor and glory of America, the home of my husband and children, and the land of my adoption."[52] The reference to her husband and children was designed to invoke sentiment, but currently she had two living husbands and had left both of them, while the plural mention of children gratuitously multiplied her largely invisible son by Bonner.

Her address to Congress died there, if it was ever even received, but before this time her interest in Cuban affairs attracted the attention of people in New York sympathetic to the Cuban revolutionaries. Back in December 1877 rumor in Washington said they had engaged her as their agent in the capital, where she pretended to be a newspaper correspondent by securing a press pass to the reporters' gallery in the Capitol.[53] Her real mission was to promote diplomatic recognition of Cuban independence in Washington. Lauretta pointed out that Peru and other South American governments had already recognized Cuba, and if the United States would do so, it would "in a short time be the 'sweetest little republic' afloat." She went on to say that the insurgents had a minister in the city even then trying to get into the Executive Mansion and the Capitol to make his case. "Perhaps he is at the backdoor," concluded one cynical reporter, "for I have not yet seen him."[54] The signing of the Pact of Zanjón a few days later, on February 10, 1878, rendered further efforts by her irrelevant, for the insurgents made peace with Spain, thus depriving her of her cause.

That same month Lauretta announced her intention to make yet another tour to promote her book, including the South and even possibly some of the western states, commencing in New Orleans. To open necessary doors, on March 1 she went to the Capitol to solicit testimonial signatures of prominent delegates attending the current session, signatures that gave some indication of states she specifically planned to visit. Among them were men from Texas, Arkansas, Maryland, Louisiana, Georgia, and Kansas, including such luminaries as John H. Reagan, former postmaster general of the Confederacy, and General Gordon of Georgia. They all attested, "She is a lady of talents, energy and high personal character" and expressed the hope that she would meet cordial reception wherever she went. This was the more important as she told them that she had a dual purpose, seeking also to promote trade between the United States and Brazil via her native Cuba. She claimed that during the past six months she had appeared before a congressional committee speaking in behalf of such trade, predicting that the United States would soon dominate all custom with South America and that within a decade a railroad would connect it through Mexico and Central America to Brazil. In service of that goal, she told the men signing her testimonial that she was a correspondent for several foreign and domestic newspapers.[55] It could have been true, though if so, she must have written without a byline or else under a pseudonym, for nothing attributed to her can be found. Far more significant, though, was her advancing interest in trade between the Americas and an international rail artery to carry that business.

To stimulate interest in her tour, and ever adept at using the press, she called on Washington correspondents of some of the Southern newspapers to announce her plans. The Raleigh *Observer*'s local man found her "sprightly" as she was about to set off. "She is canvassing for her book and otherwise making herself useful," he wrote home. Then he noted another female celebrity of the moment, the brilliant youthful sculptress Vinnie Ream, adding that Lauretta "is not as *petite* and chirrupy as Vinnie Ream, but is quite interesting."[56] If she actually made the tour, she somehow did so without attracting the least notice, which for her would be beyond unusual. Most likely other affairs forced her to cancel her plans. Her appearance as a reporter may have been more than guise, for she had already decided to publish a new journal or magazine and in April advertised for six women and six men to solicit subscriptions for her new journal, which she would publish out of her new lodging at the Windsor House at 1327 F. Street.[57] She intended to call her newspaper *Le Bulletin Courrier*.[58] Meanwhile she claimed already to be a correspondent for a Rio de Janeiro journal, *Le Buletin de Commercial*.[59]

Her magazine never went beyond an idea and may have been a scam to take subscribers' money. She did leave Washington to sell her book, however, and early in May 1878 was returning by train to the city when she met a fellow passenger from Richmond who had either read her book already or bought a copy from her. The story impressed him. He got off the train at Lynchburg and went to call on Lieutenant General Jubal A. Early, then living in a local hotel. Early was a founder and president of the Southern Historical Society and was already a self-appointed arbiter of right and wrong in Confederate history. His endorsement could boost sales and overcome Jones's criticisms, just as his condemnation could seriously damage any book's future prospects.

When the caller met with the general, however, it turned out that Early had seen the book some months before in New Orleans and looked into its contents. He told his visitor that Velasquez could not be what she pretended to be, and then, with his guest's copy of the book in hand, he pointed out its "inconsistencies, absurdities, and impossibilities." He doubted it was written by a woman or by anyone with real Confederate service. Rather, he concluded, it was the work of "a mere pretender."[60]

When Lauretta learned what Early had said, she wrote him a polite, almost pleading letter on May 18 from a seat in the press gallery in the House of Representatives. Her "high sense of honor" required that she protest his effort to "injure" her and her book "owing to some incorrect dates," she told him, then responded much as she had to Jones's earlier review. She tried to cover for errors with the story of her lost wartime notes and protested that she did not have access to the kind of detailed information generals such as Early might have. "I had to gather my information from my own personal observation of the movements of our army," she told him. She added that as he was a general and she a mere "lieutenant," naturally the two could "not see such a gigantic struggle from the same stand point." She also mentioned that she had changed the names of real people in order not to cause the living embarrassment.

Early's comments could endanger sales of her book, which she frankly said she had written to support "myself and little son." She was living close to poverty, she pleaded. Her book would have been longer, she said but she was forced to condense it "on account of Pecuniary embarrassments," meaning she had rushed to finish it or had paid some of the manufacturing cost and could not afford to make the book longer. Worse, she claimed that her health was failing. Considering her bout with convulsions back in October 1875, there might have been something to that, but more likely it was an attempt to appeal to Early's sympathy, since within a few weeks a correspondent found her hale and healthy. Continuing in that pitiable vein, she pleaded, "My whole souls devotion is the education of him who is to live after I have passed away." She continued, "I have had trials enough to have driven almost any proud spirited woman to madness, or to commit suicide." Still, her trials left her undaunted. "I have struggled and born my lot with the hope of prosperity before me, casting the buffeting of my inferiors beneath my feet." She asked him for "justice to my *child*," saying, "I live for him and him alone."[61]

No sooner did she post the letter than she decided to confront Early personally. Without warning one day she appeared at his hotel and asked him to meet her in the parlor. A brief interview followed, and when she left, he felt more convinced than ever that she had not written the book herself or else that its editor had very much changed and "improved" the work. He also concluded that she was not of Spanish birth. Certainly he heard no Spanish accent, for he found that "her appearance and voice are both those of an American, and have no resemblance to those of a Spanish lady of genteel aspirations." When he considered her book's depictions of Confederate officers as drunken braggarts and Southern women as silly flirts throwing themselves into the arms of the nearest male, he further concluded, "Madame Velasquez is no true type of a Southern woman."[62]

For a change Lauretta had misread her man. Early did not care about her testimonials from prominent Confederates such as Vice President Alexander H. Stephens and remained unconvinced. He withheld making his criticisms public, however, and she never got a second meeting with him. Any controversy between them ended, leaving her no doubt irritated that Early's was one of the portraits in her book.[63] In any case *The Woman in Battle* now attracted less attention after almost two years in print. Sales may not have met her expectation. Moreover, her magazine had come to nothing, and she needed to do something to boost support for her and her son, who presumably lived with her now if still living at all. How she supported herself is a mystery, for employment was sporadic, and writing occasional news items paid little. Most likely, as before, she obtained room and board on her promised future ability to repay, a circumstance that could not last indefinitely.

Soon after her exchange with Early, she went to Cincinnati and perhaps beyond, presumably to stir some economic advantage.[64] A few days later she went on to St. Louis, where she announced to the *Evening Post* that she was available for an interview, and it quickly obliged by sending a reporter. She put on a fine performance, if his article is any measure, and he gave her almost two full columns headlined "A Woman's Romance." On meeting her he beheld "a woman of medium height and of slightly-built form, with a pleasant face, strongly tinctured with masculinity." In her firm jaw and square chin he saw "inflexibility and persistency of purpose." Though she lacked what he called "feminine softness," he detected a "quiet, undemonstrative ladylikeness of demeanor" that seemed incongruent with her "steely gray, glittering eyes that bespeak indomitable sternness of will that no danger could turn from its aim."

She gave a full account of her life, though she laid new strata of myth over the story. Now she said she had really gotten a commission in the Confederate army on May 28, 1861, given by Governor Henry M. Rector of Arkansas, a claim not in her book. Whereas Hammond attested to her admission to his infirmary on July 26, 1863, now she said that on that date she was in the field with her men when her sex was discovered and she was forced to abandon Buford. Omitting mention of her time in Atlanta or of marrying DeCaulp, she said she then went north on Confederate secret service and was soon a "silent *attaché*" to Baker. For the rest of the war she trafficked in Yankee bonds and made nine trips to Europe. Again, it seemed important that her weight be known, and she added eleven pounds to her February statement, putting her at 139 pounds now but 159 disguised as Buford. She also said she stood five feet, five and one-half inches tall.[65]

It had been her first good newspaper interview in months. Given Lauretta's craving for fame and the waning of public interest in her, being old news left her frustrated. Her solution was to insert herself into other controversies or to create one. One of the more sensational episodes in her book, the business of alleged counterfeiting, afforded her a perfect opportunity.

CHAPTER FOURTEEN

"SHE IS A PROMOTER"

LAURETTA ALMOST DIVINELY suited the purposes of John M. Glover, a Democrat from Missouri and chairman of the House of Representatives Committee on Expenditures in the 45th Congress from March 1877 to March 1879. In his final months in office he chaired an investigation into the Treasury during the last year of the war and afterward, in part to embarrass the Republican Party. He found malfeasance in the Bureau of Printing and Engraving, and it was soon rumored that Glover was ready to listen to any information that might discredit the bureau. He would pay $3 a day to anyone giving testimony and perhaps provide stipends for people seeking evidence against the officials in his sights. "All the dead beats in Washington, when they found out what manner of man he was, sought his acquaintance and poured into his head all the scandal they ever heard and all the stories they could imagine," declared one journalist. Some of Glover's informants became professional witnesses, paid daily for months at a time or as long as they continued to provide—or invent—what he wanted to hear.[1]

They somehow came together, probably because Glover read Lauretta's narrative claiming that officials in the Treasury colluded with her to steal printing plates used to counterfeit millions in Treasury notes.[2] During the winter of 1878–79 he took testimony from her, for which she surely and gladly took her $3 a day, and she told the same lurid tale laid out in her book, this time identifying high officials in the Republican Party in 1864–65 whom she accused of corrupt involvement. The list was stunning, including Frederick Seward, son of Lincoln's secretary of state William H. Seward; Lincoln's secretary of the Treasury Salmon P. Chase; then Speaker of the House Schuyler Colfax; New York financier Jay Gould; General James A. Garfield, now a congressman; and Samuel M. Clark, now superintendent of the National Currency Bureau.

This was electrifying. If true, Glover had caught the top leadership of the Republican Party in corruption, something that could destroy the party. Glover gleaned statements from others that were even more outrageous, including charges that employees of the printing bureau printed Treasury notes for their own use to the extent of $30 million or more. When his committee report was ready to submit to the House of Representatives, where fellow Democrats held a majority, his own party refused even to print the document. After his term expired in March 1879 and his Missouri constituents declined to renominate him, he tried to get newspapers to publish the report. Even the Democratic press showed no interest, dismissing him as a crackpot and his report—and those testifying in it—as unworthy of credence. Only a much reduced version of the report ever saw print, with most reference to possible corruption excised.[3]

It incensed Lauretta that the discarded material included what she had told Glover. A public report and a congressional investigation would boost sales of her book, not to mention put her back in the headlines at a time when reporters seemed reluctant to talk with her. She and Harry Buford were old news now, the public appetite for them sated. Hoping to ignite new interest, she moved to New York in December 1879 and roomed in a boardinghouse over a plumber's shop at 78 Fourth Avenue, intending to find a publisher for a new edition of her book, now titled *The Adventures of L. J. Velasquez, the Great American Heroine.* She also hoped to find funding to revive her old magazine idea, retitling it *The North and South American Journal.*[4]

Just days after her arrival, a lodger on the floor below hers entertained an old friend from Indiana, the New York correspondent of the Indianapolis *Journal.* His host told him, "There's a lady up-stairs whom you ought to see, a character, indeed." He went on to give a précis of her story that he probably got from her, a confused mixture of elements from her book and her September 1874 Atlanta *Daily Constitution* interview.[5] Suddenly the reporter realized who she was. "See here!" he interrupted. "Isn't this Mme. Velasquez the same woman whose testimony Glover, the Missouri bilk, tried in vain to get printed last winter for the purpose of ruining the Republican party?" The journalist wanted to see her immediately and sent his calling card to her room. When she saw that a reporter wanted to see her, she invited him to meet her in the boardinghouse parlor.

On meeting her, he saw before him "a slight-built person, slender, tired-looking, with a sensitive mouth, and eyes that seem to change from gray to black as you look at them—evidently Spanish born." She held a copy of *The Woman in Battle* in one hand as she extended the other to him. "I am glad to see you," she said. "I am glad to see any journalist. Newspapers are afraid of me, and they won't print anything I say. Glover tried to print one report, but the House wouldn't allow it. Nobody dares to print the truth." Telling him its pages contained "the truth," she handed him her book, which he glanced at, noting that it was "abundantly but not very artistically illustrated." She wanted some paper to print the whole story. "They're afraid to," she complained, "and I can't get them to arrest me. If I could get Garfield to arrest me, I could prove the truth of what I say by producing the papers." That said, she named Chase, Colfax, Garfield, and all the others who profited from their involvement in the counterfeiting conspiracy.

"I should think they would arrest you, as a lunatic," blurted the shocked reporter.

"I can produce papers to prove all I say," she responded. "They are in England, locked up in a bank."

He seemed unconvinced. "Nobody will believe what you say," he told her. "Your story is quite incredible."

Unwilling to give up now that she had a newspaperman in front of her, she demanded that he take down her statement as she dictated it to him, and she would sign it before a notary. He wrote while she spoke:

> New York City, Dec. 11.—*To the Hon. James A. Garfield:* I hereby confess and allege that, with the assistance of officials of the Treasury Department, I on or about Sept. 5, 1864, procured the abstraction from that Department of two steel-plates, each capable of four United States hundred-dollar notes at each impression; that I transferred those plates to a combination of conspirators of which Salmon P. Chase, Schuyler Colfax, Jay Gould, James A. Garfield, Fred. W. Seward, Judge Burnett, Superintendent S. M. Clark, and Solicitor Jordan were members; that about $33,000,000 in bills were printed from these plates in New York, and nearly as much in England, and that these bills *were distributed between myself, the gentlemen* above named, and others not herein mentioned, and used by them; and I hereby make oath that I have in my possession a written contract signed by the persons whose names are above mentioned, and others, agreeing to a fair division of the so-called money, and that I can and will produce this document whenever legally required so to do.

"That's it to the crossing of a 't,'" she said when he read it back to her. "I'll sign it and attest it whenever you choose to go before a Notary with me."

After that, she told him more stories of the bogus money, and he asked her what she did with her portion, which came to several million.

"I spent it all in buying war vessels for the Confederacy," she boasted. "I organized the only navy that [Secretary of the Navy Stephen R.] Mallory ever had."

The interview done, the reporter left with no intention of seeing a notary. "Her story is too preposterous for consideration," he concluded, dubbing it an "utterly impossible yarn." As for Madame Velasquez, he knew not what to make of her. "She is far from being an idiot, for she is very brisk and alert in conversation, and she does not talk like a lunatic," he mused but added a caveat that "lunatics seldom do, I believe."[6]

That seemingly ended her hopes of renewed publicity. Glover's report never appeared in print in its entirety, and no one took notice of her libelous charges, not even Garfield, for whom allegations of involvement in financial scandals were nothing new. Indeed, that may have been why Lauretta felt secure in naming him, since he had been under fire for corruption for several years.[7] He would be president in fifteen months. Her visitor's account of their interview got little circulation in the press outside Indianapolis and Chicago, and perhaps it was just as well, for if she saw it in print, his depiction of her as an unbalanced fantasist would have left her fuming. Meanwhile, the new edition of her book went nowhere. She formed a partnership with printer John R. Bedan, calling their firm "L. J. Velasquez & Co.," with offices at 150 Nassau Street, but it languished without publishing her book or anything else, and by August 1880 the partnership dissolved.[8]

After the collapse of her company, she moved back to Washington and returned to her intermittent activity in Hispanic affairs. With Cuba at peace now, she approached the legation from Nicaragua and persuaded its minister to the United States, General Maximo Jerez, to employ her as an aide. It was a brief employment. His chief concern then was to keep alive plans to build a canal linking the Atlantic and Pacific across Nicaragua in the face of a challenge from parties preferring Panama. Appearing before the House Committee on Foreign Relations, he protested an American shipbuilder's insult to his country in citing it for bad faith in negotiations, and when the chairman declined to censure the speaker, Jerez stood silently, bowed, and walked out of the chamber, followed by his secretary and what a local journalist described as "the ever-faithful female attaché of the legation, Madame Velasquez."[9]

Whatever the nature of her employment, it must not have been sufficient to keep pace with her expenses, for she decided to revert once more to her old confidence game of pretending to have great wealth around the corner. On March 19, 1881, a notice appeared in the capital press announcing that "Madame L. J. Velasquez" had been directed to send an agent to Havana on her behalf in June in connection with a pending suit for "her property" in Cuba.[10] It was another variant on her December 1864 Roach personal ad, her imaginative version of the inheritance scam. There was no such property, of course, but apparently she briefly parlayed the promise of money in June into enough cash or credit that in July she announced herself as the publisher of a forthcoming magazine, *North and South American*. Moreover, she also announced that she had completed arrangements to found an agricultural college in Nicaragua, presumably with the assistance and approval of Jerez and his government.[11] The magazine never appeared, and the college was born and died in that announcement, most likely never anything but another scheme to raise immediate cash. Her connections with Nicaragua then ended abruptly a few weeks later, when Jerez died suddenly on August 11.

As she had before and would again after the failure of a confidence scheme, Lauretta dropped out of public notice, for two years this time, and changed her base. She resurfaced in the fall of 1883 at 102 Chambers Street in lower Manhattan, in the same building as the nation's most popular weekly newspaper for sport, humor, and literature, *The Spirit of the Times*.[12] Now she was proprietor of her "Continental Exporting & Importing Company," her interest in Central and South America shifting to consumer goods. "Reciprocity" proclaimed the letterhead of the company she established around November 1. It also advertised "special inducements" to manufacturers to handle exports of American goods to Mexico, Central America, and the West Indies and at the same time importation of products from those regions, probably including cigars.[13]

Convention—and the law—stood in the way of a woman taking much involvement in politics, but Lauretta had manifested intermittent interest in public affairs at least since her letter to Grant. In 1884 the presidential contest pitted New York's Democratic governor Grover Cleveland against Republican James G. Blaine. New York itself decided the election by just over eleven hundred ballots, as an emergent populist Greenback Party took enough votes away from Blaine to throw the state to Cleveland. The local adherents called themselves the People's Party, and their concerns were largely parochial. They wanted local elections separated from state and national balloting so that they could return honesty and good government to towns free of the coattail effect of national party slates. On a national scale they favored tax reform based on property ownership, demanded that only the federal government issue paper currency and coinage, and protested congressional corruption in league with monopolies to favor large corporations. They sought homestead reform, opposed importation of cheap labor, called for labor reform for wage earners, endorsed private investment in expanding and developing communications and transportation, and asked for "the amelioration of the social condition of all classes."[14]

To the extent she could, Lauretta Velasquez supported this People's Party even though, ironically, the Greenback candidate in 1884 was Benjamin F. Butler, the villain of her book chapter covering her time in New Orleans in 1862. Though she could not vote, she could attempt to speak out and perhaps did. Certainly she welcomed Cleveland's victory. Three weeks after the election, she wrote him a congratulatory letter in which she promoted her view of America's future course. It was inevitable that the United States, Mexico, and Central America must one day form a single union, she said, but to achieve that there must be free trade from the Canadian border to the Isthmus of Panama. Of course, that promised to put money in her pocket as an importer and exporter. Writing as if she were a newspaper publisher, she claimed to have a "special correspondent" placed inside the palace in Mexico City, who told her that Cleveland's election brought joy to the Mexican capital and to Presidente Porfirio Díaz himself.

Moving to a broader canvas, she declared that foreign nations must stay out of the hemisphere. "We want *no more* French invasions on our *soil*," she wrote. The United States should make no treaties with Spain, especially one then current by which Cuba, which she called "my native *land*," might be yielded to Germany to pay debt. Assuming that she spoke for Cubans in the country, she declared that annexation by the United States was what they wanted. "I could say volumes upon this subject," she closed, adding, "I now commit the whole to the care of our heavenly father," her only recorded indication of any religious awareness. For some reason she adopted a slight change in her name for the moment. Gone was the "Madame" title, and she signed herself "Loreteta J. Velasquez."[15]

Whatever notice Cleveland took of her letter, he sent a polite acknowledgment, and soon his letter joined the parcel of documents she carried as proof of her high connections. More significantly, for the first time Lauretta had given voice to a political philosophy. She was clearly an expansionist, wanting the United States to grow ever bigger until it governed the entire American hemisphere. She wanted fiscal and political reform, as well as industrial and transportation growth, and she seemed to support a degree of governmental involvement in social welfare that had about it the scent of socialism, all ideas consonant with those largely entertained in the emerging women's rights movement, though she denied being a feminist. As ever, separating genuine principles from her instinct for self-interest is difficult. Moreover, she always took it as her right to address powerful men, whose polite responses swelled her dossier of "testimonials." Still, beneath all that, it appears that she had developed, or was developing, the rudiments of a centrist or center-left political philosophy.

She stepped more prominently into the public arena at the end of the year in the hope of defeating the reciprocal trade agreement negotiated with Spain by American ambassador John W. Foster, which she dismissed as "trickery." Among other things, it reduced the duties on imported Cuban cigars and eliminated the import duty on tobacco, both of which would reduce domestic prices and force down the wages of Cuban-born cigar makers working in New York and elsewhere. She claimed to have met with several members of the Senate in Washington on the matter, notably Nathaniel Hill of Colorado, who was also, as it happened, an inveterate gold hunter.[16] On December 7 the cigar makers held a meeting to discuss efforts to defeat ratification of the treaty, and Lauretta appeared unannounced at the door. "A black-eyed and black-haired woman came into the meeting room," wrote a reporter. She gave her name to the chairman, and he introduced her to the room as Mrs. Velasquez of Washington, allowing her to address the meeting.

She told the crowd that she was a Cuban, and the first thing a New York *Times* reporter noted was that "she spoke English fluently," a good example of Lauretta's assumption that people would see and hear what she primed them to expect. She said she was "an old worker" when it came to dealing with Congress but allayed any fears the men might have by adding that she was "not a woman's rights agitator." As resistant as Caucasian American men could be to that sort of thing, she wisely calculated that Hispanic men would be even more so. She claimed that several members of the Senate had asked her to tour the nation to meet with workers affected by the treaty. That was surely a fable, even though she dropped the names of several prominent members of Congress to support what she said. Moreover, she assured them that a comfortable majority of senators opposed ratification of the treaty, whereas the numbers she quoted indicated a majority of only three. Beyond that, she declared her desire for the annexation of Cuba and assured them that many leaders in Washington felt as she did, implying that some of them called at her office in Washington to share confidences. If the meeting would send delegates to Washington to represent their interests, she promised that the treaty could be defeated.[17] In fact, the Senate did reject the treaty, though what influence, if any, Lauretta had in its defeat is unknown.

Her motive for inserting herself into the matter is unclear, but in addition to any political sentiments, she likely hoped to profit as an intermediary for the workers, perhaps gain some clout in Washington as their spokeswoman, or else establish personal relations for a future commercial enterprise. A month later she attended a meeting of New York's People's Party on January 13, 1885, to hear its leaders call on the state's senators to resign in view of their involvement in corrupt practices, endorse severing local elections from state and national elections to reduce corruption there, and unanimously approve a motion calling for the "abolition of the United States Senate as a useless appendage." During the meeting a male friend of Lauretta's asked to be recognized by the chair and then told the meeting that "Mme. Velasquez was in the audience, and would like to take the platform for five or six minutes." After her reception the month before by the cigar makers, she was ready to speak out again, but this chairman ruled her request out of order.[18] Lauretta liked the attention of an audience, but it is evident that her interest in public affairs impelled her to step outside convention to make herself heard.

Sometime that spring of 1885 she closed down her exporting and importing company and formed a new partnership under the name of "L. J. Velasquez & McCormick, importers," with offices in her former Chambers Street home. She now lived at 217 East 118th Street between 2nd and 3rd Avenues in East Harlem, a newly developed area of three-story brownstones and apartment buildings, thanks to an elevated railway, and inhabited mostly by German immigrants. Her partner in the firm, David McCormick, lived at that same address. He could have been just another boarder in the same building, or he may have been her partner in more than business. Other than the brief rumor of an engagement to a Cuban count some years prior, there are no hints of a man or men in Lauretta's personal life since she left Bobo a decade earlier. That would change soon, but McCormick disappeared from her story just as quickly as he had appeared, and nothing more is known of him.[19]

Meanwhile, she continued her professed work as an importer, though nothing indicates whether she did well at it; the brevity of her partnership argues that she did not. She also decided now to write a memoir of what she called "my travels through Central America & Mexico," to contain "my interviews with the leading men, commercial and trade relations showing the true condition of affairs." That may be what took her on a visit to Philadelphia in March 1885, to seek an editor, but she never wrote the book or else failed to find a publisher, for it never saw print. While there, she sat before the statue of George Washington in front of Independence Hall and wrote another letter to President Cleveland the day before his inauguration. "I have no voice in the politics of this gigantic country, owing to my sex," she began, "nor do I desire to have."

> I am a merchant interested in the commercial and financial welfare of the whole continent, to the Isthmus of Panama, which should be one commercially with the three local governments, U.S.A. Mexico, and Central America. With our R.R. communications, and intercourse the Latin Americans will adapt themselves to modern uses and customs as far as climate will admit of. I trust and pray that if it is consistent with the policy of the U.S. to bring about a Federal union of those five little Republics of Central America, making them self sustaining, my three years observation and knowledge of their condition has proven their inability to remain longer in there impoverished condition, with the untold hiden wealth now waiting development, and know one more thoroughly understands and deplores these facts than myself.

For the past five years she had worked as a merchant in the interest of what she called "the Aglo and Latin races" and implied that the Mexican minister to the United States, Matias Romero, was well acquainted with her efforts. There seems little point in Lauretta's letter to Cleveland. She made a couple of recommendations for appointments in New York but otherwise just repeated and expanded on what she had said months earlier. Lauretta presented herself as an expert on Latin American affairs and exaggerated her six months in Venezuela in 1868 into three years to support the claim. She might have hoped the president would employ her in some capacity, but she did not say so, and Lauretta rarely shied from saying what she wanted. She might have just been looking for another response from Cleveland, one mentioning Latin America, that she could show when useful.[20] One thing that is evident is that she looked ahead in contemplating political and trade affairs in her hemisphere. If her prediction of a future union of all the Americas failed to materialize, still it mirrored sophisticated thinking based on the United States' dominance in that part of the globe. She never shied from big ideas.

After signing that March 5, 1885, letter "Lorateta," just as she had her last to Cleveland, she all but disappeared for the next five years, in part perhaps because another man quite definitely came into her life. On August 20, 1887, she appeared before the Reverend Clayton Eddy in an Episcopal ceremony at Eddy's home at 400 West 57th Street in Manhattan. She set aside the assumed Velasquez and gave her legal name as "Loratita Juaneta Bonner," stating that this was her third marriage, thus omitting two of her first three husbands, probably Wasson and Bobo. She said that she was born in 1844 in Havana and her maiden name was Velasquez. For the first time on record, she produced full names for her fictional parents, making her father Joaquin R. Velasquez and her mother Marie Antoneta De Champ. She gave her residence as 116 Lexington Avenue, which happened to be the same address as that of her new husband.[21] Either they gave their future address as a married couple or they had been living together there already.

Standing beside her was William Beard, for whom this was his first marriage. He was a man of considerably greater horizons than her previous mates yet had some of the same attractions. Born the son of a tin miner in St. Austell, Cornwall, in 1835, he came to the United States sometime around 1860, from the outset bent on mineral exploration.[22] By the early 1870s he settled in the Southwest, where in 1878 he recorded perhaps his first strike, which he called the Odin mine, not far from Globe, Arizona Territory.[23] Two years later he was a mining superintendent at Globe.[24] Meanwhile, with his friend Con Burns, Beard located several mines around Globe and Tombstone, at the same time as the celebrated feud between the Earp brothers and local rustling elements.[25] In the spring of 1880 he made a survey of the mining fields in Colorado, only to conclude that if the mineral potential of Arizona were properly developed, "Colorado would never be heard of again."[26] He made a name as a prospector and mineralogist by the late 1880s, with some claim to prosperity, which would certainly have piqued her interest.

Beard's vision extended beyond making himself a fortune. He wanted to use the mineral wealth of the region to encourage eastern money to undertake its development. In 1882 he and Burns made multiple trips, first to Denver and then to the East, taking ore samples to show as inducements. The next year Beard went to San Francisco on the same mission.[27]

Lauretta's fifth—presumably—and last husband, the English or Welsh William Beard, who was, like her, something of a scheming opportunist. *Philadelphia Inquirer*, July 15, 1898.

His prospecting sometimes took him into danger, as in June 1884, when he found himself close to Chiricahua Apaches raising a war party to raid the mining camps.[28] He was not a man to trifle with. When he and Burns went into partnership with George H. Sissons and Major John J. Safely on the sale of mining property, Beard and Burns sued the others when their partners sold the land but kept the money.[29] The contention between them lasted for years, much of it in the New York papers, where Lauretta could not have missed it. Nor could she have missed articles reporting that Safely had secured grants from the Mexican government for fifty million acres of land in western Mexico and Baja California, along with mineral rights.[30] Since Beard knew Safely, Beard had to have known about those supposed Mexican grants as well.

He went to the December 1885–January 1886 New Orleans World's Industrial and Cotton Centennial Exposition as curator of mineral exhibits from Arizona, where he had collected ore specimens over the past two years to promote the territory's potential.[31] There is no evidence that Lauretta attended the exposition, but since it promoted trade in American products, it would certainly have been of interest to her, especially since one of the hot topics at the event was the commercial development of Mexico and Central America.[32] Thus Lauretta may have met Beard there. Soon thereafter, Beard began spending time in New York, and by 1887 he had been a resident at 116 Lexington Avenue for several years. He may not have been a celebrity, but he was known as a man of means, with excellent prospects for gold and silver wealth in the Southwest, an upscale version of Hardy Bonner. By early 1889 his interests spread to railroad building, as he tried to capitalize a road linking Salt Lake City with San Diego.[33]

Almost immediately after their marriage—or possibly before—Lauretta became pregnant, and in 1888 she gave birth to a son, whom they named Waldemar.[34] Of the five or more children she claimed to have had, he is the only one whose name is known. She was now in her middle forties, and "Wally" would be her last. Soon thereafter she signed a three-year lease at $7,600 a year for adjoining houses at 60 and 62 West 55th Street and began remodeling them to operate as a boardinghouse, perhaps with Beard's financial backing while he was away prospecting in Arizona. With permission from the owner, she removed a refrigerator and a furnace, stone wash tubs and a sink, and a cooking range, and she cut passages through walls and eliminated a chimney breast, all of which she believed would enhance the "domestic convenience and comfort" of the properties, making them more suitable for taking in roomers.

Unfortunately, the owners of the houses, Origen and Elizabeth Vandenburgh, soon defaulted on their mortgage payments to seller John Hayes, who filed foreclosure suits. Moreover, on July 28, 1890, Hayes filed a $750 suit against Lauretta for "willful and malicious injury to and destruction of" the properties by her renovations. Even before notice of his suit could be served, he secured a judge's order for Lauretta's arrest that same day, whereupon she was immediately taken to a city jail to be held for three days until she was able to post $1,000 bail.

On her release, Lauretta fought back and persuaded a court to vacate her arrest order on August 12. Eight days later Hayes tried to have her arrested again, and when that was denied, on August 21 he filed yet another complaint on the same grounds as before. Lauretta soon claimed that she suffered from nervous prostration as a result of the stress of her imprisonment and the ensuing legal battle, while the interruption of her plans for the boardinghouse resulted in her abandoning the enterprise. Worse, she had also been engaged in what she called "extensive operations" beyond the boardinghouse, but the adverse publicity attracted by Hayes's allegations and her arrest caused her investors to back out, "supposing her to be a person of bad and malicious character." Soon she commenced action against Hayes to recover $20,000 in damages.[35] It is hard to evade the irony that after escaping consequences for one shady scheme after another, she would be arrested and falsely imprisoned for possibly her first legitimate business venture to date.

While her suit slowly made its way through the court, the press took notice of her again when word spread of the Beards' railroad plans, or when Lauretta alerted the newspapers to them. On January 31, 1891, a reporter from the New York *Herald* called on her at the office the Beards shared with a real estate agent at 401 Broadway. He explained that he was writing a series of articles on women in business, and Mrs. Beard gave him more than he bargained for. "She is a promoter," he found, "and apparently an indefatigable one." Lauretta played coy at first, pretending she did not like to talk about herself for fear of being "written up" in the fashion of some of the more gushing sheets, but the reporter soon discovered that "when she got started in her plans, . . . she could talk for a year and a day on them."[36]

For perhaps the first time in a newspaper interview, Lauretta said nothing about Harry Buford and her Confederate years. Perhaps after a quarter century the Buford persona had outlived its usefulness. She was born in Cuba, she said, and now revealed for print her new father's name as Joaquin Velasquez. Claiming that she had traveled much of the world, especially South America, exploring its mineral resources, she revealed that she had written articles for a number of American and foreign journals over the years. Then she got out her packet of letters from well-known senators, congressmen, and foreign officials, as well as President Cleveland, as proof of her influential acquaintances. When he leafed through them, however, the journalist could not help noticing that most were just polite answers to her written requests.

He also saw something else. "Mrs. Beard is a typical, go-ahead Western woman, not only in manner but in dress," he thought. "She has two accents, one the normal Western, the other, when excited, the Spanish. She has a firm mouth, pale face and remarkably keen eyes." In her dozens of press interviews going back almost thirty years, this was the first time anyone ever mentioned an Hispanic accent, and an erratic one at that. Explaining that her husband was away in the West on their joint business, she said she was happy to speak of their enterprises. With Beard and three others, she had incorporated a mining investment and trading company in West Virginia, with herself as general manager. More important, however, she said she owned silver mines in Arizona—really her husband's—and then announced something more startling: she had in hand major land concessions from Mexico and Honduras for rights-of-way to build railroads, canals, and a steamship line. Thanks to her long acquaintance with Congress, she claimed, even then she had two bills before that body to advance her promotions. The *Herald* reporter left rather impressed with this "fascinating curiosity."[37]

Once again Lauretta showed that she could manage a reporter handily. In fact, nothing was ever heard of her West Virginia mining promotion, if it actually existed, and at least one of the officers of her corporation, W. Fearing Gill of New York, was a man of unsavory reputation both personally and in business, even if he was a brother-in-law to millionaire Cornelius Vanderbilt.[38] Certainly the Beards had plans for mineral prospecting and a big idea for Mexico, but she may have wanted the interview to get her name in the press for a more personal reason. Just a few months later, in June, she called on a reporter to give another story, this one crediting her as a "New York business woman and a most patriotic American." She announced that Mrs. John T. Goolrick, the president of the Mary Washington Monument Association of Fredericksburg, Virginia, had authorized her to raise a fund to place a new monument over the grave of George Washington's mother. Lauretta planned to commission an engraving of the one extant portrait of Mary Washington and then sell copies across the country. In fact, she claimed that she had already applied for a copyright on the new engraving. All proceeds from the portraits would go to erecting the new monument, she said, and any leftover she would use to purchase Washington family relics for preservation.[39] The story soon spread, and as far away as Chicago, Lauretta was soon hailed as one of Goolrick's "ablest assistants."[40]

It was the Venezuelan Emigration Company all over again. In fact, Lauretta had nothing whatsoever to do with Frances Goolrick or the Mary Washington Association.[41] What she hoped to gain by falsely associating herself with the monument is unclear, though likely it was either a quick influx of cash from sale of the engravings or a boost of cachet in society in aid of a much more extravagant plan soon to be revealed. She seems not to have been caught out publicly in her deception and never pursued the scam. It hardly mattered. By now she had something bigger on her horizon.

CHAPTER FIFTEEN

THE FIRST BIG CONS

BY THIS TIME Lauretta had other enterprises in the offing, not least the prospect of *The Woman in Battle* enjoying new life. She still owned the copyright. Ramsay was long out of business, and Dustin, Gilman & Co. folded in 1878, so no one was selling her book now. But someone else was back in business. In 1883 Alfred D. Worthington opened the house of A. D. Worthington & Co. in Hartford, and in 1888 he enjoyed a major success with another woman's memoir, Mary Livermore's *My Story of the War*, which recounted her experiences as a Union nurse and relief worker. Lauretta had more than once intended to get a new edition in print, without success, but news of Livermore's book may have prompted her to try to spur a new generation of sales after more than a decade. In 1889, coincidentally, she transferred the copyright to yet another Worthington, this time Richard Worthington, who ran Worthington Company of 747 Broadway in New York. He was no business or blood relation to Alfred D. Worthington, though both were born in England, and neither had any connection to a C. J. Worthington.

In keeping with the common practice of bringing out reissued Civil War memoirs under different titles, Lauretta and Worthington changed and much abbreviated the title of hers. It came off the press in 1890 as *Story of the Civil War; or, The Exploits, Adventures and Travels of Mrs. L. J. Velasquez (Lieutenant H. T. Buford, C.S.A.)*. Lauretta now exchanged Madame for Mrs., using only her initials instead of her adopted full name, and this time spelled her surname as she signed it. C. J. Worthington was still editor, his fictitious naval service referenced only by "U.S.N." on the title page after his name. The rest of the book ran without amendment and apparently from the original plates used in 1876.

Sales appear not to have been satisfying.[1] Richard Worthington was a questionable businessman. In three years he would declare bankruptcy while owing $130,000 to creditors, and then in June police would arrest him for embezzlement. A year later he suddenly died, presumably of diabetes and heart trouble, but some suspected suicide.[2] Meanwhile, receivers auctioned scores of cases of his books at bargain prices, and the firm of H. W. Hagemann of New York bought several titles, including the remaining stock of unbound press sheets of *Story of the Civil War.* When Hagemann brought it out once more in 1894, the publisher further streamlined the title page. Now the title was *The Story of the Civil War* and nothing more, attributed to "Madame Velasquez," and with no mention anywhere of C. J. Worthington. Instead of the old frontispiece of Lauretta, Hagemann substituted an apparently new engraving of superior quality to the other illustrations, showing her being interviewed by Colonel Lafayette C. Baker.

By the time the Hagemann edition came out, Lauretta had a new experience in store, seeing herself and her book beginning to figure as a source in a new generation of popular histories. In 1893 Ménie Muriel Dowie published in London her *Women Adventurers: The Lives of Madame Velazquez, Hannah Snell, Mary Ann Talbot, and Mrs. Christian Davies.* Besides extended excerpts from the published narratives of the women—it printed forty-seven pages from *The Woman in Battle*—it also included Dowie's own comments. Some of her heroines did not impress her, and she said so frankly. "It is difficult to take them quite seriously, these ladies of the saber," she wrote. "They are to me something of a classic jest: their day is done, their histories forgotten, their devotion dead, and they have left us no genuine descendants." Their memoirs did not stand up to scrutiny either. "It is well, too, that we have little means of investigating their exploits—or these might lose colour and fade under our sad modern microscope," she added. "Well for their reputations and for our history that we can't find the truth of such minor points."

The author of *The Woman in Battle* was another matter. "Amongst these the American soldier Loreta Velazquez cannot be counted," Dowie went on. "She stands upon a different—a more serious platform, for she is of our own day, and plenty of men now living must have known her as Lieutenant Harry Buford." Lauretta had taken her in completely. "Throughout her history upon every page" she went on, "there is an air of truthfulness which comes—dare I confess?—with very great refreshment to a connoisseur of the elaborated adventures of the average adventurer":

> Madame Velazquez was before everything a practical, single-minded woman. . . . She lived her life; she did not dream it, think it, hope for it, or regret her inability to experience it. She had the gift of actualizing her ambitions. Such a character as hers must always rouse one's

admiration, especially when one is left to read of it. It is doings that look well on paper.[3]

When the New York *Times* reviewed Dowie's book it agreed, noting that Lauretta's narrative "has to be treated with more respect" for "there is reason to believe that there is some foundation of truth in it."[4] Harry Buford's myth still held some claim to being fact.

With her husband, William, frequently away prospecting in Arizona, Lauretta had time to dream, and soon her mind conceived a new twist on an old idea. The Civil War was scarcely over before Southern leaders, seeing desperate need for rebuilding and developing their section, turned their eyes toward Europe as a source of new blood and capital via immigration. Several former Confederate states formed immigration boards to encourage an influx of new settlers, and over the next two decades one company after another tried to match immigrants with desirable Southern land. Yet by 1875 barely 10 percent of immigrants settled in the South, which still suffered the stigma of slavery.[5]

In 1888 organizers created the Southern Interstate Immigration Association, with a northern branch headquartered in New York City and a southern branch in Raleigh, North Carolina. More often called simply the Southern Immigration Association, it seemed moribund by the summer of 1892.[6] As little as 1 percent of immigrants settled in the region by that time, which one editor attributed still to "the evil legacies of slavery."[7] Then in March the governor of Virginia tried to revive hopes by calling a meeting of all Southern governors the following month.[8] That looked serious, a situation that attracted Lauretta's interest. She would even have some money to launch a new enterprise. On February 9, 1893, a New York court found in her favor in her suit against John Hayes, awarding her $4,000 in damages plus interest and costs.[9]

In May 1893 she wrote an open letter to Secretary of the Treasury John G. Carlisle, announcing that she had taken an interest in the Southern Immigration Association. Significantly, she did not claim to have any official connection with the group, unlike her 1868 effort to insert herself into the Venezuelan emigration project. She argued that the end of slavery had disrupted Southern agriculture's source of labor. Rather than be hostage to the black monopoly on unskilled workers, planters wanted to import low-cost labor from the North, Europe, and even China. Lauretta made it clear to Carlisle that she wanted nothing to do with the New York branch. "New

York of today is not the great New York of the past," she said. Throngs of eastern Europeans filled its tenements, as she well knew, having lived among them.

She proposed to establish a bureau located somewhere like Savannah, Georgia, to lure immigrants to the South, and she intended to be selective, not wanting to see her "beautiful country overrun by the Russian Jews and criminals of Siberia." She promised to have a prospectus in public hands shortly.[10] Six months later she went to Washington to promote the scheme and announced that the company would soon be incorporated, with branches in every Southern state and a European office in Paris. To promote the cause she would also publish a journal in French, German, Swiss, and Scandinavian, edited by former congressman and humorist Colonel Peter "Pat" Dornan. Her "National Immigration and Colonization Association" was chartered in November 1893, with financier William T. Riggs among the corporators and Dornan as a vice president. It had a capital stock of $500,000 and authority to increase that with future issues up to $3 million. Again she emphasized that they wanted "only good thrifty settlers; no Polish Jews or serfs."[11] She was not that socially progressive.

The press generously credited "Madame Velazquez-Beard" with being the originator of the new firm seeking to bring immigrants and capital to the South. "The time has come to change the course of the tide of immigration from the frigid wastes of Dakota, Northern Minnesota, and Wisconsin, Montana, and Manitoba, to the fertile lands and sunny climate of the South," declared an officer of the association. North Dakota, for instance, could produce only one crop a year, wheat, and the rest of the year immigrants there suffered and froze in winters that lasted five months or more. The South had far more advantages to offer—multiseasonal crops that provided work virtually year-round, hospitable weather, and natural resources in timber, coal, and minerals to offer a well-rounded environment for all manner of labor and home industry. The work was reported as well under way by December 1893, with pledges of share purchases from prominent men all over the South. Tens of thousands of acres had been made available, along with promises of assistance to new arrivals, including even offers to help build their houses. Governors sent guarantees of aid and support, and a few European steamer lines offered to transport immigrants to any Southern ports desired. "The South needs these people today," said the announcement, promising that all who participated would share in the "brighter days which are dawning in the South."[12]

Unlike her 1866 Venezuela scheme, this colonization association outwardly appeared to be legitimate, and by the summer of 1894 Vice President Dornan announced that "we are succeeding slowly but surely." They had settled many families in Southern homes and so far heard no complaints.[13] However, Madame Velasquez Beard rather quickly lost what connection she had with it, if any. The Beards' lodging business was hardly an enterprise fit for her ambitions. Most likely Lauretta ran it as her own, while her husband pursued more potentially prosperous interests. Then in 1893 a financial panic struck, thanks to the battle over silver versus gold coinage, and silver lost out. Since the government had been the major buyer of ore for specie, silver mines began closing in alarming numbers. That hit the Beards hard, and William immediately set out looking for gold and copper strikes to offset his losses on silver. He even helped rediscover the famous lost "Doc Thorn" mine, when not riding with a posse out of Globe looking for the notorious outlaw the "Apache Kid."[14]

Beard returned to Philadelphia that fall, and the couple determined to relocate to Norfolk, Virginia, to further their own immigration scheme. They rented a house at 40 Highland Avenue and, calling themselves Beard & Company, took an office at number 407 of the Columbia Building, declaring their business a brokerage.[15] Then in November 1894 they organized the International Colonization Company, Inc., with Major D. T. Taylor as president, "Colonel" Beard as vice president, Lauretta as agent for North Carolina, and headquarters in Norfolk. Thanks to Taylor, they had, or thought they had, a solid connection to Emil Lindburg, a wealthy Swede living in New York, widely reported a year earlier to have contracted to buy thirty thousand acres in Alabama on which he wanted to settle Swedish farmers.[16] They made him their company's agent in New York, but more important, they touted him as a major investor in order to persuade men in North Carolina to subscribe to their stock and fund their operations.

Lauretta stopped first at Elizabeth City, North Carolina, where she visited a local editor on November 22 before moving on to her principal target, New Bern.[17] There she set up headquarters as a guest of the city, which covered her lodging and boarding expenses while she called on potential subscribers to interest them in the project and solicited investment in a cotton factory she promised to build to process the crops their immigrants would grow.[18] Before the first week of December was out she announced that she had enough investors in line to guarantee the factory's construction, and she selected a site for it near the city.[19] At the same time she showed the public samples of the yucca plant that she found in the vicinity and proclaimed it ideal for rope making, allowing the anticipated immigrants to diversify their industry beyond just cotton.[20] Meanwhile, her husband was reported to be looking for an additional factory site between Raleigh and Goldsboro, which was bound to appeal to potential investors in both cities.[21]

Probably at her behest, Lindburg wrote a lengthy letter to the editor of the local *Weekly Journal*, setting out his aims. The South had the most fertile land in the world, with short winters and long growing seasons, as well as low prices per acre. The company would provide potential immigrants with fact-packed literature in their own languages setting forth the attributes of North Carolina's soil, which the Norfolk headquarters would do. Then it would import men with money to buy the land and ambition enough to produce more than they consumed. Such immigrants would increase the value of their land and that of their neighbors, allowing communities to fund better roads, schools, and churches, and with lower taxes. Lindburg invited the men of New Bern to contact the Norfolk office if they had land they would like to sell to the company.[22]

Meanwhile, agent Lauretta Beard moved on to Raleigh to seek more investors, as usual calling on local editors to announce her visit and its purpose. Sometimes she added a little personal information, billing herself as a "writer of note" for a number of publications in the Scandinavian countries, but in the main she focused on the project at hand, promising that she and her company would soon see colonies of prosperous immigrants adding to the common weal.[23] Back in New Bern she continued to push for investors, perhaps a bit too much, for the local newspapers suddenly felt a need for caution. "Immigration plans are now being pressed upon the consideration of the public, and so far as we are advised they are worthy of our embrace," wrote one editor while she was in town, "but it is well enough to have it distinctly understood, that ours is not a house of refuge for the ignorant, the vile and sloathful." The same day that warning appeared, Lauretta left for Raleigh again, announcing that in response to a signed petition from leading people in New Bern, her company had chosen Morehead City, forty miles south of New Bern, as the port of entry for the anticipated influx of immigrants. A little anxiously, the same editor expressed a hope that Lindburg himself would come in person and soon.[24] New Bern's mayor had already sent Lindburg and Taylor an invitation to come as guests of the city, but on December 15 Lindburg replied that they could not at present, promising to visit in the near future.[25] Lauretta also called at Greensboro and other towns, usually as a guest of the city, and at each stop she publicized her project and sought agents to locate land and sell stock in the company.

By this time she had opened an office at the Hotel Albert, where she stayed, and on December 22 she added further evidence of her sincerity when she addressed a meeting of citizens of Jones County. The first 300 families would arrive at different times, she said, and be settled in several locations. A separate company would build the cotton factory, as well as a bridge over the Trent River, and the contract for that job was now open for offers. She spoke of multiple factories now and implied that suitable land must be acquired soon, for the immigrants would be on their way before long. Then she announced that Lindburg and Taylor had accepted a new invitation and would be coming soon; after their visit she would leave to make preparations to move "her husband and family" from Norfolk. The Beards were going to make New Bern their permanent home, ample proof of their commitment to their project.[26]

On Christmas Day Lauretta arrived in Wilmington to call on the editor of the *Semi-Weekly Messenger*, where, despite the holiday, she gave him her story. Her company, she said, intended to bring 3,000 European families to the South as soon as it could secure five thousand acres of good cotton land for them. Even though Alabama and Virginia both had companies with the same goal, she declared that North Carolina could beat them both. As soon as the first colony was established, her cotton mill would process their crops. Ultimately she envisioned settlements all across the country below a line drawn from Washington to San Francisco, with as many as 1,250 families "of a desirable class of immigrants," and her company would give its bond to bring that many more each subsequent year. She wanted the "sturdy and thrifty peasantry of Finland, Norway, Denmark, Sweden and the north of Scotland, men who have means to pay for lands and then in some instances have capital left beside, who are skilled laborers." Much depended on Lindburg, whom she touted as a former consul general to Sweden. He had contacts in Scandinavia and also thousands of letters from settlers in the northwestern United States who said they wanted to move to the South. As an added attraction for local investment, she let it drop that potential immigrants from Europe were saying that they especially liked the sound of eastern North Carolina.

Lauretta told the editor that she had worked for the development of the South since 1867 and that though she was born in the West Indies, she had been raised in Louisiana and was "thoroughly Southern in attachment."

Moreover, as a writer she contributed to publications in the United States, as well as forty-two newspapers in Sweden and Scotland. She showed letters of support "from some of the most prominent men in the South, of recent date and running back for a number of years." There was no mention of Buford. That story's usefulness had passed, so far as she was concerned.[27]

Then, virtually overnight, the Beards disappeared from North Carolina. Why remains a mystery. Behind them they left a classic framework for a confidence scheme. In little more than six weeks they had started their company in Virginia, then swamped eastern North Carolina and especially New Bern with Lauretta's personal visits, speaking before the public, touting their big investor Lindburg, and promising thousands of immigrants who would pay good prices for land, factories that meant jobs, civic improvements such as the bridge at New Bern, and generally a program guaranteed to elevate the standard and quality of life for both new settlers and old residents. On top of that, they had promised to commit themselves to the region and their enterprise by becoming residents, all well calculated to build the confidence that opened purses.

The International Colonization Company may have been legitimate, but it was more likely a sham that fell through, deceiving not only New Bern but also Lindburg, for he, at least, seemed to be genuine. In January 1896 he actually did purchase more than fifteen thousand acres one hundred miles west of New Bern near Fayetteville, and he came in person in April to look over the land where he hoped to settle about 1,500 Scandinavian families before the end of the year. But when he did that, he represented his own immigration agency, Lindburg and Henzie.[28] As for New Bern, the colonists never came, and when two Finns bought property there in April 1895, it was sufficiently unusual to merit comment in the local press.[29] Neither of the Beards appears to have set foot in New Bern or North Carolina again, circumstantial evidence that they left under a cloud.

They moved to 1602 Mount Vernon Street in Philadelphia, then soon moved again to 1939 North 20th Street.[30] Meanwhile, William Beard returned to Arizona, where he prospected for copper and in 1896 registered several claims near Gila.[31] While he was away, a prospector named H. P. Bush, whom the Beards probably knew, returned from Alaska having filed four promising claims, and in September 1897 he and others formed the Alaska & Klondike Gold Mining & Prospecting Company, with Bush as president and offices on Arch Street in Philadelphia. Bush advertised anticipated capitalization at $250,000 and put shares out for sale. To promote sales, as well as to counter the competing efforts of Delaware natural gas millionaire J. Edward Atticks and his Yukon-Cariboo-British Columbia Gold Mining and Development Company, Bush engaged Lauretta as an agent to woo editors in Pennsylvania and Delaware and combat Atticks. For the first time her acknowledged skill at press relations gave her actual employment.[32]

Bush's enterprise folded almost as soon as it began and disappeared without a trace, but by this time Lauretta and her husband had plans of their own for the Klondike. In October 1897 Beard or his wife became involved forming a syndicate of investors to build "a great hotel" in Alaska's Dawson City to capitalize on the influx of prospectors. They used the name of Major General John A. Logan's widow as figurehead president, which had the distinct odor of Lauretta's Mark Twain and Mary Washington monument missteps, for no one obtained Mrs. Logan's permission first, and she killed the idea at once by writing Beard a letter denying any interest or involvement and giving it to the press.[33]

By this time new opportunities presented themselves that caused everything else the couple had attempted to pale in comparison. Back in 1891, when the Beards moved into their New York office on Broadway, Lauretta had discovered important business papers left behind by the prior occupant. She contacted his attorney, Thomas Gummey, who negotiated their purchase from her, and thereafter she maintained a professional acquaintance with Gummey. Some years later in 1897, now living in Philadelphia, she walked into the office of the investment firm of Leland and Power in the Drexel Building. That firm was then organizing and capitalizing the North Star Mining and Development Company of Alaska, one of numerous ventures that appeared in the wake of the Klondike strike that year, with up to $100,000 in shares to sell in the city at $1 per share. Having heard of the new company, Lauretta boldly told them they needed to employ her husband as their field prospector. The investors were considering several prospectors, but Lauretta proved persuasive, especially when she emphasized William's experience in the Southwest and with the Coast and Geodetic Survey. At the moment Beard worked as a mere wheelwright in nearby Delaware between prospecting trips, but they gave him the job.[34]

The investors, headed by Dr. Joseph Hancock, directed Beard to prepare an expedition to go to the Copper River region of Alaska to seek potential gold deposits. From his own pocket, Hancock gave him $1,500 to cover his expenses, and by December 17 Beard was ready to leave Philadelphia by train for Seattle.[35] On arriving there, he announced that in the spring his syndicate would have two hundred men coming to prospect. On January 3, 1898, he boarded the steam schooner *Alliance* along with seventy other passengers bound for Port Valdez on the Copper River, among them three who traveled with Beard: F. L. Hildreth of New York; H. C. Watkins, who represented himself as a New York newspaper reporter and a former broker; and one other man.[36]

It took twenty days to reach Valdez, which they found packed with hundreds of frustrated "ninety-eighters" chafing to reach the interior, held up by the impassable Valdez Glacier, which was intersected by crevasses too wide and deep to cross. Already some who had made the attempt had been swallowed in the icy depths.[37] Still, by February 1898 Beard and his three companions were on the verge of leaving for the Copper River.[38] Up to this time he sent several encouraging letters back to Lauretta and the investors, but then nothing more after they set out.[39] By March 28 the group was well on its way to the glacier. Then over the next four weeks, as they worked their way onto the ice, the weather closed in around them.

On April 29 Beard left camp to mark the trail. The others watched him go up a long cleft in the ice for nearly a mile, then he turned and they lost sight of him. When they followed, they found that he had turned into another valley, but then a heavy snowfall forced them to stop and make camp. They waited the rest of the day and all night, expecting him to return, but when he did not, they started out again at dawn. Walking about two miles to the head of the valley, they found a small glacier creased by numerous crevasses whose openings had been covered by the snow. Hildreth almost slipped into one, and the experience revealed to them what they now feared had happened to Beard.[40]

In mid-July a letter from Watkins reached Philadelphia via Seattle, informing Hancock that they had been caught in a snowstorm and Lauretta's husband was surely dead, though Watkins soon amended his story to say that the whole party was surprised by an avalanche on the Valdez Glacier and all ran for their lives, but the falling ice and snow caught Beard.[41] Hancock immediately felt uneasy. Watkins claimed that he narrowly averted the same fate as Beard, then spent ten days lost in the snow, subsisting on raw bacon and uncooked rice and oats until he got back to Valdez.[42] A letter from one of the other survivors said they remained on the glacier eight days looking for Beard before leaving to return to Valdez on May 5, which was in fact only five days after they ran into the crevasses. Moreover, a letter from another one of them was dated at Valdez on May 10. How could they have returned

Valdez, Alaska, circa 1900. The glacier where Beard disappeared is in the center background. Author's collection.

to the settlement in just five days when it had taken them six weeks to get from there to the fatal glacier?

Hancock and Lauretta knew that her husband had left Philadelphia with $1,500 in cash and should have had about $600 left when he was lost. That was enough to convince Lauretta that William's death might not be an accident, and she immediately wrote to President William McKinley asking for an investigation.[43] She grew even more suspicious a few days later, when word arrived that Beard's body had been found and there was no money on it, a report that proved to be false. Other details did not match, and Hancock sent a detective to Alaska to investigate.[44] Watkins was still there in mid-July, waiting for money for the passage back to Seattle, and did not return until July 22, followed by Hildreth three days later.[45] It might be possible to interview them to get more details and check their stories. Then Lauretta decided to go herself. Hancock gave her money to cover her trip, and she reached Seattle in early August.[46]

On arrival, she felt convinced that Beard had been murdered for the money he carried, a feeling reinforced when she believed she saw one of the survivors of the party on the city streets wearing Beard's clothes.[47] Her search for answers left her frustrated at almost every turn, however. "I found my work almost impossible for a woman to accomplish," she lamented about ten weeks later. "Fortunately I am well known in Washington and not only President McKinley but many others high in official circles, aided me." Even in grief Lauretta boasted about her high connections. In fact,

McKinley only politely acknowledged her plea for an investigation but promised nothing.[48]

Talking with those people she could reach, she pieced together a rather different story. Beard and Watkins had left to mark the trail after the snowstorm, not before it, and they left only one man behind, who was suffering from snow blindness. "When my husband left the tent he had on his person $2300 in money and gold dust," she determined, almost quadrupling the $600 she originally said he should have had, and $800 more than he took with him when he left Philadelphia. "The other man was a penniless greenhorn, so far as Alaska was concerned," she went on, "and yet he returned to the tent, well and hearty, and later on wore my husband's clothes and shoes into an Alaskan hotel."[49]

Seeing little hope of finding and recovering Beard's body, she sailed south, stopping in San Francisco and then moving on to Los Angeles, where she arrived October 13. Along the way she got word that Beard's body had been found just after she left Alaska. True to her old form, she immediately gave a press interview. "It was with the sole intention of recovering my husband's body that I went to Alaska," she told the reporter. "Dr. Hancock, president of the company, and I were both suspicious of the story of his death, but you know how things get garbled from a far-away country like that and I made my mind up to learn the truth." As she described it, "When my husband's body was found there was not a penny on it and it lay six miles away from any glacier and six miles away from any possible snowslide." She suspected he had been murdered for his money and perhaps for "other reasons" that she did not reveal. The finders buried him where found and intended to return after the snows melted to recover and return the body to Philadelphia. In passing, she mentioned her wartime care for wounded soldiers to reporters in San Francisco and Los Angeles but made no claim of being a soldier herself. She also told them that she had inherited large land holdings in her native Cuba, as well as in Louisiana and Mississippi, but lost them in the war, while another reporter understood her to say that she inherited the Cuban plantations after the war.[50]

She obviously suspected Watkins of being a murderer and thief, and indeed he was a shadowy figure. He claimed to be a journalist from New York, but none of the press there carried his byline. His real name was probably Harry Cecil Wiltshaw, a Wall Street bank clerk who embezzled $32,072 from his firm in 1888 before he walked out of the bank one day and disappeared. Authorities caught him in Buffalo, New York, in March

1894, using the alias Harry C. Watkins. Brought before a judge, he pleaded guilty, but the term of any sentence is unknown. He could have been out of jail within four years, and Alaska was a place where many a man of bad reputation went to start anew.[51] Nothing more is known of him, and though police detained him in Seattle pending investigation, he was never accused of the crime, if indeed there was one.[52]

Even in grief Lauretta used the press to aggrandize Beard and continue evolving her myth. According to her now, Beard had attended college, explored Africa and the Orient, spent four years in Alaska during the late war, and ran a silver mine in Oregon. Far from being a hired man, it was he who organized the North Star.[53] Even as she told the press of the hunt for his body and his killer, she announced she would look after the Beards' extensive mining interests and then launched new amendments to her own story.

Meanwhile, even as William's death put her name on front pages again, current events urged the nation's recall of her story of past glories. Two years earlier, when stories appeared in the press of Cuban women fighting as partisans and soldiers in the latest rebellion against Spain, editors remembered Harry T. Buford. Ménie Muriel Dowie's 1893 book had already sparked some renewed interest in *The Woman in Battle*, and in April 1896, when women were known to be taking part in the conflict in Cuba, the New York *Age-Herald* looked back to Lauretta and her story as an example of a woman of courage, declaring that "this is by no means a fictitious romance."[54] This recent insurgency continued until February 15, 1898, when the explosion of the battleship USS *Maine* in Havana Harbor propelled the United States into a war with Spain that began on April 25, just days before William Beard disappeared walking up the Valdez Glacier.

Given Lauretta's protestations of solidarity with insurgents in the Ten Years' War, it is remarkable that not a word from her about the three-year revolt appeared in the press. It may be understandable that she was silent during the sixteen-week war, since her husband's death at the conflict's outset commanded her attention through that fall. By that time Spain yielded and Cuba fell under control of the United States, which she had advocated for some time. Still, her silence is puzzling and best explained by the fact that she no longer had anything to gain from Cuba or being Cuban. She no longer tried to do business in imported goods from the island, hence she had no time to spare on concern for its situation, a possible hint of her real motive for her earlier presumed concern for Cuba and Cubans when there had been something in it for her.

She might have allied herself with the insurgents had she anticipated that after war broke out, a few editors would show some interest in the female patriots engaged and look back to earlier times for comparable warrior women. At least one writer trotted out Loreta Janeta Velasquez as an example of an American woman of action, relying without question on her story in her book. An article titled "Women as Soldiers" featured her as the sole Confederate example, though it might have rankled that her story came third following two Yankee women, and then only a handful of papers picked up the story. No one seemed to be interested anymore.[55]

CHAPTER SIXTEEN

"I HAVE NEVER MET HER EQUAL"

WHEN INTERVIEWED IN July 1898, Lauretta told reporters she came from the Spanish-American Velasquez family who had large plantations in Louisiana before the war.[1] Three months later she reiterated that she was born in Cuba and grew up in New Orleans, the heir to substantial sugar cane plantations in Cuba, Louisiana, and Mississippi. She lost her fortune in the war, she claimed, and was well known in the old Confederacy for the work she did during the war for starving soldiers. Afterward, she inherited large Cuban plantations, then went to Washington, where she met and married William Beard.[2] By October her interviews expanded their mining interests to California and Mexico.[3]

Now about eight years old, her son Waldemar was with her, a mysterious boy who flitted in and out of subsequent reports in the press, and it is evident that she intended to find a means of support for them in the West she had abandoned a quarter century before.[4] Still investigating Beard's death and his missing money, Lauretta rented rooms in Los Angeles at number 600 in the Frost Building, advertising herself as a mining broker.[5] Within months she had a new scheme that kept her up with the times. She conceived the idea of building a spa and hotel at Arrowhead Springs, in the foothills a few miles northeast of San Bernardino, and an electric railroad to feed it patrons from the city. By June 1899 she had plans for the hotel and rail route to show local businessmen in Redlands and San Bernardino, and with Waldemar in tow, she left to make her pitch.[6]

Predictably, she began with calls on local editors, displaying her file of letters from President Cleveland, assorted members of Congress, and other dignitaries, telling a reporter that "at any time" they would attest to "her capability and responsibility." She emphasized that she was the widow of a murdered man, eschewing given names and calling herself "Mrs. L. J. V. Beard," and claimed that she was in the business of mine development, mining stock, real estate, railroad construction, and other enterprises and was now head of the proposed electric line and hotel. She easily convinced a San Bernardino

Arrowhead, California, in 1900, with the white Arrowhead Springs Hotel beneath the distinctive scar on the mountain that gave the place its name. The locale would be the focus of the first of Lauretta's big confidence schemes. Author's collection.

reporter that she was "an authority upon all such deals, her sharp business acumen and indomitable energy being peculiar traits of her character." When she laid out her plans now, it is evident that she was still the Lauretta of old, in thorough command of a wealth of information to impress potential investors. "She is a walking encyclopedia on the subject and has evidently her whole soul bound up in the success of the scheme," the reporter wrote a day after meeting her. "She is a good talker, and yet talks to a purpose and not at random."

She intended to capitalize her project at $500,000 but was not interested in wealthy investors. Rather, she preferred men of moderate means for her backers, and they would profit along with her. She told the San Bernardino reporter she had sold some shares in Redlands already and investigated purchasing rolling stock, feeling so encouraged that she expected to begin construction of the railroad in a few weeks. The current owners of the land for the hotel at Arrowhead Springs wanted too much for it, she said, but she had told men in San Bernardino that while she was there she had met with the son of one of the owners, who said they might consider a partnership, joining their land with her railroad.[7]

Then she just disappeared for a year, moving back to Philadelphia to put a continent between herself and San Bernardino.[8] When or why she left remains a mystery, but she had done this before when a con was in progress, as with her sudden disappearance from North Carolina. If this scheme was legitimate, some vital elements fell through. More likely it was a scam, and once she pocketed some money from a few investors, she moved on before being found out, and as before, no charges were pressed. She counted on the willingness of businessmen to swallow losses rather than publicly admit they had been swindled by a fast-talking woman. Still, she had been onto something. In October 1902 the franchise for a railroad to Arrowhead Springs was purchased, and in 1907 the San Bernardino Valley Traction Company opened the Arrowhead Hot Springs electric line. In all of that, there was no mention of her.[9]

Her flight to Philadelphia to escape consequences from her venture did not keep her out of public notice entirely. Some newspapers continued singing the praises of a woman brought back to mind by the recent war, though for all they knew she was dead. Cuba might have produced a few Amazons, said one editor in the fall of 1899, but "none has eclipsed the fame of Lieutenant Harry Buford of the confederate army."[10]

Lauretta never stayed quiet for long. Mrs. L. J. V. Beard soon reappeared, this time with the most ambitious enterprise of her life, the Beards' other big scheme, for which the Arrowhead Springs line was a rehearsal. She revealed it in the new railroad settlement of Casa Grande, midway between Tucson and Phoenix, Arizona Territory, on May 22, 1900. The Pinal County delegation to that year's Democratic territorial convention gathered there on its way to Phoenix, and that evening she regaled the delegates with a plan for a real railroad. She told them she had ten thousand acres in Mexican land concessions from President Porfirio Díaz, who encouraged American and British investment to build industrial infrastructure in his country. Moreover, Díaz had also promised her a government subsidy of $10,000 per mile of track if she would build a line connecting Phoenix with Banderas Bay on Mexico's west coast on the Gulf of California.

From Banderas the line would run northward through the states of Jalisco, Nayarit, Sinaloa, and Sonora, crossing the border east of Nogales, and then proceed to Phoenix to connect with other lines to the east. A terminus at Banderas Bay would put goods 256 miles closer to the Philippines than any other American port, promising a lion's share of the islands' exports. She also claimed that important men in Deming, New Mexico Territory, had already offered $50,000 to reroute her proposed line to their city, but her late husband had told her that central Arizona was the most promising mineral region in the world, and she intended to follow his advice. Best of all, financiers in Holland were willing to back her up to $44 million for construction in Mexico, hence she had refused an offer of $80 million from another group, since the Dutch promise was sufficient for the job. All she needed now was money to lay the track in Arizona.[11]

In 1874 a railroad surveyor named Albert Kimsey Owen went to Topolobampo Bay, about four hundred miles up the coast from Banderas, with a very similar plan. He bought more than one hundred thousand acres from local landowners and secured concessions from Díaz, but no track was ever laid, and Mexico rescinded the concessions.[12] Lauretta claimed that Díaz had turned the Owen concessions over to her, and she had just returned from personally spending twenty-eight months surveying an eleven-hundred-mile route by mule and wagon. That would put her in Mexico since February 1898, which rather conflicted with her being in Philadelphia, Seattle, San Francisco, and Southern California until at least June 1899. With her usual cavalier attitude, she counted on no one knowing that in Arizona.

A Phoenix reporter was a bit skeptical when he reported her meeting under the headline "A Railroad for Phoenix: It Will Be a Big Thing if Its [*sic*] Ever Built," adding that it would be good news for Phoenix "if true." As for Mrs. Beard, he found her middle-aged, attractive, and possessed of "a strong flow of language."[13] She told him she had already engaged the noted engineer Lyman Bridges for the job and that Mexico's consul general at San Francisco, A. K. Coney, was helping her with the project.[14]

Within a week Lauretta arrived in Phoenix to put flesh on her story. She called her dream the American, Mexican & Pacific Railway Company and spent several days in town giving potential investors an expanded version of her Casa Grande story. Now she had German capital in addition to The Hague's promised backing up to $84 million, and to fund the Arizona portion she would make an initial stock offer of $9 million. The road was incorporated with sixteen directors from Tucson, Coney from San Francisco, Bridges and three others from Southern California, and herself in Philadelphia. She displayed the land concession documents to prove her legitimacy and said she expected real work to start in a few months and that it would be finished in December 1902.[15] She added a branch line twenty miles out to Nogales, saying that at Banderas it would connect with Mexican rail lines to Mexico City, Tampico, Veracruz, and Guatemala. She was going to open up central and southern Mexico and Central America commercially as well.[16]

On June 8, 1900, based on an interview she gave a Phoenix reporter, her story went across the country on the Associated Press wire, announcing her as "Mme. L. J. Valesquez Beard, well known throughout the country as a woman promoter."[17] Her story had changed yet again. Now she said Mexico had originally granted her concessions to Louis Huller in November 1887, to build a 1,350-mile railroad linking Deming, New Mexico Territory, to Topolobampo Bay.[18] She did not add that actually Huller was a fraud, virtually broke, and when he died suddenly in 1892, he left behind two widows but not a foot of track.[19] The concessions then supposedly went through litigation that stalled progress for years.[20] According to her now Alphonso B. Smith of Los Angeles had acquired the concessions, and she announced that he was one of the directors of her new company.[21] Lauretta claimed that Smith had engaged her to find investors, but she now represented the railroad idea and the concessions themselves as being her own. By July she embellished her mule-back survey as far south as Costa Rica, declaring that she had pursued the scheme since 1883.

For the first time in years she also made reference in interviews to her Civil War career, telling reporters she had been the Confederacy's agent in Canada to secure money for the cause.[22] She spun entirely new versions of her old story. She shaved three years from her age, saying she was born in 1845, and for the first time publicly claimed French ancestry, as well as Spanish. Her father, she said, had served in the diplomatic corps in Cuba, then moved to Mexico and fought in Santa Anna's army in the 1846–48 war with the United States, being wounded at Chapultepec. Apparently forgetting—or ignoring—the fact that in her book she had her parents living at least until 1857, and that in her December 1864 personal ad in Richmond she had her father dying that November, she now averred that both her parents had died when she was a child and that she married William E. Burnett at the age of thirteen. "It was a runaway match," she claimed, recalling a subhead from her book, "and I either had to do that or marry young Rafael Francisco Rodriguez." It was the only time she gave a full name to the man to whom her parents betrothed her.

After the outbreak of the Civil War and Burnett's death, she skipped over more than twenty years until she married Beard, with whom she had conceived her railroad idea in 1897. They would have gotten started on it immediately, but the outbreak of the Spanish-American War in April 1898 upset their plans, and she said they both went to Alaska, forgetting the fact that Beard had left for Alaska in December 1897 and she did not go there until after his death. She maintained now that she had just returned from Alaska around the first of the year, neatly placing herself outside the country during the time she was in Southern California promoting her Arrowhead Hot Springs electric railroad.[23]

Lauretta's enterprise attracted a lot of attention. When a Chicago journalist commented that "women have entered even to the field of the promoter," he very likely had her in mind.[24] A Los Angeles editor referred to her as "the woman railroad promoter," adding that though her plans seemed extravagant, she was winning over prominent men.[25] What is amazing is that with as much publicity as she received, no one connected the Mrs. Beard of the American, Mexican & Pacific Railway Company with the Mrs. Beard of the Arrowhead Hot Springs, the International Immigration Company, the bogus Dawson City Hotel, or the Mary Washington monument promotion. Moreover, she gave more than enough details of her earlier life to connect her with Loreta Velasquez, she of the letter accusing President Garfield of embezzlement and the false claims of collaboration with Mark Twain. Lauretta may not have been fortunate in her schemes, but she was almost always lucky in that the knowledge of her failures rarely followed her from one con to the next.

Now she would be fortunate in failure again. As rapidly as Lauretta could invent and expand a story, so also it could collapse. By July 19 the American, Mexican & Pacific Railway was dead. She announced that there had been a falling out with the engineer Bridges, accusing him and other directors of "treachery" that forced her to abandon the project. Immediately she organized a new company, announcing that she had new investors and would commission the New York engineering firm of Roosevelt & Sullivan to complete the survey. She called the new concern the American-Mexican Commercial Railway and projected a total capitalization of $55 million, saying that most of the company's stock was already subscribed in Europe. It was all a lie, of course, and by the end of the month she was broke. Money contributed by sympathetic citizens paid her hotel bill and bought a train ticket out of Phoenix. When she left on July 28, she variously gave her destination as Chicago or El Paso in search of new investors. Behind her, men in Phoenix complimented her energy but found her aggressive self-promotion "tactless," a local reporter concluding that "Mrs. Beard's case is a pathetic instance of a woman's effort to fulfill a man's mission, and the consequent failure."[26]

Lauretta went to neither El Paso nor Chicago, but first to Albuquerque, New Mexico Territory, taking Waldemar with her.[27] She then turned up in Denver on August 22 and tried to start her con over again, announcing that she sought $40 million in capital for her railroad. Now she displayed letters from Díaz; senators and governors; prominent capitalists such as Chauncey Depew, J. Pierpont Morgan, and Henry Clews; and even the noted Chinese statesman Li Hongzhang. She said her real reason for coming to the city was to campaign for the election of William Jennings Bryan in the fall presidential election.[28]

Four weeks later, having done no campaigning, she arrived in Chicago, giving her residence as Washington, D.C., and announcing that she was returning to Mexico to build her railroad. She also added a new fillip to her history, claiming that she had spent two years with Beard hunting diamond mines in Kimberley, South Africa. Giving up on Phoenix, she now expected her line to connect in Denver. Those she met seemed impressed, unaware of her troubles in Phoenix. "She is 50 years old, tall and vigorous," wrote one reporter, who also offered only the second known mention of any Spanish accent, though he found her "entirely American in her sentiments and her energy."[29]

Moving east from Chicago, she stopped in Springfield, Illinois, to give an interview and added yet more conflicting nuances, which may be why the local press thought her an "eccentric lady." With no mention of her supposed sojourn in Mexico, she said she was now on her way home from Alaska after collecting her husband's body and evidence of his murder. She intended to go to St. Louis and then New Orleans, bound ultimately for Washington to lobby for support for her railroad, and added to her list of supporters President Díaz's brother-in-law, half of the members of the U.S. Senate, "and nearly all the cabinet officers." Her packet of letters also included one from President William McKinley, no doubt his condolences on her husband's death.[30]

By October 24 she reached New Orleans, announcing it as her former home, and no one seemed to connect her with Lauretta Williams of old. She called on businessmen, looking to raise $150,000 in immediate capital, and once again changed the northern terminus of her railroad. Phoenix and Denver were forgotten now in favor of Tampico on the Gulf of Mexico and from there via steamship to New Orleans. She unveiled a newfound localism when she put aside her Cuban nativity and claimed she was "a native of this state" and would not allow the trade route to end anywhere else. She sought the "co-operation of the people here to consummate what she believes would be a splendid thing for the city." At the same time, the cost of the railroad was reduced to $35 million.[31]

New Orleans proved to be another Phoenix and Denver. No one came forward with the $150,000 initial subscription she sought, probably all she ever really looked for from her scheme. So she left for Savannah and by the last week of December moved on to Atlanta, Waldemar still with her, to spend several days calling on prospects. She promised she had wealthy investors elsewhere, including Savannah, and would have them come to Atlanta to meet with her and local investors on the last day of the year. It is evident that she was desperate to raise something. Having started out looking for millions, now she reduced her $150,000 expectations and announced that she would organize a development company with capital of just $30,000 to $50,000. She also cut the capitalization for building the railroad to between $10 million and $15 million, a far cry from the $55 million she had projected in Phoenix. She made no mention now of concessions already in hand but said only that she had "applied" for the rights to build the line in Mexico. Any concessions she got would go to the Atlanta development company.

On the evening of December 26, 1900, a reporter for the Atlanta *Constitution* called on Lauretta. She could not then have known that it was probably the last time the press would come to her for an interview.[32] For the occasion, she continued evolving her personal history. Having given up on New Orleans, she reverted to her Cuban nativity and Spanish parentage. After marrying Burnett, she said, she joined him in the ranks. "I carried a gun just as my husband," she declared, "and I was right in the front ranks." Dismissing DeCaulp, Wasson, Bonner, and Bobo from her history, she said that William Beard was only her second husband, and the two of them had possessed "vast mining interests in Arizona." After his murder she managed the mines with the aid of an unnamed partner, whom she never mentioned again, and resurrected her late husband's plan for a Mexican railroad. As for herself, she had traveled extensively and spoke many languages.

She gave her current residence as Arizona but made it clear that she wanted the railroad to link the Pacific coast with the South, presumably at Atlanta. She believed the track and the steamship line she also projected would bring the riches of the Orient to the South, rather than to New York, and be the means of regional prosperity and rebuilding. She thought her prospects for attracting local money in Atlanta were bright, but if not, then she would move on to New York where, she assured the reporter, wealthy men drooled at the opportunity. He came away impressed by Lauretta's ambition, if nothing else. "Many enterprises have been undertaken by women and prosecuted to success, but probably the record for the most daring business venture ever made by a woman is held by Mrs. L. J. Velasquez Beard," concluded the journalist. "Whether she proves equal to the task of rendering this immense undertaking a success remains to be seen."[33]

Aspects of Lauretta's last interview raise anew the question that slowly emerged from her declarations going back more than twenty years to her reckless accusations about Garfield. Though she was only fifty-eight now, she increasingly showed signs of intermittent irrational behavior and memory loss. No doubt the life she had led for years, moving—sometimes running—from city to city, constantly on the grift, had placed physical, emotional, and psychological strain on a woman who may have been something of a fantasist from youth. Constant failure only added to the pressure on her, and whatever her true relation to Waldemar, she kept him closer to her than she had her son by Bonner, or any child by DeCaulp if there was one, adding concern for his support to her burden. It did not help that the press she had used so adroitly in past years to build and spread her celebrity was now her enemy, thanks to wire services that quickly spread the story of her failed swindles. Now sometimes word of her schemes reached the next city before she did. Then, too, the first section of a genuine American & Pacific Railroad was under construction, connecting the mines of Arizona to the Mexican border near Nogales, with a longer segment continuing on to Topolobampo Bay planned as soon as concessions from Mexico could be obtained. It was virtually the line Lauretta promoted, and the spreading news of the railroad compromised her ability to pass herself off as representing another line proposing the same route.[34]

Her shifts of focus and numbers and details on the railroad scheme might have been improvisations, as she tailored her pitch to the prospects at hand, but her wanderings in her personal past could have had no real purpose. Even given her carelessness—if not frivolity—about contradicting herself, for some time she had been saying things that made no sense. Back in July she said Beard had been killed "three years ago," when it was just two.[35] Omitting four husbands in her Atlanta interview exceeded the bounds of carelessness, even if it was politic to omit DeCaulp in case locals remembered his desertion. She was always inconsistent on other details of her real life and her mythical creation Buford, but in recent years her claims were becoming more exaggerated and erratic. Actions soon to unfold demand questioning the state of her mental health and whether she was and had been experiencing episodes of nascent dementia.

Atlanta proved to be no more susceptible to her confidence scheme than Savannah or New Orleans, Denver or Phoenix, so a few weeks later she took it to Tampa, Florida. Lauretta appeared in the city on or about February 2, 1901, and registered at the Palmetto Hotel, but only after giving the desk clerk a thorough grilling as to who the more wealthy and influential men in Tampa might be. The next day she took up what observers now called a "heavy bundle" of all her letters and endorsements and set off to make her calls. She boasted to one potential investor after another of having millions of dollars at her disposal, with Díaz and a syndicate from The Hague behind her. J. Pierpont Morgan, the great New York financier, had offered her $50,000 if she would allow him to put the deal together, she said, and she came to the South as his representative to select a port to be the terminus for the projected steamship line, while the railroad would now bypass the unimaginative cities of Arizona, Louisiana, and Georgia, to cut across Mexico from west to east. It would bring the goods of the Far East to the Gulf of Mexico, from which her new line of steamers would carry it to the United States. Tampa, she argued, was the right place for those vessels to land their cargoes. When one "mark" pointed out that the river linking Tampa to the Gulf was not deep enough for ocean traffic, she dismissed his objection by declaring that she would dredge a ship channel fifty-five feet deep right to the city docks.

The city council refused to give her an audience, but five of the men she called on agreed to a meeting to discuss her plans. They met at an attorney's chambers on the afternoon of February 22 with a reporter for the Tampa *Morning Tribune* present, most likely at Lauretta's invitation, hoping the publicity would attract more investors. Giving her project the unwieldy name of Pacific-Atlantic, Trans-Mexican, Orient-Occident, Penuka-Peninsula Railroad and Steamship Company, Mrs. Beard rhapsodized on what she and her railroad would do for Tampa. It seemed to go well until Judge George P. Raney proposed that if she expected them to put up substantial money, it was only fair that she deposit $10,000 in cash with him as a token of good faith. At that the reporter heard Colonel C. C. Whitaker give "a little goo-goo laugh," and the others broke into guffaws. None of them took her seriously, meeting only to have fun with a mountebank.

"Angered to desperation," according to the reporter, Lauretta picked up her bundle of letters and stalked out of the room, telling them they would be sorry when she took her steamship line and its yield of riches to another port. Shortly before dawn on February 23, she stealthily departed the Palmetto

Hotel without paying her bill for three weeks' room and board, leaving nothing behind but a small purse containing several business cards. The next day the *Morning Tribune* carried the bold headline "Big Scheme of One Woman." Describing Lauretta as almost a double for the temperance activist Carrie Nation but for a hatchet, the article told the story of her time in the city and her humiliation in the meeting as "the large, cruel world scoffed with a large, cruel scoff."[36] Fifteen years later Tampa still remembered her as "a mysterious woman."[37]

She returned to Philadelphia, virtually destitute, and employed a female con artist's standard weapon, sentiment. It had worked once on Dr. Hancock, so she tried him again, and it worked a second time. Out of regard for her late husband, he agreed to cover lodging for her and fifteen-year-old Wallie at William F. Binder's home at 1545 Bouvier Street. Meanwhile, they would dine at Hancock's home.[38] With her basic necessities secured, she determined to try one more con. Mrs. L. J. Velasquez Beard was not done yet.

That same month Lauretta called at the office of attorney Thomas Gummey, carrying with her what he called a "mass of documents," including her Mexican land concessions, and presented her new plan for the Mexican railroad. Now she would run it five hundred miles from Banderas Bay east to Tampico, with branch lines to other cities and ports. Its connections in the United States would bring Philadelphia within eighty hours of the Pacific coast by train, and a steamship line from Tampico to Pensacola, along with telephone and telegraph lines, would cut seventeen hundred miles from the route to the Philippines.[39]

It sounded good, though informed men in the Northeast should have heard something of her efforts in the South and Southwest. If she really had the concessions, then it might be worth the risk of dealing with her. Gummey asked for "the most explicit proof" that she really had them, and she showed him some of her documents but refused to display them all, since she said they had bearing on other business schemes and she did not want to reveal their details. What Gummey saw looked to him legal and plausible, and he agreed to act as attorney for her project and lend his influence and perhaps monetary assistance. Soon he took her proposal to Philadelphia financiers, including James F. Horton and Henry Hile, president of the Quaker City Mining Company.[40]

Meanwhile, in the first week of April Lauretta approached Albert L. Johnson, noted builder of urban electric trolley systems, and soon afterward may have gone to Cleveland to see his brother and fellow trolley line builder, mayor-elect Thomas L. Johnson.[41] She claimed that a grateful President Díaz promised her the land concessions whenever she organized a corporation with herself as an officer or investor. She and her son had traversed the projected route on mules in 1899 and 1900 and knew it was suitable for rails. All she needed was an initial capitalization of $150,000 to qualify for the concessions, which she told her hosts she "expected every day." Once they arrived she would send teams of surveyors to Mexico, and construction would commence by the end of the year.[42] Her story intrigued other Philadelphians associated with her husband in the North Star Mining Company, especially her gullible benefactor, Hancock, who joined with Hile in mid-July to incorporate the Mexican National Telephone Company.[43] She even claimed to have enlisted the interest of eighty-year-old General Longstreet, whom she continued to use as a reference long after their only meeting nearly thirty years before.[44]

Gummey assembled the investors in August and, satisfied that her documents were genuine, Horton undertook organizing and incorporating the Mexican Continental Railway and Steamship Company late that month, with Hile as president, Horton as secretary and treasurer, and Gummey as counsel. Investors were to pay Lauretta $10,000 for the rights to her plans and holdings and give her an allotment of stock.[45]

The new railroad and steamer company attracted notice and a little publicity for Lauretta, which proved to be the final glimpse of her at large. A reporter thought her "a little woman, not much more than five feet high, and of slight build." She dressed only in black. She told people that she came to Philadelphia not from Florida, Atlanta, or the Southwest, but from Tepic, the capital city of the state of Nayarit, Mexico, not far from Banderas Bay. She changed her birthplace back to Louisiana, still claiming her parents were Cuban, and now made a dramatic departure in her late husband's background: William Beard had been an officer in the Mexican Army, serving close to then-general Díaz in one of that officer's several conflicts before he assumed the presidency. A man of great wealth, Beard had left Lauretta a fortune in mineral land in Arizona and Mexico, she claimed, and before then a grateful Díaz had promised her that railroad right-of-way across Mexico. "She is said to be a very good business woman," commented a Philadelphia newsman, adding that she was "a firm believer in the rights of secession."[46] Her partners in the new venture were said to credit her with "much shrewdness."[47]

Soon her partners feared she was too shrewd. Without the knowledge of the others, she sold her alleged Mexican grants to Charles E. Foster, a partner and agent for the brokerage firm Douglas, Lacey & Company of New York, whom the other partners no doubt enlisted to oversee sales of stock when issued. It was a classic confidence artist's scheme. Having formed a partnership to which others brought cash investment while her only contribution was her documents, she cashed out by selling them to one of the partners, leaving her presumably free from liability or responsibility and legally untouchable since she had sold the documents "in good faith." When the partners learned what she had done, Gummey investigated Foster and learned that he had left Douglas, Lacey & Company. In fact, Foster's successor as agent told Gummey that the firm "would like to know where Foster is." It had had him arrested for embezzlement and knew of other warrants for his arrest after he made bail and then disappeared. Before he vanished, he told friends that he disdained his paltry office in the brokerage, "as he would soon be president of a Mexican railway company, at a salary of $25,000 a year."

Meanwhile, Gummey wrote to F. L. De La Barra, whom Lauretta cited as her counsel in Mexico City. He denied any dealings with her, though she had written him to send her government maps and documents. Further, he told Gummey that a search of appropriate archives found no record of any concession grants to her, while inquiries revealed that she was unknown personally to any Mexican officials. De La Barra's response, atop the Foster business, convinced Gummey that Lauretta was a fraud, especially after Wallie Beard indiscreetly said he knew nothing about Mexico and had never ridden a mule, putting the lie to her stories of personally reconnoitering the proposed line. Gummey summoned her to his office and accused her to her face of "gross deception." As she had before when found out, she attacked him with invective designed to deflect suspicion. "She became abusive," he said later, "and I ordered her from my office." Convinced of her power of persuasion, she returned, but Gummey "threatened her with arrest if she did not at once leave and never again show herself."

All this time Lauretta had been living on the goodwill and gullibility of others. While Hancock provided her lodging and meals, she got Philadelphia merchants to advance her goods on the promise of stock in the new company. One elderly man at a major department store succumbed to her promise of a job at $10,000 a year with the railroad and made himself guarantor with his employers for payment of several hundred dollars' worth of goods that she "bought" at the store. Worse, he sold some property of his own to buy more stock from her, then quit his job against the advice of friends, saying he would soon be "a railway magnate." He had fallen for the same pitch as Foster.

By early November 1901 her behavior became increasingly erratic. Hancock was fed up, telling Gummey that "Mrs. Beard was a great source of annoyance on account of her imperative and exacting temperament." He refused to give her any more meals and stopped paying her rent. Lauretta then convinced her landlords to let her and Wallie dine with them and to extend her credit for her rooms. "I believe in Senora Beard," Binder's wife told a reporter afterward. "Why, she has letters from Diaz, of Mexico, and from every member of his cabinet, all with big red official seals attached, and President Diaz says that all concerned m[a]y place implicit trust in Senora Beard." She added, "Only three weeks ago, a gentleman interested in the Senora's project guaranteed the lodging bill, of which I have not yet received one dollar." Soon Lauretta took meals at a 9th Street restaurant, running up a bill for $150, no doubt on the promise of future wealth.[48]

Finally on November 20 Horton went to Washington to call at the Mexican legation to investigate further. That same day Lauretta and Wallie told the Binders they were leaving for New York, expecting to return in two days. Two days later Horton announced the recall of all outstanding stock in the Mexican Continental Railway and Steamship Company pending an investigation, confessing that the directors believed Mrs. Beard did not legally own the concessions that were the basis of the company.[49]

Then it all came out in the press. "Senora Velasquez Beard, the Cuban Princess," as one headline called her, had not returned to Philadelphia as promised and owed money to any number of friends now anxious to hear from her. Horton announced that Mexican officials knew her only as "a persistent applicant for maps, pamphlets, etc." He said there was nothing to do except call in the stock and close the company's books. He had just learned that she was running a concurrent confidence scheme in New York while defrauding her Philadelphia investors, but news of the Mexican Continental swindle frightened potential New York backers away before they gave her any money. She had been provided with room and board for almost a year, plus cash, clothing, jewelry, and similar things for her son, without paying a cent. She owed hundreds to restaurants and stores. Horton further estimated that she had received between $1,500 and $2,000 in cash advances from each of her "partners." "The woman is one of the most plausible and fluent I have ever met. She seems to be able to persuade her fellow humans to almost anything—until her absolutely appalling deceptions are found out. Meantime she gets money to support her while her schemes are being investigated or acted upon. I have never met her equal."[50]

Few had. The Civil War accelerated changes in female roles, with new degrees of independence that gave rise to a generation of not just confidence men but women as well. It unlocked the door to a flood of corruption both within and outside government, especially for manufacturers of poor-quality goods profiteering on government contracts. The passing of a few decades opened up limited opportunities that allowed some women to rise moderately in more legitimate endeavors, but that would not be Lauretta's trajectory. From first to last she delineated the archetype of the career confidence woman over the span of forty years, virtually pioneering techniques those coming after her would use. She demonstrated an unscrupulous instinct for human nature, choosing as targets those who thought themselves too shrewd to be fooled in business and would be reluctant to admit their victimization by filing charges. Victims repeatedly described her as a "remarkable woman" and an "excellent talker," hallmarks of the swindler. Behind a feminine front, she was smarter, tougher, more unconventional, and less morally restrained than most other women. Lauretta was no dime novel adventuress, for they rarely broke the law. She had unlimited confidence in herself that led her to take great risks in expectation of great gain.

To the extent that Americans were aware that female con artists existed in the late nineteenth century, they did not expect these women to step so far into the male world as to imitate a robber baron such as James "Big Jim" Fisk by selling stocks worth millions in bogus companies. They expected the con woman still to be a "lady," but not Lauretta. Using disguise during the war and deception and manipulation always to achieve her ends, she made the rules she played by and refused to be pigeonholed with the pious, domestic, and submissive sisters in her trade.[51] In her era, she genuinely was unique. Horton was right: no one had "met her equal."

CHAPTER SEVENTEEN

"THE OLD BATTLE-LIGHT"

IN LATE 1901 Lauretta and her son took a hotel room on New York's Greenwich Street after leaving Philadelphia and as usual maintained a low profile.[1] Unlike the marks in her previous confidence games, her victims this time were not keeping quiet, frankly and publicly admitting that they had been taken. Still, she had little to fear. After all, her room and board had been gifts, and she had given stock as surety for her retail purchases. The money from the pockets of the investors was to buy her interest in the *promise* of the concessions. She did not claim she actually had them. While she often skirted illegality, she may not have broken any laws other than what appears to have been a swindle of Foster, and he was a felon on the run. She had played a bold game with her railroad schemes for years, and she was fortunate that she was still free and at large. If the promised investigation took place, it resulted in no prosecution, though there were repercussions on others. In a little more than two years the amiable Dr. Joseph Hancock would file for bankruptcy.[2]

She rapidly faded from public view, though she was not entirely forgotten. A genuine American-Mexican Pacific Railway company surveyed a roadbed throughout 1902, and that sparked recollections in Arizona.[3] An Albuquerque editor ran the headline "Mrs. Beard's Railroad," recalling the "weird female" who "exhibited her reticule of documents, and tried to organize a corporation at Albuquerque, El Paso and Phoenix, and then disappeared." He credited her with originating the idea for the line now being run.[4] At the same time an editor in Phoenix remarked on the new railroad's progress and recalled Lauretta's weeks in his city in 1900 as she "for a time worked up great enthusiasm among those she met" for what he called her "paper railroad."[5]

Just how much money Lauretta took with her when she fled Philadelphia is unknown, but it may have been enough to form the basis for her subsistence for some time. She disappeared for more than three years before she reemerged in May 1905 at about age sixty-two, still living in New York

City in a Manhattan hotel run by a Cuban immigrant.[6] After letting her railroad scheme rest for some time, she gave it one last effort, this time in Portland, Maine, where she joined six men to incorporate the Mexican American Construction Company. They announced plans to issue stock in the amount of $10 million to build and operate railroads in Mexico and broker real estate. Two of the incorporators were George F. Gould and John J. Whittemore, surnames that instantly suggested the nation's most prominent railroad industrialists. But these were not the tycoons, for the real Gould's middle initial was J. and the real Whittemore's middle initial was H. In fact, the sixty-year-old John J. Whittemore was a lawyer lodging at the same hotel as Lauretta, though whether he was her partner in anything more than business is unknown. It seems certain that the two of them deliberately used the names Gould and Whittemore to add cachet to their company and attract investors.[7]

Lauretta's Mexican railroad plots were just too well known by now, for this last one garnered little notice, and nothing came of the venture. She did not emerge again for nearly three years, still in New York in pitiable circumstances, in a March 21, 1908, New York *Times* article. "Mrs. Beard Ill and in Want," it read, billing her as a "once wealthy war nurse and friend of ex-President Cleveland." She lay critically ill in New York Hospital, where doctors said she would die if not given a private room and special treatment, but she was destitute, "too poor" to afford such care. For the past quarter century she had been a familiar figure in New York, Washington, and the South, but now she was helpless, and her son, though by this time he would have been nearly twenty, was yet too young to support her. Implicit in the notice was an appeal for donations to save her life, and in aid of that, the brief news item reminded readers that during the late war, she had spent time in Canada securing money to aid the Confederacy and nursing wounded soldiers. Without mentioning DeCaulp, the notice promoted him to a position on the personal staff of General Joseph E. Johnston.[8] Nothing indicated that the article's content came from anyone at the hospital, while the personal details, exaggerations, and shifts of fact are redolent of Lauretta's past press announcements, making it likely that she or Waldemar was the source and her "helpless" condition just a classic tool of the female con artist to play on the sympathy of potential donors. Still, for one who had once seen her name in bold headlines as a dashing heroine, it must have been humiliating

Perhaps the donations came, for Lauretta rallied, if indeed she had been ill at all. Seven months later she and J. G. B. Woolworth, another of the partners in her Mexican American Construction Company bearing a surname similar to a prominent millionaire's, incorporated in New York their World Finance Company at 200 Broadway, announcing an immediate capitalization of $50,000.[9] It sank without a trace. The confidence game had moved beyond Lauretta now, even though for so long she helped pioneer the craft.

By 1911 she was nearly seventy. Her son, Waldemar, was in his early twenties and probably out on his own, and she had nothing to show for her decades of ambitious schemes.[10] She moved back to Washington and tried to go into business selling real estate as L. J. Velasquez Beard at 1329 G Street NW.[11] She announced in June 1912 that she was gathering new material to produce a revised edition of *The Woman in Battle*, as well as a new book on relations between the United States and Mexico based on her recent "protracted study of political and social conditions in the latter republic."[12]

It was all pipe dreams now. She suffered increasingly from arterial sclerosis and the onset of dementia, which had been manifesting for some years. Just two months after her last announcement, on August 5, 1912, she went into Washington's Government Hospital for the Insane, better known as St. Elizabeth's. Admitted as case number 20081, she was listed as indigent, sixty-nine years old, and a resident of the District of Columbia. Still clinging to an old ambition, she claimed an occupation as a "writer," and despite so long maintaining Hispanic origins, she left the question of where she was born unanswered. Perhaps by now she had forgotten. She listed herself as Episcopalian, an echo of DeCaulp though she had claimed she became a Methodist on marrying Burnett before the war. She had changed so many faces over the years that she may have changed what faith she had as well. She had contradicted herself so many times on so many things that it is virtually impossible to tell where her lies left off and her dementia began.[13]

Indeed, we may wonder if she even knew anymore. She had created a glamorous world all her own in her newspaper stories as far back as 1861 and in and since *The Woman in Battle*. The characters she created may have had the names of real people—Lafayette Baker, John H. Winder, and especially Thomas DeCaulp—but her imagination remolded them just as it invented or reshaped the events of her life. In her dementia now, was she able to remember her reality and distinguish it from her own creation? Did she revisit either or both now? Could she any longer tell the difference between the facts and her own myth?

Government Hospital for the Insane, better known as St. Elizabeth's, where, on August 5, 1912, Lauretta entered the doors and never left. National Archives.

St. Elizabeth's could be an interesting place despite Lauretta's reason for being there. Among the other patients at the moment was William Chester Minor, probably the greatest contributor to the compilation of the Oxford English Dictionary. Still, these were increasingly sad years as Lauretta flickered in and out of reality. She occasionally got into print, though she may not have known of it. Back in 1907 a Birmingham, Alabama, writer retold much of *The Woman in Battle* in an article that saw modest circulation.[14] Two years later a series of articles on "Twenty Women Soldiers of the World" appeared in Salt Lake City and elsewhere, and the ninth installment detailed at length the story given in *The Woman in Battle*, meanwhile failing to link her with the Lauretta Bonner who had left Utah under a bit of a cloud. It also managed via a typographical error to make a claim more outlandish than any of hers—namely, that she had decided to follow her husband into the Confederate army when she was "only 1 years old."[15]

As time passed, however, some people increasingly doubted her story. That same year a Dallas newspaper, talking about women in wartime, mentioned "a Spanish girl, Loreta Velasquez; a Confederate sympathizer," as an example of a small host of her kind from the Civil War "responsible for reams and volumes of writing—autobiographical, biographical, apocryphal and frankly fictitious."[16]

Now with Europe on the verge of war, interest renewed in the woman warrior motif, and inevitably a few recalled Harry T. Buford of the last Great War. The writer of a forgettable 1913 encyclopedia of adventurous men and women gave her three sentences as his only example from the Civil War in a chapter on female fighters, managing to make a mistake in every sentence.[17] Within weeks of Europe erupting in conflict, the issue of women in combat warmed, and articles briefly appeared recounting the histories of such heroines back to ancient times. In September 1914 a Cincinnati reporter mentioned "Loreta Velazquez, who wore a Lieutenant's shoulder straps in the Confederate army," oblivious of the fact that Confederate officers wore insignia on their collars.[18] By 1917, with the United States now in the war, a West Virginia journalist remembered that Lauretta had been "wild about war" and, as Harry Buford, fought "for the sheer joy of fighting."[19] In the last year of the conflict the New York *Times*, which spilled little ink on her in decades past, placed "Mme. L. J. De Velazquez" second only to Belle Boyd in celebrity among female warriors of the Confederacy, a ranking sure to rankle Lauretta if she saw it. Six weeks later a Wyoming writer credited "Señora Loreta" with action at Bull Run and great success as a spy.[20]

It was on the eve of the outbreak of war, in June 1914, that the indefatigable writer on Civil War spies and espionage William Gilmore Beymer gave Lauretta the last major press notice in her lifetime. He published an article on her in *Pearson's Magazine*, a popular and sometimes sensational monthly proclaiming that it published "facts which you want to know but which no magazine that lives on advertising could 'afford' to print." Forthrightly admitting that he based his article on *The Woman in Battle*, Beymer further confessed that when he first read her book he did not believe it, but after a while he came to the conclusion that it was genuine, a judgment he based on his perception of her character as it shone through in her book. "To believe Loreta Janeta's story you have to know what was in the blood," he said, accepting completely her story of her parentage and ancestry. He wondered why she did not explain gaps in her story but remained convinced of its authenticity. "If this narrative were fiction the sneering comment would here be made 'it always happens so in stories,'" he concluded. "But this is not fiction."

Dazzled though he might have been by her character, Beymer did not avoid a hard judgment at the end when he mentioned her activities blockade

Section 10 of Cedar Hill Cemetery in Suitland, Maryland. In the unmarked ground at center is plot 59, where lies Lauretta in complete—and unaccustomed—anonymity. Author's collection.

running and brokering bounties, as well as the bond and stock manipulations she supposedly perpetrated. "Little by little she slipped down," he wrote, "down from the position of a woman unselfishly serving a great cause to that of a woman who turns warfare into a means to serve her own selfish ends." Her war ended, Beymer found the balance of her autobiography dull and plodding, closing with jarring abruptness during her trip east in 1874. "How does it all end?" he asked, wondering what later became of her. In resignation he could only conclude, "God knows." "Doubtless, it is all we shall ever know," he said. He then went on to speculate, "Perhaps she is living to-day a dear old granddame of seventy-odd. Perhaps she may chance upon this story, and as she reads there will again come the old battle-light into 'Lieutenant Harry Buford's' age-dimmed eyes."[21]

She still lived in 1914 and for nearly a decade beyond, though the "battle-light" came not again into her little world at St. Elizabeth's. Except perhaps in imagination and cloudy memory, she never left it until January 6, 1923, when she died at about eighty years old, her death attributed to "serious and persistent mental illness" caused by an organic heart disease and general arteriosclerosis that had advanced over the previous five years. Two days later undertaker W. W. Deal took her body to Cedar Hill Cemetery in Suitland, Maryland, just a few blocks from the District of Columbia boundary, and there laid her to rest in plot 59 of section 10.[22] Just days after this mentally ill "veteran" of the Civil War era passed, a new program commenced at St. Elizabeth's to train doctors to deal with mental disorders caused by World War I.[23]

There would be no funeral or memorial service. The burial was done at government expense. In a crowning irony, the woman who lived a fictionalized life largely of her own creation in the newspapers died without a single mention or obituary in the press. It was as if she had never lived. A woman who craved renown more than anything else went to an unmarked grave, where she still lies today.[24] As for her son Waldemar, who would have been about thirty-four, nothing more is known. As Lauretta herself had done so many times, he simply vanished.

Yet she was not forgotten. Her creation outlived her in public memory. At the end of that same year a judge in Dallas, Texas, published a notice in the *Confederate Veteran* magazine asking if the woman who had posed as a lieutenant was still living. He could not remember her female name, but he did recall that she had been known as Lieutenant Buford.[25]

CHAPTER EIGHTEEN

LEGEND, LEGACY, AND LEGERDEMAIN

LAURETTA WAS NO better remembered in the years following her death. Occasionally a book or essay about women at war recalled her. Perhaps the first was Reginald Hargreaves in his *Women-at-Arms: Their Famous Exploits throughout the Ages*, published in London, England, in 1930, which gave her a chapter titled "Loreta Velasquez: A Swashbuckler of Secession," based solely and unquestioningly on her book. Another approaching war in 1939 brought her to mind in Perrin F. Shaw Jr.'s "A Lady in Gray Fighting for the Confederacy," in the Richmond, VA, *Times-Dispatch Magazine* on May 21, it too based on her memoir. In March 1941 a newspaper article on Greek women fighting the Italians and on Chinese women resisting the Japanese mentioned her as one of two examples from the Civil War.[1] That August, with America still four months away from war, she got brief mention in an essay about women fighting in Germany and Japan, titled "When Women Go to War," though it dismissed her with the comment that "except for her rather boastful memoirs, however, little is known of her military career."[2] By June 1942, with millions of women engaged in war efforts around the globe, the past seemed irrelevant. Perhaps her last wartime press appearance was on June 4, when an obscure newspaper mentioned her book and cited her as a woman warrior of yore.[3]

In the peace that followed, Loreta Velasquez and Harry T. Buford were relegated almost to pulp fantasy, the most bizarre being the claim in a July 1946 article that when her war began, she lived in Cuba with her American army officer husband and was disguised as "a beautiful boy." Then, the writer went on to say, she stowed away on a vessel bound for New Orleans and wandered its docks until she met a vagrant Welshman named John Rowlands. They enlisted in the Confederate army to get bed and board, and she signed up as Harry Buford. The next morning, however, Rowlands discovered that Buford was a woman, and she then gave him her story. Rowlands later became Sir Henry Morton Stanley. The story, falsely attributed to Stanley's 1909 autobiography, was complete nonsense.[4]

Scarcely better was Lauretta's appearance as the stuff of the Sunday supplement. In June 1950 a slightly fictionalized one-page distillation of her book appeared in the *American Weekly*, titled "The Girl in Gray." A sultry illustration of a blondish beauty with a darkly handsome mustached man dominated, while to the side a bosomy Lauretta in full uniform astride her white charger held the Confederate battle flag aloft as she led soldiers into battle. Lauretta herself could have written the headline: "Three Times the Beautiful Loreta Velasquez Lost a Husband at the Hands of Death, but Her Love of Adventure Always Sustained Her."[5]

The approaching Civil War Centennial in 1961 generated some interest, but always based on her book. From August 1958 until October 1960 a two-sentence filler ran in dozens of newspapers saying only that "Loreta J. Velazques" was a noted Confederate spy who wore a special brace to make her appear masculine.[6] Then in June 1961 a Washington Sunday supplement addressed the subject of "Women in the Civil War," in particular Sarah Edmonds, Emma Brownell, and Loreta Velazquez. For perhaps the first time a modern journalist cast a skeptical eye at *The Woman in Battle*. "Mme. Velazquez' account of her military adventures is also a lively one but somehow doesn't seem to ring true," wrote author Ruth Dean. "The reader gets the impression she was more of a spectator than a participant, and even hazards a guess that such a lively-imagined raconteur might even have purloined others' war experiences as her own." Finding Lauretta's book less believable than Edmonds's, Dean added that *The Woman in Battle* was one that "historians pretty much discount."[7] Seventeen years later, continuing that skepticism, another columnist writing on "Antebellum Amazons," rhetorically asked "if the book describing the adventures of Madame Velasquez of New Orleans be true."[8]

One who certainly did not question its authenticity was Jacob Mogelever, an executive with the U.S. Treasury who in 1961 published a biography of Lafayette C. Baker that was almost as fictional as *The Woman in Battle*, which he accepted without question. Mogelever invented scenes and dialogue that reversed her duping Baker and instead had him manipulating her, describing her always as "the slim Cuban girl," "the Cuban adventuress," or "the dark-eyed Cuban charmer, a woman to tempt any man with the lure of her sex," as he styled her. "Who could resist this Latin beauty, with her flashing dark eyes, provocative lips, and slender figure?"[9] Nonsense though it was, Mogelever inaugurated the notion that she was a femme fatale.

By then Lauretta and her book had fallen into the hands of historians, and earlier questions of authenticity turned into serious doubts. In 1940 Ella

Lonn commented that of all the women's memoirs from the Civil War, "none was stranger," though she did not appraise its content.[10] Fifteen years later Katherine Jones published an extended excerpt from *The Woman in Battle* but prefaced it by noting that research in New Orleans newspapers challenged some of Lauretta's statements.[11] Then in 1966 scholar Mary Elizabeth Massey took direct aim at the book. Admitting the possibility that Lauretta could have done some of the feats in her book, Massey charged that "it seems impossible that any one woman could have done all she claimed." Massey concluded that this "questionable" book was "the most fantastic of all accounts which claimed to be factual," a set of "sensational exaggerations" designed to encourage higher book sales.[12]

In the first extended scholarly examination of Lauretta and her book, historian Sylvia D. Hoffert in 1978 went well beyond Massey. Accepting that C. J. Worthington was a genuine character, Hoffert highlighted the narrative's generalities and lack of specifics in names and dates. Focusing on Lauretta's claim of enlistment in Company B of the 21st Louisiana, Hoffert was the first to go to official documents to check facts. She found no record of any enlistment, as well as several other factual errors, leading her to conclude that *The Woman in Battle* was "more bizarre than most," and though some portions might be authentic, it revealed a high degree of literary opportunism.[13]

Fifteen years later amateur historian Richard Hall went to greater lengths of investigation in his 1994 *Patriots in Disguise: Women Warriors of the Civil War*. After encapsulating Lauretta's memoir, he made a commendable effort to reach an objective judgment, though it is clear that he wanted to find in favor of authenticity. More than once he interpreted her admissions of thwarted plans and failed ventures as "lending credence," reasoning that a writer producing fiction would claim only successes. "On balance," he wrote, "this tends to support the interpretation that she was trying to give an honest account of her experiences, rather than consciously trying to deceive anyone for some ulterior motive." It may have been a fair judgment of human nature, but Hall forgot that a charlatan has to work ultimate failure into any narrative of bold risks, for claiming success would highlight outcomes subject to verification. Hall also saw confirmation in her description of her Venezuelan adventure, since it was an otherwise "little known" historical footnote, making that account "of exceptional interest in evaluating the reliability and veracity of Velazquez." Among other arguments in favor of her book, he also cited James D. Horan's erroneous statement that Felix

Stidger met her in St. Louis in the "summer of 1863 [1864]," whereas Horan's statement is a mix of his own imagination and flawed readings of Lauretta's and Stidger's memoirs.[14]

To his credit, Hall kept asking questions, even if he preferred answers supporting *The Woman in Battle.* He wondered whether the gross errors in chronology and dates might have resulted from "concocting fiction for personal gain." He leaped on the glaring discrepancies between her account of Thomas C. DeCaulp and what his official record disclosed and admitted that several of Jubal Early's caveats on her narrative were difficult to refute. Hall was the first to highlight the fact that her assertion of Spanish blood and Cuban birth rest wholly on her own claims. On the other hand, he lauded the general accuracy of her descriptions of battles and places, without acknowledging that such material was all available in popular histories when she wrote.

In the end, Hall concluded that in her book, "Velasquez mixed fiction with fact in some unknown but significant proportions," but that "we know it is not entirely a work of fiction," arguing that it had been established that "she did serve in male uniform as 'Lieutenant Buford.'" That conclusion is now unsupportable. She did put on a uniform at times while traveling on trains and on arriving in cities such as New Orleans, Lynchburg, and Jackson, but that does not translate into her having served in action on the battlefield or even having traveled with the army in the field. Meanwhile, Hall did not deny the "major discrepancies" in her narrative or the fact that "serious questions remain unanswered."[15]

A few years later historian Elizabeth D. Leonard thoughtfully assessed the known evidence to conclude that "it is a fantastic tale in many ways, but there is evidence as well that the narrative's elements . . . are rooted in real experience."[16] She too accepted Worthington as a genuine entity, and she acknowledged that almost nothing in *The Woman in Battle* could be authenticated independently. She offered several bits of evidence in its favor, in particular the Mary Ann Keith episode in 1861; Lauretta's June 1863 Jackson *Mississippian* interview; her July 27, 1863, application for a commission in the name of Harry Buford; and the January 1867 New Orleans *Daily Picayune* article about Mary DeCaulp. Unfortunately, she also cited Charles Dunham's Sanford Conover letter from October 1865 regarding Alice Williams and the November 1863 pass referring to Mrs. Alice Williams as a Union "special agent." The former, of course, is suspect, while the latter is genuine but relates to the wrong woman.[17]

Leonard concluded that Lauretta was indeed Buford and that her "wartime movements, activities, and use of aliases" matched those appearing in her book. When she went on to say that Lauretta "served in a number of battles, and became a spy and a smuggler," Leonard went beyond the evidence. In accepting Lauretta's account of her desire to pose as a man, serve as a soldier, see battle, and win glory, Leonard took *The Woman in Battle* at face value, rather than as a narrative designed to titillate readers and sell copies, though she acknowledged Lauretta's financial motivation.[18]

Most recently two authors, DeAnne Blanton and Lauren M. Cook, echoed Leonard in solidly, if not emphatically, endorsing Lauretta's narrative as being in the main genuine, though they admitted that she embroidered the truth to make her story more exciting and marketable. They asserted that "the veracity of much of her narrative is corroborated in Civil War-era newspapers, the testimony of fellow Confederates, and government documents" and again that it is "largely corroborated by contemporary sources." Though their 2002 book, *They Fought like Demons: Women Soldiers in the American Civil War*, appeared before the discovery of a mass of new material on Lauretta, they took into account all sources then known before coming to that conclusion and in the process broke some new ground. They were the first to assert that Velasquez might have been a nom de plume used for her book and not her maiden name, as indeed it was not. They also seconded Hall in questioning her Spanish blood and Cuban nativity.[19]

Occasionally they misread evidence, accepting editorial errors in Lauretta's name as actual aliases. They interpreted her 1878 letter to Early as meaning that she had moved to Rio de Janeiro, which she certainly had not, and cited Longstreet's 1888 letter as evidence that he personally knew of a woman who served in the ranks as Lieutenant Buford, whereas he made it clear that all he knew of her was what she had told him in 1874, hardly a corroboration of her claims.[20] They also accepted that the November 1863 "secret agent" document for Mrs. Alice Williams applied to Lauretta.[21]

That same year Richard Hall returned with another look after the passage of a decade, believing that he had uncovered additional material corroborating portions of *The Woman in Battle*. Yet his evidence was mostly just confirmation of some dates and names that she got correctly, while he abandoned his earlier skepticism and now asserted that her myriad errors and chronological impossibilities were due to well-meaning bad memory. "Overall," said Hall, "the internal evidence suggests that she was not consciously fabricating." His only new evidence was a soldier's "recollection" of seeing her in Georgia in the later part of 1864, written forty years after the fact, based probably on hearsay, and clearly written after seeing her book. More to the point, at the time that soldier supposedly saw her in Georgia, she had been in the North fully a year.

Hall still forthrightly admitted that serious problems remained. Confronted with official records of Thomas C. DeCaulp that conflicted dramatically with Lauretta's claims, he concluded that she might have fabricated her account of him in *The Woman in Battle* "to protect someone." She certainly did that. While not all of her published narrative about DeCaulp was invention, she certainly covered up his desertion and subsequent "galvanization into the Union Army," as well as her own departure for the North to meet him. Hall was also perturbed that he could find no record of the hamlet named Hurlburt where she claimed to have raised her battalion in 1861, though it was quite genuine and still survives vestigially, but its existence in no way authenticates that portion of her story. Anyone in Memphis in the 1860s would have heard of Hurlburt, and it remained a railroad stop for some years after the war.[22]

Some scholars have been impressed with the quality of Lauretta's descriptions of campaign and battle. Cultural anthropologist David E. Jones, in his 1997 *Women Warriors: A History*, devoted fully a third of his narrative on the Civil War to Lauretta's battle accounts without addressing the issue of authenticity. Instead, he cited her book as "the most complete account" of a woman warrior in the Civil War and declared that it entitled her to a place in the world's "pantheon of historic woman warriors."[23]

Going beyond that, her book has been used and reused to bolster modern assumptions that hundreds of women in disguise populated the Civil War armies, a fascinating field of study, albeit the numbers are seriously exaggerated. Lauretta's invented adventures should not be used in support, however, and the rush to ignore or gloss over the question of her authenticity in order to employ her narrative only aims harsh light on the paucity of genuine evidence to support most claimants.

There her story remained as of 2002. Some unquestionable facts were known of Lauretta's life, and innumerable instances in her book were identified as flawed, if not erroneous. The vast expanse of her life remained a void. Yet more than a decade earlier, an emerging phalanx of scholars from a different discipline discovered her, finding that the paucity of authentic information that so frustrated historians made her a useful palette for applying new and quite contemporary colors of interpretation to her life and times. Much had happened in the academic world as the end of the century approached. African American studies burgeoned among young scholars in the 1960s, followed immediately by women's studies, and then minority studies in general. Scholars sought to rectify an imbalance that had resulted in women, nonwhites, and the poor being treated in conventional scholarly inquiry as less worthy, their voices insignificant. Such objects of multiple inequities came to be identified as "the other." These efforts cut across multiple disciplines—not just history but also literature and economics. New work focusing on race, class, and gender has enjoyed great success, especially among younger scholars, and has nudged aside older, more established areas of inquiry in the academy.

Concurrently, newer interrelated schools of thought characterized as postmodernism and poststructuralism emerged, primarily in literary theory, but soon applied to other disciplines such as linguistics, anthropology, and sociology. Part of this new paradigm was a shift of emphasis from the concept of fixed reality—absolute facts in historian's terms—to a "third order" that sought to act as a buffer and link between fact and the abstract. It is taken for granted that a text has no single "authentic" meaning, but rather multiple interpretations, each potentially as valid as the others. Having many meanings, any narrative is thus self-contradictory. Ultimately, if no single reading is authoritative, then the concept of fact itself is compromised, and "there are no truths, only interpretations," as one critic averred.[24] Lauretta's book was ideal for postmodernists, poststructuralists, and other related theorists, providing a neutral mannequin on which scholars could drape any raiment they chose, unbothered about the conflicts and falsehoods in her story. They could massage her claims of Hispanic birth to align her with other racial underdogs. Her initial poverty and radical departure from the stereotypical behavior of a "Southern lady" brought class into the discussion. Being a woman who claimed to have posed as a man raised gender issues, with attendant questions about sexuality, while the fact that she claimed to have been a soldier invited attention in another modern realm of study, that of the "woman warrior." What has ensued would have both amused and mystified Lauretta.

It is profoundly interesting that virtually all of these new interpretations of Lauretta, and *The Woman in Battle* in particular, came not from historians but from professors of English and American literature, particularly scholars emphasizing literary analysis, feminist theory, and even creative writing.[25] It should be immediately apparent that their training and experience brought them to the subject via a radically different vector from that driving the historians. Certainly the latter engage in interpretation and analysis based on their research, and they often differ on the picture their sources present, but ultimately they are obliged to judge between what is reliable and what is not, what to use and what to reject. Facts, so far as they can be ascertained as definitive, are the heart of their matter. These literary scholars, however, sought different things in Lauretta's text from what the historians looked for. In their realm the reading of the narrative is paramount. To them even history can—and ought to—be considered as literature apart from factual content, a dynamic that allies them with the postmodernists and others. Lauretta's story offered them a rich field to plow.

Perhaps first in this new wave was Julie Wheelwright, a British professor of creative writing who in 1989 essentially accepted *The Woman in Battle* at face value for her book *Amazons and Military Maids: Women Who Dressed as Men in the Pursuit of Life, Liberty and Happiness*. She observed that even in Lauretta's own time, her audience was willing to believe her regardless of concern for authenticity—which the contemporary reviews to some degree affirmed—thus tacitly implying that a modern readership ought to do the same.[26]

Five years later Jesse Alemán, a professor of English and American literary studies, went much farther in capitalizing on what Lauretta offered and addressed the issue of her authenticity. In his foundational 1994 essay, "Crossing the Mason-Dixon Line in Drag: The Narrative of Loreta Janeta Velasquez, Cuban Woman and Confederate Soldier," Alemán wrote, "I am less concerned with finding a historical Velazquez than I am with exploring how *The Woman in Battle* generates an ontological and epistemological crisis in gender identity that not only calls into question the distinction between Confederate and Cuban nationalities but also challenges the process of authenticating the text's authorship and, in the greater picture, the existence of Velazquez."[27] The issue of fact or fiction was largely irrelevant. Lauretta's narrative challenged definitions of what it meant to be male or female, Cuban or Confederate, as well as the extent to which humans could know one from the other. More than that, Alemán seemed to declare that separating truth from fiction in Lauretta's book was fruitless, if not meaningless. Indeed, even whether Lauretta ever existed in any of her claimed incarnations was a pointless question. What mattered was what she wrote.

Two areas of her story attracted the most speculation, not surprisingly her sexuality and her claimed Cuban origins. Alemán asserted that Jubal Early's caustic remarks were the result of his feeling threatened as a man by the challenge she presented to gender norms and national identities by dressing as Buford.[28] Indeed, Early became a prime target for other scholars seeking gender issues at work. They charged him with dismissing her because of her sex and accused him of slander by insinuating that he suggested she was a prostitute when he said she appeared to have been coarsened by "associations with camp life." It is an accusation rendered rather meaningless by the fact that she actually had been a prostitute in New Orleans.

It is worth reiterating that only three actual instances of Lauretta posing as Buford are independently documented, while her own account of her adventures as a man constitutes barely a quarter of her book. Yet Alemán portrayed her primarily as a cross-dresser and a transvestite, and incidentally as nonwhite despite her claims of European parents and Cuban birth.[29] In addition, he concluded that her accounts of Buford's flirtations with Southern belles revealed that she was "protolesbian." Thereby he inaugurated a whole new subfield of interpretation of her life through her writing. Certainly one could speculate from these romantic—but by her account completely nonsexual—dalliances that Lauretta might have felt a latent or repressed desire to blossom into a lesbian. Alemán read further evidence of repressed lesbianism into Lauretta's marriage to DeCaulp. He saw DeCaulp as having his own latent homoerotic desire, because he told her he loved her at a moment when she was dressed as Buford. Thus her readers experienced the unsavory yet titillating hint of two "men" marrying each other. Even though DeCaulp was the only husband ever—allegedly—to have seen Lauretta as Buford, Alemán maintained that when Lauretta married him and her later husbands, she brought Southern masculinity "to a homoerotic crisis."[30]

She may have faced a similar crisis within herself, for Alemán read a seam of homophobia into her narrative that left her both attracted to and repelled by the very lesbianism he thought she craved. He ignored the alternative that her aversion to coarse women may have been evidence of her being quite heterosexual. As for the apparent instances of lesbian seduction in her narrative, Lauretta wrote only of flirtation, but Alemán read Lauretta's sharing a room—and perhaps a bed—with a woman during her western travels as evidence of something more. This is a prime example of the misconceptions that can arise when a scholar from one discipline ventures into another. Most historians would see nothing out of the ordinary in the shared bed, because they would know that men and women traveling alone in that era routinely shared beds with others of their gender, even if strangers, in the crowded inns and small hotels of the West.

Dismissing the question of authenticity in *The Woman in Battle*, Alemán maintained that her cross-dressing made authentication impossible. "Gender, race, and nation are sartorial performances that dislodge stable identity markers," he wrote, "wreaking havoc, as they did for Jubal Early, on ideologies, national institutions, and literary histories that demand readable signs of subjectivity." Alemán declared that his primary interest was in her sexuality, because "transvestism in *The Woman in Battle* brings the Americas into a transnational crisis of identity as it blurs the line between Cuba and the Confederacy, self and Other, America and América." Her "homoerotic" marriage to DeCaulp fomented a gender crisis and a "criollo desire to merge Cuban independence with southern secession."[31]

Concern with her Cubanness drew equally puzzling conclusions. Arguing that Lauretta's Cuban origin had been ignored because it challenged her essential identity as a Southern woman, Alemán suggested that no historian had tried to trace her roots in Havana because of the preoccupation with her Buford incarnation. Going on to say that she became Cuban in her memoir at the Confederate surrender, he was unaware that as of 1865 Lauretta still claimed to have been born in the British Bahamas to an Englishman and his Franco-American wife; by her own declarations she did not "become" Cuban until 1874 or Velasquez until a year later.[32]

Alemán laid the groundwork and sharply defined the issues for those who followed. In just two years Lauretta leaped to the forefront as a virtual definer of gender and "the other." Feminist literary scholar Elaine K. Ginsberg argued in a 1996 essay that in *The Woman in Battle*, masculinity "is authenticated only through the subordination and abjection of white women and black men."[33] Elizabeth Young, a specialist in feminist theory and women's literature of the Civil War, echoed Alemán when she characterized "the charge of 'fiction' as a point of departure for literary analysis rather than as a cause for historical censure." *The Woman in Battle* was a "picaresque novel," but factual truths could be drawn from that.[34] Her truth was that *The Woman in Battle* was a dissertation on gender in America. Cuba signified uncontrolled femininity, while Lauretta's "Cuban origins symbolically combine the hazards of femininity and the implicitly racial 'otherness' of Cuba in relation to the United States." For Young the whole point of *The Woman in Battle* was the "cross-dressing plot" that occupied a fraction of its pages. "In its covert narratives of sexuality and race as well as its overt focus on gender, the cross-dressing plot of *The Woman in Battle* enacts the consequences of Southern feminization," she declared. "By literalizing a gender iconography that is supposed to remain only metaphorical, Velazquez's cross-dressing plot threatens the male anatomy of regional fantasy."[35]

Beyond that, Young argued that Lauretta's "story of wartime cross-dressing illuminates a series of cultural fears that move in two figurative directions: metaphorically, between bodies and costumes; and metonymically, from counterfeit women to counterfeit men, from femininity to feminization, and from gender inversion to homosexual invasion." Young read Lauretta's scanty account of DeCaulp and dismissive references to her other three husbands as of 1876 to be subconsciously revealing when measured against the greater space given to her flirtations with women while posing as Buford. Following on the path blazed by Alemán, Young concluded that all of this was evidence of Lauretta's repressed protolesbianism.[36]

Even considered in the overall context of this new school of approach to Lauretta, some of Young's interpretations challenge credulity. She declared that Lauretta and the Confederacy were "metaphorically inseparable" and that when Harry Buford's fortunes declined, so did the Confederacy's. Into Velasquez's protolesbianism and cross-dressing Young read a metaphor for the exchange of "intersections between individual bodies and the national body politic." Moreover, her relationship with Worthington mirrored the "heterosexual dynamics of Confederate defeat," for he held control over her text, just as the North had power over a South "feminized" by loss. When Lauretta used the phrase "Attack on the Federal Rear" in a chapter subhead, Young saw in it "a strand of imagery that constructs Southern military aggression as anal penetration."[37] The Civil War, it seems, was just a battle of the sexes.

For several years there was nothing more until Alemán returned to the field in 2003 with a paperback reprinting of *The Woman in Battle*, for which he penned an introduction that remains the most thoughtful and inventive essay to date. In it he declared that "Velazquez's very existence, as with the narrative attributed to her, rests somewhere between history and story, where even a seemingly inauthentic author can nonetheless produce an authentic cultural text that embodies and enacts the prevailing beliefs and anxieties of its historical context."[38] Fictional or not, as a literary construct the book demonstrated truths about human nature, her culture and society, the Civil War, the United States, Hispanic America, and the world at large.

Alemán concluded with renewed emphasis that cross-dressing was "central to *The Woman in Battle*." "North and South collapse in a book ostensibly about the Civil War just as comfortably as Cuba and the Confederacy converge on Velazquez's corselette," he argued in an elegant turn of phrase. "Instead of a fixed state of being, identity in *The Woman in Battle* is a series of performances that render authenticity an impossibility," yet somehow give an "accurate picture of the Civil War's gender crises." Expanding on his earlier conclusions, Alemán asserted that authenticity had less to do with finding the real Lauretta than with "understanding *The Woman in Battle* and its author as embattled national allegories that offer cultural truths about the instability of gender, race, and nation during the Civil War and in its literature." He saw allegories in medieval abundance as the book offered "an ideologically authentic cultural text that reflects—through cross-dressing—the gender and national crises the Civil War generated." The text's transvestism was "an authentic symptom of the Civil War."[39]

He was not the only modern scholar drawn to read transvestism into her occasional pose as Buford. A transvestite is a "third sex," they have argued, someone who disrupts the "binary opposition between One and the Other."[40] Some have even argued that transvestism is an essential component of culture and that Lauretta's attiring herself as a man propelled her headlong into a no-person's-land inhabited by the flotsam of a traditional white male-dominated world with room only for heterosexual men and women. The transvestite and the cross-dresser presented frightening challenges to concepts of order and normality and were powerful agents of destabilization, something Lauretta presumably promoted by her journeys across the border between the genders.[41] Alemán agreed when he further maintained that "her transnational transvestism keeps Velazquez on the move between national boundaries and gender categories to the point that her only authenticity is as a symbolic, historical embodiment of a pro-slavery Cuban Confederate with no place in the Americas."[42] That is difficult to square now with our knowledge that she spent more years living in the North as a gilded age con artist than she ever did in the South, that she may not have been Cuban at all, and that during the war she demonstrated at best a loose loyalty to the Confederacy. She did stay "on the move," a necessity of the confidence artist's trade needing no explanation in sexuality or worldliness.

Alemán was on better ground when his reading of her book saw significance shifting "from a suspicious autobiography to a cultural narrative that accurately represents the historical instabilities of the war years," though using the word "accurately" in the same sentence with *The Woman in Battle* is always risky. Its most important allegorical cultural truth, he argued, was that "gender, race, and nation are simple matters of clothing that, when cross-dressed, challenge the ideologies of authenticity that determine the battle lines between masculinity and femininity, black and white, North and South, autobiography and fiction, and ultimately, self and Other."[43] Alemán stops short of forthrightly asserting that this was her intention, but if such was not her goal, then we are left to suppose that she unwittingly created this complex allegory by accident, which is hard to swallow. More logically, this is Alemán's conclusion engrafted onto the framework she left behind. What happens to "authenticity" when motives are attributed to a writer that she never actually entertained? What would Lauretta make of these assertions, when she was so frank in admitting that she just wanted to make some money and knew enough of human nature and nineteenth-century prudery to realize that the spicier her suggested sexual encounters, the better the potential sales?[44] Her writing reveals far more about the era's interest in the prurient among both men and women than it does about behavioral and power inequities, though she was surely aware of the latter.

More puzzling still, as a literary scholar Alemán acknowledged an American tradition of cross-dressing common in female memoirs and novels about war going back to the Revolution—including several from the Civil War, such as those by Sarah Emma Edmonds, Pauline Cushman, and the popular 1862 novel *The Lady Lieutenant.* Yet he chose not to include Lauretta's entry in that tradition as the obvious literary device that it was, even though he recognized that such narratives usually ended with a return to the sanctity of male-female romance, the very denouement that Lauretta chose when she set Buford aside to marry DeCaulp.[45] In fact, she repeatedly opted for romance, with Wasson, then Bonner, Bobo, and finally Beard. If anything, she appears to have been rampantly heterosexual in pursuit of the conventional.

Four years after the appearance of Alemán's new edition of *The Woman in Battle,* in 2007 Coleman Hutchison, a distinguished specialist on Civil War literature, attempted to spread Lauretta's utility over an even wider scale of narrative significance. Hers was not an insular outlook on the world. He read from her descriptions of wartime travels back and forth between Union and Confederacy, and in and out of the country on blockade runners to Cuba and other foreign ports, cause to declare that "Velazquez's awareness of a world outside of the United and Confederate States helps to disrupt the insularity of Civil War narrative convention and to tell the belated story of a Confederacy in and of the world." Hers was "a restless text, one that moves dexterously and recurrently across lines of nation and region," hence her book "elegantly 'embodies and enacts' the international dimensions of the American Civil War." He saw her book as remapping the conflict in a global system of immigration, foreign intervention, transnational capital, transatlantic slavery, and competing nationalisms involving Europe, South America, and the Caribbean. Granting her a cosmopolitan background that gave her "a particularly keen eye for the international aspects and implications of the war," Hutchison argued that *The Woman in Battle* forced readers to the realization that the war exceeded the boundaries of North and South, thereby disrupting "the insularity of Civil War narrative convention."[46]

In this same vein, Caroline Levander, a distinguished scholar of humanities and English, contended that same year that Lauretta's alleged movements in the North, South, and abroad reinforced "her desire to imagine an independent Cuba aligned with an independent South," for Cuba and the Confederacy might jointly maintain "a colonial fantasy of white privilege through black slave labor."[47] In so arguing, she fell in line with Alemán's contention that Lauretta saw Cuba and the Confederacy as twins in revolutionary spirit and proslavery values, which only piqued her desire to see the two joined.[48]

A year later Matthew Teorey, a specialist on American humanities and postmodern narrative techniques, attempted to collect most of the multiple strands of Lauretta's new story under one umbrella. He accepted the conclusion that *The Woman in Battle* was essentially genuine, though he admitted that "Velazquez did add a little embellishment." He agreed with Alemán that early critics "only attacked the authenticity of Velazquez's text because it 'challenged the supposed gentility of Southern gender codes.'" In fact, Teorey argued, the book "revealed the true, brutal nature of warfare." He called it a "patriotic, honest, and realistic" account of her "four years of military service," even though by her own account she spent less than two years with the army. Highlighting her harsh critiques of "the utter contemptibleness of some [male] individuals," he suggested that Lauretta did not like men, further evidence of her cross-gender complexity. *The Woman in Battle*, Teorey concluded, "implicitly argued that only transgendered people, who reject society's rigid gender roles, deserve to 'wear male attire' and enjoy a male level of freedom and responsibility."

Velasquez, he argued, was "quintessentially American," imbued with the United States' "promise of personal freedom and socio-economic opportunities," a statement hard to square with her eagerness to go to war with the United States in 1861 or to trade it for Venezuela and the fact that virtually all of her "socio-economic" endeavors were confidence schemes.

Ultimately returning to the question of authenticity, Teorey asserted that Lauretta conveyed a message that was important, "regardless of whether or not these experiences actually happened or not."[49]

Then in 2010 Hutchison returned to her, concluding that the "signal achievement of the narrative" was "to situate the American Civil War in a truly international context."[50] In fact, Lauretta's multiple postwar interests in developing Nicaragua, Mexico, and Cuba and in seeing North, Central, and South America united under a single commercial umbrella certainly did speak to an internationalist outlook on trade, at least, though most of that came years after the appearance of *The Woman in Battle.* As for Lauretta's account of her postwar wanderings, Hutchison thought her narrative of her western travels "inadvertently burlesques Confederate remasculinization."[51] Once more the road led back to gender.

The precipice awaiting all of these theories is that in varying degrees they are founded on the assumption that *The Woman in Battle,* though admittedly flawed, provides enough narrative fact to serve as a basis for coming to "authentic" conclusions about Lauretta and her times. Aware of the multiple questions raised about her book's reliability, their authors chose not to venture beneath the surface, finding security for their themes by invoking the tenets of literary analysis and the postmodern creed of the primacy of narrative over fact. Viewing the book as literature, even if fictive, their constructs work because no rules bind them once they assert that even a fictional *The Woman in Battle* has historical significance. Those appraising the book for cultural significance are forced to make the same claim. Approaching the book on any other basis sets them on a collision course with its overwhelming fictionalization.[52] They may not all make claims about actual history based on what Lauretta wrote, but all do assert that in her fictions are to be found truths about the social and cultural currents running through her times. Stepping thus across disciplines without adequate grounding in the new environment virtually prescribes problems. Consider the reverse of the case, should a historian cross disciplines into literature to use Margaret Mitchell's *Gone with the Wind* as a source for a study of slavery in the Civil War era. However much that "narrative" might tell us about white Southern attitudes *of the 1930s* toward that institution, anything it says about the reality of slavery *in the 1860s* is worthless.

Inevitably, Lauretta's story had to attract filmmakers. *Full Metal Corset: Secret Soldiers of the Civil War,* produced by the Arts and Entertainment Network, appeared in 2007. Half of it dealt with Lauretta, but uncritically in a wholesale adoption of her story from her book. Far more nuanced was 2013's *Rebel: Loreta Velazquez, Secret Soldier of the American Civil War*, written and directed by María Agui Carter. It too accepted *The Woman in Battle* as narratively authentic, but it delved thoughtfully into side issues such as the status of Hispanic women in the Old South, the importance of "passing" for white even for Spanish-born Europeans, the genuine desire of an unknown number of women to serve with the armies, and the challenge that presented to contemporary ideas of womanhood. The production was dramatically effective, and it was laced with commentary by a number of historians and literary scholars. Unfortunately, the filmmakers compromised objectivity by editing out the historians' caveats about Lauretta's book, while including endorsements of authenticity from Alemán, Ginsberg, and others. It seems clear that the production's intent was not to tell Lauretta's story, but to present *The Woman in Battle* as presumed fact.[53]

Rebel offered only one document as verification, that same misapplied November 1863 Alice Williams appointment as a Union "secret agent." The docudrama implied other corroboration by flashing a number of 1861–63 newspaper articles on the screen, failing to note that most were inaccurate and all were based on what Lauretta told the press. Most troubling, though, was an effort to suggest that white male Southern leaders tried to write Lauretta and her story out of Civil War history after her book challenged Southern sensibilities, particularly those of General Early. Early did condemn the book, but only in one private letter known to survive. He wrote and said nothing else about it publicly that has come down to us. The *Southern Historical Society Papers*, the organ he wielded like a sword in sculpting the "Lost Cause myth," published not a word about her or *The Woman in Battle* after the John William Jones review, which appeared more than a year before Early read the book. That hardly suggests that there was an operating imperative to suppress the book. Neither was there an effort to prevent reissuing the book in 1890 or again in 1894, nor to stifle the dozens of favorable reviews that appeared in Southern newspapers or the articles on Lauretta and the book that continued to appear for years thereafter. Where are the private letters or published articles or speeches by Confederate mythmakers discrediting Lauretta and thereby erasing her from approved memory? There are none. The alleged effort to repress the book and evict her from history is a fiction—a "narrative"—calculated to bolster the implicit suggestion that her book was so authentic and so threatening that self-appointed guardians of Confederate history kept it from the public.[54]

Thus she stands. There never seemed to be a final version of her saga. Even after she put her story through 1874 fully on record, presumably immutable, she continued its evolution. Lauretta found the journey more interesting than its destination. With her book done, the urge to revise, invent, and add new layers to her account, even at the risk of self-contradiction, overtook the wisdom of leaving it alone, until at some point for her the myth became the reality, as what began as carelessness or overactive imagination turned into dementia. It is tragically fitting that a woman who spent her life concealing her own real identity should come to her end with no sure grasp of who she really was.

There are perverse ironies as a result of what we now know about her. When she was just the Loreta Velasquez of her book, our ignorance of so much of her life allowed imagination and ingenuity full rein to shape her to suit any purpose: proud Latina, Confederate patriot, woman warrior, secret agent, social and sexual rebel, woman of the world, pathbreaking journalist, and more. The crowning irony now is that in discovering so much more about her life, the new detail and context confound all of them. The more we learn about Lauretta, the more she is somehow diminished.

It is worth noting that virtually all of these writers accept Lauretta's claims of Hispanic blood and Cuban birth. Yet what do her prior claims of birth in New York, the Bahamas, and the West Indies do to her later adoption of Cuba? What do her adopted sequential parentages of the Clarks, the Anglo-Franco-American Roaches, or the Mississippi and Louisiana Clapps make of her 1875 declaration at age thirty-three that then and thereafter she was blood of the Spaniard Velasquez and his French wife, whom she waited decades longer to identify by name? If Cuban freedom from Spain was so dear to her, why did she remain completely silent about it through the first seven years of the Ten Years' War and adopt the cause only after she changed her name to Velasquez and her nativity to Havana? Moreover, why did she say little more than a sentence on Cuban independence in *The Woman in Battle* but devote much of a chapter to detailing her quite pleasant relations with its Spanish rulers? "I begrudged that this fair island should be the dependency of a foreign power," she wrote during that part of her narrative rather shakily established by context as early 1862. The only thing that could have persuaded her to abandon the Confederate cause, she went on, would be "an attempt on the part of the Cubans to have liberated themselves from the Spanish yoke." Wondering whether they would actually rise up one day, she said she resolved to join them if they did.[55] Her effort to depict herself as prescient in 1862 is obvious, since she well knew that Cuba had been in revolt for several years when she wrote that passage in 1875–76.

Coleman Hutchison counted just twenty-four instances of the words *Cuba* and *Cuban* in her six-hundred-page book, which seems hardly impressive, let alone patriotic. Still, he proclaimed her to be an example of "ethnic otherness."[56] Caroline Levander saw her as an exemplar of Cuban independence, one who also favored an alliance between the island and the Confederacy, perhaps unaware that the men running the Confederacy had a few years before advocated actual annexation and thereby the extinction of a Cuban political identity.[57] While Lauretta showed intermittent interest in Cuban and Central and South American affairs, how does one explain her complete silence during that later Cuban revolt that eventually pulled the United States into war with Spain in 1898?

Even her claims to be a devoted Confederate and Southerner are suspect. Her work for the Union war effort making cartridges and offering to supply information, not to mention abetting DeCaulp's desertion and encouraging his transformation into a Yankee soldier, speaks for itself. She left the Confederacy in the summer of 1863 and did not return to live there until 1874. By 1876 she had spent perhaps as much as half of her life outside the region, and she lived most of her last forty-five years in the North. Worse, when she did return to the old Confederacy, it was only to practice her confidence schemes in Tampa, Atlanta, New Orleans, North Carolina, and elsewhere, thereby making her supposedly beloved South her repeated victim. It seems clear that for all her protestations even after the war, Lauretta felt only a tenuous loyalty to the region, and that made it easy for her write the things that so outraged General Early. The overwhelming preponderance of pure fiction in her book reduces it to just one more confidence scheme, another vehicle for making money by lies and deception, and one for which, in a rare moment of candor, she frankly admitted that her motive was money.

Lieutenant Harry T. Buford remains both Lauretta's most attractive creation and the least believable. It is apparent from her book, the contemporary accounts of her repeated unmaskings, and her lifelong behavior afterward that her intent in the Buford pose was always to gain attention. Her habit of parading around in her uniform virtually begged for discovery, behavior hardly calculated to conceal her masquerade if she attempted it in camp and field with the army. Her established timeline reduces even her *possible* time with the soldiers to a few months of 1861, the first third of 1862, and a few weeks in the summer of 1863. Future documentary discoveries will likely further contract those limits. Moreover, the only eyewitness testimonials she ever offered to establish her actual service with the army turn out not to have been as she represented them. To date there is still no independent, directly contemporaneous eyewitness testimony to support her claims. We have only her word, and given her record with the truth, accepting that word would be folly. The same must be said of the secret service and spying activities that make up so much of her book. Only a single document unequivocally refers to her as being engaged in "secret service" for the Union, yet that expression, so loaded to the modern ear, is undefined, while for many at the time like her, it amounted to nothing more than occasionally informing on suspicious persons. As for her clandestine work for the Confederacy, we again have nothing but her own unsubstantiated claims. The argument that establishing some of those claims lends credence to the rest is a logical absurdity.

To modern readers the most sensational aspect of *The Woman in Battle* is Lauretta's alleged "cross-dressing" as Buford and his (her) flirtatious dalliances with unsuspecting women drawn by his irresistible allure, redolent as they are with hints of transgender issues, actual transvestism, and latent lesbianism. A bare half dozen instances of this, occurring over just two of the roughly fifteen adult years covered by the memoir, have generated a considerable literature. Yet no one has asked the question that if Lauretta's doing this in 1861–63 established her "other" sexuality, then what conclusion is to be drawn from the remaining eleven years covered in her book, or the forty-six years of her life after its publication, during which there was not a hint of anything other than conventional heterosexual behavior? Certainly many lesbians married men during her time, as many still do rather than challenge prevailing—though shifting—mores, but Lauretta took at least five husbands, and her sole surviving letter to one of them, her May 1864 missive to DeCaulp, betrays nothing if not a typical married woman's concern, longing, and frustration. On top of all that, the fact that the entire Civil War period text of *The Woman in Battle* is seriously compromised by what we now know of her inevitably argues that these flirtations as Buford were nothing but mildly salacious dramatic inventions aimed at titillating her audience, while her supposed "cross-dressing" had little if anything to do with repressed transexuality but much to do with attracting public and press attention.

Certainly she deserves credit for being far more well traveled than most men and women of her time. She can be placed definitively in all of the Confederate states but Arkansas during or after the war, and it seems reasonable to include that state as well, though no evidence but her own claims puts her there. Hutchison argued that her very independence as Buford forced her to be itinerant and that somehow her peripatetic status from 1865 to 1874 helped place her constant travel during the war into the context of global civil war.[58] We now know, however, that much of the time she claimed in her book to have been going back and forth to Cuba and elsewhere through the Union blockade was time she actually spent in the Orleans Parish Prison in 1862–63 and in Indiana, Wisconsin, and Minnesota in late 1863–64. Her only instance of verifiable foreign travel came in 1867 after the war ended.

The Woman in Battle is indeed an unusual memoir and has been so judged for generations, even by those who acknowledged that it contained exaggeration and fictionalization. According to Hutchison, "Because of her careful manipulation of narrative sequence, it is as though Velasquez and her readers are together in time." Certainly it falls well outside the mold of the "Lost Cause" literature of the postwar generation. Far from idealizing the Confederacy, she found fault with the behavior and morals of Confederate men and women and questioned the value of Southern institutions, though without questioning slavery.[59]

How do we continue to regard her as an authentic memoirist whose commentary offers useful illumination of her times and places when we realize that she rarely witnessed what she claimed to have seen or was rarely where she claimed to have been, while when she actually did write authentically about a time and place of her experience, she combined invention and obfuscation to drain the moment of its true context? Alemán frankly called the book "sensationalist, secessionist, and suspicious," as well as "seemingly impossible," averring with more understatement than he realized that it is "undeniably part pulp fiction." Still, he and others have concluded that it contains enough details to make it a "legitimate Civil War narrative."[60] That begs a definition of what constitutes a "Civil War narrative." Must it be an eyewitness account, a factual compilation or history, or just anything that includes some "facts"? Whatever issues there may be with her other conclusions on *The Woman in Battle*, Elizabeth Young's characterization of it as a "picaresque novel" is as good as any.

These recent works are thought-provoking, often insightful, and certainly imaginative. They have had to be, for in the absence of concrete data on Lauretta, the authors have had to accept *The Woman in Battle* at face value. That decision comes at a price. Did she lie all the time in her book? No. Did she ever tell a complete truth without reshaping it or its circumstances to suit some purpose other than accuracy? No. Faced with the myriad half-truths and exaggerations in the book, added to the far greater quotient of lies, equivocations, and inventions she promulgated in the press about these same events for years both before and after the book's appearance, the only rational conclusion is that accepting anything Lauretta said or wrote, at any time, involves unwarrantable risk. Remove the security of her text, and these otherwise often elegant theories are reduced to a handsome wardrobe of clothing in considerable need of an emperor.[61]

Nevertheless, Lauretta has had her relevance and continues to have it, even if it is based on a fiction. As newspaperman Maxwell Scott said in John Ford's film *The Man Who Shot Liberty Valance*, "when the legend becomes fact, print the legend." The legend Lauretta created has become spiritual fact, and many still prefer it to be literal, choosing to "print the legend" even while fearing they should not. Succeeding generations did see significance in her and her story. In every war subsequent to her own, she has been revived as the woman warrior, spiritual progenitor of the female in uniform risking her all on the battlefields of freedom. Every time that happens, every time her story appears yet again in a gullible anthology of women warrior memoirs, every time the fictions in *The Woman in Battle* are cited in support of statements offered as fact, Lauretta is back in command again through the myth she so consciously, if unsystematically, constructed.

Aside from admiring the ambition it must have taken for this moderately literate woman to create so large and broad a work—fiction or not—it is her actual life that merits reflection, grudging admiration even, for her sheer unstoppability. She was a sign of her times but not a mirror to them, a dark doppelganger of a Horatio Alger heroine, with too little luck, inordinate pluck, and almost no virtue.

Meanwhile, she remains what she always wanted to be—the center of attention, herself her only successful confidence scheme, and one still working on new generations of marks she never imagined.[62]

ACKNOWLEDGMENTS

NOTES

BIBLIOGRAPHY

INDEX

ACKNOWLEDGMENTS

I OWE A great many thanks to the people who have generously given their time and expertise to aid in this work. Archivists always deserve first notice, for without them historians would be dead in the water. DeAnne Blanton proved yet again to be a national treasure, assisting with the location of documents in the labyrinthine National Archives. Also at the National Archives, Chris Killillay helped try to track down the elusive C. J. Worthington. At the Library of Congress, Michelle Krowl was most helpful with the presidential papers housed there, while Bonnie Mangan lent aid with the records of the copyright office. Dominique Dery of the David M. Rubenstein Rare Book and Manuscript Library at Duke University was most helpful, as was old friend Norwood Kerr at the Alabama Department of Archives and History. John Coski, a friend to all who work in the realm of the Confederacy and the Civil War, never failed to take on a question or provide a copy, and I am indebted to him for many years of such aid and friendship. Yvonne Loiselle and Irene Wainwright of the Louisiana Division and City Archives at the New Orleans Public Library were always prompt and helpful in opening up that wonderful, and still underappreciated, wealth of material. Heidi Stringham at the Salt Lake County Court House undertook more than one quest for a document and always with kindness. Thanks, too, to Graham Duncan at the University of South Carolina's wonderful Cooper Library. Closer to home in Lynchburg, Virginia, Greg Starbuck generously helped in the search for local records and newspapers.

It was necessary to employ freelance researchers on some occasions, and Joanne Smalley was a real boon at the Georgia State Archives in Atlanta. James Snider undertook several digs into Montgomery, Alabama, newspapers, and Kelly Summers of Provo, Utah, was more than generous in taking on the task of looking for records of Lauretta's divorces, of which it appears she had none. Avi Mowshowitz in New York was relentless in pursuit of details of Lauretta's days on Manhattan. Especially, Vonnie Zullo put in long hours and turned up many a find in obscure places, well justifying her reputation as an indefatigable researcher.

Friends have been ever generous with their time, especially Tony Hall in London; Greg Starbuck in Lynchburg, Virginia; J. D. Humphries in Atlanta; Robert K. Krick of Fredericksburg, Virginia, and dear Chris Vella in New Orleans. Kathryn Canavan and Dr. Patrick Canavan put me in touch with Cassandra Jackson at St. Elizabeth's Hospital in Washington in the quest for more on Lauretta's final days, and Anita J. Morgan and Stephen Towne at the University of Indiana–Purdue University at Indianapolis both generously shared some of their discoveries on Lauretta in Indiana. Descendants were also untiring in their desire to help. Amanda Gault, distant relative of Thomas C. DeCaulp, tirelessly combed Little Rock archives, and Andrene Messner helped add background on her cousin, Lauretta's last husband, William Beard. Sylvia Rodrigue of Southern Illinois University Press has been all that an editor should be and more. Most of all, I owe a great debt to Carman Cumming, who researched Lauretta for some years yet shared much of his research with me and read a late draft of this work, which has benefited immeasurably from his generosity.

Then there is Sandra Davis, who is everything Lauretta was not.

NOTES

CSR	Compiled Service Record
LC	Library of Congress
NA	National Archives, Washington, DC
OR	United States War Department. *War of the Rebellion: Official Records of the Union and Confederate Armies.* 128 vols. Washington, DC: Government Printing Office, 1880–1901.
RG	Record Group
WIB	Loreta Janeta Velazquez. *The Woman in Battle: A Narrative of the Exploits, Adventures, and Travels of Madame Loreta Janeta Velazquez, Otherwise Known as Lieutenant Harry T. Buford, Confederate States Army.* Edited by C. J. Worthington. Richmond, VA: Dustin, Gilman & Co., 1876.

INTRODUCTION: MYSTERIES ON MYSTERIES

1. The other memoir by a woman claiming—truthfully—to have posed as a man to serve in the army was Sarah Emma Edmonds's *The Female Spy of the Union Army* (Boston: DeWolfe, Fiske & Co., 1864).

2. Carman Cumming to the author, June 8, 2015.

3. It is thanks to modern technology that we can begin to know her now. A generation ago, even a decade ago, this book could not have been written. The sources needed to discover the extent of that life were there all the time, hidden by the sheer impracticability of finding them. Given her aptitude at press manipulation, it is hardly coincidental that the major source of information on her should be the newspapers of her time. The challenge of newspaper research has been daunting. The millions of pages of newsprint that survive are housed in hundreds of archives and libraries, available only in dim microfilm and microfiche files, incomplete transcriptions, and often fragile originals. Few were indexed, and those indexes were scarcely more than guides to headlines. The historian had no choice but to spend hours, days, weeks, even months scanning randomly in hopes of finding something useful. More often than not,

it simply was not practical to do so. Now, however, we have optical character recognition (OCR). Thanks to the sophisticated programs recently developed, key or search words can be entered on a site that surveys millions of pages of newsprint to retrieve hits for further investigation. Sites such as genealogybank.com, newspapers.com, newspaperarchive.com, and chroniclingamerica.loc.gov, among others, along with digital databanks produced independently by several states, have opened an incalculable trove of previously untapped material. Any historians hereafter who ignore these sites knowingly compromise the content of whatever they produce.

Of course, there are hazards and pitfalls. Every such database employs different protocols for searches. That lack of uniformity makes the work more cumbersome and the results inconsistent. Moreover, no OCR program is infallible. All are subject to interference in the digital search thanks to dim or worn type—a particular problem with Confederate newspapers and early American journals—faded pages, poor photography of the original, and more. Sometimes a program misses a potential hit that is standing out boldly. Then as today, compositors inadvertently made typographical errors. Moreover, journalists could hear one thing and write down another, and their handwriting was sometimes such that a typesetter simply misread one word for another. To realize the full potential of these databases, the researcher must go beyond identified search terms to try every conceivable alternative spelling or misspelling. A program searching for Smith is not going to notice Smiht. The subject of this book went by the given name Lauretta much of her life, but in print it sometimes appeared as Laure, Laura, Loretto, and wildest of all, Jeruth. One journal actually identified her as James. Velasquez turned up as Velazquez and Velazques, and her alter ego Buford as Bufort, Beaufort, Bufford, Benford, and more.

It should go without saying that these newspaper sites do not provide "one-stop shopping" and are no substitute for ingenuity, intuition, and patient hard work. The researcher also must be ever aware that virtually everything found may reflect only what someone *told* a reporter, as opposed to a journalist's actual eyewitness observations or knowledge, or it may be what the reporter remembered hours or days later.

If there is one realization that several years of research for this book has led me to, it is that no matter how much has been found, there is likely to be more. An informal estimate would be that all of the hits found for this book in these digital searches amount to no more than about 80 percent of the potential total. If a researcher were content to make this single subject a life's work, surely more would be found. It is a brave new world for historians in the digital age. The trick is to learn to master the full potential of what we have wrought.

1. WHO WAS SHE?

1. Journalists sometimes truncated Lauretta into Laura, a variant she never used, and in 1863 a Richmond typesetter misread his reporter's cursive Lauretta as Jeruth. Lauretta and Jeruth do not look so similar in type, but when written in cursive, they are very much so. Initial appearances of all variants are cited and annotated when they appear.

2. Jesse Alemán states that he believes Velasquez to be her genuine birth name, an insupportable contention. See Jesse Alemán, "Authenticity, Autobiography, and Identity: *The Woman in Battle* as a Civil War Narrative," introduction to *The Woman in Battle* (1876; repr., Madison: University of Wisconsin Press, 2003), xxxiv–xxxv.

3. *WIB*, 40.

4. A Lauretta Clark was born in 1844, but in Maine, and nothing seems to connect her with the young woman in Louisiana. A Mary Ann Williams, a variant by which she sometimes was known, was born in 1842 and living in St. Tammany Parish, Louisiana, with her farmer parents in July 1860. Meanwhile, Laura J. Williams, also born in 1842 in Arkansas, lived with her well-to-do father, slave owner Cokely P. Williams, at Mine Creek in Hempstead County, Arkansas, which fits with her later claims to have come from a planter family in Arkansas. At the same time, an orphan named Lauretta Williams, born in 1842 in Louisiana, lived in Richmond, Fort Bend County, Texas, with her younger brother, Clarence, in the home of Marian Shaw. Lauretta could have been any one of them, or none, though the young woman in Richmond, Texas, seems a reasonable candidate, in part because her first name was spelled as the Lauretta in question spelled hers. As Lauretta Williams, she and three others presented a flag to Captain John T. Holt's Richmond Mounted Riflemen on January 30, 1861, when they mustered immediately after secession to go to war. United States Census, Lebanon, York County, ME, 1850, 1860; United States Census, St. Tammany Parish, LA, 1860; United States Census, Hempstead County, AR, 1860; United States Census, Fort Bend County, TX, 1860; New Orleans *Daily Delta*, February 15, 1861.

5. *WIB*, 41, 48–49.

6. Laura Ewen Blokker, "Education in Louisiana" (Greensburg: State of Louisiana, Department of Culture, Recreation and Tourism, Office of Cultural Development, Division of Historic Preservation, 2012), 11–12, 14; Edwin Whitfield Fay, *The History of Education in Louisiana* (Washington, DC: Government Printing Office, 1898), 69–71.

7. *WIB*, 319–25. She does not actually name the author, the collection, or the specific story by title and gives evidence of familiarity with it only by writing an extended paraphrase of the story.

8. Lauretta DeCaulp to Oliver P. Morton, December 7, 1863, Papers of Governor Oliver P. Morton, 401-A-3, microfilm roll 10, Indiana State Archives, Indiana Commission on Public Records, Indianapolis; Lauretta J. DeCaulp to James Stockdale, July 26, 27, 29, 1864, Lauretta DeCaulp File, Union Provost Marshal's File of Papers Relating to Individual Citizens, Pub. #345, RG 109, NA (hereafter cited as DeCaulp Provost File).

9. Lauretta J. DeCaulp to Thomas DeCaulp, May 12, 1864, DeCaulp Provost File; L. J. Wasson to U. S. Grant, February 24, 1876, Letters from the President, RG 60, NA.

10. Cleveland *Plain Dealer*, February 2, 1864.

11. Janet E. Kaufman asserts that Lauretta incorporated into her *WIB* narrative the wartime newspaper accounts of another Lauretta J. Williams, presenting that story as her own. "'Under the Petticoat Flag': Women Soldiers in the Confederate Army," *Southern Studies* 23 (Winter 1984), 373. Irrefutable links, including handwriting in a score of her personal letters, clearly disprove that, establishing that the Lauretta J. Williams DeCaulp of 1862–64 is incontestably the Lauretta DeCaulp of the postwar years. Similarly, questions arise over which newspaper accounts of 1861–62 refer to Lauretta by different names. Fortunately, we can construct a direct chain linking most of them.

Working backward, there is no basis to conclude that any of the postwar newspaper accounts or documentary evidence of her activities from 1866 to 1923 deals with anyone other than Lauretta. Internal evidence and story continuity tie it all together. From there her newly found letters and official government documents take her story back to the fall of 1863, at which point accounts in the Confederate press and a few official documents press it earlier to June 1863, when she reappeared following her imprisonment. Her interview on June 6 in the Jackson *Mississippian* directly links her with the Lauretta Williams Clark who was in the New Orleans press in October and November 1862, and those accounts inextricably link her with news items from April 1862 in which she appears as M. M. Arnold and Ann/Anne Williams.

A critical issue arises with the Mary Ann Keith episode of September–October 1861. Key points are her claims that before the war she was married in Arkansas to a man who by September 1861 was a Union soldier; that when arrested and sent to Richmond, she was trying to get to General Leonidas Polk's command in western Kentucky; that she was again arrested in Lynchburg and held in jail until freed by the mayor on orders from Richmond; that she claimed to have met the secretary of war and obtained from him a passport; and finally, that she used the alias Lieutenant Buford. All of these features figured in Lauretta's postwar interviews and in *WIB*, but that does not mean she could not have read the Keith story in the press episode and borrowed it. Also, the John B. Jones diary (cited below) was published in 1866, in which he recounted his interview with a woman who said she fought at the Battle of First Bull Run and was then on her way to join Polk at Columbus. The dates in Jones's diary do not match the date of the Keith visit to Richmond as established by newspaper coverage, but Jones often wrote after the fact, depending on his memory for dates. Otherwise his account is entirely consonant with the Keith episode and with Lauretta's telling of her story. Lauretta certainly could have borrowed details from it as she compiled her book.

However, significant material from the Keith episode was already part of her story well before 1866. Keith's account has her married to a man who went north at the outbreak of war and was in the Union army in late 1861. Lauretta's June 6, 1863, interview in the Jackson *Mississippian* echoes that. Keith's account has her arrested in October 1861. Lynchburg *Republican*, September 28, 1861. Lauretta's account in April 1862 spoke of her arrest and release and by context placed it prior to November 1861. Keith asserts that before the war she lived in Arkansas, and so does Lauretta in her statements in New Orleans in April. New Orleans *Daily Picayune*, April 24, 1862. Hence Lauretta cannot have borrowed such details from Jones's diary. She provided further corroboration that she was Keith when she spoke with General Samuel P. Heintzelman on January 27, 1864, telling him she had been a "prisoner" in Richmond twice. One occasion was in July 1863, of course. There was no second time as Lauretta Williams or DeCaulp, but Keith's detention for posing as Lieutenant Buford made a second. Samuel P. Heintzelman Journal, January 27, 1864, Heintzelman Papers, LC.

Finally, the fact that both Keith and Lauretta chose the alias Buford and the rank of lieutenant is beyond coincidence. Either they were one and the same or Lauretta adopted Keith's story in the Confederate press as her own by the spring of 1862. Yet the Keith story did not appear in any of the New Orleans papers at the time. New Orleans regarded Lauretta as a notorious character, and details like her alleged prewar marriage to a man in Arkansas were general rumor associated directly with her as early as April 1862. The notable decline in arrests of an Ann Williams during the period of Keith's trip to Richmond is suggestive, if circumstantial, and Lauretta's later repeated connections with Memphis, Keith's supposed home, provide further circumstantial interest. On balance, the weight of evidence suggests that Lauretta was Mary Ann Keith, taking her confirmed story back to late summer of 1861, a time when 1862 sources agree that she was known in New Orleans as Ann or Anne Williams. There her verifiable story begins.

12. New Orleans *Daily Picayune*, July 20, November 15, 1852, June 3, 1853.

13. Ibid., February 22, May 1, 1855.

14. Ibid., October 30, 1856; New Orleans *Daily Creole*, October 31, 1856.

15. Judith Kelleher Schafer, *Brothels, Depravity, and Abandoned Women: Illegal Sex in Antebellum New Orleans* (Baton Rouge: Louisiana State University Press, 2009), 48.

16. New Orleans *Daily True Delta*, November 2, 1862.

17. New Orleans *Daily Picayune*, April 4, 1857; New Orleans *Bee*, April 6, 1857.

18. One Ann Williams was fined for being drunk and disorderly in May 1858. It seems unlikely that this was Lauretta, now age sixteen, for whatever her other weaknesses, she seems never to have been fond of the bottle. New Orleans *Daily Picayune*, May 7, 1858.

19. New Orleans *Daily True Delta*, November 2, 1862; New Orleans *Bee*, November 3, 1862.

20. Adjutant General's Office, *Official Army Register, for 1856*. Washington, DC: Public Printer, 1856), 18–19.

21. Entry for Lauretta Williams, November 8, 1862, New Orleans Charity Hospital Admission Books, 1818–1899, Louisiana Division & City Archives, New Orleans Public Library, New Orleans; Atlanta *Constitution*, September 4, 1874. Her statement that Williams was not her maiden name could also refer to her claim that she was married to Private John Williams, with whom she was staying before her arrest. In *WIB*, 50–51, she later claimed that she stayed in New Orleans while her husband was away on the Utah expedition, but that when he returned in the summer of 1858 he took her to Fort Leavenworth, Kansas, where they remained until the spring of 1860. However, no officers named Arnold, Williams, or Burnett were stationed at Fort Leavenworth from June 1858 to April 1860. Returns from U.S. Military Posts, 1806–1916, M 617, RG 94, NA.

22. Estelle C. Jelinek, *The Tradition of Women's Autobiography from Antiquity to the Present* (New York: Macmillan, 2003), 119.

23. A letter was being held at the New Orleans post office for Mrs. M. M. A. Arnold in early April 1861, but nothing connects it to Lauretta and her use of a similar alias. New Orleans *Daily Picayune*, April 5, 1861.

24. New Orleans *Daily True Delta*, June 15, 1859; New Orleans *Daily Picayune*, June 15, 1859; New Orleans *Daily Crescent*, June 15, 1859. The assailant couple was variously identified as William and Eliza Powley or Dowby.

25. Record of Prisoners Committed to the Parish Prison, 1852–1862, City Archives, TX420, New Orleans Public Library, 134.

26. New Orleans *Daily Crescent*, October 7, 11, 1859; New Orleans *Bee*, October 11, 1859.

27. Record of Prisoners Committed to the Parish Prison, 1852–1862, 156, 180; New Orleans *Daily Picayune*, June 27, 1861. In 1862 the press would refer to her as Mrs. Williams for no immediately apparent reason.

28. United States Census, Third Ward, New Orleans, LA, 1860. There was also an Ann Williams, also age nineteen and born in Louisiana, working as a "servant" in the much smaller house on Gravier Street operated by Bridget Malloy, who until recently had also run a house on Dryades. Fisher's was the better-known establishment, and Lauretta's earliest known claim of nativity was in New York, suggesting that she was with Fisher and not Malloy. New Orleans *Daily Picayune*, October 7, 1857, June 13, August 26, 1858.

29. New Orleans *Daily Picayune*, July 13, 1862; New Orleans *Daily Crescent*, November 13, 26, 1860.

30. Record of Prisoners Committed to the Parish Prison, 156.

31. Lauretta was definitely not the Mary Ann Williams charged with an assault on Ida Durand in June 1861. That woman signed by mark, whereas Lauretta was literate. *State of Louisiana v. Mary Ann Williams*, Case File 15410, First General District Court Case Files, New Orleans Public Library; New Orleans *Daily Picayune*, November 14, 17, 1861; New Orleans *Bee*, November 14, 1861; New Orleans *Daily Crescent*, November 18, 1861; New Orleans *Daily True Delta*, November 17, 1861.

32. New Orleans *Daily True Delta*, November 2, 1862; New Orleans *Bee*, November 3, 1862.

33. New Orleans *Bee*, November 1, 1861; Charles Gardner, *Gardner's New Orleans Directory for 1861* (New Orleans: Charles Gardner, 1861), 76, shows Mrs. E. Bremer at 82 Dauphine.

34. United States Census, Orleans Parish, Louisiana, 1860.

35. New Orleans *Daily Picayune*, May 24, July 16, October 10, 1857, July 29, 1865; New Orleans *Daily True Delta*, July 24, 1861.

36. Schafer, *Brothels, Depravity, and Abandoned Women*, 145.

37. New Orleans *Daily Picayune* July 13, 1861; New Orleans *Bee*, July 13, 1861.

38. New Orleans *Daily Picayune*, August 23, October 31, 1861; New Orleans *Daily Crescent*, August 24, November 1, 1861; New Orleans *Bee*, August 24, November 1, 1861.

39. Bachman was not a common name in Arkansas or Louisiana, yet he is impossible to pin down. Christian Bachman of Union County, Arkansas, was more than twice Lauretta's age. William S. Bachman of Carroll County was a more likely candidate, but he was hardly a man of wealth. Only three men of that name lived in Louisiana, each already married with a family. New Orleans *Daily True Delta*, November 2, 1862; New Orleans *Bee*, November 3, 1862;

United States Census, Orleans Parish, LA, 1860; William S. Bachman CSR, 27th Arkansas Infantry, RG 109, NA. A Theodule Bachman Jr. lived in New Orleans in 1866 but apparently not earlier. New Orleans *Daily Southern Star*, January 27, 1866.

40. New Orleans *Daily True Delta*, November 2, 1862; New Orleans *Bee*, November 3, 1862. A further, though entirely speculative, reason to suspect that the Bachman episode took place in the summer of 1861 is that in 1862 Lauretta claimed to have participated in the Battle of Manassas, Virginia, on July 21, 1861. Had she been in New Orleans at that time, she could hardly claim to have been in Virginia without fear of contradiction. It is also remotely possible that Bachman was really her later husband Thomas C. DeCaulp, since postwar she often said they had courted before the war in Arkansas. This would conflict with DeCaulp's claim that his real surname was Irwin and also call into question the accuracy of the *Daily True Delta*'s statement that Bachman was the name of the man who took her to Arkansas. It was surely hearsay or secondhand information in any case, with plenty of opportunity for error to have inserted itself.

41. "Letter from a Patriotic Woman," Vernon, LA, May 27, 1861, New Orleans *Daily Picayune*, June 8, 1861.

42. V. E. W. to the editors, Memphis *Daily Appeal*, April 18, 1861.

43. "Some Account of Hannah Snell, the Female Soldier," *Gentleman's Magazine* 20 (July 1750): 291–93.

44. Madison *Daily Patriot*, June 14, 1861.

45. New Orleans *Daily Picayune*, June 16, 1861.

46. Ibid., June 29, 1861.

47. Schafer, *Brothels, Depravity, and Abandoned Women*, 4–5, 14, 54.

48. Memphis *Avalanche*, September 12, 1861, quoted in New Orleans *Daily True Delta*, September 14, 1861. This story may be conflated with another, for two days earlier Memphis police arrested a twenty-year-old woman named Ellen Bosquis or Helen Voskins, caught wearing man's trousers tied at the ankles and "a handsome uniform of the Confederate army." "Her jaunty cap, Bloomer pants and close fitting coat rendered her the observed of all observers," writes one reporter. She turned out to be a *vivandiere* who had accompanied her regiment to Richmond, now returned on furlough to visit friends in Memphis. It is unlikely that this was Lauretta, since Voskins stood five feet, ten inches tall, while no physical description of Lauretta ever put her close to that height. Memphis *Daily Appeal*, September 10, 1861; Memphis *Daily Avalanche*, September 10, 1861, in Nashville *Union and American*, September 12, 1861.

49. The Memphis *Avalanche* notice dated September 12, 1861, appeared in New Orleans *Daily True Delta*, September 14, 1861; Nashville *Union and*

American, September 14, 1861; Richmond *Daily Dispatch*, September 18, 1861; Janesville, WI, *Daily Gazette*, September 19, 1861; Columbus *Daily Ohio Statesman*, September 20, 1861; Milwaukee *Daily Milwaukee Press and News*, September 21, 1861; Charlotte *Western Democrat*, September 24, 1861; Wilmington *Journal*, September 26, 1861; Fremont, OH, *Journal*, September 27, 1861; Manitowoc, WI, *Pilot*, September 27, 1861; Rochester, IN, *Sentinel*, October 19, 1861; Mineral Point, WI, *Weekly Tribune*, October 22, 1861. No one later seems to have connected this woman with Lauretta as Harry T. Buford.

50. There is no definitive source for identifying officer casualties from these states, but the Record of Events cards that accompany CSRs in RG 109, NA, for individual Confederate units are the surest source regarding officers killed, wounded, or missing in action.

51. Kathleen De Grave, *Swindler, Spy, Rebel: The Confidence Woman in Nineteenth-Century America* (Columbia: University of Missouri Press, 1995), 4, 8, 10, 247.

52. John B. Jones, *A Rebel War Clerk's Diary at the Confederate States Capital* (Philadelphia: J. B. Lippincott, 1866), 1:94, November 20, 1861.

53. Lynchburg *Republican*, September 26, 1861, in Richmond *Daily Dispatch*, September 27, 1861.

54. Richmond *Daily Dispatch*, September 27, 1861.

55. In her book Lauretta states that she was in Virginia nonstop from mid-June through October, but almost that entire portion of the narrative is fluff and anecdote and two highly fanciful accounts of the battles at Bull Run and Ball's Bluff. *WIB*, 88ff.

56. Lynchburg *Republican*, September 26, 1861, in Richmond *Daily Dispatch*, September 27, 1861. A Mary Keith was living in Memphis in 1860, born about 1835 in Tennessee, so she was seven years older than Lauretta and was married with three living children. United States Census, Memphis, TN, 1860.

57. Lieutenant Richard Arnold was in that same artillery unit, but he was on the Pacific coast throughout the early 1850s until June 1855, when he became an aide to General John E. Wool, first on the Pacific, and then from 1857 to 1861 at Troy, New York. In light of her 1862 claim to have been in Minnesota sometime before the war (see chapter 2, note 29), it is interesting that Company E of the 3rd U.S. Artillery was stationed in Minnesota from 1853 to 1861, but Arnold certainly was not there, and no connection can be made placing Lauretta there either.

58. Lynchburg *Republican*, September 26, 1861, in Richmond *Daily Dispatch*, September 27, 1861; Richmond *Enquirer*, September 28, 1861. When this article was reprinted in the Memphis *Daily Appeal*, October 3, 1861, there was no

mention of the editors recognizing in Keith the woman or women detained in Memphis on September 9–11.

59. Richmond *Daily Dispatch*, September 27, 1861; Staunton, VA, *Spectator*, October 1, 1861; Raleigh *Weekly Standard*, October 2, 1861; Memphis *Daily Appeal*, October 3, 1861; Baltimore *Sun*, October 3, 1861; Washington *National Republican*, October 4, 1861; Milwaukee *Daily Milwaukee Press and News*, October 11, 1861; San Francisco *Evening Daily Bulletin*, October 25, 1861.

60. Lauretta later corroborated that she was Keith when she told General Heintzelman she had "been twice in the Richmond prisons" and there met Union generals James B. Ricketts and Michael Corcoran, captured at First Manassas. The mention of the generals must refer to the fall of 1861, the only time both were in the city. Certainly she did not meet them, however. Ricketts was in a military hospital until October 11, and Corcoran was moved from the city on September 10. Hence neither was in a prison while Lauretta/Keith was there on September 25–27. The other occasion of her arrest was in July 1863. Heintzelman Journal, January 27, 1864. In *WIB*, 284, 286, she correctly implies that the Lynchburg jail was on a second floor, though she speaks only of confinement in "comfortable quarters" and makes no mention of the jail specifically. Neither her postwar interviews nor *WIB* indicates that she ever saw the actual jail, but Mary Ann Keith/Lieutenant Buford certainly did.

61. Jones, *War Clerk's Diary*, 1:94, November 20, 1861. The dates in Jones's published diary do not match the dates established by newspaper coverage of Keith/Buford, but Jones often made such mistakes, depending on his memory for dates. Otherwise his account is consistent with the Keith episode and with Lauretta herself.

62. Richmond *Daily Dispatch*, September 27, 1861.

63. Jones, *War Clerk's Diary*, 1:94, November 21, 1861.

64. Lynchburg *Republican*, September 28, 1861, in Nashville *Union and American*, October 4, 1861.

65. Jones, *War Clerk's Diary*, 1:94, November 21, 1861.

66. Lynchburg *Republican*, October 14, 1861, in Nashville *Union and American*, October 18, 1861.

67. It is probably only coincidental that letters addressed to Mrs. Mary J. Keith and Mrs. M. E. Keith arrived at the Richmond post office a week after she left the city. Richmond, *Daily Dispatch* October 5, 1861.

68. Richmond *Daily Dispatch*, September 27, 1861, from Lynchburg *Republican*, September 26; Staunton *Spectator*, October 1, 1861; Raleigh *Weekly Standard*, October 2, 1861 (much abridged); Memphis *Daily Appeal*, October 3, 1861; Nashville *Daily Patriot*, October 3, 1861; Nashville *Union and American*,

October 4, 18, 1861; Baltimore *Sun*, October 3, 1861; Boston *American Traveller*, October 4, 12, 1861; Philadelphia *Inquirer*, October 4, 1861; Washington *National Republican*, October 4, 1861; Wheeling *Daily Intelligencer*, October 5, 1861; Cincinnati *Daily Press*, October 10, 1861; Louisville *Daily Journal*, October 9, 1861; Milwaukee *News*, October 11, 1861; New Bedford *Whalemen's Shipping List, and Merchants' Transcript*, October 15, 1861; San Francisco *Evening Daily Bulletin*, October 25, 1861. This list covers only those papers known to have run the story. It surely appeared in many more that have not been found or no longer survive.

2. "HEROINE IN A FIX"

1. New Orleans *Daily Picayune*, October 18, 1861; New Orleans *Daily Crescent*, October 18, 1861.

2. New Orleans *Daily Picayune*, December 6–7, 1861; New Orleans *Daily Crescent*, January 17, February 13, 1862. On November 16, 1861, a judge fined an Ann Williams for assault and battery, but this seems definitely not to have been Lauretta (New Orleans *Daily True Delta*, November 17, 1861; New Orleans *Bee*, November 18, 1861).

3. New Orleans *Daily Picayune*, April 6, 1862.

4. New Orleans *Daily True Delta*, April 24, 1862. She makes no mention of being at Belmont in her book, but in *WIB*, 161–73, she gives a lengthy account of experiences at Fort Donelson, which, though vivid, seems unreliable given her omission of Donelson from any of her earliest accounts. On 225, she also changes her Shiloh wounds to her right arm and shoulder.

5. *WIB*, 150.

6. Ibid., 153.

7. The absence of any Ann or Mary Ann Williams court cases after February 17, just days before Beauregard's call, may be because she was elsewhere, or it may be meaningless.

8. New Orleans *Daily True Delta*, April 15, 20, 1862.

9. New Orleans *Daily Picayune*, January 5, 1867. The unidentified writer of this article, titled "Mrs. Mary De Caulp," conflated his sighting of Lauretta with bandaged foot and crutch in April 1862 with a recollection of her arrest that October.

10. She could have been influenced by the sensational publicity given in 1861 to Fanny Sweet of New Orleans, who posed as a man occasionally and attracted considerable attention as a result. Fannie Bliss of Memphis, who volunteered in early 1862 with the 1st Tennessee, also gained some press attention. New Orleans *Daily Picayune*, March 26, 1862.

11. New Orleans *Daily True Delta*, April 24, 1862.

12. Ibid., April 26, 1862.

13. No instances have been found of Lauretta using the alias Gibbons. It may be only coincidence that in 1861 a Thomas Gibbons enlisted in the 3rd Arkansas Cavalry on the same day and at the same place as Lauretta's future husband, Thomas C. DeCaulp. Gibbons died or deserted on September 10, 1861, "while riding express between Pocahontas and Memphis." It was the next day, September 11, that the mysterious unidentified widow in uniform who may have been Lauretta appeared in Memphis. Two weeks later Lauretta appeared as Mary Ann Keith in Lynchburg. Thomas Gibbons CSR, 3rd Arkansas Cavalry, RG 109, NA.

14. New Orleans *Daily Picayune*, January 5, 1867.

15. Lauretta Williams entry, November 8, 1862, New Orleans Charity Hospital Admission Books, 1818–1899, New Orleans Public Library, Louisiana Division and City Archives, New Orleans, LA.

16. New Orleans *Daily Picayune*, November 2, 1862.

17. Augusta, GA, *Daily Constitutionalist*, May 1, 1862; Augusta, GA, *Southern Watchman*, May 14, 1862.

18. In July a "Mrs. Williams" was twice arrested for being drunk and assaulting her own child, which hardly sounds like Lauretta, since there is no reliable indication to date of her having had any children. New Orleans *Daily Picayune*, July 26, 1862.

19. New Orleans *Bee*, August 22, September 4, 1862.

20. New Orleans *Daily True Delta*, October 3, 1862.

21. Augusta, GA, *Daily Constitutionalist*, September 9, 1862.

22. New Orleans *Daily Picayune*, November 2, 1862.

23. John Williams CSR, RG 109, NA.

24. New Orleans *Daily Picayune*, June 1, July 19, 30, August 30, September 20, October 1, 1862.

25. Homer B. Sprague, *History of the 13th Infantry Regiment of Connecticut Volunteers during the Great Rebellion* (Hartford: Case, Lockwood & Co., 1867), 74, 78.

26. Ibid., 74, 78; Williams CSR; New Orleans *Daily Picayune*, November 2, 1862.

27. The *Daily True Delta*'s brief articles on her appeared in North Carolina's Wilmington *Journal*, May 8, 1862, but scarcely anywhere else.

28. De Grave, *Swindler, Spy, Rebel*, 13.

29. New Orleans *Daily True Delta*, October 30, 31, 1862; New Orleans *Daily Picayune*, November 2, 1862. The *Picayune* article says she knew the Chesters

from meeting them in Minnesota before the war, but no evidence corroborates Lauretta having visited Minnesota prior to 1864.

30. New Orleans *Daily True Delta*, October 31, November 2, 1862.

31. New Orleans *Picayune*, November 2, 1862. In *WIB*, 198, she writes that she sat for a photograph in Memphis in March 1862, which could be true.

32. New Orleans *Bee*, October 31, 1862; New Orleans *Daily True Delta*, October 31, 1862.

33. New Orleans *Bee*, October 31, 1862; New Orleans *Daily True Delta*, October 31, November 2, 1862; New Orleans *Daily Picayune*, November 2, 1862; New Orleans *Daily Delta*, November 2, 1862, in New York *Evening Post*, November 20, 1862. No original copy of the November 2 *Daily Delta* appears to have survived, but it was republished widely, and internal evidence establishes the date as November 2. The accounts in the November 2 *Daily True Delta* and *Bee* are identical, suggesting a shared reporter, or the provost court may have issued its own reports. The *Daily Picayune* and *Daily Delta* had their own reporters present, providing details not included in the other papers.

34. New Orleans *Daily Picayune*, November 2, 1862; New Haven, CT, *Columbian Weekly*, December 6, 1862. Unfortunately, the Fifth District Court Docket book for 1862 no longer survives in the City Archives at the New Orleans Public Library, and the Record of Prisoners Committed to the Parish Prison, 1852–1862, extends only through May 1862, so no official record of her sentencing or any notes about her incarceration exist. City Archives, TX420, New Orleans Public Library.

35. New Orleans *Daily Picayune*, November 2, 1862.

36. The Northern accounts all derive from the November 2, 1862, New Orleans *Daily Delta*, which no longer exists in the original. There are two variants. The first began in the New York *Evening Post* for November 20, 1862, and subsequently appeared in New England papers. The second was published in the Madison *Wisconsin Daily Patriot* of December 2, 1862, and later in Wisconsin and Illinois. It contains two distinctive errors, one of considerable significance. In the sentence originally reading, "she resided in this city several years ago, in a house of questionable character," the later version changed "questionable" to "unquestionable," thereby turning a condemnation into a compliment.

37. She also gave her age, which the registrar first entered as thirty-eight, then changed to twenty-eight, and perhaps altered again to eighteen, probably through simple carelessness.

38. Lauretta Williams entry, November 8, 1862, New Orleans Charity Hospital Admission Books.

39. New Orleans *Bee*, November 15, 1862; New Orleans *Daily True Delta*, November 15, 1862; New Orleans *Daily Picayune*, November 15, 1862; New

Orleans *Daily Delta*, November 15, 1862. The first two of these accounts give her name as "Lorett*o*" rather than Loretta. She never used that spelling, meaning it was a typographical error, and it has been corrected here.

40. Lauretta Williams entry, November 8, 1862, New Orleans Charity Hospital Admission Books.

41. New Orleans *Bee*, November 15, 1862; New Orleans *Daily True Delta*, November 15, 1862; New Orleans *Daily Delta*, November 15, 1862; New Orleans *Daily Picayune*, November 15, 1862.

42. One Ann Williams was arrested at Christmas for selling liquor to occupying soldiers, and another identified only as "Mrs. Williams" was charged in January 1863 for being publicly drunk and using seditious language. New Orleans *Daily True Delta*, December 27, 1862.

43. An Ann Williams came before the provost court on April 30 for drunkenness, but this was not likely Lauretta, as excessive drinking did not seem to have been one of her vices. New Orleans *Daily Picayune*, May 1, 1863.

44. General Orders 35, April 27, 1863, New Orleans *Daily Picayune*, May 1, 1863. No record of her incarceration seems to survive in the Federal records. Selected Records of the War Department relating to Confederate Prisoners of War, 1861–1865, RG 109, roll 106, vols. 338–43; Records relating to Individual Prisons or Stations, RG 109, New Orleans, LA, Register of Prisoners and Hospital Register, 1863–1865, M598, NA, begins with July 9, 1863, thus missing her. Similarly, Union Provost Marshal's File of Papers Relating to Two or More Civilians, RG 109, Prisoners: Gallatin, TN–New Orleans, M416, roll 88, NA, carries no documents mentioning her.

45. [W. C. Corsan], *Two Months in the Confederate States, Including a Visit to New Orleans under the Domination of General Butler. By "An English Merchant"* (London: Richard Bentley, 1863), 43.

46. New Orleans *Daily Picayune*, May 17, 1863. In her interview with Henri Garidel on September 14, 1863, in Richmond, Lauretta told him she had been transported on the *Brown*. Michael Bedout Chesson and Leslie Jean Roberts, eds., *Exile in Richmond: The Confederate Journal of Henri Garidel* (Charlottesville: University Press of Virginia, 2001), 70. Interestingly, the original deportation order specifies that registered enemies would leave in alphabetical order, with those whose surnames began with A, B, and C departing on May 15. That ought to have meant that the May 17 contingent would be those whose surnames started with G, H, I, and J, which clearly would not have included Williams. The deadline was extended to May 20, but the alphabetical order of departure may have proved impractical, so the date she left is no sure key to what name she used. Sent to prison as Williams, she would have been so

on any list of enemies (New Orleans *Bee*, May 15, 1863; New Orleans *Daily Picayune*, May 19, 1863).

47. New Orleans *Daily Picayune*, March 8, 1863. This is an account by a New York *Tribune* writer from February 1863, but the experience would have been much the same for Lauretta.

48. New Orleans *Daily Picayune*, May 22, 1863.

49. New York *Daily World*, December 10, 1862; Philadelphia *Inquirer*, December 10, 1862.

50. Mary Anna Clark to Mrs. Kate Huffman and Mrs. Tucker, n.d. [early to mid-December 1862], E. A. W. Burbage to Kate Huffman, December 27, 1862, Mary Ann Clark Letters, Kentucky Historical Society, Frankfort.

51. Jackson *Mississippian*, December 30, 1862, as excerpted and reprinted in the Atlanta *Daily Constitution*, January 8, 1863; Montgomery *Weekly Advertiser*, January 7, 1863; Charleston *Daily Courier*, January 8, 1863; Staunton *Spectator*, January 20, 1863. That issue of the *Mississippian* no longer survives. As excerpted in the other papers, its article shows some differences in content and wording from the original in the New York *Daily World*, though it is clearly credited to that paper.

3. THE SUMMER OF HARRY BUFORD

1. United States Census, Hinds County, MS, 1860; Dallas *Herald*, March 31, 1866.

2. Jackson *Mississippian*, December 30, 1862, in Montgomery *Weekly Advertiser*, January 7, 1863.

3. It has occasionally been suggested that she may have been the woman believed to have served in a Louisiana regiment who was pointed out to Arthur J. Fremantle on a train from Chattanooga to Atlanta. Ella Lonn, *Foreigners in the Confederacy* (Chapel Hill: University of North Carolina Press, 1940), 381–82. As dated in Fremantle's diary, this sighting took place on June 5, 1863, when Lauretta was demonstrably still in Jackson, Mississippi. Arthur J. L. Fremantle, *Three Months in the Southern States, April–June 1863* (London: William Blackwood & Sons, 1863), 175. Alemán, "Authenticity, Autobiography, and Identity," xvi, rightly dismisses the Fremantle account but errs in concluding that another by Fitzgerald Ross (see chapter 4) does not involve her.

4. No copy of the *Mississippian* for June 6, 1863, appears to have survived. However, internal evidence indicates that the article's republication in the Natchez *Daily Courier* of June 13 was based directly on a copy of the *Mississippian* in hand.

5. The *Mississippian* article published the name as Benford, which was picked up by other papers and widely disseminated, but this is clearly another example

of a typographical error, where the *u* in Buford in Purdom's notes was transformed into *en*, a mistake easily made, as with the earlier mention of Lauretta being printed as Jeruth.

6. "Adventures of a Young Lady in the Army," Jackson *Mississippian*, June 6, 1863, as reprinted in Natchez *Daily Courier*, June 13, 1863.

7. Houston *Star* in Dallas *Herald*, April 14, 1866.

8. Natchez *Daily Courier*, June 13, 1863; Mobile *Register & Advertiser*, June 13, 1863; Memphis *Daily Appeal*, June 15, 1863; Richmond *Whig*, June 19, 1863; Houston *Tri-Weekly Telegraph*, June 24, 1863; Raleigh, NC, *Register*, June 24, 1863; Richmond *Daily Dispatch*, June 25, 1863; Savannah *Republican*, June 29, 1863; Staunton, VA, *Spectator*, June 30, 1863; Dallas *Herald*, July 1, 1863; Augusta, GA, *Daily Chronicle & Sentinel*, July 26, 1863; Wilmington, NC, *Journal*, August 6, 1863; Personne [Felix DeFontaine], *Marginalia; or, Gleanings from an Army Note-book* (Columbia, SC: F. G. DeFontaine & Co., 1864), 65–66. The total 1860 population in the referenced cities was nearly two hundred thousand, half of that number adults. By June 1863 all Confederates cities saw their population swelled by an influx of refugees from territory occupied by Union forces, especially Richmond and Atlanta. Allowing for that, as well as the inevitable number of other newspapers that would have picked up Purdom's story but are not available now for examination, makes it seem reasonable that a quarter million adults could have read the interview or been told of it by others.

9. Knoxville *Chronicle*, July 6, 1863, in Milledgeville, GA, *Southern Recorder*, August 4, 1863.

10. Adjutant and Inspector General's Office, RG 109, Register of Letters Received, April–July 1863, M–Z, chap. 1, vol. 56, file 1145 W 1863, NA. This entry has been misread in the past as saying Lauretta Fennett Williams.

11. Richmond *Daily Richmond Examiner*, July 2, 1863.

12. Letter from Jackson, June 24, 1863, Memphis *Daily Appeal*, June 29, 1863.

13. Adjutant and Inspector General's Office, Register of Letters Received, file 1145 W 1863. Notation indicates receipt of her letter on June 25 and adds her alias, suggesting either that she used it in her letter or that it was already known in Richmond, perhaps as a result of telegraphic notification from the provost in Mobile.

14. Augusta, GA, *Daily Constitutionalist*, July 18, 1863.

15. It is hardly probable that Lauretta gave the false first name herself, for she immediately proclaimed that she was the Lieutenant Buford widely touted in the press, married to a man in the Union forces but herself a loyal Southerner. She wanted to be recognized as the heroine of the *Mississippian* article, and confusing the matter with a different given name hardly served that purpose.

16. Richmond *Enquirer*, July 2, 1863. The *Enquirer* copied the error of an earlier newspaper in giving her alias as "Benford" rather than Buford.

17. Richmond *Daily Richmond Examiner*, July 2, 1863.

18. Staunton *Spectator*, July 7, 1863; Knoxville *Chronicle*, July 6, 1863, in Milledgeville, GA, *Southern Recorder*, August 4, 1863.

19. New Orleans *Item*, October 6, 1879. This article, which first appeared in an undetermined September or October issue of the Richmond *Southern Intelligencer*, was clearly written by a Confederate who was at Castle Thunder when Lauretta was there. According to Robert E. L. Krick of Richmond in an e-mail message, the only likely candidates for authorship are Captain Alexander, Dennis Callahan, the prison adjutant, and a clerk known only as Timberlake. Having been written sixteen years after the fact, it obviously suffers from faulty memory and erroneous chronology. The account of Lauretta's adventures agrees most closely with the *Mississippian*'s, making it likely that the author was truthful when he said he wrote it "as [he] heard it from Harry herself and from others who were conversant with it at the time."

20. Ibid.

21. Richmond *Daily Richmond Examiner*, July 16, 1863.

22. Harvey Birch [Charles Dunham] to the editor, October 17, 1863, New York *Herald*, October 19, 1863.

23. Richmond *Enquirer*, July 11, 1863; Selma, AL, *Morning Reporter*, July 18, 1863; Adjutant and Inspector General's Office, Register of Letters Received, file 1145 W 1863. Docketing on the entry shows her July 10 release with the abbreviation "Presd," which could mean that "Pres[i]d[ent]" Davis ordered it or perhaps "P[risoner] re[lea]s[e]d."

24. Birch [Dunham] to the editor, October 17, 1863, New York *Herald*, October 19, 1863. In his letter Birch/Dunham also said, based on hearsay, that Alexander had told some unnamed source that three weeks after Lauretta's departure from Richmond—which would have been about August 6—he had received a letter from her posted in Washington. That was clearly impossible, as she was demonstrably in Montgomery, Alabama, as late as August 3.

25. Frances H. Casstevens, *George W. Alexander and Castle Thunder* (Jefferson, NC: McFarland, 2004) is an excellent and thorough work on its subject, but it unfortunately casts no additional light on Lauretta's time in the Castle.

26. Richmond *Daily Richmond Examiner*, July 11, 1863.

27. *WIB*, 89, 93, 96, 98.

28. Ibid., 118, 121–22, 165, 223, 271.

29. Ibid., 72, 96, 118, 218, 259, 355, 385, 535.

30. Richmond *Enquirer*, July 15, 1863.

31. Richmond *Daily Dispatch*, July 16, 1863.

32. Richmond *Sentinel*, July 16, 1863.

33. Richmond *Enquirer*, July 18, 1863.

34. Ibid.; Richmond *Daily Dispatch*, July 16, 1863; Richmond *Sentinel*, July 16, 1863; Augusta, GA, *Daily Constitutionalist*, July 18, 1863.

35. For instance, Savannah *Republican*, July 15, 1863.

36. Quoted in Abbeville, SC, *Abbeville Press*, July 24, 1863.

37. Charleston *Daily Courier*, July 20, 1863.

38. Yorkville, SC, *Enquirer*, July 22, 1863.

39. The Richmond *Enquirer*'s July 2, 1863, article was picked up by the Staunton *Spectator* on July 7, 1863, and its July 11, 1863, piece headlined "Discharge of the Fair Lieutenant" was republished in the July 19, 1863, Columbia, SC, *Carolinian*. Meanwhile, the Richmond *Daily Richmond Examiner*'s July 16, 1863, piece on her release and departure saw print in the Augusta *Daily Constitutionalist* of July 18, 1863; in an undated reduced version in the Columbia, SC, *Carolinian*; and in the Abbeville, SC, *Abbeville Press* of July 24, 1863. The Yorkville, SC, *Enquirer* of July 22, 1863, carried its own original article on her trip back to Atlanta, while the Staunton *Spectator* of July 21, 1863, republished a variant from an undated issue of the Richmond *Sentinel*. Her visit to Montgomery, Alabama, at the end of July was mentioned in passing by the Montgomery *Mail* in an undated issue referred to in the Chattanooga *Daily Rebel* of August 4, 1863.

40. Yorkville, SC, *Enquirer*, July 22, 1863.

41. Lauretta J. Williams to Samuel Cooper, July 20, 1863, Letters Received by Confederate Adjutant-General, July–October 1863, RG 109, M474, roll 88, frame 0101, rile W1310, NA; Augusta, GA, *Daily Constitutionalist*, July 18, 1863.

42. Montgomery *Daily Mail*, July 26, 1863; Montgomery *Daily Mail*, no date, quoted in Chattanooga, *Daily Rebel*, August 4, 1863. The latter article says that she had been in town "several days." Given that it was republished in Chattanooga on August 4, an issue of the *Mail* with the article could not have reached that town later than August 3, meaning it left Montgomery August 1–2. Hence "several days" back from August 1–2 suggests that Lauretta reached Montgomery no later than July 31.

4. "IN SECRET SERVICE"

1. A tantalizing coincidence is that DeCaulp enlisted at Pocahontas, seven miles from the home of a Miss Williams, daughter of Isaac Williams, who helped her father raise a small company of armed men in May 1861 as detailed in the Pocahontas, AR, *Advertiser*, May 31, 1861, in the New Orleans *Daily*

Picayune, June 16, 1861. After the war Lauretta claimed that she and DeCaulp had been engaged before the war. This young woman was sixteen-year-old Margaret Williams, however. She was still living near Pocahontas in 1870, when Lauretta was demonstrably in the Far West.

2. DeCaulp gave his age as twenty-five when he enlisted in 1861 and stated that he was born in Pennsylvania. Undated Descriptive Roll of Officers of the 3rd Regiment of Arkansas Cavalry, Thomas C. DeCaulp CSR, RG 109, NA. His age is shown as twenty-eight on a certificate of disability for discharge dated January 14, 1865, as well as on a September 20, 1865, muster-out roll. Irwin, CSR.

3. Thomas C. DeCaulp et al. to Sterling Price, August 26, 1862, as printed in Calvin L. Collier, *The War Child's Children: A Story of the Third Regiment, Arkansas Cavalry, Confederate States Army* (Little Rock, AR: Pioneer Press, 1965), 30–31.

4. With no attribution of source, Collier says DeCaulp was shot through both legs at Corinth. Ibid., 28. DeCaulp's CSR shows discrepancies in his promotion dates and also the details of his capture, saying Iuka in one document and Corinth in another.

5. DeCaulp CSR. Unless otherwise cited, all information on his Confederate service comes from his CSR.

6. Documents in his CSR say both May 4 and May 14.

7. Certificate of disability for discharge, January 14, 1865, Irwin CSR. In her 1876 book, Lauretta largely echoes that description, saying he was "tall in stature," with auburn hair and dark hazel eyes. *WIB*, 337.

8. United States Census, Pulaski County, AR, 1860. The census listing shows him born in New York rather than Pennsylvania, but given Irwin/DeCaulp's subsequent economy with the truth, this seems not too significant. Given Lauretta's later claim that he was a native of Scotland, it is just possible that he was also the William Irwin, born in 1839–40 in England, listed in the 1860 census as a carpenter living in Ward 23, Precinct 7, Philadelphia, Pennsylvania.

9. Alex Arnold statement, March 31, 1864, Irwin CSR.

10. The 1860 United States Census lists no DeCaulps anywhere, nor any close variants of the name. There were a handful of DeKalbs, including one in the Philadelphia area.

11. Pulaski County, Arkansas, Marriage Record, 12, Marriage Book B2, 66, Pulaski County Circuit Court, Little Rock, AR. These are the only extant documents placing anyone with a name similar to DeCaulp in Arkansas before or during the war.

12. The marriage record was not actually recorded in the courthouse until February 10, 1863. Regardless of the dates of marriages, officiants sometimes

recorded several at a time on the same day, as with the marriage directly above DeCaulp's in the county marriage book, which took place in November 1862 but also was recorded on February 10, 1863. No surviving original marriage document is known, and hence the only record is what the county clerk copied more than two months after the ceremony, raising the possibility of error through faulty memory or carelessness. The union might have taken place some day or days earlier, allowing DeCaulp time for a more leisurely return to Camp Rogers.

13. That Thomas R. DeCalp and Thomas C. DeCaulp were not one and the same is so improbable as to be dismissed. All descendants of the DeCalp-Haralson union spelled their name DeCaulp and used that spelling on Sarah's headstone. Their marriage is Thomas R. DeCalp's sole appearance in the documentary record. There is no record of his death or a divorce before Sarah married a third time, on March 4, 1868. That raises the theoretical possibility that there was no actual marriage. If she was pregnant, registering a fictitious marriage would be a convenient way around the problem, and there would be no need for a divorce when she later remarried if DeCaulp were still living or believed to be alive. The 1870 census for Pulaski County, Arkansas, shows their son Edwin, age six, and lists both of his parents as being foreign born. In her various accounts of Thomas C. DeCaulp, Lauretta placed his birth in both England and Scotland.

14. Sarah Ann Hollingshead Haralson DeCaulp Straughn died February 19, 1894, and lies buried in Cato United Methodist Church Cemetery in Pulaski, Arkansas. Her son, who in youth went by both Edward and Edwin DeCaulp, married Nellie Rice on November 4, 1886, and lived virtually all his life in Little Rock, where he died July 20, 1894. His widow, Nellie, lived until 1940. United States Census, Pulaski County, AR, 1870, 1880. Virtually all DeCaulps in the United States descend from Thomas Edwin DeCaulp.

15. *WIB*, 335, gives his name as "Rev. Pinkington," a false recollection, as Pinkerton was the chaplain at the Atlanta hospital where she and DeCaulp probably met. Lauretta refers to the venue as the Thompson House, a name by which it had been known in the early 1860s, but by 1863 it advertised itself as the Atlanta Hotel. An 1866 mention of their wedding, erroneously dating it to 1864, says it took place at the Atlanta Hotel (Pulaski, TN, *Citizen*, May 18, 1866). A search of Marriage Book B, Fulton County, Georgia, Marriages, 1854–1921, covering the years 1862–66 shows no record of a DeCaulp-Williams marriage. It does reveal that Samuel J. Pinkerton performed at least three weddings in 1863 and 1864, including one on August 6, 1863, not long before the alleged DeCaulp-Williams marriage, so it is certainly plausible that he joined Thomas and Lauretta but for some reason failed to get the record to the court for registration.

Delays in recording marriages were common, often extending to several weeks, and some records were lost or destroyed in the disruption of wartime. No marriages were recorded in Atlanta in the months of October and November 1863, which seems unusual and probably reflects documents somehow lost. The record of the DeCaulp-Williams marriage may be among the lost, which leaves three options for Lauretta and Thomas's nuptials: there was no marriage; Pinkerton married them but failed to get the record to the court; or the court recorder received the record but it was lost with others received in October and November. Given that by September 15 the story of their marriage reached Augusta, Georgia, it seems certain that they did in fact wed. Fulton County, GA, Probate Court, General Index to Marriages, 1854–1921, microfilm 106/66; Marriage Book B, 1862–1866, microfilm 110/66, Georgia Department of Archives and History, Atlanta.

16. The earliest contemporary reference to the wedding found to date is in the Augusta, GA, *Daily Constitutionalist*, September 16, 1863.

17. Lucius A. Gartrell to James A. Seddon, January 17, 1863, Pinkerton CSR.

18. In *WIB* she says she converted, and her case record from St. Elizabeth's Hospital gives her religion as Episcopalian. Case #20081, Beard, Loretta J., Records of St. Elizabeth's Government Hospital for the Insane, RG 418, Entry 64, Registers of Cases, 1855–1941, 115–16, NA.

19. Savannah *Republican*, September 25, 1863.

20. Augusta, GA, *Daily Constitutionalist*, September 16, 1863.

21. Thomas C. DeCaulp to Lauretta J. DeCaulp, May 1864, DeCaulp Provost File.

22. Applications for Appointments in Military Service, Confederate States and Civil Service under War Department, July 1, 1863, to December 31, 1863, chap. 9, vol. 90, RG109, NA.

23. *WIB*, 336, 342.

24. Richmond *Enquirer*, September 17, 1863.

25. Chesson and Roberts, *Exile in Richmond*, 70, 73. Later that day Garidel wrote that "her first name was Alice Williams and her second Mrs. Deschamps." His sentence is best read to mean that she had been known previously in Richmond as Alice Williams, as the press erroneously gave her name back in July. There is no verifiable instance of her using Alice, so Garidel's use here must have had its origin in that press error.

26. Richmond *Daily Richmond Examiner*, September 16, 1863. The paper reports her as "Mrs. Jeruth DeCaulp," which is almost certainly a typesetter's misreading of Lauretta or Loretta, and not yet another alias. It says she arrived in Richmond "the other day" and was still in town as of September 16.

27. Ibid. Bromfield Ridley, *Battles and Sketches of the Army of Tennessee* (Mexico, MO: Missouri Printing and Publishing, 1906), 495, says, "I recollect" a woman arriving at Tyner's Station near Chattanooga at Stewart's headquarters with orders from Bragg's adjutant Kinloch Falconer to report to him as a scout. Immediately discovered to be a woman, she was sent back. Ridley's account is both forty-three years after the fact and obviously based on reading about Lauretta rather than witnessing the alleged incident.

28. Adjutant and Inspector General's Office, Register of Letters Received, file 1145 W 1863; Applications for Appointments in Military Service, Bound Records, chap. 9, vol. 90, file 1549, RG 109, NA.

29. See Staunton, VA, *Spectator*, September 22, 1863, and Columbus, GA, *Weekly Enquirer*, October 6, 1863.

30. Richmond *Enquirer*, September 17, 1863.

31. Richmond *Daily Richmond Examiner*, September 16, 1863; Columbus, GA, *Columbus Daily Enquirer*, October 2, 1863; Staunton *Spectator*, September 22, 1863.

32. Fitzgerald Ross, *Cities and Camps of the Confederate States*, ed. Richard Barksdale Harwell (Urbana: University of Illinois Press, 1958), 115–16. Ross says a "Colonel Geary" found her, but the context makes it clear that this was Gary. Lauretta is not identified by name, but the woman's story and the timing are such that it can only have been she.

33. The Atlanta *Daily Intelligencer*, September 18, 1863, reported an interesting coincidence within a week of Lauretta's departure. A young woman who had posed as a soldier named Charley Green decided just then to stop her masquerade and resume feminine dress. Reportedly, she had passed through many battles but now would work as a nurse in the military hospitals instead. The press, while complimenting her on her bravery, heartily approved an end to her pose, which "sooner or later would have demoralized her beyond all reach." Her real name, or at least the one she would use now in her crinolines, was "Mrs. Irvin." Assuming that DeCaulp was telling the truth, Lauretta was now Mrs. Irwin, at least in Pennsylvania.

34. Mrs. L. J. DeCaulp to James Stockdale, July 27, 1864, DeCaulp Provost File. It seems unlikely that she would have invented the story of the pistols and the belt in a letter to Stockdale, since they were details easily checked if not already known to him. Her account of taking them from a courier of Ferguson's could be an invention, of course, for Stockdale might have had no means of checking that.

35. Mrs. Lauretta J. DeCaulp to Joseph D. Webster, July 30, 1864, DeCaulp Provost File.

36. The actual date of DeCaulp's desertion is cloudy. Confederate records list it as October 13 or 15, and the promotion of his successor on October 16 suggests the day before as the more accurate (DeCaulp CSR; William J. Bass CSR, RG 109, NA). DeCaulp claimed on April 1, 1864, that he deserted on October 13 (Irwin CSR). Federal records date his desertion to September 14, however (DeCaulp CSR). In the end, October seems more likely to be correct.

37. Thomas C. DeCaulp to Lauretta J. DeCaulp, May 12–15, 1864, DeCaulp Provost File.

38. In 1876 she suggested in print that at this juncture she was discouraged and more than a bit put out with Confederate officialdom for what she called "the non-recognition of the value of my services." She went on to reiterate "the disappointments I have felt at different times at not being able to obtain exactly the kind of official recognition I desired." She was no longer Lieutenant Buford, and she found that woman's attire attracted far less respect than a uniform. "All my plans seemed to have gone amiss," she recalled, "and I certainly was not in the most pleasant state of mind imaginable." *WIB*, 345–47.

39. Curiously, the Indianapolis *Daily Journal*, September 5, 1863, advertised a letter being held in the city post office for a Harry Buford as of September 3. It seems only coincidence, but it does raise the faint possibility that Indianapolis was in their plans before they left the Confederacy, though who would have written the letter or what might have been in it cannot be guessed. Similarly, during their time in the city, letters were also advertised for Mary Williams, Mary E. Williams, and Mrs. M. E. Williams, all of whom appear to have been one and the same, but there is no reason to connect them to Lauretta. *Indianapolis Daily Journal*, November 7, 14, 21, 28, 1863.

40. Thomas C. DeCaulp to Lauretta J. DeCaulp, May 12–15, 1864, DeCaulp Provost File. In *WIB* Lauretta erroneously dates her work at the Indianapolis arsenal to the summer of 1864. In May 1864 Thomas linked it in time with his enlistment in mid-December 1863, which is correct, as subsequent citations show.

41. Paymaster's statements for Mrs. Lauretta J. DeCaulp, December 1, 1863, January 1, 1864, Indiana State Arsenal Payroll Ledger, Civil War Miscellany, 47-I-5, drawer 107, folder 43, Indiana State Archives, Indiana Commission on Public Records, Indianapolis.

42. Anita J. Morgan, "Indiana Arsenal," *Hoosier Voices Now*, accessed March 25, 2016, http://www.in.gov/history/4057.htm.

43. Thomas C. DeCaulp to Lauretta DeCaulp, May 12, 1864, DeCaulp Provost File.

44. Richard N. Current, *Lincoln's Loyalists: Union Soldiers from the Confederacy* (Boston: Northeastern University Press, 1992), 113–14.

45. Lauretta J. DeCaulp to Oliver P. Morton, December 7, 1863, Oliver P. Morton Papers, 401-A-3, microfilm roll 10, Indiana State Archives, Indiana Commission on Public Records, Indianapolis. On the verso Morton or someone has annotated, "wants recruiting commission for husband," but says nothing of any further action.

46. Thomas C. DeCaulp to Lauretta DeCaulp, May 12, 1864, DeCaulp Provost File.

47. William Irwin [Thomas C. DeCaulp] to Assistant Adjutant General, April 1, 1864, Certificate of Disability for Discharge, January 14, 1865, Irwin CSR.

48. Statement of Captain Alex W. Arnold, March 31, 1864, Irwin CSR. It is possible that Lauretta made the trip with him, since her pay at the arsenal for December was half that for November, suggesting she could have been absent for some time during the month.

49. William Irwin [Thomas C. DeCaulp] to Assistant Adjutant General, April 1, 1864, Irwin CSR.

50. Collier, *War Child's Children*, 70, says that while researching at the National Archives, he found a letter from an unnamed U.S. senator to "Commander, Minnesota Department, USA," which was probably Brigadier General Henry H. Sibley. It introduced a soldier who wanted to enlist, saying he was really Thomas C. DeCaulp, "forced into the Rebel Service," and that he "was from the beginning a good Union man." The senator apparently garbled what DeCaulp told him, for he went on to say that Thomas wanted to enlist under an assumed name and that his real name was Thomas C. DeCaulp, which must be kept secret, exactly the reverse of all other statements by both Thomas and Lauretta. The fact that the surname DeCaulp is entirely absent from records of any kind prior to his enlistment in Arkansas in 1861, and that his later statements about residing in Philadelphia, and particularly saying his home was in Holmesburg, a Philadelphia suburb, were so definite, argues strongly that DeCaulp was an assumed name, even if William Irwin was as well. Since this letter is—or was—in the National Archives, it is evident that DeCaulp did give it to some official, presumably Sibley. Collier gave no source citation other than "Official Records at the NA," a useless reference. The letter was probably written by one of Minnesota's two senators, Alexander Ramsey or Morton S. Wilkinson; it is not in the Irwin CSR and has not been found in Sibley's department records.

51. New Orleans *Daily Picayune*, November 2, 1862.

52. In July 1864 she claimed that she had spent most of December 1863 and January 1864 in Washington. Lauretta DeCaulp to Joseph D. Webster, July 30,

1864, DeCaulp Provost File. However, it is definitely Lauretta's signature on the December statement of her wages, dated January 1, 1864. This does not appear to have been an interim or midmonth payment, and since it was among much larger sums, and each was signed for by the recipient, it is unlikely that she was paid before January 1. Hence this places her in Indianapolis as of January 1, 1864. Paymaster's statement, January 1, 1864, Indiana State Arsenal Payroll Ledger.

53. Washington *Evening Star*, February 9, 1864. General Heintzelman's letter to Pelouze after hearing Lauretta's story and Pelouze's reply suggest that she saw him. See the following chapter.

54. This is what she told General Heintzelman just a few days later on January 27, and it is reasonable to assume that she would have said the same to Pelouze, whether true or not. Samuel P. Heintzelman Journal, January 27, 1864, Samuel P. Heintzelman Papers, Library of Congress, Washington, DC.

55. Ibid.

56. Pass, January 26, 1864, DeCaulp Provost File. This is the only known documentary evidence connecting her with work or "secret service" for the Union. In recent years the discovery of Major General Robert C. Schenck's order appointing a Mrs. Alice Williams, on November 15, 1863, as "U.S. Special Agent to act in Middle Dept until further orders" has been taken by historians as confirmation that Lauretta did work as an agent for the Union military in or around Baltimore. Schenck ordered Mrs. Williams "scrupulously to avoid notoriety or permitting any person to learn that she is acting in such capacity unless absolutely necessary." Alice Williams File, Records of the Provost Marshal General's Bureau, RG 110, Entry 36, Correspondence, Reports, Accounts, and Other Records relating to Individual Scouts, Guides, Spies and Detectives, 1861–1868, box 21, NA. However, this was definitely not Lauretta, who was demonstrably living and working in Indianapolis in November 1863. Moreover, on subsequent dates in January and February 1864 when Mrs. Williams filed reports from Baltimore, Lauretta was undeniably in Columbus and Cleveland, Ohio. Finally, Mrs. Williams did not write her reports but had them written for her, whereas Lauretta could write more than adequately, and Mrs. Williams's signatures are not a match for Lauretta's. Lauretta never used the alias Alice, simply acquiescing to its use when the Richmond press got her name wrong. Definitively, the genuine pass given to her in January 1864 shows that she was known to the Union War Department as Lauretta DeCaulp, making an alias pointless.

57. This scenario of her "mission," if there was one, is speculation, but it is supported by Lauretta's and Thomas's documented contemporary claims. No record of transportation passes for her has been found in Records of the Office

of the Secretary of War, RG 107, NA, Entry 56, Records Concerning Travel Passes, 1862–1865, box 13; Entry 57, Travel Passes of Visitors to Union Army Units or Installations, 1863; or Entry 54, Letters Received Applying for Passes to Enter Union Territory, box 1.

5. "WIN MY GLORY BACK"

1. *OR*, ser. I, 33, pt. 2, 79.

2. Heintzelman Journal, January 27, 30 [29], February 5, 13, 1864, Samuel P. Heintzelman Pocket Diary, January 27, 29, February 5, 12, 1864, Heintzelman Papers, LC. Unfortunately, Heintzelman's letter to Pelouze and his response do not appear in the Index to General Correspondence of the Adjutant General's Office, 1809–1917, roll 306, RG 94, NA.

3. Cleveland *Plain Dealer*, February 3, 1864; Macon, GA, *Daily Telegraph*, June 12, 1862.

4. Springfield, MA, *Daily Republican*, November 16, 1863.

5. Cleveland *Plain Dealer*, February 3, 1864.

6. Springfield, MA, *Daily Union*, February 11, 1864.

7. Cleveland *Plain Dealer*, February 2, 1864.

8. Philadelphia *Inquirer*, February 15, 1864; Milwaukee *Wisconsin Daily Patriot*, February 17, 1864; Springfield, MA, *Daily Union*, February 13, 1864.

9. Milwaukee *Daily Sentinel*, February 5, 1864; Janesville, WI, *Daily Gazette*, February 6, 1864.

10. Milwaukee *Semi-Weekly Wisconsin*, February 20, 1864; Cleveland *Plain Dealer*, February 2, 1864.

11. Milwaukee *Daily Milwaukee News*, February 5, 1864.

12. Milwaukee *Daily Sentinel*, February 5, 1864.

13. Milwaukee *Daily Milwaukee News*, February 6, 1864.

14. Columbus *Daily Ohio Statesman*, February 5, 1864; New Orleans *Daily Picayune*, February 28, 1864.

15. Milwaukee *Semi-Weekly Wisconsin*, February 3, 1864.

16. Alexander W. Arnold statement, March 31, 1864, Irwin CSR.

17. Milwaukee *Daily Sentinel*, March 7, 1864.

18. Alexander W. Arnold statement, March 31, 1864, Irwin CSR. Arnold further stated, "I learn that his true name is T. C. DeCaulp but [he] enlisted in the U.S. Service as William Irwin." This is the same version that the unnamed senator wrote in the introduction for DeCaulp that historian Collier found in the National Archives. Taken together, they do raise the question of which was the real name and which the alias, DeCaulp or Irwin, or even if both were aliases, as the complete absence of any other DeCaulps in the United States would

argue. Still, it seems reasonable to conclude that the senator, and now Captain Arnold, both jumped to the wrong conclusion when Thomas told them he had been DeCaulp in the Confederate service but was now using the name Irwin.

19. William Irwin to the Assistant Adjutant General, April 1, 1864, Irwin CSR; Note of receipt on April 16, 1864, of Irwin to Assistant Adjutant General, April 1, 1864, Records of United States Army Continental Commands, 1821–1920, RG 393, part 1, Department of the Northwest, entry 3445, Register of Letters Received, September 1862–July 1865, NA.

20. Thomas C. DeCaulp to Lauretta J. DeCaulp, May 12–15, 1864, DeCaulp Provost File. The 30th Wisconsin was not an entirely happy regiment, chafing at long garrison duty and sensitive to accusations that it had frittered away a year and a half "without honor, glory, or hope of reward." Milwaukee *Daily Sentinel*, April 15, 1864. H. Winslow to J. C. Denis, March 15, 1864, *OR*, ser. I, 32, pt. 3, 633–34, has been cited erroneously as relating to Lauretta when it speaks of the writer placing "a highly intelligent and observant lady" in northwest Mississippi to observe suspected disloyal Confederates and report to Richmond in April 1864. In March and April 1864 Lauretta was in Milwaukee.

21. A. Bailey, comp., *Milwaukee City Directory for 1863* (Milwaukee: Starr & Son, 1863), 92; *Edwards' Annual Directory of the Inhabitants . . . in the City of Milwaukee, for 1866* (Milwaukee: Edwards, Greenough & Deved, 1866), 230.

22. Thomas C. DeCaulp to Lauretta J. DeCaulp, May 12–15, 1864, DeCaulp Provost File.

23. *Roster of Wisconsin Volunteers, War of the Rebellion, 1861–1865* (Madison: Democrat Printing Co., 1886), 1:424, dates the transfer to April 17, 1864, while Irwin's CSR gives both April 16 and 17.

24. Lauretta J. DeCaulp to Thomas C. DeCaulp, May 12, 1864, DeCaulp Provost File.

25. Thomas C. DeCaulp to Lauretta J. DeCaulp, May 12–15, 1864, ibid.

26. *WIB*, 337.

27. Lauretta J. DeCaulp to Thomas C. DeCaulp, May 12, 1864, DeCaulp Provost File.

28. Richmond *Enquirer*, July 18, 1863.

29. Lauretta J. DeCaulp to Thomas C. DeCaulp, May 12, 1864, DeCaulp Provost File.

30. A Colonel Benjamin F. Carter had commanded the 4th Texas Infantry until killed at Gettysburg, and the 3rd Arkansas Infantry was in the same brigade with his regiment, but that seems a very tenuous connection.

31. Thomas C. DeCaulp to Lauretta J. DeCaulp, May 12–15, 1864, DeCaulp Provost File.

32. Lauretta J. DeCaulp to Thomas C. DeCaulp, May 12, 1864, Thomas C. DeCaulp to Lauretta J. DeCaulp, May 12–15, 1864, ibid.

33. Lauretta J. DeCaulp to Martha Davidson, July 22, 1864, ibid.

34. As is the case with all of her supposed children, which, from known references, could have totaled five or more, virtually nothing more can be said about this child except that in 1874 Lauretta did supposedly leave a young son with friends in New Orleans. If that child was DeCaulp's son, then he would have been about ten years old, but it was more likely her later son by E. H. Bonner, then about age five.

35. Thomas C. DeCaulp to Lauretta J. DeCaulp, May 12–15, 1864, DeCaulp Provost File.

36. Ibid.

37. Lauretta DeCaulp to Joseph D. Webster, July 30, 1864, DeCaulp Provost File; Detachment Muster Roll, November–December 1864, Irwin CSR. When it arrived at Fort Snelling, Company G, 1st Connecticut Cavalry, was commanded by Captain James R. Straut. *OR*, ser. I, 41, 997. Straut became captain of the company in Minnesota on December 3, 1864. There is no official record of DeCaulp being elected.

38. Lauretta J. DeCaulp to Webster, July 30, 1864, DeCaulp Provost File; Detachment Muster Roll, November–December 1864, Certificate of Disability for Discharge, January 14, 1865, Irwin CSR.

39. An envelope addressed to "Mrs. Adams, Boarding House, Fort Snelling, Minn" was among papers seized when Lauretta was arrested in July 1864. It seems probable that this was meant for her landlord when she was at Fort Snelling. DeCaulp Provost File.

40. Sibley to Hascall, August 11, 1864, Records of United States Army Continental Commands, 1821–1920, RG 393, part 3, entry 343, Letters and Telegrams Sent, November 1862–June 1873, NA. In his letter Sibley stated, "Mrs. Irwin (or Mrs. Delcamp) came to see me in person shortly after her husband had been assigned to duty in this Military District and her representations of the facts agrees with your own."

41. Lauretta J. DeCaulp to Webster, July 30, 1864, DeCaulp Provost File.

6. "YOU WILL LEARN A LITTLE MORE OF ME"

1. Lauretta J. DeCaulp to J. D. Webster, July 30, 1864, DeCaulp Provost File.

2. Thomas DeCaulp to Lauretta J. DeCaulp, May 12, 1864, Lauretta J. DeCaulp to Webster, July 30, 1864, ibid. The fact that the insurance company that gave her a job was headquartered in New York City argues strongly that

that was where she went, even though her letter could be interpreted to mean she met the Youngs and Chamberlyn at Suspension Bridge.

3. This assumes that the Ann Williams working in Clara Fisher's brothel in 1860 was indeed Lauretta.

4. Lauretta J. DeCaulp to Webster, July 30, 1864, DeCaulp Provost File.

5. New York *Evening Post*, January 28, 1864; Cleveland *Plain Dealer*, December 24, 1864; Philadelphia *Inquirer*, October 4, 1880.

6. No one named Chamberlyn/Chamberlain seems to have been a diplomat to Mexico in the 1860s. If he was real, he was perhaps vice consul for New York.

7. Charles A. Dunham, the Harvey Birch who claimed to have known her at Castle Thunder, was in Canada in December 1864. There is no evidence that they met there or that she actually crossed the border, but in light of his subsequent claim that she was involved in the Lincoln assassination conspiracy, the possibility of a meeting is worth mention. Clearfield, PA, *Republican*, September 12, 1867.

8. Pass, July 4, 1864, DeCaulp Provost File. No such document survives, but it is implicit in this pass that Lauretta had displayed her bona fides from Young and that it was genuine. Her spelling and grammar would have given her away had she tried to forge her own commission.

9. Lauretta J. DeCaulp to Webster, July 30, 1864, ibid. In her letter to Webster she writes of "Col Young & Lady and Mr. Chamberlyn, the vice council to Mexico who was interested in the National Life & Limb Insurance co." Her grammar is so erratic that it is hardly certain that her use of "who was interested" applied only to Chamberlyn; she could have meant all three.

10. Milwaukee *Daily Milwaukee News*, February 14, 1864.

11. New York *Daily Tribune*, April 25, June 30, July 19, 1864. It is still flourishing in the twenty-first century as the Metropolitan Life Insurance Company.

12. Lauretta J. DeCaulp to Webster, July 30, 1864, DeCaulp Provost File.

13. One copy of the application, an envelope addressed but not mailed to Sylvester O. Post, general agent of the company in New York, and an unfinished letter to J. L. Donaldson, July 23, 1864, making reference to letters of introduction, are in ibid.

14. Erastus B. Tyler to Assistant Provost Marshal, June 26, 1864, ibid.

15. Lauretta J. DeCaulp to Webster, July 30, 1864, ibid.

16. The envelope is in ibid., but not its contents.

17. Nashville *Daily Union*, March 13, 1864. It is implicit in the fact that the envelope was in her possession in late July 1864 that she did not deliver it to Grant.

18. Pass, July 4, 1864, DeCaulp Provost File. This solicitation at Fort Columbus may have been the origin of her claim in the August 25, 1874, Mobile

Daily Register to have raised several hundred dollars for soldier relief from a fleet, only to give it to the Confederacy, and her subsequent revision of that story in *WIB*, 496.

19. Lauretta J. DeCaulp to J. L. Donaldson, July 23, 1864, DeCaulp Provost File.

20. W. W. Tuttle to S. B. Brown, July 12, 1864, and docket of same date, ibid.

21. D. T. Monsarrat to Lauretta J. DeCaulp, July 18, 1864, ibid.

22. Flyer, n.d. [July 1864], ibid.

23. "Met Life Begins," accessed March 26, 2016, https://www.metlife.com/about/corporate-profile/metlife-history/metlife-begins/index.html.

24. All in DeCaulp Provost File; New York *Times*, August 28, 1864.

25. Lauretta J. DeCaulp to J. L. Donaldson, July 23, 1864, DeCaulp Provost File.

26. Nashville *Daily Union*, July 17, 1864.

27. Sidney A. Stockdale to Hunter Brooke, July 25, 1864, Records of United States Army Continental Commands, 1821–1920, RG 393, part 1, entry 2517, Military Division of Mississippi, 1863–1866, Letters Sent by Provost Marshal, March 1864–January 1865, vol. 1 21/37, 38 MDM, NA.

28. Lauretta J. DeCaulp to Stockdale, July 26, August 1, 1864, DeCaulp Provost File.

29. Richmond *Daily Richmond Examiner*, September 16, 1863; Augusta, GA, *Daily Constitutionalist*, September 16, 1863.

30. Lauretta J. DeCaulp to Webster, July 30, 1864, DeCaulp Provost File.

31. Lauretta J. DeCaulp to Stockdale, July 26, 1864, ibid. Nothing more on this Hubbard or Hubbards has been found.

32. Lauretta J. DeCaulp to Stockdale, July 27, 1864, ibid.

33. Lauretta J. DeCaulp to Webster, July 30, 1864, ibid.

34. Lauretta J. DeCaulp to Stockdale, July 26, 27, 1864, ibid.

35. Lauretta J. DeCaulp to Stockdale, July 27, 29, 1864, ibid.

36. Lauretta J. DeCaulp to Stockdale, July 29, August 1, 1864, ibid.

37. Lauretta J. DeCaulp to Stockdale, July 29, 1864, ibid.

38. Lauretta J. DeCaulp to Webster, July 30, 1864, ibid.

39. Webster to Stockdale, July 30, 1864, docket on verso of ibid.

40. Lauretta J. DeCaulp to Martha Davidson, July 22, 1864, ibid. The only other explanation for ordering suits of clothes for three- and four-year-old boys would have been if she had sons that age, for which there is no evidence whatsoever, and if she had, she would certainly have been haranguing Stockdale about taking her away from them. At the same time, if she was pregnant by DeCaulp, it would have been three or four years before a son—if they had one—

would be big enough for the suits. On the other hand, while Lauretta was by all accounts slim, she was not petite, and the suits would surely have been too small for her to wear. However, disassembled, the three suits might have provided more than enough gray cloth for her to construct a waist-length military jacket, or basque. If she added the "staff" buttons to ornament the sleeves and collar, using the coat-gauge thread to put it together, she could have made a credible replica of the uniform coat she had worn in the Confederacy. As for the blue cloth, with ten yards of it she could easily have made a similar military jacket and trousers, and at $5 a yard, the cloth was surely of a heavy uniform-grade weight. Other than for this possible use, the boys' suits remain for the moment inexplicable.

41. This is how it is found in ibid.

42. Lauretta J. DeCaulp to Stockdale, August 1, 1864, ibid.

43. James D. Horan, in *Confederate Agent: A Discovery in History* (New York: Crown, 1954), states that after the Indiana arrests, Felix Stidger, the man credited with breaking up the conspiracy, went to St. Louis in August, and there "he saw the beautiful Madam Valesque, the Confederate whose black eyes bewitched passes from Union generals" (106). There is no citation, and the chapter sources list only Stidger's 1903 memoir and some wartime reports, none of which in fact mention any meeting with Lauretta under any alias. Referring to her incorrectly as Valesque means that Horan's source, if he had one, was post-1875, when she started using the name Velasquez. In *WIB* she places herself in St. Louis in August 1864 but makes no mention of meeting Stidger or any Federal agent (449). Stidger's memoir, *Treason History of the Order of Sons of Liberty, Succeeded by Knights of the Golden Circle, Afterward, Order of American Knights* (Chicago: privately printed, 1903), says he went to Louisville, not St. Louis. It seems that Horan read Lauretta's book and conflated some of its content with Stidger's to produce a wholly erroneous statement.

44. H. B. Adams to Stockdale, July 29, 1864, Records of United States Army Continental Commands, 1821–1920, RB 393, part 1, entry 2518, Military Division of Mississippi, 1863–1866, Endorsements Sent by the Provost Marshal General, July–December 1864, vol. 9/40 MDM; Statement of John Knoedler, August 1, 1864, Louise Oyster Provost File, RG 109, Stockdale to Brook, July 31, 1864, entry 2517, RG 393, NA.

45. Statement of John Knoedler, August 1, 1864, Oyster Provost File.

46. Selected Records of the War Department relating to Confederate Prisoners of War, 1861–1865, RG 109, entry 202, Roll of Paroled & Exchanged Prisoners of War at Camp Morton, Indiana, Microfilm Publication M598, roll 3, 86, line 12, roll 8, 81, NA.

47. Stockdale to Brooke, August 1, 1864 [two documents], entry 2517, RG 393, NA.

48. Evidence that Lauretta did not hear from her husband after she left Fort Snelling on June 14 is that as of July 30, in her letter to Webster, she still believed him to be with Company G of the 1st Connecticut Cavalry (which she mistakenly called the 2nd). In fact, four days after she left, on June 18, DeCaulp and his comrades were detached from the Connecticut unit and simply designated as "Unassigned Minnesota Volunteers." Lauretta J. DeCaulp to Webster, July 30, 1864, DeCaulp Provost File, Detachment Muster Roll, November–December 1864, Irwin CSR.

49. M. D. Hascall to Henry Hastings Sibley, August 4, 1864, Irwin CSR.

50. Sibley to Hascall, August 11, 1864, part 3, entry 343, Letters and Telegrams Sent, November 1862–June 1873, RG 393, NA.

51. Certificate of Disability for Discharge, December 26, 1864, Irwin, CSR.

52. Interestingly enough, by November the institute was trying a fund-raising scheme involving selling portraits of General Grant for $2 each to people whose receipts then became lottery tickets for $50,000 worth of real estate. Just a few weeks after the war was over, this was revealed to be a lottery, in violation of New York state laws, and a brief scandal erupted, though the institute's intentions appear to have been upright. Some years later Lauretta briefly tried to launch what appears to have been a swindle involving prints of George Washington's mother being sold to raise money for a monument. Cleveland *Plain Dealer*, December 24, 1864; Milwaukee *Daily Sentinel*, January 5, 1865; Albany, NY, *Evening Journal*, May 23, 1865.

7. LOST MONTHS IN THE SHADOWS

1. Charlotte, NC, *Times*, September 30, 1864, in Macon, GA, *Daily Telegraph*, October 7, 1864.

2. Ibid.

3. Endorsement, November 9, 1864, on James Jones to James Seddon, n.d., Secretary of War, Endorsements on Letters Received, Agent of Exchange of Prisoners, 1863–1865, chap. 9, vol. 228, RG 109, NA.

4. Richmond *Enquirer*, December 22, 1864.

5. Charleston *Daily Courier*, December 29, 1864; Atlanta *Daily Constitution*, December 31, 1864.

6. Richmond *Daily Richmond Examiner*, July 11, 1863.

7. M. D. Hascall to Henry Hastings Sibley, August 4, 1864, Irwin CSR.

8. St. Louis *Republican*, March 7, 1866, in Cleveland, *Plain Dealer*, March 13, 1866.

9. Consultation of the Navy Lists for 1855–1866 at the Caird Library of the National Maritime Museum, Greenwich, England, found no names even close to this on the active lists, reserve lists, retired lists, or pension lists. The National Archives at Kew, which has service records for British seamen, also contains no record of such a person.

10. Nothing in her surviving interviews or recollections ever mentions her having a brother. He appears only in this and a similar advertisement in 1869 and a few places in *WIB*, and then only fleetingly and not at all connected with Haiti or the British foreign service.

11. Colin Mackie, "A Directory of British Diplomats," last modified March 12, 2015, http://gulabin.com.

12. De Grave so regards the women-turned-soldiers of this era. *Swindler, Spy, Rebel*, 96–97.

13. Ibid., 58–64, 68, 246. These are all early variants of what in more modern times is generically known as the Nigerian bank scam.

14. Ibid.; Certificate of Disability for Discharge, January 14, 1865, Irwin CSR. As an ironic aside, a detachment of his regiment participated in the March 1865 hunt to capture Jerome Clark, a Kentucky Confederate erroneously identified as the fictional guerrilla disguised as a woman named Sue Mundy.

15. DeCaulp as William Irwin is not listed in *A Diary of the 30th Regiment, Wisconsin Volunteers. A History of the Regiment since Its Organization* (Madison: Martin & Judson, 1864), which failed to include his February assignment to the regiment by the time it went to the printer in March. Neither does his name appear in Thirtieth Wisconsin Infantry Association, *Roster of the Thirtieth Wisconsin Infantry Volunteers* (Madison: M. J. Cantwell, 1896), a volume chiefly concerned with the postwar lives of veterans.

16. Memphis *Daily Avalanche*, March 1, 1866.

17. St. Louis *Republican*, March 7, 1866, in Cleveland *Plain Dealer*, March 13, 1866.

18. Nashville *Daily Union and American*, June 16, 1866.

19. *WIB*, 343.

20. Almost half of the burials at Fort Snelling were already unknown by 1866. A report from 1879 tells much the same story—only 82 of the 176 known burials could be identified. In 1905 all of these graves were moved to the newer 1885 cemetery to make room for a trolley line extension. All of the burials from the 1885 "Old Cemetery" were exhumed and moved to Fort Snelling National Cemetery in the late 1930s and early 1940s. Neither DeCaulp nor Irwin appears on a list of identifiable graves from the 1866 and 1879 reports. If he was buried here, there appears to be no record of that burial.

21. A. McElroy, *McElroy's Philadelphia City Directory for 1865* (Philadelphia: A. McElroy, 1865), 343; A. McElroy, *McElroy's Philadelphia City Directory for 1866* (Philadelphia: A. McElroy, 1866), 360; Isaac Costa, comp., *Gopsill's Philadelphia City and Business Directory for 1867–68* (Philadelphia: James Gopsill, 1867), 470; Isaac Costa, comp., *Gopsill's Philadelphia City Directory for 1870* (Philadelphia: James Gopsill, 1870), 793; A. McElroy, *McElroy's Philadelphia City Directory for 1863* (Philadelphia: A. McElroy, 1863), 378; A. McElroy, *McElroy's Philadelphia City Directory for 1862* (Philadelphia: A. McElroy, 1862), 324; A. McElroy, *McElroy's Philadelphia City Directory for 1861* (Philadelphia: A. McElroy, 1861), 476; E. J. Cowell, *Cowell's Philadelphia Business Directory* (Philadelphia: E. J. Cowell, 1860), 470.

22. United States Census, Frankford Station [23rd District], Philadelphia County, PA, 1870; Isaac Costa, comp., *Gopsill's Philadelphia City Directory for 1880* (Philadelphia: James Gopsill, 1880), 855; Isaac Costa, comp., *Gopsill's Philadelphia City Directory for 1881* (Philadelphia: James Gopsill, 1881), 824.

23. United States Census, Caln Township, Chester County, PA, 1880.

24. Memphis *Daily Avalanche*, March 1, 1866.

25. Boston *Journal*, May 25, 1866; Augusta, GA, *Daily Chronicle & Sentinel*, May 12, 1866.

26. Nashville *Daily Union and American*, June 16, 1866.

27. New Orleans *Item*, October 6, 1879. The *Item* article, by an unknown author, is taken from an unidentified issue of the Richmond *Southern Intelligencer*.

8. THE RETURN OF MRS. DECAULP

1. Sanford Conover to Joseph Holt, October 10, 1865, *OR*, ser. II, 8, 936.

2. *New York, Passenger Lists, 1820–1957*, Ancestry.com.

3. Memphis *Daily Avalanche*, March 1, 1866.

4. Whereas the article always shows her surname as De Camp, his is always presented as DeCamp, a perhaps meaningless inconsistency.

5. St Louis *Republican*, March 7, 1866.

6. Memphis *Daily Avalanche*, January 31, 1866.

7. St. Louis *Republican*, March 7, 1866, in the Cleveland *Plain Dealer*, March 13, 1866.

8. De Grave, *Swindler, Spy, Rebel*, 13, 67.

9. While not all of the article's appearances in Mississippi River cities have been located, the piece appeared in the Augusta, GA, *Daily Constitutionalist*, March 14, 1866; Cleveland *Plain Dealer*, March 13, 1866; Columbus, GA, *Daily Columbus Enquirer*, April 11, 1866; and Augusta, GA, *Daily Chronicle & Sentinel*, April 19, 1866. It even appeared in the Milwaukee *Semi-Weekly Wisconsin*, March 17 1866, and the Brattleboro *Vermont Phoenix*, June 1, 1866, among others.

10. Dallas *Herald*, April 14, 1866.

11. Mexico City *Mexican Times*, April 14, 1866.

12. Memphis *Daily Avalanche*, March 21, 1866.

13. New Orleans *Daily Southern Star*, March 30, 1866.

14. Cincinnati *Daily Enquirer*, February 6–7, 1866.

15. Augusta, GA, *Daily Chronicle & Sentinel*, May 12, 1866.

16. Ibid.

17. De Grave, *Swindler, Spy, Rebel*, 53.

18. Augusta, GA, *Daily Chronicle & Sentinel*, May 12, 1866.

19. De Grave, *Swindler, Spy, Rebel*, 143.

20. Philadelphia *Evening Telegraph*, May 15, 1866; Springfield, MA, *Daily Republican*, May 12, 1866. The original Mobile *Tribune* carrying her notice has not been found.

21. Belfast, Ireland, *Morning News*, June 20, 1866; Edinburgh *Evening Courant*, June 14, 1866; London *Standard*, June 13, 1866. Notice of it also appeared in the Aylesbury *Bucks' Herald, Uxbridge Advertiser, Agricultural Journal, and Advertiser, Windsor and Eton Journal*, June 16, 1866; Gravesend, *Gravesend and Dartmouth Reporter*, June 16, 1866; Glasgow *Falkirk Herald and Journal*, June 30, 1866; and Londonderry, Ireland, *Londonderry Journal*, June 23, 1866.

22. Nashville *Daily Union and American*, June 16, 1866.

23. Atlanta *Intelligencer*, in Augusta, GA, *Daily Chronicle & Sentinel*, May 12, 1866.

24. Pulaski, TN, *Citizen*, May 18, 1866.

25. De Grave, *Swindler, Spy, Rebel*, 131–32.

26. Boston *Journal*, May 25, 1866; Dayton *Daily Empire*, June 6, 1866.

27. Philadelphia *Daily Evening Telegraph*, May 29, 1866.

28. Ibid.; Albany *Evening Journal*, June 25, 1866; Brattleboro *Vermont Journal*, June 16, 1866.

29. Atlanta *Daily Constitution*, May 22, 1866.

30. New Orleans *Times*, June 12, 1866; Newberry, SC, *Herald*, May 30, 1866, reprinted from a Charleston correspondent's report in an unidentified issue of the Columbia *South Carolinian*.

31. Atlanta *Daily Constitution*, May 22, 1866.

32. Atlanta *Daily Intelligencer*, May 24, 1866.

33. Meridian, MS, *Messenger*, June 2, 1866, in New Orleans *Times*, June 5, 1866.

34. Nashville *Daily Union and American*, June 16, 1866.

35. *WIB*, 294.

36. Nashville *Daily Union and American*, June 20, 1866.

37. Pulaski, TN, *Citizen*, June 22, 1866.

38. Memphis *Public Ledger*, June 27, 1866.

39. Richmond *Whig*, August 10, 1866.

40. Washington *Evening Star*, August 13, 1866.

41. New Castle, IN, *Courier*, August 23, 1866.

42. Charleston *Daily Courier*, March 10, 1866.

43. New York *Evening Post*, September 18, 1866.

44. New Orleans *Daily Picayune*, December 20, 1866; Baltimore *Sun*, December 21, 1866.

45. New York *Herald*, December 23, 1866; New Orleans *Daily Picayune*, January 5, 1867.

46. New Orleans *Daily Picayune*, January 5, 1867.

47. This claimed connection with a Texas cavalry unit somewhat echoes the Lauretta Williams who, on January 30, 1861, presented a flag to the Richmond Mounted Riflemen at Richmond, Texas. They later became Company H of the 8th Texas Cavalry. It was not at Manassas, however.

48. New Orleans *Daily Picayune*, January 5, 1867.

49. New York *Commercial Advertiser*, December 24, 1866; New Orleans *Times*, December 22, 1866; Providence, RI, *Evening Press*, December 26, 1866; Baltimore *Sun*, December 21, 1866; New Orleans *Daily Picayune*, December 20, 1866. Brigadier General John G. Walker had been in St. Louis in November and December 1866, while Lauretta was in New York for some time before sailing on December 22, making it unlikely that they really met. Alfred Jackson Hanna and Kathryn Abbey Hanna, *Confederate Exiles in Venezuela* (Tuscaloosa, AL: Confederate Publishing Co., 1960), 23.

50. New Orleans *Daily Picayune*, February 9, 1867.

51. *WIB*, 536–37, 545.

52. De Grave, *Swindler, Spy, Rebel*, 11.

53. *WIB*, 539–40.

54. Marriage license, John Wasson and Lauretta J. DeCaulp, January 17, 1867, Louisiana Justices of the Peace, Marriage Records 1846–1880, VED vol. 658, 126, vol. 678, 265, New Orleans Public Library, Louisiana Division and City Archives, New Orleans, LA.

55. It seems evident that Wasson was from Missouri, since the March 1867 letter sent home to people in Lincoln County, Missouri, published in the Troy *Lincoln County Herald*, May 31, 1867, explicitly stated that it was excerpted for publication because the news of local people might interest its readers. Since Wasson is the first name mentioned, it is logical to assume that he either was from Lincoln County or

had recently lived there. His marriage witness being Daniel Clary from Missouri also suggests a Missouri origin for Wasson, and Lincoln County is very close to St. Louis, where the group was formed. Efforts to identify or locate Wasson prior to 1867 have been unsuccessful. The 1860 census shows a John Wasson born in 1845–46 in Missouri living in St. Louis County. He does not appear there in the 1870 census, so this was possibly him, but it is hardly conclusive.

56. *WIB*, 539–40.

57. Memphis *Daily Avalanche*, February 16, 1869.

58. New Orleans *Times*, January 24, 1867; New Orleans *Daily Picayune*, January 24, 1867.

59. "Derby" [Frederick Derbyshire] to the New Orleans *Picayune*, March 13 1867, New Orleans *Daily Picayune*, May 20, 1867.

60. Troy, MO, *Lincoln County Herald*, May 31, 1867.

61. Henry M. Price to A. F. Rudler, July 6, 1867, Atlanta *Daily Constitution*, September 8, 1867.

62. *WIB*, 543, 552. Her 1876 letter to President Grant to stop the abuse of convicts in Georgia certainly would have benefited the black people who made up the majority of the convicts, but nothing in her plea acknowledged awareness of that. Two years later her arguments in favor of aid to the Cuban revolution included an observation that the rebels opposed slavery as did the United States, but again they revealed nothing of her own feeling. In 1893 she commented on how the end of slavery had disrupted Southern agriculture's source of labor, and she endorsed white European immigrant labor in preference to a black monopoly on unskilled workers, which at least revealed some resentment, but she was far more forthcoming in her denunciation of eastern European Jews.

63. *WIB*, 544–45.

64. "Derby" to the New Orleans *Picayune*, March 23, 1867, in New York *Commercial Advertiser*, May 17, 1867; "Derby" to the New Orleans *Picayune*, April 23, 1867, in New Orleans *Daily Picayune*, June 9, 1867.

65. *WIB*, 543, 545.

66. Ibid., 553–69.

67. New York *Herald*, November 11, 1867; Record for Laura Wasson, 1867, Passenger Lists of Vessels Arriving at New York, New York, 1820–1897, M237, Records of the U.S. Customs Service, RG 36, NA.

9. GOLD, SILVER, AND BIGAMY

1. *WIB*, 570.

2. Austin, NV, *Daily Reese River Reveille*, August 3, 1867; Salt Lake City *Daily Telegraph*, December 27, 1867.

3. Lauretta describes this accident briefly in *WIB*, 581–82, and her account is substantially confirmed in Salt Lake City *Daily Telegraph*, December 28, 1867, January 4, 1868. She described the trip quite differently to General James Longstreet by letter or in person around 1874, or else Longstreet seriously confused the story. According to him, she traveled through the Rocky Mountains disguised as Harry Buford with a number of men. They met trouble with Indians, lost their horses, and had to continue "a great distance" on foot. Lauretta gave out from exertion, and the others assisted her on the rest of the journey. James Longstreet to Emily W. Park, June 18, 1888, James Longstreet Papers, David M. Rubenstein Rare Book & Manuscript Library, Duke University, Durham, NC.

4. *WIB*, 571–83; San Francisco *Daily Alta California*, December 25, 1867.

5. *WIB*, 583.

6. Austin, NV, *Daily Reese River Reveille*, August 3, 1867; Salt Lake City *Daily Telegraph*, December 27, 1867.

7. Her arrival in Salt Lake and her departure cannot be precisely dated. As for her arrival in Austin, if she reached Salt Lake on December 26–27, 1867, as fixed by the stagecoach accident, and if she stayed "a day or two" as she says in *WIB*, then she would have departed December 28–29 and should have reached Austin December 31–January 1.

8. *WIB*, 583.

9. Austin, NV, *Daily Reese River Reveille*, August 3, 1867.

10. Adam Wilson to Editor, January 5, 1875, Atlanta *Constitution*, January 15, 1875.

11. *WIB*, 585.

12. United States Census, Yuba County, CA, 1860, shows on October 29, 1860, an "Edward Bonner, 26, miner, born in Ten."

13. San Francisco *Evening Daily Bulletin*, March 2, 1865, March 31, April 24, 1866; Austin, NV, *Daily Reese River Reveille*, April 24, 1865, October 4, 1867, April 21, 1868; Fort Whipple *Arizona Miner*, April 20, 1867; Wilson to Editor, January 5, 1875, Atlanta *Constitution*, January 15, 1875.

14. Austin, NV, *Daily Reese River Reveille*, December 20, 21, 1867.

15. E. H. Bonner to Lauretta J. Wasson, Index to Marriages, Lander County, NV, Book 1, 20, Lander County Court House, Recorder's Office, Battle Mountain, NV. Lauretta gave this same date for her marriage to Bonner in an interview in the Atlanta *Constitution*, September 4, 1874.

16. Austin, NV, *Daily Reese River Reveille*, January 30, 1868.

17. *WIB*, 585–86.

18. The Bonners' movements are established in part by announcements in the Austin, NV, *Daily Reese River Reveille* concerning letters being held for them at

the post office and by their names appearing on lists of passengers coming and going on coaches. No letters were held for them from the date of their marriage through the end of February, suggesting they were in town and got their mail. Letters being held for E. H. Bonner on March 5, 1868, suggest his absence but not necessarily hers. Austin, NV, *Daily Reese River Reveille*, March 5, 1868.

19. Ibid., March 27, 1868.

20. *WIB* fails to mention the murder committed by Rufus Anderson on May 8, 1868, in Austin or his brutally botched hanging on October 30. Since Lauretta's book comments on other newsworthy events that occurred while she was in Austin, her failure to do so in these instances suggests her absence. San Francisco *Evening Daily Bulletin*, May 7, 1868; Boise *Idaho Statesman*, November 10, 1868.

21. Wilson to Editor, January 5, 1875, Atlanta *Constitution*, January 15, 1875.

22. Austin, NV, *Daily Reese River Reveille*, September 2, 24, 1868.

23. Ibid., October 4, 5, 1868.

24. Sacramento *Daily Union*, September 2, 1873; Austin, NV, *Daily Reese River Reveille*, December 20, 1867.

25. San Francisco *Daily Alta California*, January 9, 1869.

26. This is Lauretta's first mention of San Luis Potosí. A few years later in *WIB*, 40–41, she claims that her father, Velasquez, had vast lands there "in Central Mexico" prior to the war with Mexico, but that when the war ended his estates were part of "the northern part of Mexico" ceded to the United States. Not only did her war wounds migrate on her person, but whole Mexican states changed location in her writing.

27. New York *Herald*, January 4, 1869; New York *Evening Standard*, January 4, 1869.

28. *WIB*, 50. The bases for identifying the time of this child's birth conflict dramatically. Lauretta first mentions this son in an interview with the Atlanta *Constitution*, September 4, 1874, when she gives his age as five, dating his birth to 1868–69. In 1876 in *WIB*, 597, she writes of leaving Salt Lake "with my little baby boy—born during my sojourn in Salt Lake City—in my arms." She lived in Salt Lake from March 1871 to September 1872. Assuming her 1874 statement more likely to be truthful, the winter of 1868–69 would have been roughly the season of his birth. She mentions him as "my little son" in her May 18, 1878, letter to Jubal A. Early (Tucker Family Papers, Southern Historical Collection, University of North Carolina, Chapel Hill), but she never afterward gives his name or says what became of him. He was certainly genuine, corroborated by one independent source when the Galveston *Daily News*, February 24, 1874, refers to "A. G. Bobo, lady and child."

29. *WIB*, 586–87.

30. San Francisco *Chronicle*, October 12, 20, December 1, 7, 8, 15, 22, 29, 1869. A letter addressed to her was also being held in Austin, Texas, probably a postal confusion with her home in Nevada. Austin, TX, *Daily Austin Republican*, December 16, 1868.

31. The Marysville, CA, *Daily Appeal*, December 11, 1869, reports that the home of a Mr. Bonner west of the F Street slough was entered by robbers but Mrs. Bonner frightened them away. This may or may not have been Hardy and Lauretta. However, letters held in the Sacramento post office for "Mrs. E. H. Bannar" and "Mrs. E. H. Barner" were almost certainly meant for Lauretta. Sacramento *Daily Union*, December 17, 24, 1869, January 13, 14, 20, 21, 1870.

32. The Salt Lake City *Daily Herald* records Bonner coming to town on February 23, March 5, 9, 10, 16, 17, 1871, so he was clearly already spending a lot of time in the vicinity since late February at least. It reports Lauretta's arrival as "Mrs. E. H. Bonner, Sacramento," on March 19 and 21, 1871.

33. The timing of their move to Salt Lake City is derived from sources cited subsequently, as well as Lauretta's statement in 1874 that she spent eighteen months living among the Mormons. Since she moved to New Mexico in or around November 1872, that would put her arrival at Salt Lake in about March 1871. Mrs. E. H. Bonner to S. P. [*sic*] Clemens, 1874, Mark Twain Papers, University of California, Bancroft Library, Berkeley, CA.

34. *WIB*, 587; Wilson to Editor, January 5, 1875, Atlanta *Constitution*, January 15, 1875.

35. *WIB*, 589, mistakenly placed this in Nevada, a case of simple confusion on Lauretta's part. She mentions an avalanche that took place at the Wellington mine, killing its foreman, "while I was there," and this can be dated to April 12, 1872. On the same page she recalls snow in August and September, placing her there in the fall of 1872.

36. Salt Lake City *Daily Herald*, September 22, 1871; Leavenworth *Bulletin*, March 22, 1871.

37. Salt Lake City *Daily Herald*, November 3, 1871, April 20, May 18, 1872. As of September 27 a letter was being held for Lauretta in Salt Lake City. Salt Lake City *Deseret News*, October 2, 1872.

38. San Francisco *Chronicle*, April 30, 1872.

39. In 1888 Longstreet told a correspondent that Lauretta "became a belle of course in Nevada & she referred her suitors to me, but I had not known of her in the ranks, nor as Lieutenant, and could only attest of points she gave for identification." He did not date this business, but context in his letter makes it clear that these contacts occurred while she was in the West and before her

return to New Orleans in 1874. Her courtship with Bonner was too fast for her to have time to refer him to Longstreet, and considering Adam Wilson's allegations that she left Bonner for an unnamed man in San Francisco, it seems a reasonable inference that on her visits to that city, she encouraged other men to woo her. Longstreet to Park, June 18, 1888, Longstreet Papers.

40. *WIB*, 590. This is the last page on which Lauretta refers to Bonner, though she never mentions him by name in the book, saying simply, "my husband."

41. San Francisco *Chronicle*, June 11, July 7, August 30, 1870.

42. Tucson *Arizona Weekly Citizen*, March 21, 1874.

43. Louisville *Courier-Journal*, September 7, 1874, quoted in San Francisco *Evening Daily Bulletin*, September 14, 1874.

44. Mrs. E. H. Bonner "to the Public Press," [September 6, 1874], Louisville *Courier-Journal*, September 7, 1874.

45. Louisville *Courier-Journal*, September 7, 1874, quoted in San Francisco *Evening Daily Bulletin*, September 14, 1874. See Robert Wilson, "The Great Diamond Hoax of 1872," *Smithsonian* 35 (June 2004): 70–79.

46. The time of their arrival in Silver City is based on Lauretta's statement that she spent seven months living in Apache territory, which meant New Mexico. Since she appears to have gone to San Francisco in May 1873, that would date her arrival at Silver City as roughly in November. Mrs. E. H. Bonner to S. P. [*sic*] Clemens, 1874, Mark Twain Papers. Clemens says she wrote to him "some months" prior to October 7, 1874. That would argue for this letter dating from no later than July, and perhaps as early as the spring.

47. Santa Fe *Daily New Mexican*, February 7, March 10, 1873; Santa Fe *Weekly New Mexican*, March 18, 1873.

48. Las Cruces, NM, *Borderer*, February 1, 1873. Since the *Borderer* of this date mentions a ball catered "last week" by Bonner of the Keystone House, he and Lauretta must have been running their establishment at least since mid to late January.

49. *WIB*, 590.

50. The last advertisement for the Keystone House under the Bonners' ownership ran in the Santa Fe *Daily New Mexican*, April 16, 1873. Her 1874 letter to Clemens puts her departure around May. Hence April–May seems the likely time for her move.

51. Wilson to Editor, January 5, 1875, Atlanta *Constitution*, January 15, 1875. *WIB* does not say when she left Salt Lake, and she or her editor badly confused the chronology of her Utah years. *WIB*, 590, 593.

52. Salt Lake City *Deseret News*, May 21, 1873; San Francisco *Daily Alta California*, September 7, 1873; San Francisco *Chronicle*, May 28, 1873.

53. Heidi Stringham to author, February 23, 2015, says no record of a divorce application or grant for Lauretta Bonner, L. J. Bonner, or E. H. Bonner can be found in the Salt Lake County 3rd District Court records or Salt Lake County probate records. Edward H. Bonner remained a miner for some time after Lauretta left him. According to the San Francisco *Evening Daily Bulletin*, August 18, 1873, a "Mr. Bonner, miner," was prospecting in San Bernardino County, California, in late summer 1873, at virtually the same time that Lauretta was leaving Salt Lake City, meaning that he may have been away when she decided to leave him. In December 1874 he was back in Salt Lake City, at least for a time, and by 1880 he was living in a boardinghouse in Silver City and curiously listing himself as married though he had no wife with him, which circumstantially supports the conclusion that there was no divorce. As of June 1885 he was boarding at Lone Mountain in Grant County, and by 1900 he was back in Silver City living as a boarder and now reporting himself to be a widower, though no record of a subsequent marriage after Lauretta has been found. He disappeared from the census after 1900. Salt Lake City *Deseret News*, October 14, 1874; United States Census, Silver City, Grant County, New Mexico Territory, 1880, 1900; New Mexico Territorial Census, Silver City, Grant County, June 1885.

54. Chicago *Daily Inter Ocean*, September 8, 1874.

55. *WIB*, 590, 597–604.

56. San Antonio, TX, *Daily Express*, December 6, 1873.

57. Galveston *Flake's Daily Galveston Bulletin*, April 29, 1868.

58. Houston *Daily Union*, June 18, 1869.

59. United States Census, Talladega District, Alabama, 1850, 1860.

60. Andrew Jackson Bobo CSR, RG 109, NA. Two of the several documents relating to Bobo's capture say he was actually taken at Moorfield, Virginia, and Mt. Sterling, Kentucky, but the majority agree on Atlanta. A letter in the Galveston *Weekly News*, May 28, 1877, says that Bobo was wounded at Shiloh and Nashville, but nothing in his CSR indicates that he participated in the former battle, and he was captured months before the latter.

61. New Orleans *Daily Picayune*, August 3, 1869; United States Census, Bexar District, TX, 1870.

62. J. J. H. letter April 13, 1871, Cincinnati *Commercial Tribune*, April 26, 1871.

63. Las Cruces, NM, *Borderer*, October 5, 1872.

64. Galveston *Flake's Semi-Weekly Galveston Bulletin*, March 26, 1870; Cincinnati *Commercial Tribune*, May 2, 1871.

65. Las Cruces, NM, *Borderer*, January 25, 1873.

66. Houston *Daily Union*, November 2, 1871.

67. San Antonio *Daily Express*, August 21, 1869, August 22, 1873.

68. Galveston *Weekly News*, May 28, 1877; New Orleans *Daily Picayune*, June 22, 1870.

69. Galveston *Weekly News*, May 28, 1877.

70. This is inferred from the advertisement of a letter waiting at the Galveston post office for "Mrs. L. J. Wasson" as of January 31, 1874. Bonner would not have addressed her so, if he even knew where she was, which seems unlikely. Nor would anyone in the East have known her by that name, making her new friend Bobo the only likely writer. Galveston *Daily News*, February 1, 1874.

71. Ibid., February 22, 1874, lists a letter at the Galveston post office awaiting collection by A. J. Bobo, so he certainly gave that town as his address sometime before.

72. Ibid., February 1, 1874, advertises a letter waiting for "Mrs. L. J. Wasson."

73. Ibid., February 21, 1874. A notation with the advertisement indicates that it was originally placed to run from February 19.

74. Marriage license, A. J. Bobo to Loretta J. Wasson, February 21, 1874, Waller County Marriage Book "A," October 1873–December 1881, Grooms Letter "B," 28, Waller County Court House, Hempstead, TX.

75. Galveston *Daily News*, February 24, 1874. The "G." in Bobo's name is an editorial or typographical error. The exact wording is "A. G. Bobo, lady and child, Austin," which could imply that the child's name was Austin, but editorial style in these announcements was to specify the visitors' homes following their names.

76. Ibid., March 1, 8, 1874, announces letters held for "Laurette J. Wasson" and "miss L J Wasson." By that time, however, she was Mrs. Bobo.

77. Ibid., May 12, 1874.

78. *WIB* stops just at the point where Lauretta would have married Bobo, and he is not mentioned in the book, either by name or by implication. No record of a divorce has been found to date. Whether divorced or not, he married Lee Ann Draper on October 23, 1878, and soon moved to Bumble Bee, in Yavapai County, Arizona, where he served as postmaster briefly before spending five years driving coaches for the Ben Ficklin Stage Coach Line. When the coming of the railroad put the stages out of business, the Bobos returned to Hood County, Texas, where he farmed until his death May 24, 1911. He was buried at Acton. A patriotic Confederate, he named two of his sons Robert E. Lee Bobo and Jefferson Davis Bobo. Yuma *Arizona Sentinel* July 5, 1879; Dallas *Morning News*, January 15, 18, 1945; United States Census, Phoenix, Maricopa County, AZ Territory, 1880; United States Census, Precinct 4, Harris County, TX, 1910; Application of Mrs. L. A. Bobo, July 24, 1917, Andrew Jackson Bobo pension

file 34524, United States Confederate Pensions, 1884–1958, Ancestry.com; Texas Death Index, 1903–2000, Ancestry.com, 2281.

79. Chicago *Daily Inter Ocean*, September 8, 1874.

10. "AN IMPOSTER OF NO ORDINARY RANK"

1. McKinney to Clemens, October 31, 1874, Twain Papers.

2. Mrs. E. H. Bonner to Clemens, 1874, Ibid. Clemens said she wrote to him "some months" prior to October 7, 1874. She headed her letter 155 East 29th Street, New York City, and according to an 1879 fire insurance map at the New-York Historical Society, the structure at that address was a four-story residential building.

3. Clemens to Henry Watterson, October 9, 1874, Samuel L. Clemens Papers, LC.

4. A letter addressed to Mrs. E. H. Bonner was being held at the New Orleans post office as of September 5, so someone knew she expected to be there at that time. New Orleans *Daily Picayune*, September 6, 1874.

5. Longstreet to Park, June 18, 1888, Longstreet Papers. Longstreet did not date their meeting, but the context, as well as the fact that he said he met her in New Orleans, clearly places it in 1874, after her return from the West.

6. Atlanta *Daily Constitution*, September 4, 1874.

7. Mobile *Daily Register*, August 25, 1874, in Indianapolis *Evening News*, September 2, 1874. The Mobile paper could not be located, and in the Indianapolis and subsequent reprintings of the story, Bridgeport is given as the location where she raised money from U.S. soldiers, but there is no Bridgeport. It should have been Bridgetown, though whether the mistake was made by Lauretta, the *Daily Register*, or the *Evening News* cannot be determined.

8. The article from the Mobile *Daily Register* of August 25 appeared in the Indianapolis *Evening News*, September 2, 1874; Albany, NY, *Argus*, September 4, 1874; Chicago *Daily Inter Ocean*, September 8, 1874; Jackson, MI, *Citizen Patriot*, September 12, 1874; Salina, KS, *Saline County Journal*, September 17, 1874; Orangeburg, SC, *Orangeburg Times*, September 17, 1874; Columbia, TN, *Herald and Mail*, September 18, 1874; New Haven, CT, *Columbian Register*, September 26, 1874; Trenton, NJ, *State Gazette*, October 15, 1874; San Francisco *Evening Daily Bulletin*, October 16, 1874; Sacramento *Daily Union*, October 24, 1874; Opelousas, LA, *Journal*, October 30, 1874; New Bern, NC, *Newbernian*, November 4, 1874; and New York *Frank Leslie's Illustrated Newspaper*, November 14, 1874.

9. Atlanta *Daily Constitution*, September 4, 1874.

10. Ibid.; McKinney to Clemens, October 31, 1874, Twain Papers.

11. David G. Burnet to Jefferson Davis, March 28, 1861, William E. Burnet to R. Potts, January 21, 1865, Burnet CSR. In his letter to Davis, David G. Burnet mentioned members of the family, living and deceased, but made no

mention of his son being married. More conclusively, in a long series of letters written home to his father from his frontier posting in 1858–60, Burnet made no mention whatsoever of a wife either at home in Galveston or with him on post. Raymond Estep, ed., "Lieutenant William E. Burnet Letters: Removal of the Texas Indians and the Founding of Fort Cobb," pts. 1 and 2, *Chronicles of Oklahoma* 38 (Autumn 1960): 274–309; 38 (Winter 1960): 369–96.

12. Mark Twain [Samuel L. Clemens] to editor, October 9, 1874, Indianapolis *Journal*, October 17, 1874.

13. Cloverport, KY, *Breckenridge News*, January 12, 1881.

14. Louisville *Courier-Journal* in Cincinnati *Enquirer*, September 8, 1874.

15. Louisville *Courier-Journal*, September 7, 1874.

16. Louisville, *Courier-Journal*, September 7, 1874, quoted in San Francisco *Evening Daily Bulletin*, September 14, 1874. See Wilson, "Great Diamond Hoax of 1872," 70–79. Arnold was killed in August 1878 in a street shooting in Elizabethtown, Kentucky, where he was president of Arnold and Polk's Bank. He had started the bank with his swindle income. Louisville *Courier-Journal*, August 19, 1878; Cloverport, KY, *Breckenridge News*, August 21, 1878; Cincinnati *Enquirer*, August 31, 1878.

17. No such letter from Casey appears in the thirty-two-volume *Papers of Ulysses S. Grant*, edited by John Y. Simon (Carbondale, IL: Southern Illinois University Press, 1967–2012).

18. McKinney to Clemens, October 7, 1874, Twain Papers.

19. McKinney to Clemens, October 31, 1874, Ibid.

20. Clemens to Watterson, October 9, 1874, Ibid.

21. Mark Twain [Samuel L. Clemens] to editor, October 9, 1874, Louisville *Courier-Journal*, October 16, 1874.

22. Clemens to McKinney, October 13, 1874, Twain Papers.

23. McKinney to Clemens, October 31, 1874, Ibid.

24. Boston *Daily Advertiser*, October 13, 1874.

25. New York *Daily Graphic*, September 9, 1874.

26. Augusta, GA, *Daily Chronicle & Sentinel*, November 1, 1874.

27. Wilson to Editor, January 5, 1875, Atlanta *Daily Constitution*, January 15, 1875. Thus far, efforts to further identify Wilson have been unavailing.

28. Atlanta *Daily Constitution*, March 9, 1876.

11. THE APPEARANCE OF "MADAME VELASQUEZ"

1. The Memphis *Daily Avalanche*, n.d., as republished in Bolivar, TN, *Bulletin*, April 30, 1875. Efforts to confirm that there was such a firm in Paris or New York have been unavailing.

2. Chicago *Daily Inter Ocean*, April 16, 1877.

3. Hartford, CT, *Daily Courant*, December 19, 1874; New York *Daily Graphic*, October 6, 1876.

4. Atlanta *Constitution*, February 27, May 4, 19, June 6, September 11, 1875.

5. Ibid., September 26, 1876.

6. New York *Herald*, August 9, 1875; Tarborough, NC, *Southerner*, August 27, 1875.

7. Atlanta *Sunny South*, October 2, 1875.

8. Atlanta *Daily Constitution*, October 6, 1875.

9. Ibid., October 15, 1875.

10. Ibid., October 31, 1875.

11. Ibid., November 3, 1875; Marietta, GA, *Journal*, November 19, 1875.

12. Atlanta *Sunny South*, December 18, 1875.

13. Marietta, GA, *Journal*, November 19, 1875; Mad. L. J. Velazquez to Editors of the Courier Journal, October 7, 1875, Twain Papers.

14. Mad. L. J. Velazquez to Editors of the Courier Journal, October 7, 1875, Henry Watterson to Clemens, nd. [October 1875], Twain Papers.

15. Envelope dated October 30, 1875, letter missing, ibid.

16. Atlanta *Sunny South*, December 18, 1875.

17. See, for instance, Bainbridge, GA, *Weekly Democrat*, December 23, 1875.

18. Athens, GA, *Weekly Banner-Watchman*, September 4, 1888.

19. Copies have been found imprinted T. Belknap in Hartford and H. W. Kelley in Philadelphia. Possibly other variants exist.

20. For instance, the two woodcuts opposite pages 576 and 596, "The Trapper's Last Shot" and "The Buffalo Hunt," come from Frances Fuller Victor, *The River of the West. Life and Adventure in the Rocky Mountains and Oregon; Embracing Events in the Life-Time of a Mountain-Man and Pioneer: With the Early History of the North-Western Slope* (Hartford, CT: R. W. Bliss, 1870).

21. Not all of the woodcuts are signed, and those that are say only "B." or "E. B. B. del[ineator]." This artist (or artists) has not been identified. Rea signed six of the steel engravings "REA Phila."

22. "One of the most skillful engravers of facial expression in the United States," he was called in 1896. "Dr. Burrowes Portrait," *Pennsylvania School Journal* 44 (March 1896): 416. Only six of the ten illustrations carry his "REA Phila" identification.

23. Tarborough, NC, *Southerner*, August 27, 1875.

24. Atlanta *Sunny South*, December 18, 1875; Bainbridge, GA, *Weekly Democrat*, December 23, 1875.

25. *WIB*, 6, 9–12.

26. Atlanta *Sunny South*, March 9, 1876.

27. See Carman Cumming, *Devil's Game: The Civil War Intrigues of Charles A. Dunham* (Urbana: University of Illinois Press, 2004), 260. Cumming speculates that Dunham was Worthington on circumstantial—though logical—grounds and could be right. On the only two *known* intersections of Dunham's and Lauretta's careers in July 1863 and October 1865, he attempted to hazard her reputation and safety, but she may not have known of that and hence would have had no reason not to engage him.

28. Alemán, "Authenticity, Autobiography, and Identity," xxii, implicitly hints that Lauretta was Worthington.

29. Macon *Georgia Weekly Telegraph*, February 1, 1876.

30. In *WIB*, 194, she specifically says that she had a diary in 1862 at least, though she nowhere indicates when she began keeping it, when she stopped, or what she wrote.

31. Ibid., 5–6.

32. Ibid., 7–13.

12. *The Woman in Battle*

1. *WIB*, 40–41. On page 40 she puts San Luis Potosí in central Mexico, and on page 41 she has moved it to northern Mexico. It was hundreds of miles from any territory taken over by the United States.

2. Ibid. A Mrs. F. Roberson appears in the 1849 New Orleans city directory, living at the corner of Dauphine and Esplanade, and "Madame Robert" appears in the directories from 1849 to 1851, at 93 Dauphine and 125 Esplanade. The wealthiest Creoles did not live on Esplanade or in that section of the city at the time, however. Since 1830 Esplanade had divided the Vieux Carré from the downriver section inhabited by laborers, free black people, and immigrants.

3. *WIB*, 45.

4. Ibid., 46–51.

5. Richard Hall and others have made much of Lauretta's mention of the little town of Hopefield as evidence that she actually did make this trip, hence supporting in some degree the authenticity of her book, even while admitting that no record of Hurlburt Station could be found. Richard Hall, *Patriots in Disguise: Women Warriors of the Civil War* (New York: Marlowe and Co., 1994), 210n. In fact, Hurlburt Station does appear on a *Map of the Lands of the Memphis & Little Rock Railroad Company (as reorganized), 1878* (St. Louis: Woodward, Tiernan and Hale, 1878), in the Geography and Map Division of LC. It is today a neighborhood called Hulbert just off U.S. Route 63 in the southwestern corner of the city limits of West Memphis, Arkansas. Lauretta

had been in Memphis in 1861 as Mary Anne Keith, possibly again in the spring of 1862 before its fall, and certainly more than once from 1866 on, so there was nothing unusual about her being aware of a town just across the river. DeCaulp also could have mentioned it to her, as he probably passed through it in late 1862 on his furlough to Arkansas. She could even have become aware of it during her prewar time in Arkansas with the mysterious Bachman.

6. *WIB*, 38, 71–88, 91–93, 110–11, 156–58, 191–99, 221–22, 286, 365, 539, 585–86.

7. Ibid., 15–19.

8. Ibid., 91–92.

9. Ibid., 38, 87–88.

10. Ibid., 92–93.

11. Ibid., 93–106.

12. Ibid., 107–18.

13. Ibid., 150–52.

14. Ibid., 176–81.

15. *A True Heroine. The Woman in Battle: The Adventures, Exploits, and Travels of Madame Loreta Juaneta Velasquez* (N.p.: 1876). This flyer appeared in at least two versions. One lists H. W. Kelley as a subscription agent, and the other shows Lauretta as agent for North Carolina and South Carolina, based in Raleigh. Both are in the David M. Rubenstein Rare Book & Manuscript Library, Duke University, Durham, NC. Coleman Hutchison says this document was printed in Philadelphia in 1876 by H. W. Kelley. This does not appear on the document, however. He fails to note that on the broadside, Lauretta's middle name is spelled "Juaneta," not "Janeta." Coleman Hutchison, "On the Move Again—Tracking the 'Exploits, Adventures, and Travels of Madame Loreta Janeta Velazquez,'" *Comparative American Studies* 5, no. 4 (December 2007): 423, 438. The flyers also reprinted notices from the Augusta, GA, *Constitutionalist*; Kennesaw, GA, *Gazette*; Atlanta *Daily Commonwealth*; and Atlanta *Daily Constitution*. This suggests that both versions appeared after the book's release.

16. Alemán declares that "the 'unsolicited testimonials' from Hammond, Alexander, Anderson, and Newman confirm the book's veracity" and regards the flyer's evidence as "compelling." Alemán, "Authenticity, Autobiography, and Identity," xviii. This misreads the testimonials, missing the unmistakable signs that they were solicited, and ignoring the contexts in which any of the testators could have known Buford/Lauretta.

17. *True Heroine.*

18. John F. Hammond file (Joel's papers are misfiled here), Confederate Papers relating to Citizens or Business Firms, Joel F. Hammond CSR, RG 109, NA.

19. *WIB*, 306–9.

20. Ibid., 315.

21. Atlanta *Southern Confederacy*, March 24, 1863; Augusta *Daily Constitutionalist*, May 15, 1863.

22. *True Heroine.*

23. James W. Beasley, *Beasley's Atlanta Directory for 1875* (Atlanta: James W. Beasley, 1875), 106; Atlanta *Constitution*, February 20, 1889. It further came out that Hammond had announced that he wanted to move to Texas and needed medical instruments. When the lunatic burgled instruments from another physician, there was speculation that he had done it for Hammond. Hammond remained in Atlanta the rest of his life as a professor at Georgia Eclectic Medical College. He died on January 14, 1893, on a visit to Indiana. Atlanta *Constitution*, January 16, 1893.

24. *True Heroine.*

25. Madame L. J. Velasquez to William L. De Rosset, January 22, 1877, Special Collections, D. H. Hill Library, North Carolina State University, Raleigh.

26. In *WIB* she says on page 144 that she left Virginia "nearly six months" after her arrival, which she earlier put at June 1861.

27. Madame L. J. Velasquez to William L. De Rosset, January 22, 1877.

28. New Orleans *Daily True Delta*, February 11, March 9, 1862.

29. This is derived from the CSRs of members of the two companies. The four 1862 enlistees are Conrad Crowl, John George Miller, Samuel S. Scott, and Leobold Selenger. Desertion was rampant in these companies, with seventy-three absent by summer 1862.

30. *WIB*, 182.

31. New Orleans *Daily True Delta*, April 24, 1862.

32. *WIB*, 38.

33. Ibid., 204–6, 213, 225.

34. Ibid., 301.

35. Ibid., 337–38, 352–80.

36. Ibid., 38, 283, 339, 394–97, 446–49.

37. Lafayette C. Baker, *History of the United States Secret Service* (Philadelphia: L. C. Baker, 1867), and *The Secret Service in the Late War* (Philadelphia: John E. Potter, 1874).

38. *WIB*, 462–63; New York *Herald*, September 22, 1864; Philadelphia *Daily Age*, July 3, 1865.

39. *WIB*, 464–98; Baker, *Secret Service in the Late War*, 249–75.

40. This is particularly so in their descriptions of enlistment bounty fraud. See Baker, *Secret Service in the Late War*, 251, and *WIB*, 489.

41. *WIB*, 496; Baker, *Secret Service in the Late War*, 253–54, 262.

42. *WIB*, 470–71, 476–87.

43. Columbus *Daily Ohio Statesman*, May 3, 1864; Washington *National Republican*, May 13, 20, July 20, 1864; Washington *Evening Star*, August 11, 1864; Stephen Mihm, *A Nation of Counterfeiters: Capitalists, Con Men, and the Making of the United States* (Cambridge, MA: Harvard University Press, 2007), 343–44.

44. Baker, *Secret Service in the Late War*, 380–82.

45. The most recent authoritative study of counterfeiting in America, Mihm's *Nation of Counterfeiters*, makes no mention of anything of this sort, even as rumor.

46. *WIB*, 477. The actual date that Baker commenced his investigation is obscure, but December seems the likely target, since Clark was rumored to have been relieved of his job in the first week of January 1864. Cleveland *Morning Leader*, January 8, 1864.

47. *WIB*, 467.

48. United States Congress, *Reports of Committees of the House of Representatives Made during the First Session, Thirty-Eighth Congress, 1863–'64* (Washington, DC: Government Printing Office, 1864), 1, Report no. 140, June 30, 1864, 207–8; *WIB*, 466, 483.

49. She also could have drawn her account of the scandal from the Washington, DC, *Daily Constitutional Union*, July 2, 9, 11, August 5, 1864, and other newspapers. However, her mention of having read the congressional report points to it as her most obvious source.

50. Ibid., 509–10.

51. Derek Marlowe employed essentially this same plot twist in his 1966 novel, *A Dandy in Aspic*, having his spy protagonist assigned to kill another agent, who turned out to be himself in disguise.

52. Manzana died on September 24, 1867, and she says she left soon after for the United States, whereas she actually departed on October 31. Philadelphia, *Inquirer*, September 25, 1867; *WIB*, 568; Record for Laura Wasson, 1867, Passenger Lists of Vessels Arriving at New York, New York, 1820–1897, M237, Records of the U.S. Customs Service, RG 36, NA.

53. *WIB*, 605–6.

54. For these and other traits of nineteenth-century confidence women, see De Grave, *Swindler, Spy, Rebel*, 5, 10, 114, 127, 135.

55. *WIB*, 363–64.

13. EMBATTLED WOMAN

1. Copyright No. 3046G, March 10, 1876, Copyright Book for 1876, Records Research Section, Copyright Office, LC, shows that two copies of the book

were deposited at the Library of Congress on August 3, which would suggest a late-July publication.

2. Copyright No. 3046, March 10, 1876, Copyright Ledger for 1876, ibid.

3. Atlanta *Sunny South*, December 18, 1875.

4. Atlanta *Daily Constitution*, March 9, 1876.

5. No record of bankruptcy filing for Ramsay has been found in the Bankruptcy Dockets in U.S. District Court, Northern District of Georgia, Atlanta Division, August 1875–August 1878, RG 21, NA at Atlanta, Morrow, GA. Significantly, the Southern Publishing Company is listed in the 1875 *Atlanta City Directory*, but not in subsequent editions.

6. Atlanta *Daily Constitution*, March 26, 1876.

7. Ibid., April 9, 1876.

8. Ibid., April 11, 1876; Marietta *Journal*, April 14, 1876; Macon, GA, *Georgia Weekly Telegraph*, April 18, 25, 1876.

9. Atlanta *Daily Constitution*, July 19, 1876.

10. Ibid., May 2, 1876.

11. Columbus, GA, *Daily Enquirer*, September 7, 1876.

12. Americus, GA, *Weekly Sumter Republican*, September 15, 1876.

13. Salt Lake City *Daily Herald*, October 10, 1876.

14. Tarborough, NC, *Southerner*, September 29, 1876.

15. Wadesboro, NC, *Pee Dee Herald*, October 4, 1876.

16. Raleigh *Observer*, December 20, 1876.

17. Raleigh *News*, January 7, 1877.

18. John William Jones, "Book Notices," *Southern Historical Society Papers* 2 (October 1876): 208.

19. For more on this theme, see De Grave, *Swindler, Spy, Rebel*, 140.

20. Jones, "Book Notices," 208.

21. Madame L. J. Velasquez to J. William Jones, October 27, November 12, 1876, Southern Historical Society Collection Correspondence Files, Museum of the Confederacy, Richmond, VA.

22. Atlanta *Daily Constitution*, July 19, 1876.

23. Macon, GA, *Georgia Weekly Telegraph*, February 1, 1876.

24. *WIB*, 566.

25. Matthew J. Mancini, *One Dies, Get Another: Convict Leasing in the American South* (Columbia: University of South Carolina Press, 1996), 82–87.

26. L. J. Wasson to Grant, February 24, 1876, Letters from the President, RG 60, NA; Galveston *Daily News*, March 21, 1876.

27. Atlanta *Daily Constitution*, March 23, 1876.

28. Trenton, NJ, *State Gazette*, March 21, 1876.

29. Atlanta *Daily Constitution*, March 25, April 19, 1876.

30. Augusta *Chronicle & Sentinel*, March 22, 23, 1876.

31. Atlanta *Daily Constitution*, March 23, 1876.

32. Macon *Georgia Weekly Telegraph*, March 26, 1876.

33. Ibid., March 30, 1876.

34. Ibid., March 28, 1876.

35. Ibid.; Augusta *Chronicle & Sentinel*, March 28, 1876.

36. *WIB*, 539.

37. Macon *Georgia Weekly Telegraph*, March 26, 1876.

38. Ibid., April 18, 1876.

39. Raleigh *Sentinel*, August 24, 1876; Wadesboro, NC, *Pee Dee Herald*, October 4, 1876.

40. Tarborough, NC, *Southerner*, September 29, 1876.

41. Oxford, NC, *Torchlight*, November 7, 1876.

42. Wilmington *Morning Star*, January 25, 28, 1877. The Charlotte, NC, *Democrat*, November 20, 1876, announced that she had unclaimed mail at the local post office.

43. Baltimore *Sun*, May 5, 1877. No record of her activities from May to December 1877 has been found.

44. Jasper, IN, *Weekly Courier*, August 24, 1877; Holton, KS, *Recorder*, August 23, 1877.

45. New Orleans *Daily Picayune*, April 17, 1877.

46. Galveston *Daily News*, September 23, 1876; New Orleans *Daily Picayune*, April 17, 1877; Baltimore *Sun*, May 5, 1877; Chicago *Daily Inter Ocean*, April 6, 1877; Washington, DC, *Evening Star*, January 26, 1878.

47. Dallas *Weekly Herald*, September 21, 1878.

48. Holton, KS, *Recorder*, August 23, 1877.

49. Cleveland *Leader*, January 12, 1878.

50. Charleston *News* in Atlanta *Daily Constitution*, February 7, 1878.

51. *WIB*, 56.

52. Madame L. J. Velasquez, "Address to the American Congress on 'Cuba'" (n.p.: [January–February 1878?]), Rose Reading Room, Schwarzman Building HOL p.v. 13, New York Public Library. Internal content suggests this was written after 1877 trade figures were available and before the Pact of Zanjón, concluded on February 10, 1878.

53. Chicago *Daily Inter Ocean*, December 5, 1877.

54. Charleston *News* in Atlanta *Daily Constitution*, February 7, 1878.

55. Cincinnati *Enquirer*, June 29, 1878, reprinting an article from the St. Louis *Evening Post* of June 27 or 28, 1878.

56. Raleigh *Observer*, March 12, 1878.

57. Washington, DC, *Evening Star*, March 30, 1877, January 24, April 11, 1878.

58. Cincinnati *Daily Star*, May 30, 1878.

59. Velasquez to Jubal A. Early, May 18, 1878, Tucker Family Papers, Southern Historical Collection. Lauretta's statement about Rio de Janeiro has been read to mean that she was actually living there, which was demonstrably not the case, since she headed her May 18 letter "House of Representatives, Washington, DC." Until recently her May 1878 business with Jubal Early has been assumed to mark her disappearance from history. DeAnne Blanton and Lauren M. Cook, *They Fought like Demons: Women Soldiers in the American Civil War* (Baton Rouge: Louisiana State University Press, 2002), 183.

60. Early to William F. Slemons, May 22, 1878, Tucker Family Papers. It is unclear from Early's letter how much time passed between his meeting the unnamed caller and Lauretta's appearance at his hotel.

61. Velasquez to Early, May 18, 1878, ibid. This letter is Early's *verbatim* copy of her letter, the original of which does not survive.

62. Early to Slemons, May 22, 1878, ibid.

63. Velasquez to Early, May 18, 1878, ibid.

64. Cincinnati *Daily Star*, May 30, 1878.

65. Cincinnati *Enquirer*, June 29, 1878.

14. "SHE IS A PROMOTER"

1. Portland *Oregonian*, July 28, 1879.

2. *WIB*, 476–87.

3. Baltimore *Sun*, July 8, 1879; Portland *Oregonian*, July 28, 1879; Cincinnati *Daily Gazette*, May 20, 1879.

4. *The New York City Directory* (New York: Trow City Directory Co., 1881), 1584; Raleigh *News*, December 12, 1879.

5. For instance, *WIB* never mentions William Burnet as Lauretta's first husband, but he appears so in the host's capsule account. Since it seems hardly likely that he would remember a five-year-old Atlanta newspaper article, conversation with Lauretta seems the only logical source.

6. Chicago *Daily Tribune*, December 23, 1879, reprinting the Indianapolis *Journal* of unknown date. The Burnett referred to was Ward R. Burnett, Jordan was Solicitor of the Treasury Edwin Jordan, and Mallory was Confederate secretary of the navy Stephen R. Mallory.

7. In 1872 it was revealed that the Crédit Mobilier of America construction company had given Garfield shares of its stock at significantly below market value as part of a scheme to overcharge for construction of the transcontinental

railroad. He also accepted a fee in the awarding of a paving contract for Washington that opponents regarded as a conflict of interest.

8. *New York City Directory*, 1584; United States Census, De Ruyter, Madison County, NY, 1880; New York *Truth*, August 21, 1880.

9. Washington, DC, *National Republican*, January 19, 1881.

10. Ibid., March 19, 1881.

11. San Francisco *Evening Bulletin*, July 6, 1881.

12. New York *Herald*, March 19, 1881; *The New York City Register* (New York: Trow City Directory Co., 1884), 1799. She listed her occupation as "sec.," presumably meaning secretary, but this may have been a corporate title.

13. An advertising card attached to a letter from Velasquez to Grover Cleveland, March 3, 1885, carries her notation "my house. 16 months old," which would put its founding at the beginning of November 1883. Grover Cleveland Papers, LC.

14. New York *Tribune*, August 13, 1885.

15. Velasquez to Cleveland, November 29, 1884, Cleveland Papers.

16. Washington, DC, *National Republican*, December 8, 1884.

17. New York *Times*, December 8, 1884; Washington, DC, *National Republican*, December 8, 1884.

18. New York *Herald*, January 14, 1885.

19. *The New York City Register* (New York: Trow City Directory Co., 1885), 1188, 1967.

20. Velasquez to Cleveland, March 5, 1885, Cleveland Papers.

21. Marriage certificate 73085, August 20, 1887, Marriage Registers, Extracts from Manhattan (1869–1880) and Brooklyn (1895–1897), New York City Department of Health, Division of Vital Statistics, New York, NY. Her interview published in the Los Angeles *Herald*, October 14, 1898, says she met Beard in Washington, DC, and implied that they were married there, which is manifestly untrue. Lauretta alternately claimed he was from England or Wales, depending on when she spoke of him.

22. Marriage certificate 73085; Census Returns of England and Wales, 1841, Ancestry.com. Lists of Vessels Arriving at New York, New York, 1820–1897, M237, Records of the U.S. Customs Service, RG 36, NA, show three William Beards immigrating from England, one born circa 1833 coming on May 16, 1866; the second born circa 1836 coming on the same ship; and the third born circa 1829 and arriving on September 15, 1869, on the *City of Antwerp* out of Liverpool. Lauretta's husband could have been any one of them, or someone else not recorded. In 1891 she said that Beard was born around 1835 in Wales, that he came to the United States with a brother, and that in the 1850s the

two of them explored the Mackenzie River and up the Yukon to the Brandywine, producing survey and geological reports that were later published. She claimed that he also explored from the Alaska and Cascade ranges to the Rockies in California, and that in 1859–60 he was one of the first to explore Alaska with the Geodetic Survey Commission. Thereafter, she said he spent a few years in the 1860s in South Africa in the diamond fields; that she spent two years there with him at Kimberley, which is clearly not true; and that from 1871 until 1888 he lived mostly in Arizona. It is just possible that she could have met him there when she was Mrs. Bonner. New York *Herald*, February 1, 1891.

23. Globe, AZ, *Arizona Silver Belt*, May 30, 1878.

24. United States Census, Pinal County, AZ, 1880.

25. Tucson, AZ, *Daily Arizona Citizen*, November 1, 1882; Tombstone, AZ, *Epitaph*, April 17, 1882.

26. Globe *Arizona Silver Belt*, November 20, 1880.

27. Ibid., August 12, December 23, 1882, August 25, 1883.

28. Ibid., June 28, 1884.

29. New York *Times*, January 18, 1884.

30. New York *Herald*, November 20, 1884.

31. Globe *Arizona Silver Belt*, September 13, 1884.

32. New York *Herald*, November 19, 1884.

33. Ibid., February 23, 1889; Marriage certificate 73085, August 20, 1887.

34. To date, no record of his birth has been found. Waldemar Beard is referred to specifically by name, and as being ten years old, in Springfield, MA, *Republican*, July 22, 1898, and Philadelphia *Inquirer*, July 15, 1898. Presumably, Lauretta was the source.

35. *The New York City Register* (New York: Trow City Directory Company, 1891), 80–81; New York *Herald*, December 30, 1890; Loratita J. V. Beard complaint, *Loratita J. V. Beard v. John Hayes*, June 18, 1891, John Hayes response, July 10, 1891, Supreme Court Law Judgments 1799–1910, 1893 H-42, *Beard, Loratita J. V. v. Hayes, John*, New York City Department of Records and Information, Surrogates Court, New York, NY.

36. New York *Herald*, February 8, 1891.

37. Ibid., February 8, 1891.

38. Ibid., June 30, 1888.

39. Kalamazoo, MI, *Gazette*, June 16, 1891.

40. Chicago *Daily Inter Ocean*, June 20, 1891.

41. A printed appeal dated 1890 from "The National Mary Washington Memorial Association" lists supporters and advisory board members, including

the president, and coordinators for various states, but Lauretta's name appears nowhere. The definitive source, Susan Riviere Hetzel, *The Building of a Monument: A History of the Mary Washington Associations and Their Work* (Lancaster, PA: Press of Wickersham Company, 1903), contains no mention anywhere of Lauretta Beard or Velasquez, nor does her name appear in a listing of six hundred members of the association in the back of the book.

15. THE FIRST BIG CONS

1. This is inferred from the fact that, while all original copies of the book are rare today, the Worthington edition is especially so, as is the 1894 Hagemann edition that followed.

2. New York *Herald*, October 9, 1894.

3. Ménie Muriel Dowie, ed., *Women Adventurers: The Lives of Madame Velazquez, Hannah Snell, Mary Ann Talbot, and Mrs. Christian Davies* (London: T. Fisher Unwin, 1893), x–xi, xix, 51.

4. New York *Times*, June 19, 1893.

5. New York *Commercial Advertiser*, March 25, 1875.

6. Charlotte *Observer*, August 7, 1892.

7. Jersey City, NJ, *Evening Journal*, April 17, 1893.

8. New Orleans *Daily Picayune*, March 18, 1893.

9. Supreme Court finding, *Loratita J. V. Beard v. John Hayes*, February 9, 1893, Clerk's statement, February 10, 1893, Supreme Court Law Judgments 1799–1910, 1893 H-42, *Beard, Loratita J. V. v. Hayes, John*, New York City Department of Records and Information, Surrogates Court, New York, NY; New York *Times*, February 10, 1893.

10. Columbus, OH, *Daily Enquirer*, May 14, 1893.

11. L. J. V. Beard to W. B. Whaley, November 18, 1893, Charleston *News and Courier*, November 22, 1893; Washington, DC, *Evening Star*, November 30, 1893; New York *Times*, June 24, 1894.

12. Roanoke, VA, *Times*, December 14, 1893.

13. New York *Times*, June 24, 1894.

14. Prescott, AZ, *Weekly Journal-Miner*, January 24, 1894; Tombstone, AZ, *Epitaph*, June 25, 1893.

15. J. H. Chataigne, *Chataigne's Directory of Norfolk, 1895–6* (Norfolk: J. H. Chataigne, 1895), 101.

16. Wilmington, NC, *Morning Star*, November 10, 1893; Hickory, NC, *Press*, November 16, 1893.

17. Elizabeth City, NC, *Weekly Economist*, November 23, 1894.

18. Wilmington, NC, *Semi-Weekly Messenger*, December 27, 1894.

19. Wilmington, NC, *Morning Star*, December 4, 1894.

20. New Bern, NC, *Weekly Journal*, December 6, 1894.

21. Smithfield, NC, *Herald*, December 6, 1894.

22. New Bern, NC, *Weekly Journal*, December 6, 1894.

23. Raleigh *News and Observer*, December 7, 1894.

24. New Bern, NC, *Weekly Journal*, December 6, 13, 1894.

25. Ibid., December 20, 1894.

26. Ibid., December 27, 1894.

27. Wilmington *Semi-Weekly Messenger*, December 27, 1894.

28. Fayetteville *Observer*, February 3, April 21, 22, 1896.

29. New Bern, NC, *Weekly Journal*, April 4, 1895.

30. Philadelphia *Times*, September 19, 1897; Philadelphia *Inquirer*, July 15, 1898.

31. Phoenix *Weekly Herald*, June 25, 1896.

32. Philadelphia *Times*, September 19, 1897; Philadelphia *Inquirer*, September 5, 1897.

33. Chicago *Inter Ocean*, October 2, 1897. Nothing more has been found on this curious incident to shed light on the Beards' involvement, if any. Lauretta may also have become involved with the "cuban hospital relief association of Rochester NY" in some fashion, as it protested President Cleveland's policy toward Spain's treatment of Cuban rebels. When it sent a telegram to the president on February 21, 1898, decrying his administration's unwillingness to support the rebels, the name William S. Beard was first among the signatories. However, since the Beards had no known connection with Rochester, it is possible, if not probable, that this was another William Beard entirely. William Beard et al. to Cleveland, February 21, 1898, Cleveland Papers.

34. Philadelphia *Times*, November 21, 1901; Philadelphia *Inquirer*, September 26, 1897.

35. Philadelphia *Times*, November 21, 1901.

36. Seattle *Post-Intelligencer*, January 4, 1898.

37. Butte, MT, *Weekly Miner*, March 31, 1898.

38. Seattle *Post-Intelligencer*, January 4, 1898; Portland *Oregonian*, January 10, 1898; Springfield, MA, *Daily Republican*, July 22, 1898.

39. Philadelphia *Times*, November 21, 1901.

40. Seattle *Post-Intelligencer*, July 23, 1898.

41. Ibid.; Tacoma, WA, *Daily News*, July 14, 1898.

42. Springfield, MA, *Daily Republican*, July 22, 1898.

43. Philadelphia *Inquirer*, July 15, 1898.

44. Springfield, MA, *Daily Republican*, July 22, 1898.

45. Tacoma *Daily News*, July 14, 1898; Seattle *Post-Intelligencer*, July 23, 1898; Cleveland *Leader*, July 26, 1898.

46. The Kansas City *Star*, October 15, 1898, carried a story headlined "San Francisco October 15," saying that Lauretta was in that city preparing to go to Alaska, but it must have been an editorial error, as she could hardly have been leaving for Alaska on or after October 15 and arriving in Los Angeles two days earlier.

47. Philadelphia *Times*, November 21, 1901.

48. Phoenix *Weekly Herald*, August 18, 1898; Jersey City *Evening Journal*, September 1, 1898; John Addison Porter to Mrs. William Beard, September 26, 1898, William McKinley Papers, LC.

49. Los Angeles *Herald*, October14, 1898.

50. Ibid.; Baltimore *Sun*, October 15, 1898.

51. New York *Herald*, April 14, 15, 1892, March 7, 1894; New York *Tribune*, March 6, 1892, March 15, 1894.

52. Los Angeles *Herald*, October 14, 1898. A Henry C. Watkins was involved in the October 3, 1901, strangling of David Levy in Boise, Idaho. A purported will left by Levy bequeathed his $100,000 estate to Watkins, but it was found to have been written on Watkins's typewriter, and there was evidence of Watkins imitating Levy's signature. Another man was wrongfully convicted, but the death sentence was set aside in 1904. There is nothing specifically connecting this Watkins with the one who may have murdered Beard, but the similarities are suggestive. San Francisco *Call*, April 12, 1904; Idaho Falls *Idaho Register*, October 11, 1901; Boise *Idaho Statesman*, October 7, 1901.

53. Los Angeles *Herald*, October 14, 1898.

54. New York *Age-Herald*, April 12, 1896.

55. Mrs. T. Woods Hopely, "Women as Soldiers," Harrisburg *Telegraph*, August 16, 1898. This article appeared later in the San Diego *Union*, September 30, 1898, and elsewhere, but it seems to have gotten only limited circulation.

16. "I HAVE NEVER MET HER EQUAL"

1. Philadelphia *Inquirer*, July 15, 1898.

2. Los Angeles *Herald*, October 14, 1898; Baltimore *Sun*, October 15, 1898.

3. Los Angeles *Herald*, October 14, 1898.

4. Ibid.

5. *Classified Business Directory of the City of Los Angeles* (Los Angeles: Los Angeles Directory Company, 1899), 1018, 1120.

6. San Bernardino *Daily Sun*, June 13, 1899.

7. San Bernardino *Weekly Sun*, June 16, 1899.

8. She does not appear in any Los Angeles city directories for 1900, and in the Phoenix, AZ, *Republican-Herald*, June 7, 1900, she listed her residence as Philadelphia.

9. San Bernardino *Evening Transcript*, October 9, 1902.

10. Grand Rapids, MI, *Sunday Herald*, November 19, 1899.

11. Phoenix, AZ, *Republican-Herald*, May 24, 1900.

12. *Monthly Bulletin of the Bureau of the American Republics, International Union of American Republics* 9 (1900): 325.

13. Phoenix, AZ, *Republican-Herald*, May 24, 1900.

14. Tucson, AZ, *Arizona Daily Citizen*, May 25, 1900; New York *Times*, June 7, 1900; Phoenix, AZ, *Republican-Herald*, June 7, 1900.

15. Phoenix, AZ, *Republican-Herald*, June 7, 1900. The company sometimes appeared with variant names, such as American, Pacific & Mexico Railroad.

16. Phoenix, AZ, *Arizona Sentinel*, June 13, 1900.

17. San Diego *Evening Tribune*, June 8, 1900.

18. Cleveland *Plain Dealer*, May 7, 1890.

19. New York *Herald*, February 16, August 24, 1889; Prescott, AZ, *Weekly Journal Miner*, April 6, 1892.

20. Cleveland *Plain Dealer*, May 7, 1890; New York *Herald*, August 26, 1896.

21. San Diego *Weekly Union*, July 5, 1900; *McGue v. Rommel*, C. P. Pomeroy, *Reports of Cases Determined in the Supreme Court of the State of California* (San Francisco: Bancroft-Whitney Co., 1906), 148, 543ff.

22. New York *Herald*, July 7, 1900.

23. Phoenix, AZ, *Republican-Herald*, July 26, 1900.

24. Honolulu *Republican*, September 23, 1900, quoting the Chicago *Record Mine.*

25. Los Angeles *Herald*, June 19, 1900.

26. Phoenix, AZ, *Republican-Herald*, July 26, August 2, 1900; Sausalito, CA, *News*, August 4, 1900.

27. Sausalito, CA, *News*, August 4, 1900; Albuquerque, NM, *Daily Citizen*, August 2, 1900.

28. Denver *Post*, August 23, 1900.

29. Davenport, IA, *Republican*, September 21, 1900.

30. Phoenix, AZ, *Republican*, September 27, 1900.

31. New Orleans *Daily Picayune*, October 16, 25, 1900.

32. This is a supposition. Research has located no later articles based on interviews.

33. Atlanta *Constitution*, December 27, 1900.

34. Bisbee, AZ, *Cochise Review*, October 19, 1900; New York *Tribune*, October 29, 1900.

35. Phoenix, AZ, *Arizona Republican*, July 30, 1900.

36. Tampa *Morning Tribune*, February 24, 1901.

37. Ibid., February 23, 1916.

38. Philadelphia *Times*, November 21, 1901.

39. Cleveland *Leader*, August 28, 1901; Philadelphia *Times*, November 21, 1901.

40. Philadelphia *Times*, November 21, 1901.

41. New York *Times*, April 4, 1901.

42. Cleveland *Leader*, August 28, 1901; Philadelphia *Times*, November 21, 1901.

43. Philadelphia *Inquirer*, July 19, 1901.

44. Longstreet to Park, June 18, 1888, Longstreet Papers.

45. Philadelphia *Inquirer*, July 19, 1901; Philadelphia *Times*, November 21, 1901.

46. Cleveland *Leader*, August 28, 1901.

47. Philadelphia *Times*, November 21, 1901.

48. Ibid., November 21, December 10, 1901.

49. Ibid., November 21, 1901.

50. Ibid., December 10, 1901.

51. For more discussion of the confidence woman in this period, and especially the traits demonstrated by Lauretta, see De Grave, *Swindler, Spy, Rebel*, 4, 8, 15, 53, 114–15, 245–46.

17. "THE OLD BATTLE-LIGHT"

1. Philadelphia *Times*, December 10, 1901.

2. Philadelphia *Inquirer*, February 20, 1904.

3. Albuquerque, NM, *Daily Citizen*, February 15, 1902; Globe, AZ, *Arizona Silver Belt*, March 6, 1902; Bisbee, AZ, *Daily Review*, March 18, November 21, 1902.

4. Albuquerque, NM, *Daily Citizen*, March 13, 1902.

5. Phoenix, AZ, *Arizona Republican*, March 13, 1902.

6. Boston *Herald*, May 25, 1905. She did not appear in the New York or Washington directories for 1901–10. She is "J. L. W. Beard" in the New York State Census for 1905, age sixty, a lodger in Manhattan, occupation "promoter." The fact that many others at the boardinghouse were Cubans, and especially that her partner, John J. Whittemore, also lodged there, makes it certain that this is Lauretta. New York City: Manhattan County—State Population Census Schedules, 1905; Election District A.D. 05 E.D. 14, 34, New York State Archives, Albany, NY. The Cubans on the roll are interesting. One of the final statements in María Agui Carter's docudrama, *Rebel: Loreta Velazquez, Secret Soldier of*

the American Civil War (Arlington, VA: Iguana Films, ITVS, WPBT/Miami and Latino Public Broadcasting, 2013), is that Lauretta was last known in a reference connecting her with Cuban revolutionaries in 1902. That reference has not been found.

7. Boston *Herald*, May 25, 1905.

8. New York *Times*, March 21, 1908.

9. Ibid., October 23, 1908.

10. She was probably not the Mrs. William K. Beard elected president of the Philadelphia chapter of the United Daughters of the Confederacy for 1910–11. Philadelphia *Inquirer*, January 27, 30, May 19, 1910.

11. *Boyd's 1911 District of Columbia Directory* (Detroit: R. L. Polk & Co., 1911), 267.

12. Washington, DC, *Times*, June 4, 1912.

13. Case #20081, Beard, Loretta J., Records of St. Elizabeth's Government Hospital for the Insane, RG 418, Entry 64, Registers of Cases, 1855–1941, 115–16, NA; *WIB*, 49.

14. Athens, GA, *Weekly Banner*, September 13, 1907.

15. Salt Lake City *Herald-Republican*, May 2, 1909.

16. Dallas *Morning News*, July 5, 1909.

17. Roger Pocock, *Captains of Adventure* (Indianapolis: Bobbs-Merrill, 1913), 317.

18. "Women Who Were Warriors," Cincinnati *Enquirer*, September 26, 1914.

19. Beckley, WV, *Raleigh Herald*, April 20, 1917.

20. New York *Times*, May 20, 1918; Cheyenne *Wyoming State Tribune*, July 1, 1918.

21. William Gilmore Beymer, "Secret Service of Miss 'Harry Buford,'" *Pearson's Magazine* 31 (June 1914): 739, 743–46.

22. Ibid.; Cedar Hill Cemetery Burial Register, Beard, Loretta J., page 23, interment 1076, Cedar Hill Cemetery offices, 4111 Pennsylvania Ave., Suitland, MD; Family History Library film 2115943, District of Columbia, Select Deaths and Burials, 1840–1964, FamilySearch.org; Loretto [*sic*] J. Beard death certificate, record 275406, District of Columbia Department of Health, Washington, DC. Her birthplace is listed as the United States on her death certificate, but no informant is shown, so any such information could have been assumption. Her death record says she was seventy-nine, but if she had been born in 1842, as she maintained for most of her life, that would put her just past eighty.

23. Washington, DC, *Evening Star*, January 21, 1923.

24. A search through the entire listing of nearly three thousand patients at St. Elizabeth's in the United States Census, District of Columbia, 1920, failed

to find her, so either she was away when the census taker came or she gave another name. That would not have been unusual, since among the others listed are Abraham Lincoln and Thomas Jefferson. An interesting listing is Lorena D. Cropp, which is not all that far from Lauretta Clapp.

25. "Inquiry," *Confederate Veteran* 31 (December 1923): 442.

18. LEGEND, LEGACY, AND LEGERDEMAIN

1. "Women as Warriors," Mexia, TX, *Weekly Herald*, March 14, 1941.

2. Andreas Dorpalen, "When Women Go to War," San Bernardino *Daily Sun*, August 10, 1941.

3. Kannapolis, NC, *Daily Independent*, June 4, 1942.

4. Henry W. Shoemaker, "This Morning's Comment," Altoona, PA, *Tribune*, July 15, 1946.

5. Stewart Kelsey, "The Girl in Gray," *American Weekly*, June 18, 1950, 21; Cleveland *Plain Dealer*, June 18, 1950. Kelsey erroneously claimed that she wrote two volumes of memoirs, confusing the 1894 edition of *WIB* as being a second volume rather than a reissue.

6. See, for example, Paris, TX, *News*, August 14, 1958.

7. Ruth Dean, "Women in the Civil War," Washington, DC, *Evening Star*, June 4, 1961. The only other 1961–65 newspaper account found was in the Deming, NM, *Highlight*, April 18, 1963, and it dealt only with local interest in her postwar comments on Mowry City, New Mexico.

8. Fred Brooks, "Antebellum Amazons," Baton Rouge, LA, *State Times Advocate*, January 8, 1978.

9. Jacob H. Mogelever, *Death to Traitors: The Story of General Lafayette C. Baker, Lincoln's Forgotten Secret Service Chief* (New York: Doubleday, 1961), 196–201.

10. Lonn, *Foreigners in the Confederacy*, 380–82.

11. Katherine Jones, *Heroines of Dixie: Confederate Women Tell Their Story of the War* (Indianapolis: Bobbs-Merrill, 1955), 290–98.

12. Mary Elizabeth Massey, *Bonnet Brigades* (New York: Alfred A. Knopf, 1966), 82, 195, 310.

13. Sylvia D. Hoffert, "Madame Loreta Velasquez: Heroine or Hoaxer?" *Civil War Times Illustrated* 17 (June 1978): 29–31.

14. Hall, *Patriots in Disguise*, 107–53, 189n, 190n, 191n, 192n, 193–94n.

15. Ibid., 208–11.

16. Elizabeth D. Leonard, *All the Daring of the Soldier: Women of the Civil War Armies* (New York: W. W. Norton, 1999), 252.

17. Ibid., 256, 258, 259.

18. Ibid., 260–61.

19. Blanton and Cook, *They Fought like Demons*, 2, 178, 181, 232n3. Blanton and Cook spell the name Velazquez, as do others.

20. Longstreet to Park, June 18, 1888, Longstreet Papers; Blanton and Cook, *They Fought like Demons*, 197.

21. Blanton and Cook, *They Fought like Demons*, 119.

22. Richard Hall, "Laureta Janeta Velazquez: Civil War Soldier and Spy," in *Cubans in the Confederacy: José Agustín Quintero, Ambrosio José Gonzales, and Loreta Janeta Velazquez*, ed. Philip Thomas Tucker (Jefferson, NC: McFarland, 2002), 229–31, 235–36. Hall also misspells her name.

23. David E. Jones, *Woman Warriors: A History* (Washington, DC: Brassey's, 1997), 233–37.

24. Daniel C. Dennett, "Dennett on Wieseltier v. Pinker in the New Republic: Let's Start with a Respect for Truth," *Edge*, September 10, 2013, http://edge.org/conversation/dennett-on-wieseltier-v-pinker-in-the-new-republic.

25. An early historian's voice in this chorus of literature scholars was Drew Gilpin Faust, who in 1998 observed of Belle Boyd's memoir, *Belle Boyd in Camp and Prison*, that while "most historians have dismissed the memoir as so filled with invention and embellishment as to stand closer to fiction than history," if her book is approached "as a text carefully fashioned to impart a particular view of herself and her time, we will find it contains its own sort of truth—one ultimately more important than the accuracy or inaccuracy of Boyd's assessment of her impact." Drew Gilpin Faust, foreword to 1998 edition of *Belle Boyd in Camp and Prison*, by Belle Boyd (Baton Rouge: Louisiana State University Press, 1998), xi–xii.

26. Julie Wheelwright, *Amazons and Military Maids: Women Who Dressed as Men in the Pursuit of Life, Liberty and Happiness* (London: Pandora, 1989), 140. In this Lauretta paralleled Belle Boyd in popular culture. "Any attempt to arrest the story guaranteed further subversion," Sharon Kennedy-Nolle observed in her introduction to the 1998 edition of Boyd's memoir, quoting a 1929 journalist who observed that Boyd was "one of those persons who are hard to keep down, even after they're dead and gone." *Belle Boyd in Camp and Prison*, 53.

27. Jesse Alemán, "Crossing the Mason-Dixon Line in Drag: The Narrative of Loreta Janeta Velasquez, Cuban Woman and Confederate Soldier," in *Look Away! The U.S. South in New World Studies*, ed. Jon Smith and Deborah Cohn (Durham, NC: Duke University Press, 1994), 125n5.

28. Ibid., 110–11.

29. Ibid., 113.

30. Ibid., 116–17.

31. Ibid., 122, 124, 118.

32. Ibid., 112, 120.

33. Elaine K. Ginsberg, introduction to *Passing and the Fictions of Identity*, ed. Elaine K. Ginsberg (Durham, NC: Duke University Press, 1996), 15.

34. Elizabeth Young, *Disarming the Nation: Women's Writing and the American Civil War* (Chicago: University of Chicago Press, 1999), 156, 160–61.

35. Elizabeth Young, "Confederate Counterfeit: The Case of the Cross-Dressed Civil War Soldier," in *Passing and the Fictions of Identity*, ed. Elaine K. Ginsberg (Durham, NC: Duke University Press, 1996), 198, 203, 208.

36. Ibid., 193, 205.

37. Young, *Disarming the Nation*, 173, 181–82.

38. Alemán, "Authenticity, Autobiography, and Identity," xix.

39. Ibid., xix, xxii, xxvi–xxvii.

40. Marjorie Garber, *Vested Interests: Cross-Dressing and Cultural Anxiety* (London: Routledge, 1992), 13, 16, 22, 71.

41. De Grave, *Swindler, Spy, Rebel*, 117–19.

42. Alemán, "Authenticity, Autobiography, and Identity," xxxvi.

43. Ibid., xxxvi–xxxvii.

44. She is used in classroom studies on social psychology for her flaunting of social norms. See Kenneth S. Bordens and Kristin Sommer, *Instructor's Manual/Test Bank to Accompany Social Psychology*, 2nd ed. (Mahwah, NJ: Lawrence Erlbaum Associates, 2002), 27–29.

45. Alemán, "Authenticity, Autobiography, and Identity," xxix–xxx.

46. Hutchison, "On the Move Again," 423, 425–26.

47. Caroline Levander, "Confederate Cuba," in *Imagining Our Americas: Toward a Transnational Frame*, ed. Sandhya Shukla and Heidi Tinsman (Durham, NC: Duke University Press, 2007), 94.

48. Alemán, "Authenticity, Autobiography, and Identity," xxxi, xxxvi.

49. Matthew Teorey, "Unmasking the Gentleman Soldier in the Memoirs of Two Cross-Dressing Female US Civil War Soldiers," *War, Literature and the Arts* 20 (November 2008): 74–78, 80–81, 84, 87, 89n.

50. Coleman Hutchison, *Apples & Ashes: Literature, Nationalism, and the Confederate States of America* (Athens: University of Georgia Press, 2010), 200.

51. Ibid., 192.

52. Alemán declares that "Blanton and Cook have established the historical veracity of most of the events in the narrative." Today that contention would be difficult to support. Alemán, "Crossing the Mason-Dixon Line," 126n4.

53. Carman Cumming, Gary W. Gallagher, and Christina Vella in discussions on various dates with the author.

54. Carter, *Rebel.*

55. *WIB*, 248.

56. Hutchison, *Apples & Ashes*, 193, 199.

57. Levander, "Confederate Cuba," 94.

58. Hutchison, "On the Move Again," 426, 433.

59. Hutchison, *Apples & Ashes*, 178, 183.

60. Alemán, "Authenticity, Autobiography, and Identity," v, xii, xv.

61. It is interesting to note that Alemán, Young, Hutchison, Hall, and others spell her name Velazquez, as it appears in the text of her book, though it is spelled correctly as Velasquez in the caption to her frontispiece portrait and in her 1876 promotional leaflet. The definitive fact is that in all of her surviving holographic letters, she signed her name Velasquez, as it also appears in published letters. One inclined to overinterpretation might see in this a conspiracy to "other" her even further by denying her own name to her, but since it was never her real name in the first place, she apparently "othered" herself.

62. In recent years Lauretta continues to appear regularly in uncritical general works that regurgitate the *WIB* story while adding nothing new. See, for instance, Norma Jean Perkins, "The Soldier: Loreta Janeta Velazquez Alias Lt. Harry T. Buford," in *Confederate Women*, ed. Muriel Phillips Joslyn (Gretna, LA: Pelican, 2004), 63–76; Anita Silvey, *I'll Pass for Your Comrade: Women Soldiers in the Civil War* (New York: Clarion, 2008); H. Donald Winkler, *Stealing Secrets: How a Few Daring Women Deceived Generals, Impacted Battles, and Altered the Course of the Civil War* (Naperville, IL: Cumberland House, 2010); and Michael Walbridge, *Latino Heroes of the Civil War* (Portland, ME: J. Weston Walch, 1997).

BIBLIOGRAPHY

MANUSCRIPTS

California Digital Newspaper Collection

Cedar Hill Cemetery, Suitland, MD

Burial Register, Beard, Loretta J.

Census Returns of England and Wales, 1841, Ancestry.com

Chroniclingamerica.loc.gov

Cooperative libraries automated network

District of Columbia Department of Health, Washington, DC

Record 275406, Loretto [*sic*] J. Beard death certificate

Duke University, David M. Rubenstein Rare Book & Manuscript Library, Durham, NC

A True Heroine. The Woman in Battle: The Adventures, Exploits, and Travels of Madame Loreta Juaneta Velasquez. Printed flyer. N.p.: 1876

James Longstreet Papers

Family History Library film 2115943, District of Columbia, Select Deaths and Burials, 1840–1964, FamilySearch.org

Genealogybank.com

Georgia Department of Archives and History, Atlanta

Marriage Book B, Fulton County, Georgia, Marriages, 1854–1921

Fulton County, Probate Court, General Index to Marriages, 1854–1921, microfilm 106/66

Marriage Book B, 1862–1866, microfilm 110/66

Indiana State Archives, Indiana Commission on Public Records, Indianapolis

Indiana State Arsenal Payroll Ledger, Civil War Miscellany, 47-I-5, drawer 107, folder 43

Papers of Governor Oliver P. Morton

Kentucky Historical Society, Frankfort, KY

Mary Ann Clark Letters

Lander County Court House, Recorder's Office, Battle Mountain, NV
    Index to Marriages, Lander County, NV, Book 1
Library of Congress, Washington, DC
    Samuel L. Clemens Papers
    Grover Cleveland Papers
    Samuel P. Heintzelman Papers
    William McKinley Papers
Library of Congress, Copyright Office, Records Research Section
    Copyright No. 3046G, March 10, 1876, Copyright Book for 1876
    Copyright No. 3046, March 10, 1876, Copyright Ledger for 1876
Library of Congress, Geography and Map Division
    Map of the Lands of the Memphis & Little Rock Railroad Company (as reorganized), 1878. St. Louis: Woodward, Tiernan and Hale, 1878
Museum of the Confederacy, Richmond, VA
    Southern Historical Society Collection Correspondence Files
National Archives, Washington, DC
    Records of the U.S. Customs Service, Record Group 36
        Passenger Lists of Vessels Arriving at New York, New York, 1820–1897, M237
    Letters from the President, Record Group 60
    Compiled Service Records of Union Soldiers, Record Group 94
        William Irwin
        John Williams
    Index to General Correspondence of the Adjutant General's Office, 1809–1917, roll 306, Record Group 94
    Returns from U.S. Military Posts, 1806–1916, M 617, Record Group 94
    Records of the Office of the Secretary of War, Record Group 107
        Entry 54, Letters Received Applying for Passes to Enter Union Territory, box 1
        Entry 56, Records Concerning Travel Passes, 1862–1865, box 13
        Entry 57, Travel Passes of Visitors to Union Army Units or Installations, 1863
    Adjutant and Inspector General's Office, Record Group 109
        Register of Letters Received, April–July 1863, M–Z, chap. 1, vol. 56, RG 109, file 1145 W 1863
    Applications for Appointments in Military Service, Record Group 109
        Confederate States and Civil Service under War Department, July 1, 1863, to December 31, 1863, chap. 9, vol. 90

Applications for Appointments in Military Service, Record Group 109
Bound Records, chap. 9, vol. 90, file 1549
Compiled Service Records of Confederate Soldiers, Record Group 109
William S. Bachman
William J. Bass
Andrew Jackson Bobo
William E. Burnet
Thomas C. DeCaulp
Thomas Gibbons
Joel F. Hammond
Samuel J. Pinkerton
Confederate Papers Relating to Citizens or Business Firms, Record Group 109
John F. Hammond File
Letters Sent, Andersonville Prison, Georgia, May 1864–March 1865, Record Group 109
Letters Received by Confederate Adjutant-General, July–October 1863, Record Group 109
M474, roll 88, frame 0101, file W1310
Records relating to Individual Prisons or Stations, Record Group 109
New Orleans, LA, Register of Prisoners and Hospital Register, 1863–1865, M598
Secretary of War, Endorsements on Letters Received, Agent of Exchange of Prisoners, 1863–1865, chap. 9, vol. 228
Selected Records of the War Department relating to Confederate Prisoners of War, 1861–1865, Record Group 109
Roll 106, vols. 338–43
Entry 202, Roll of Paroled & Exchanged Prisoners of War at Camp Morton, Indiana, Microfilm Publication M598, rolls 3, 8
Union Provost Marshal's File of Papers relating to Individual Citizens, Record Group 109
Lauretta DeCaulp File
Louise Oyster Provost File
Union Provost Marshal's File of Papers relating to Two or More Civilians, Record Group 109
Prisoners: Gallatin, TN–New Orleans, M416, roll 88

Records of the Provost Marshal General's Bureau, Record Group 110
Entry 36, Correspondence, Reports, Accounts, and Other Records relating to Individual Scouts, Guides, Spies and Detectives, 1861–1868
Records of St. Elizabeth's Government Hospital for the Insane, Record Group 418
Entry 64, Registers of Cases, 1855–1941
Records of United States Army Continental Commands, 1821–1920, Record Group 393
Part 1, entry 2517, Military Division of Mississippi, 1863–1866, Letters Sent by Provost Marshal, March 1864–January 1865, vol. 1 21/37, 38 MDM
Part 1, entry 2518, Military Division of Mississippi, 1863–1866, Endorsements Sent by the Provost Marshal General, July–December 1864, vol. 9/40 MDM
Part 1, entry 3445, Department of the Northwest
Register of Letters Received, September 1862–July 1865
Part 3, entry 343, Letters and Telegrams Sent, November 1862–June 1873
National Archives at Atlanta, Morrow, GA
Bankruptcy Dockets, U.S. District Court, Northern District of Georgia, Atlanta Division, August 1875–August 1878, Record Group 21
National Maritime Museum, Caird Library, Greenwich, England
Royal Navy Lists, 1855–1866
New Mexico Territorial Census, Silver City, Grant County, 1885
New Orleans Public Library, Louisiana Division and City Archives, New Orleans, LA
Louisiana Justices of the Peace, Marriage Records 1846–1880, VED vols. 658, 678
New Orleans Charity Hospital Admission Books, 1818–1899
Record of Prisoners Committed to the Parish Prison, 1852–1862, TX420
State of Louisiana v. Mary Ann Williams, Case File 15410, First General District Court Case Files
New York City Department of Health, Division of Vital Statistics, New York, NY
Marriage Registers, Extracts from Manhattan (1869–1880) and Brooklyn (1895–1897)
New York City Department of Records and Information, Surrogates Court, New York, NY

Supreme Court Law Judgments, 1799–1910, 1893 H-42, *Beard, Loratita J. V. v. Hayes, John*

New York Passenger Lists, 1820–1957, Ancestry.com

New York State Archives, Albany, NY

New York City: Manhattan County—State Population Census Schedules, 1905; Election District A.D. 05 E.D. 14

Newspaperarchive.com

Newspapers.com

North Carolina State University, D. H. Hill Library, Raleigh

L. J. Velasquez to William L. De Rosset, January 22, 1877, Special Collections

Pulaski County Circuit Court, Little Rock, AR

Pulaski County, Arkansas, Marriage Record

Marriage Book B2

Salt Lake County Court House, Salt Lake City, UT

Salt Lake County 3rd District Court records

Salt Lake County probate records

Southern Historical Collection, University of North Carolina, Chapel Hill

Tucker Family Papers

Texas Death Index, 1903–2000, Ancestry.com

United States Census, Bexar District, TX, 1870

United States Census, Caln Township, Chester County, PA, 1880

United States Census, Chester County, PA, 1880

United States Census, De Ruyter, Madison County, NY, 1880

United States Census, District of Columbia, 1920

United States Census, Fort Bend County, TX, 1860

United States Census, Frankford Station [23rd District], Philadelphia County, PA, 1870

United States Census, Hempstead County, AR, 1860

United States Census, Hinds County, MS, 1860

United States Census, Memphis, TN, 1860

United States Census, Ninth and Eleventh Wards, Orleans Parish, LA, 1860

United States Census, Orleans Parish, LA, 1860

United States Census, Philadelphia County, PA, 1860, 1870

United States Census, Phoenix, Maricopa County, AZ Territory, 1880

United States Census, Pinal County, AZ, 1880

United States Census, Precinct 4, Harris County, TX, 1910

United States Census, Pulaski County, AR, 1860, 1870, 1880

United States Census, Silver City, Grant County, NM Territory, 1880, 1900
United States Census, St. Tammany Parish, LA, 1860
United States Census, Third Ward, New Orleans, LA, 1860
United States Census, York County, ME, 1850, 1860
United States Census, Yuba County, CA, 1860
United States Confederate Pensions, 1884–1958, Ancestry.com
University of California, Bancroft Library, Berkeley, CA
Mark Twain Papers
Waller County Court House, Hempstead, TX
Waller County Marriage Book "A," October 1873–December 1881, Grooms Letter "B"

PUBLISHED PRIMARY SOURCES

Adjutant General's Office. *Official Army Register, for 1856*. Washington, DC: Public Printer, 1856.

Bailey, A., comp. *Milwaukee City Directory for 1863*. Milwaukee: Starr & Son, 1863.

Baker, Lafayette C. *History of the United States Secret Service*. Philadelphia: L. C. Baker, 1867.

———. *The Secret Service in the Late War*. Philadelphia: John E. Potter, 1874.

Beasley, James W. *Beasley's Atlanta Directory for 1875*. Atlanta: James W. Beasley, 1875.

Boyd's 1911 District of Columbia Directory. Detroit: R. L. Polk & Co., 1911.

Chataigne, J. H. *Chataigne's Directory of Norfolk, 1895–6*. Norfolk: J. H. Chataigne, 1895.

Chesson, Michael Bedout, and Leslie Jean Roberts, eds. *Exile in Richmond: The Confederate Journal of Henri Garidel*. Charlottesville: University Press of Virginia, 2001.

Classified Business Directory of the City of Los Angeles. Los Angeles: Los Angeles Directory Company, 1899.

[Corsan, W. C.]. *Two Months in the Confederate States, Including a Visit to New Orleans under the Domination of General Butler. By "An English Merchant."* London: Richard Bentley, 1863.

Costa, Isaac, comp. *Gopsill's Philadelphia City and Business Directory for 1867–68*. Philadelphia: James Gopsill, 1867.

———. *Gopsill's Philadelphia City Directory for 1870*. Philadelphia: James Gopsill, 1870.

———. *Gopsill's Philadelphia City Directory for 1880*. Philadelphia: James Gopsill, 1880.

———. *Gopsill's Philadelphia City Directory for 1881*. Philadelphia: James Gopsill, 1881.

Cowell, E. J. *Cowell's Philadelphia Business Directory*. Philadelphia: E. J. Cowell, 1860.

A Diary of the 30th Regiment, Wisconsin Volunteers. A History of the Regiment since Its Organization. Madison: Martin & Judson, 1864.

Edwards' Annual Directory of the Inhabitants . . . in the City of Milwaukee, for 1866. Milwaukee: Edwards, Greenough & Deved, 1866.

Estep, Raymond, ed. "Lieutenant William E. Burnet Letters: Removal of the Texas Indians and the Founding of Fort Cobb." Pts. 1 and 2. *Chronicles of Oklahoma* 38 (Autumn 1960): 274–309; 38 (Winter 1960): 369–96.

Fremantle, Arthur J. L. *Three Months in the Southern States, April–June 1863*. London: William Blackwood & Sons, 1863.

Gardner, Charles. *Gardner's New Orleans Directory for 1861*. New Orleans: Charles Gardner, 1861.

Jones, John B. *A Rebel War Clerk's Diary at the Confederate States Capital*. 2 vols. Philadelphia: J. B. Lippincott, 1866.

Jones, John William. "Book Notices." *Southern Historical Society Papers* 2 (October 1876): 208.

McElroy, A. *McElroy's Philadelphia City Directory for 1861*. Philadelphia: A. McElroy, 1861.

———. *McElroy's Philadelphia City Directory for 1862*. Philadelphia: A. McElroy, 1862.

———. *McElroy's Philadelphia City Directory for 1863*. Philadelphia: A. McElroy, 1863.

———. *McElroy's Philadelphia City Directory for 1865*. Philadelphia: A. McElroy, 1865.

———. *McElroy's Philadelphia City Directory for 1866*. Philadelphia: A. McElroy, 1866.

Monthly Bulletin of the Bureau of the American Republics, International Union of American Republics 9 (1900).

The New York City Directory. New York: Trow City Directory Co., 1881.

The New York City Register. New York: Trow City Directory Co., 1884.

The New York City Register. New York: Trow City Directory Co., 1885.

The New York City Register. New York: Trow City Directory Co., 1891.

Personne [Felix DeFontaine]. *Marginalia; or, Gleanings from an Army Notebook*. Columbia, SC: F. G. DeFontaine & Co., 1864.

Ross, Fitzgerald. *Cities and Camps of the Confederate States.* Edited by Richard Barksdale Harwell. Urbana: University of Illinois Press, 1958.

Simon, John Y., ed. *Papers of Ulysses S. Grant.* 32 vols. Carbondale: Southern Illinois University Press, 1967–2012.

"Some Account of Hannah Snell, the Female Soldier." *Gentleman's Magazine* 20 (July 1750): 291–93.

Stidger, Felix. *Treason History of the Order of Sons of Liberty, Succeeded by Knights of the Golden Circle, Afterward, Order of American Knights.* Chicago: privately printed, 1903.

United States Congress. *Reports of Committees of the House of Representatives Made during the First Session, Thirty-Eighth Congress, 1863–'64.* 2 vols. Washington, DC: Government Printing Office, 1864.

United States War Department. *War of the Rebellion: Official Records of the Union and Confederate Armies.* 128 vols. Washington, DC: Government Printing Office, 1880–1901.

Velasquez, Madame L. J. "Address to the American Congress on 'Cuba.'" N.p.: [January–February 1878?]. Rose Reading Room, Schwarzman Building HOL p.v. 13, New York Public Library.

Velazquez, Loreta Janeta. *Story of the Civil War; or, The Exploits, Adventures and Travels of Mrs. L. J. Velasquez (Lieutenant H. T. Buford, C.S.A.).* New York: Worthington & Co., 1890.

———. *The Story of the Civil War.* New York: H. W. Hagemann, 1894.

———. *The Woman in Battle: A Narrative of the Exploits, Adventures, and Travels of Madame Loreta Janeta Velasquez, Otherwise Known as Lieutenant Harry T. Buford, Confederate States Army.* Edited by C. J. Worthington. Richmond, VA: Dustin, Gilman & Co., 1876.

NEWSPAPERS

Abbeville, SC, *Abbeville Press*, 1863

Albany, NY, *Argus*, 1874

Albany, NY, *Evening Journal*, 1865, 1866

Albuquerque, NM, *Daily Citizen*, 1900, 1902

Altoona, PA, *Tribune*, 1946

Americus, GA, *Weekly Sumter Republican*, 1876

Athens, GA, *Weekly Banner*, 1907

Athens, GA, *Weekly Banner-Watchman*, 1888

Atlanta, GA, *Constitution*, 1874, 1875, 1876, 1889, 1893, 1900

Atlanta, GA, *Daily Constitution*, 1863, 1864, 1866, 1867, 1876, 1878

Atlanta, GA, *Daily Intelligencer*, 1863, 1866
Atlanta, GA, *Southern Confederacy*, 1862, 1863
Atlanta, GA, *Sunny South*, October 2, 1875
Augusta, GA, *Chronicle & Sentinel*, 1876
Augusta, GA, *Daily Chronicle & Sentinel*, 1863, 1866, 1874
Augusta, GA, *Daily Constitutionalist*, 1862, 1863, 1866, 1874
Augusta, GA, *Southern Watchman*, 1862
Austin, NV, *Daily Reese River Reveille*, 1865, 1867, 1868
Austin, TX, *Daily Austin Republican*, 1868
Bainbridge, GA, *Weekly Democrat*, 1875
Baltimore, MD, *Sun*, 1861, 1866, 1867, 1877, 1879, 1898
Baton Rouge, LA, *State Times Advocate*, 1978
Beckley, WV, *Raleigh Herald*, 1917
Bisbee, AZ, *Cochise Review*, 1900
Bisbee, AZ, *Daily Review*, 1902
Boise, ID, *Idaho Statesman*, 1868, 1901
Bolivar, TN, *Bulletin*, 1875
Boston, MA, *American Traveller*, 1861, 1862
Boston, MA, *Daily Advertiser*, 1874
Boston, MA, *Herald*, 1905
Boston, MA, *Journal*, 1866
Brattleboro, VT, *Vermont Journal*, 1866
Butte, MT, *Weekly Miner*, 1898
Charleston, SC, *Daily Courier*, 1863, 1864, 1866
Charlotte, NC, *Democrat*, 1876
Charlotte, NC, *Observer*, 1892
Charlotte, NC, *Times*, 1864
Charlotte, NC, *Western Democrat*, 1861
Chattanooga, TN, *Daily Rebel*, 1863
Cheyenne, WY, *Wyoming State Tribune*, 1918
Chicago, IL, *Daily Inter Ocean*, 1874, 1877, 1891, 1897
Chicago, IL, *Daily Tribune*, 1879
Cincinnati, OH, *Commercial Tribune*, April 26, 1871
Cincinnati, OH, *Daily Enquirer*, 1866
Cincinnati, OH, *Daily Gazette*, 1879
Cincinnati, OH, *Daily Press*, 1861
Cincinnati, OH, *Daily Star*, 1878
Cincinnati, OH, *Enquirer*, 1874, 1878, 1914

Clearfield, PA, *Republican*, 1867
Cleveland, OH, *Leader*, 1878, 1898, 1901
Cleveland, OH, *Morning Leader*, 1864
Cleveland, OH, *Plain Dealer*, 1864, 1866, 1890, 1950
Cloverport, KY, *Breckenridge News*, 1878, 1881
Columbia, TN, *Herald and Mail*, 1874
Columbus, GA, *Daily Columbus Enquirer*, 1863, 1866
Columbus, GA, *Daily Enquirer*, 1876
Columbus, GA, *Weekly Enquirer*, 1863
Columbus, OH, *Daily Enquirer*, 1893
Columbus, OH, *Daily Ohio Statesman*, 1861, 1864
Dallas, TX, *Herald*, 1863, 1866
Dallas, TX, *Morning News*, 1909, 1945
Dallas, TX, *Weekly Herald*, 1878
Davenport, IA, *Republican*, 1900
Dayton, OH, *Daily Empire*, 1866
Deming, NM, *Highlight*, 1963
Denver, CO, *Post*, 1900
Elizabeth City, NC, *Weekly Economist*, 1894
Fayetteville, NC, *Observer*, 1896
Fort Whipple, AZ, *Arizona Miner*, 1867
Fremont, OH, *Journal*, 1861
Galveston, TX, *Daily News*, 1874, 1876
Galveston, TX, *Flake's Daily Galveston Bulletin*, 1868
Galveston, TX, *Flake's Semi-Weekly Galveston Bulletin*, 1870
Galveston, TX, *Weekly News*, 1877
Globe, AZ, *Arizona Silver Belt*, 1878, 1880, 1882, 1883, 1884, 1902
Grand Rapids, MI, *Sunday Herald*, 1899
Harrisburg, PA, *Telegraph*, 1898
Hartford, CT, *Daily Courant*, 1874
Hickory, NC, *Press*, 1893
Holton, KS, *Recorder*, 1877
Honolulu, HI, *Republican*, 1900
Houston, TX, *Daily Union*, 1869, 1871
Houston, TX, *Tri-Weekly Telegraph*, 1863
Idaho Falls, ID, *Idaho Register*, 1901
Indianapolis, IN, *Daily Journal*, 1863
Indianapolis, IN, *Evening News*, 1874

Jackson, MI, *Citizen Patriot*, 1874
Jackson, MS, *Mississippian*, 1862, 1863
Janesville, WI, *Daily Gazette*, 1861, 1864, 1866
Jasper, IN, *Weekly Courier*, 1877
Jersey City, NJ, *Evening Journal*, 1893, 1898
Kalamazoo, MI, *Gazette*, June 16, 1891
Kannapolis, NC, *Daily Independent*, 1942
Kansas City, MO, *Star*, 1898
Knoxville, TN, *Chronicle*, 1863
Las Cruces, NM, *Borderer*, 1872, 1873
Leavenworth, KS, *Bulletin*, 1871
London, UK, *Standard*, 1866
Los Angeles, CA, *Herald*, 1898, 1900
Louisville, KY, *Courier-Journal*, 1874, 1878
Louisville, KY, *Daily Journal*, 1861
Lynchburg, VA, *Republican*, 1861
Macon, GA, *Daily Telegraph*, 1862, 1864
Macon, GA, *Georgia Weekly Telegraph*, 1876
Madison, WI, *Daily Patriot*, 1861, 1862
Madison, WI, *Weekly Wisconsin Patriot*, 1862
Manitowoc, WI, *Pilot*, 1861
Marietta, GA, *Journal*, 1875, 1878
Marysville, CA, *Daily Appeal*, 1869
Memphis, TN, *Daily Appeal*, 1861, 1863
Memphis, TN, *Daily Avalanche*, 1861, 1866, 1869
Memphis, TN, *Public Ledger*, 1866
Meridian, MS, *Messenger*, 1866
Mexia, TX, *Weekly Herald*, 1941
Mexico City, Mexico, *Mexican Times*, 1866
Milledgeville, GA, *Southern Recorder*, 1863
Milwaukee, WI, *Daily Milwaukee News*, 1864
Milwaukee, WI, *Daily Milwaukee Press and News*, 1861
Milwaukee, WI, *Daily Sentinel*, 1864, 1865
Milwaukee, WI, *Semi-Weekly Wisconsin*, 1864, 1866
Milwaukee, WI, *Wisconsin Daily Patriot*, 1864
Mineral Point, WI, *Weekly Tribune*, 1861
Mobile, AL, *Daily Register*, 1874
Mobile, AL, *Register & Advertiser*, 1863

Montgomery, AL, *Daily Mail*, 1863
Montgomery, AL, *Weekly Advertiser*, 1863
Nashville, TN, *Daily Patriot*, 1861
Nashville, TN, *Daily Union*, 1864, 1865
Nashville, TN, *Daily Union and American*, 1866
Nashville, TN, *Union and American*, 1861
Natchez, MS, *Daily Courier*, 1863
New Bedford, MA, *Whalemen's Shipping List, and Merchants' Transcript*, 1861
New Bern, NC, *Newbernian*, 1874
New Bern, NC, *Weekly Journal*, 1894, 1895
New Castle, IN, *Courier*, 1866
New Haven, CT, *Columbian Register*, 1874
New Haven, CT, *Columbian Weekly Register*, 1862
New Orleans, LA, *Bee*, 1857, 1859, 1861, 1862, 1863
New Orleans, LA, *Daily Creole*, 1856
New Orleans, LA, *Daily Crescent*, 1859, 1860, 1861, 1862
New Orleans, LA, *Daily Delta*, 1861, 1862
New Orleans, LA, *Daily Picayune* 1852, 1853, 1855, 1857, 1858, 1859, 1861, 1862, 1863, 1864, 1865, 1866, 1867, 1869, 1874, 1877, 1893, 1900
New Orleans, LA, *Daily Southern Star*, 1866
New Orleans, LA, *Daily True Delta*, 1859, 1861, 1862
New Orleans, LA, *Item*, 1879
New Orleans, LA, *Times*, 1865, 1866, 1867
New Orleans, LA, *Tribune*, 1865
New York, NY, *Age-Herald*, 1896
New York, NY, *Commercial Advertiser*, 1866, 1867, 1875
New York, NY, *Daily Graphic*, 1874, 1876
New York, NY, *Daily Tribune*, 1864
New York, NY, *Daily World*, 1862
New York, NY, *Evening Post*, 1862, 1864, 1866
New York, NY, *Evening Standard*, 1869
New York, NY, *Frank Leslie's Illustrated Newspaper*, 1874
New York, NY, *Herald*, 1863, 1864, 1866, 1867, 1869, 1875, 1881, 1884, 1885, 1889, 1890, 1891, 1892, 1894, 1896, 1900
New York, NY, *Times*, 1864, 1865, 1884, 1893, 1894, 1900, 1901, 1908, 1918
New York, NY, *Tribune*, 1885, 1888, 1892, 1894, 1900
Newberry, SC, *Herald*, 1866
Opelousas, LA, *Journal*, October 30, 1874

Orangeburg, SC, *Orangeburg Times*, 1874
Oxford, NC, *Torchlight*, 1876
Paris, TX, *News*, 1958
Peoria, IL, *Morning Mail*, 1862
Philadelphia, PA, *Daily Age*, 1865
Philadelphia, PA, *Daily Evening Telegraph*, 1866
Philadelphia, PA, *Inquirer*, 1861, 1862, 1864, 1867, 1880, 1897, 1898, 1901, 1904
Philadelphia, PA, *Times*, 1897, 1901
Phoenix, AZ, *Arizona Republican*, 1900, 1902
Phoenix, AZ, *Arizona Sentinel*, 1900
Phoenix, AZ, *Republican-Herald*, 1900
Phoenix, AZ, *Weekly Herald*, 1896, 1898
Pocahontas, AR, *Advertiser*, 1861
Portland, OR, *Oregonian*, 1879, 1898
Prescott, AZ, *Weekly Journal Miner*, 1892, 1894
Providence, RI, *Evening Press*, 1866
Pulaski, TN, *Citizen*, 1866
Raleigh, NC, *News*, 1877
Raleigh, NC, *News and Observer*, December 7, 1894
Raleigh, NC, *Observer*, 1878
Raleigh, NC, *Register*, 1863
Raleigh, NC, *Sentinel*, 1876
Raleigh, NC, *Weekly Standard*, 1861
Richmond, VA, *Daily Dispatch*, 1861, 1863, 1865
Richmond, VA, *Daily Richmond Examiner*, 1863
Richmond, VA, *Enquirer*, 1861, 1863, 1864
Richmond, VA, *Sentinel*, 1863
Richmond, VA, *Whig*, 1863, 1866
Roanoke, VA, *Times*, 1893
Rochester, IN, 1861
Sacramento, CA, *Daily Union*, 1869, 1870, 1873, 1874
Salina, KS, *Saline County Journal*, 1874
Salt Lake City, UT, *Daily Herald*, 1871, 1876
Salt Lake City, UT, *Daily Telegraph*, 1867
Salt Lake City, UT, *Deseret News*, 1872, 1873, 1874
Salt Lake City, UT, *Herald-Republican*, 1909
San Antonio, TX, *Daily Express*, 1869, 1873
San Bernardino, CA, *Daily Sun*, 1899, 1941

San Bernardino, CA, *Evening Transcript*, October 9, 1902
San Bernardino, CA, *Weekly Sun*, 1899
San Diego, CA, *Evening Tribune*, 1900
San Diego, CA, *Weekly Union*, 1900
San Francisco, CA, *Call*, 1904
San Francisco, CA, *Chronicle*, 1869, 1870, 1872, 1873
San Francisco, CA, *Daily Alta California*, 1867, 1869, 1873
San Francisco, CA, *Evening Daily Bulletin*, 1861, 1865, 1866, 1868, 1873, 1874, 1881
Santa Fe, NM, *Daily New Mexican*, 1873
Santa Fe, NM, *Weekly New Mexican*, 1873
Sausalito, CA, *News*, 1900
Savannah, GA, *Republican*, 1863
Seattle, WA, *Post-Intelligencer*, 1898
Selma, AL, *Morning Reporter*, 1863
Smithfield, NC, *Herald*, 1894
Springfield, MA, *Daily Republican*, 1863, 1866, 1898
Springfield, MA, *Daily Union*, 1864
St. Louis MO, *Evening Post* 1878
St. Louis, MO, *Republican*, 1866
Staunton, VA, *Spectator* 1861, 1863
Tacoma, WA, *Daily News*, 1898
Tampa, FL, *Morning Tribune*, 1901, 1916
Tarborough, NC, *Southerner*, 1875, 1876
Tombstone, AZ, *Epitaph*, 1882, 1893
Trenton, NJ, *State Gazette*, 1874, 1876
Troy, MO, *Lincoln County Herald*, 1867
Tucson, AZ, *Arizona Citizen*, 1874
Tucson, AZ, *Arizona Daily Citizen*, 1900
Tucson, AZ, *Daily Arizona Citizen*, 1882
Wadesboro, NC, *Pee Dee Herald*, October 4, 1876
Washington, DC, *Daily Constitutional Union*, 1864
Washington, DC, *Evening Star*, 1864, 1866, 1877, 1878, 1923, 1961
Washington, DC, *National Republican*, 1861, 1864, 1881, 1884
Washington, DC, *Times*, 1912
Wheeling, VA [WV], *Daily Intelligencer*, 1861
Wilmington, NC, *Journal*, 1861, 1862, 1863
Wilmington, NC, *Morning Star*, 1877, 1893 1894

Wilmington, NC, *Semi-Weekly Messenger*, 1894
Windsor, VT, *Vermont Journal*, 1862
Yorkville, SC, *Enquirer*, 1863
Yuma, AZ, *Arizona Sentinel*, 1879

SECONDARY WORKS

Alemán, Jesse. "Authenticity, Autobiography, and Identity: *The Woman in Battle* as a Civil War Narrative." Introduction to *The Woman in Battle*, by Loreta Janeta Velazquez, ix-xli. 1876. Reprint, Madison: University of Wisconsin Press, 2003.

———. "Crossing the Mason-Dixon Line in Drag: The Narrative of Loreta Janeta Velasquez, Cuban Woman and Confederate Soldier." In *Look Away! The U.S. South in New World Studies*, edited by Jon Smith and Deborah Cohn, 110–29. Durham, NC: Duke University Press, 1994.

Beymer, William Gilmore. "Secret Service of Miss 'Harry Buford.'" *Pearson's Magazine* 31 (June 1914): 739–46.

Blanton, DeAnne, and Lauren M. Cook. *They Fought like Demons: Women Soldiers in the American Civil War*. Baton Rouge: Louisiana State University Press, 2002.

Blokker, Laura Ewen. *Education in Louisiana*. Greensburg: State of Louisiana Department of Culture, Recreation and Tourism, Office of Cultural Development, Division of Historic Preservation, 2012.

Bordens, Kenneth S., and Kristin Sommer. *Instructor's Manual/Test Bank to Accompany Social Psychology*. 2nd ed. Mahwah, NJ: Lawrence Erlbaum Associates, 2002.

Brooks, Fred. "Antebellum Amazons." Baton Rouge, LA, *State Times Advocate*, January 8, 1978.

Carter, María Agui. *Rebel: Loreta Velazquez, Secret Soldier of the American Civil War*. Arlington, VA: Iguana Films, ITVS, WPBT/Miami and Latino Public Broadcasting, 2013.

Casstevens, Frances H. *George W. Alexander and Castle Thunder*. Jefferson, NC: McFarland, 2004.

Collier, Calvin L. *The War Child's Children: A Story of the Third Regiment, Arkansas Cavalry, Confederate States Army*. Little Rock, AR: Pioneer Press, 1965.

Cullum, George W. *Biographical Register of the Officers and Graduates of the U.S. Military Academy at West Point, N.Y.* Boston: Riverside Press, 1891.

Cumming, Carman. *Devil's Game: The Civil War Intrigues of Charles A. Dunham*. Urbana: University of Illinois Press, 2004.

Current, Richard N. *Lincoln's Loyalists: Union Soldiers from the Confederacy.* Boston: Northeastern University Press, 1992.

Dean, Ruth. "Women in the Civil War." Washington, DC, *Evening Star*, June 4, 1961.

De Grave, Kathleen. *Swindler, Spy, Rebel: The Confidence Woman in Nineteenth-Century America.* Columbia: University of Missouri Press, 1995.

Dorpalen, Andreas. "When Women Go to War." San Bernardino *County Sun*, August 10, 1941.

Dowie, Ménie Muriel, ed. *Women Adventurers: The Lives of Madame Velazquez, Hannah Snell, Mary Ann Talbot, and Mrs. Christian Davies.* London: T. Fisher Unwin, 1893.

"Dr. Burrowes Portrait." *Pennsylvania School Journal* 44 (March 1896): 416.

Faust, Drew Gilpin. Foreword to 1998 edition of *Belle Boyd in Camp and Prison*, by Belle Boyd, xi–xii. Baton Rouge: Louisiana State University Press, 1998.

Fay, Edwin Whitfield. *The History of Education in Louisiana.* Washington, DC: Government Printing Office, 1898.

Full Metal Corset: Secret Soldiers of the Civil War. New York: Arts and Entertainment Network, 2007.

Garber, Marjorie. *Vested Interests: Cross-Dressing and Cultural Anxiety.* London: Routledge, 1992.

Ginsberg, Elaine K. Introduction to *Passing and the Fictions of Identity*, edited by Elaine K. Ginsberg, 1–18. Durham, NC: Duke University Press, 1996.

Hall, Richard. "Laureta Janeta Velazquez: Civil War Soldier and Spy." In *Cubans in the Confederacy: José Agustín Quintero, Ambrosio José Gonzales, and Loreta Janeta Velazquez*, edited by Philip Thomas Tucker, 225–39. Jefferson, NC: McFarland, 2002.

———. *Patriots in Disguise: Women Warriors of the Civil War.* New York: Marlowe & Co., 1994.

Hanna, Alfred Jackson, and Kathryn Abbey Hanna. *Confederate Exiles in Venezuela.* Tuscaloosa, AL: Confederate Publishing Co., 1960.

Hargreaves, Reginald. *Women-at-Arms: Their Famous Exploits throughout the Ages.* London, UK: Hutchinson & Company, 1930.

Hetzel, Susan Riviere. *The Building of a Monument: A History of the Mary Washington Associations and Their Work.* Lancaster, PA: Press of Wickersham Company, 1903.

Hoffert, Sylvia D. "Madame Loreta Velasquez: Heroine or Hoaxer?" *Civil War Times Illustrated* 17 (June 1978): 24–31.

Hopely, Mrs. T. Woods. "Women as Soldiers." Harrisburg, PA, *Telegraph*, August 16, 1898.

Horan, James D. *Confederate Agent: A Discovery in History*. New York: Crown, 1954.

Hutchison, Coleman. *Apples & Ashes: Literature, Nationalism, and the Confederate States of America*. Athens: University of Georgia Press, 2010.

———. "On the Move Again: Tracking the Exploits, Adventures, and Travels of Madame Loreta Janeta Velazquez." *Comparative American Studies* 5, no. 4 (December 2007): 423–40.

"Inquiry." *Confederate Veteran* 31 (December 1923): 442.

Jelinek, Estelle C. *The Tradition of Women's Autobiography from Antiquity to the Present*. New York: Macmillan, 2003.

Jones, David E. *Women Warriors: A History*. Washington, DC: Brassey's, 1997.

Jones, Katherine. *Heroines of Dixie: Confederate Women Tell Their Story of the War*. Indianapolis: Bobbs-Merrill, 1955.

Kaufman, Janet E. "'Under the Petticoat Flag': Women Soldiers in the Confederate Army." *Southern Studies* 23 (Winter 1984): 363–75.

Kelsey, Stewart. "The Girl in Gray." *American Weekly*, June 18, 1950, 21.

Kennedy-Nolle, Sharon. Introduction to the 1998 edition of *Belle Boyd in Camp and Prison*, by Belle Boyd, 1–53. Baton Rouge: Louisiana State University Press, 1998.

Leonard, Elizabeth D. *All the Daring of the Soldier: Women of the Civil War Armies*. New York: W. W. Norton, 1999.

Levander, Caroline. "Confederate Cuba." In *Imagining Our Americas: Toward a Transnational Frame*, edited by Sandhya Shukla and Heidi Tinsman, 88–110. Durham, NC: Duke University Press, 2007.

Lonn, Ella. *Foreigners in the Confederacy*. Chapel Hill: University of North Carolina Press, 1940.

Mackie, Colin. "A Directory of British Diplomats." Accessed March 12, 2015. http://gulabin.com.

Mancini, Matthew J. *One Dies, Get Another: Convict Leasing in the American South*. Columbia: University of South Carolina Press, 1996.

Massey, Mary Elizabeth. *Bonnet Brigades*. New York: Alfred A. Knopf, 1966.

"Met Life Begins." Accessed March 26, 2016. https://www.metlife.com/about/corporate-profile/metlife-history/metlife-begins/index.html.

Mihm, Stephen. *A Nation of Counterfeiters: Capitalists, Con Men, and the Making of the United States*. Cambridge, MA: Harvard University Press, 2007.

Mogelever, Jacob H. *Death to Traitors: The Story of General Lafayette C. Baker, Lincoln's Forgotten Secret Service Chief.* New York: Doubleday, 1961.

Morgan, Anita J. "Indiana Arsenal." *Hoosier Voices Now.* Accessed March 25, 2016. http://www.in.gov/history/4057.htm.

Perkins, Norma Jean. "The Soldier: Loreta Janeta Velazquez Alias Lt. Harry T. Buford." In *Confederate Women*, edited by Muriel Phillips Joslyn, 63–76. Gretna, LA: Pelican, 2004.

Pocock, Roger. *Captains of Adventure.* Indianapolis: Bobbs-Merrill, 1913.

Pomeroy, C. P. *Reports of Cases Determined in the Supreme Court of the State of California.* San Francisco: Bancroft-Whitney Co., 1906.

Ridley, Bromfield. *Battles and Sketches of the Army of Tennessee.* Mexico, MO: Missouri Printing and Publishing, 1906.

Roster of Wisconsin Volunteers, War of the Rebellion, 1861–1865. 2 vols. Madison: Democrat Printing Co., 1886.

Schafer, Judith Kelleher. *Brothels, Depravity, and Abandoned Women: Illegal Sex in Antebellum New Orleans.* Baton Rouge: Louisiana State University Press, 2009.

Shaw, Perrin F., Jr. "A Lady in Gray Fighting for the Confederacy." Richmond, VA, *Times-Dispatch Magazine*, May 21, 1939.

Shoemaker, Henry W. "This Morning's Comment." Altoona, PA, *Tribune*, July 15, 1946.

Silvey, Anita. *I'll Pass for Your Comrade: Women Soldiers in the Civil War.* New York: Clarion, 2008.

Sprague, Homer B. *History of the 13th Infantry Regiment of Connecticut Volunteers during the Great Rebellion.* Hartford, CT: Case, Lockwood & Co., 1867.

Teorey, Matthew. "Unmasking the Gentleman Soldier in the Memoirs of Two Cross-Dressing Female US Civil War Soldiers." *War, Literature and the Arts* 20 (November 2008): 74–93.

Thirtieth Wisconsin Infantry Association. *Roster of the Thirtieth Wisconsin Infantry Volunteers.* Madison: M. J. Cantwell, 1896.

Victor, Frances Fuller. *The River of the West. Life and Adventure in the Rocky Mountains and Oregon; Embracing Events in the Life-Time of a Mountain-Man and Pioneer: With the Early History of the North-Western Slope.* Hartford, CT: R. W. Bliss, 1870.

Walbridge, Michael. *Latino Heroes of the Civil War.* Portland, ME: J. Weston Walch, 1997.

Wheelwright, Julie. *Amazons and Military Maids: Women Who Dressed as Men in the Pursuit of Life, Liberty and Happiness*. London: Pandora, 1989.
Wilson, Robert. "The Great Diamond Hoax of 1872." *Smithsonian* 35 (June 2004): 70–79.
Winkler, H. Donald. *Stealing Secrets: How a Few Daring Women Deceived Generals, Impacted Battles, and Altered the Course of the Civil War*. Naperville, IL: Cumberland House, 2010.
"Women as Warriors." Mexia, TX, *Weekly Herald*, March 14, 1941.
"Women Who Were Warriors." Cincinnati, OH, *Enquirer*, September 26, 1914.
Young, Elizabeth. "Confederate Counterfeit: The Case of the Cross-Dressed Civil War Soldier." In *Passing and the Fictions of Identity*, edited by Elaine K. Ginsberg, 181–218. Durham, NC: Duke University Press, 1996.
———. *Disarming the Nation: Women's Writing and the American Civil War*. Chicago: University of Chicago Press, 1999.

INDEX

Given Lauretta's many aliases, including *Velasquez*, all references to her under any name are indexed under *Velasquez, Loreta Janeta*, and she is herein referred to as *LJV*.

WILLIAM C. DAVIS, formerly a professor of history and the executive director of the Virginia Center for Civil War Studies at Virginia Tech, has written or edited more than fifty books on Civil War and Southern history, most recently *Crucible of Command: Ulysses S. Grant and Robert E. Lee—the War They Fought, the Peace They Forged.* He is, to date, the only four-time winner of the American Civil War Museum's Jefferson Davis Award, given for the best book in Civil War history.